Deco Body, Deco City

THE MEXICAN EXPERIENCE

William H. Beezley, *series editor*

Deco Body, Deco City

Female Spectacle and Modernity
in Mexico City, 1900–1939

AGEETH SLUIS

University of Nebraska Press
Lincoln and London

Portions of chapters 2 and 5 were previously published as "*Bataclanismo!* Or, How Deco Bodies Transformed Postrevolutionary Mexico City," *The Americas* 66, no. 4 (2010): 469–99. Portions of chapters 3 and 4 were previously published as "Projecting Pornography and Mapping Modernity in Mexico City," *Journal of Urban History* 38, no. 3 (May 2012): 467–87.

Library of Congress Cataloging-in-Publication Data
Sluis, Ageeth, 1964–
Deco body, deco city: female spectacle and
modernity in Mexico City, 1900–1939 / Ageeth Sluis.
pages   cm. — (The Mexican experience)
Includes bibliographical references and index.
ISBN 978-0-8032-9382-3 (paperback: alk. paper)
ISBN 978-0-8032-9390-8 (epub)
ISBN 978-0-8032-9391-5 (mobi)
ISBN 978-0-8032-9392-2 (pdf)
1. Women's studies—Mexico—Mexico City.
2. Feminism—Mexico—Mexico City.
3. Transgenderism—Mexico—Mexico City.
4. Mexico City (Mexico)—History—20th century.
I. Title.
HQ1181.M6S58 2015   305.420972'53—dc23
2015019355

Set in Sabon Next Pro by L. Auten.

CONTENTS

ILLUSTRATIONS

ACKNOWLEDGMENTS

Writing a book is a long and often arduous journey. From dissertation to manuscript, the writing of *Deco Body, Deco City* was complicated by long hiatuses due to heavy loads of pre-tenure teaching and service commonplace at a small university, big life changes, and—well, life in general. It also benefited from spurts of new energy and ideas, the infusion of new research collected on summer trips, inspiration from new secondary sources and theoretical works, and helpful critiques collected on the conference circuit. And, various experiences sparked ideas and influenced how I engaged with the project—those moments of stasis in motion or motion in stasis experienced while sitting on a bus, seeing the landscape go by, and making connections. This made the journey much more interesting, richer, and deeper, and all the more worthwhile undertaking. Though frustrating at times, these periods of starts, stops, spurts, and "stalling" ultimately enriched the book.

Needless to say, although I undertook the journey as one person, I was never really alone. I owe enormous debts of gratitude for those fellow travelers who were extremely generous with their time and insights. This book would have not been possible without the help and support of many mentors, colleagues, and friends. *Deco Body, Deco City* began as a dissertation completed at the University of Arizona, and many of the ideas that form its bedrock were inspired by courses and discussions with faculty and fellow graduate students. I am indebted to Kevin Gosner for calm yet engaged criticism. Bert Barickman's enthusiastic, at times bewildering, but always stimulating comments and inquiry sustained me throughout my studies. From the very beginning, as an undergraduate in the 1990s, when I first wandered into their classrooms, they fostered my interest in and helped me understand this place called Latin America. I was very fortunate to work with Stacy Widdifield, who deepened my fascination with Mexico City and photography; Karen Anderson, who set me on a lifelong path to learning about the politics of gender; and Donna Guy, who made sure I asked the right questions. I am especially grateful to my adviser, Bill Beezley, for his infectious enthusiasm, patience, support, eagle-eye editorial skills, and never-ending quest to eliminate jargon. A very special thanks goes to the irreplaceable Adrian Bantjes.

I also owe an enormous debt to my cohort at the University of Arizona, whose insights, criticism, and stimulus enriched this project and my life. Throughout my graduate career at the University of Arizona I was surrounded by a group of amazing individuals with whom I was lucky to share course work, passionate debate, and camaraderie. I want to thank Tracy Alexander, Glenn Avent, Michelle Berry, Celeste González de Bustamante, Rachel Kram-Villareal, Amanda Lopez, Michael Matthews, Gretchen Pierce, Monica Rankin, and especially my *compañeras*—Lean Sweeney, Melissa Guy, and Tracy Goode—for our ongoing conversations and friendship. Thank you.

In Mexico City, I need to thank the staff at the Archivo General de la Nación, Fideicomiso Plutarco Elías Calles y Fernando Torreblanca, and especially the Archivo Histórico del Distrito Federal. Guillermo Palacios at Colegio de México graciously offered his support, library, and contacts. I owe a very special thanks to Carmen Nava at UAM–Xochimilco, whose kind hospitality, intellectual generosity, and vast knowledge of Mexican history never ceased to amaze me. I had the good fortune to attend the Oaxaca Summer Institute for Mexican History, which greatly benefited my project. I am grateful to the faculty, staff, and students who provided the fertile ground upon which this project grew and offered helpful suggestions, feedback, and criticism. I especially want to thank Ann Blum, Katherine Bliss, Diane Davis, John Hart, Gil Joseph, Alan Knight, Pablo Piccato, Debra Poole, and Gabriela Soto-Laveaga, as well as all 2001, 2003, and 2009 fellows, especially Rob Alegre, Jeff Banister, Sarah Beckhart, Robert Jordan, Aurea Toxqui, and Eddie Wright-Rios. I owe a very special thanks to *comadre* María Muñoz for her relentless criticism and unqualified friendship, and Bill French for the suggestion of the book's much improved title. My time in Mexico would have not been the same without two very remarkable women and scholars, Anne Rubenstein and Eileen Ford, who in realms professional and personal became my mentors, counselors, champions, and, in one case, a dissertation committee member. *Mil gracias.*

During many years of drafts and revisions, the book has benefited tremendously from the critical eye of many amazing scholars. I want to thank Melissa Guy, Michael Matthews, Anne Rubenstein, Kristin Swenson, and especially Tracy Goode for their invaluable advice, edits, and suggestions. A big thanks also to Pamela Voekel, Elliott Young, Reiko Hillyer, and all at the Tepotzlán Institute for Transnational History of the Americas for their stimulating work and discussions. At Butler University, I would like to thank the Butler Awards Committee, whose generous funding supported additional research in Mexico, Brazil, and the United States, and my colleagues in the History and Anthropology Department and the Gender, Women, and Sexuality Studies program. I especially thank the participants of several writing groups that sustained me and prodded me forward. The book would have not have been completed if not for the opportunity afforded me by the School for Advanced Research, where I had the great fortune of working during my sabbatical. Thanks to the wonderful community of fellows, artists, researchers, and staff, Nicole Taylor, James Brooke, John Kantner, and Nancy Owens in particular. I also want to acknowledge my anonymous reviewers for their helpful insights, comments, and questions, as well as Bridget Barry at the University of Nebraska Press. Needless to say, any remaining errors are my own.

Lastly, I want to express my everlasting gratitude to family: my mother, Marry Dijksman, who supported me and helped me in ways too many to enumerate; my sister, Miriam Sluis, whose intelligence and enduring attraction to realms unknown and spaces unexplored has inspired me from childhood; and sweet Aidan-Xenon, whose amazing imagination, boundless creativity, endless curiosity about the world, and patience with the completion of "that book" have been a constant inspiration. I do not have enough words to express my gratitude to Elise, not only for her keen insights, sharp critique, and sustained help with this project, but also—and more importantly—for her continual support, near impossible optimism, infectious enthusiasm, and undying friendship and love. I dedicate this work to all of you.

deco body, deco city

Introduction

During and after the armed phase of the Mexican Revolution (1910–20), which claimed over one million lives and displaced many more, Mexico City experienced a drastic influx of female migrants. Some hoped to escape the ravages of war in the countryside, while others sought refuge after losing male protection due to the death of their husbands, fathers, and brothers. Poor female migrants generally settled in crowded *vecindades* (slums) or in *viviendas* (tenements) in the city center. For these disadvantaged women new to the capital, the informal economy of street vending, domestic service, and prostitution often provided the only means of survival. Destitute, vulnerable, and sexualized as *mujeres callejeras* (women of the street), they were seen by upper- and middle-class residents as shameful spectacles of poverty and a powerful reminder of revolutionary upheaval in the heart of the capital city.

The revolution, however, also carved out new social spaces in which women could exercise agency, propelled women to take up traditionally male roles in the absence of men, and created new jobs in the public sphere that were open to women. High levels of urbanization only added new opportunities for women. Swept up in the revolution, whether by force or choice, women became part of a transnational movement connecting them to both revolutionary politics and nascent consumerism. Like other early-twentieth-century burgeoning cities, Mexico City experienced the influx of a heterogeneous population that allowed for a rise in new activities that facilitated female mobility. By moving through new physical places and social territories, these women—especially lower-class women of rural origin—were exposed to novel ways of thinking, living, and expressing themselves. Entertainment, especially theatergoing, exposed them to actresses performing new roles of female comportment, while new publications on fashion, sports, and leisure changed the way they visualized the capital. In short, the revolution had the unintended consequence of urbanizing women, forcing them into public spaces and making them more cosmopolitan.

These gendered effects of the revolution would lead the new government officials to reinvigorate and "civilize" Mexico City through a series of urban reforms and public works. From the 1920s to the 1940s the country experienced the "institutionalized revolution," an intense period of state-led social reforms aimed at overhauling cultural norms and modernizing the citizenry. Concern over women in public places resonated strongly throughout this period as political leaders linked nation building with family reform. State anxieties over "free women" and the impending disintegration of society mounted during the 1920s and 1930s with the arrival of "New Women," such as the flapper, and a proliferation in women's activism. Governmental elites reacted to changes in female identities and accompanying activism by attempting to regulate women's bodies and sexuality. They feared the spectacle of "public women," including prostitutes, actresses, *chicas modernas* (modern girls), and working-class women. These figures, as women and archetypes, all occupied visible positions in social movements of the day and were seen as undermining revolutionary efforts to strengthen nuclear families and socialize women to embrace their "proper roles" as mothers and wives.

Revolutionary leaders promoted urban reform to create a healthy, safe, and, above all, modern urban utopia to reflect revolutionary reform based on a gendered view of the city's social and spatial geography. Fearing the spectacle of "public women," they created spaces of containment within the public sphere such as indoor markets, theaters, and the *zonas libres* (prostitution districts; literally, "free zones") set aside for legalized prostitution. These feminized containment areas contrasted sharply with other burgeoning sites of urban development, such as stadiums, schools, and monuments intended to memorialize the revolution and its heroes. In analyzing the construction of this revolutionary, utopian city, *Deco Body, Deco City* focuses on the intersections of urban reform, public-works projects, and new gender norms to show how changing gender roles—in the form of new behavior but especially new bodily ideals—influenced the reshaping of Mexico City in the 1930s.

The large public-works projects, such as markets, parks, and monuments, as well as upscale, middle-class *colonias* (neighborhoods), such as colonia Condesa, were not only conceived to augment living conditions in Mexico City and make the city appear more modern, but also occurred because of concern over—and infatuation with—the new female types of embodiment. The "Deco body" was a new, ideal female physique that stressed length, height, and androgyny, and this new aesthetic echoed in urban landscapes. By linking new forms of femininity with transnational cosmopolitanism, female Deco bodies helped to usher in new gender ideals and visualize an urban "mestizo modernity." Consequently, while much revolutionary urban reform worked to control women's movements in the public sphere, female bodies as concept and form also inspired urban-renewal efforts.

Deco Body, Deco City explores Mexico City from the turn of the century, the heyday of the Porfiriato, through the armed and institutional phases of the Mexican Revolution. It not only looks at structural change in the city but also humanizes those changes by following the movements, actions, and lives of Mexican New Women such as the actresses Esperanza Iris and Maria Conesa and the columnists Cube Bonifant and Carmina, in addition to the artists, writers, and less-famous (but just as interesting) women who appear in police, medical, and other governmental records and in newspaper and magazine articles. By analyzing representations of "modern women" in popular media, theater productions, film, art, and architecture, this book inquires into the intersections of gender, embodiment, sexuality, and urban space at a moment of great change.

CITY

Mexico City experienced great changes in its transition from Porfirian showcase to revolutionary city. In 1899, counting but 344,721 inhabitants, it was rather small.[1] Although it had undergone drastic changes during the early Porfiriato, the city still bore distinct traces from its colonial past, with the division of eight districts, for example, that went back to viceregal regulations.[2] The center consisted of the remainder of the old *traza*, ten to fifteen blocks around the Zócalo (main square in Mexico City) that had been set aside for elite *peninsulares* (Spaniards born in Spain) during early colonization. Large colonial structures— mansions, churches, government palaces—dominated the city center (now *centro histórico*), and their characteristic red tezontle stones, re- cycled from Mexica temples, reminded all who moved through this cityscape of the city's colonial foundations. These structures, as well as public places such as the Alameda Central, a park that dated to the 1590s and had been the centro's premier space of leisure for the city's well-to-do since the eighteenth century, were physical cues ensconced in the urban landscape that spoke to the colonial past.

Modernization projects mapped onto this colonial structure re- flected the changing economic, social, and political conditions of the late Porfiriato. Like rapidly growing cities elsewhere in Latin America, Mexico City absorbed a continual stream of displaced rural migrants.[3] The city's population nearly tripled between 1870 and 1910, when it reached 471,066. Roughly half of the capital's inhabitants came from other states, many from the countryside.[4] Most of these migrants crowded the tenement belt east of the Zócalo, which doubled in size from 1880 to 1900, at which point more than a third of the city's population lived in an area that composed less than 15 percent of the overall urban landmass.[5] This influx informed the formation of both symbolic and structural demarcations of an impoverished eastern district positioned against an affluent western district.

The western district in many ways represented the regime's "show- case of progress and peace," a barometer by which to measure Porfirian success.[6] Covering the area from the Zócalo in the east to the Alameda Park in the west, this district had a distinctly performative charac- ter, representing elite increase in consumption and leisure. With its grandiose architecture, Plateros Street (today's Avenida Madero), the west side's main artery that connected the Zócalo with the Alameda, functioned as a stage where the elite performed their identity as *gente decente* (as the wealthy referred to themselves; literally, "decent people") by showing off their wealth, fashion tastes, and enviable levels of comfort. They shopped at fancy department stores such as Liverpool and El Palacio de Hierro, dined at French restaurants like Sylvain, sipped tea from English china at Sanborns, and mingled with other rich and powerful citizens at the Jockey Club. With its palaces of consumption, fine restaurants, and European airs, Plateros Street joined the political space of the Zócalo with the realm of leisure of Alameda Park and functioned as a gateway to new, modern neighborhoods along the grand Reforma Boulevard. As such, the west, as historian Michael Johns notes, not merely represented a separate neighborhood but also harbored "a distinct way of life" that symbolized an "urbane, civilized and modern Mexico" that evoked Europe.[7]

The spatial expression, in keeping with this show of affluence that William Beezley has called the "Porfirian persuasion," shaped the city in new ways at the turn of the twentieth century. It played out on the city's west side in the many upscale theaters. Teatros Principal, Arbeu, and Fábregas were just a block away from Plateros Street. The famous Coliseo, which had been in operation since the colonial period and had come under control of the city upon independence, was but a few streets over.[8] At the end of the street at Alameda, the Palacio de Bellas Artes (Palace of Fine Arts), destined to become the new Teatro Nacional (National Theater), was under construction by the early 1900s.[9] Further west of the centro lay the neighborhoods that had come of age in the late nineteenth century, such as Santa María de la Ribera (1861), Guerrero (1874), and San Rafael (1891). They accommodated the *pequeña burguesía* (petit bourgeois) who worked as shopkeepers, skilled workers, lower-rung administrators, and professionals to create the opulence that the elite enjoyed.[10] And it was in the new, elite neighborhoods of Roma and Juárez that the Porfirian city—in celebration of the positivist dictum of order and progress—found its greatest expression. Around 1900, elites again moved further west of the center to these new colonias along Reforma Boulevard toward Chapultepec Castle and the adjacent park in an attempt to escape from the unwashed masses in the centro once and for all.[11]

Indeed, the Porfirian city was not the place of affluence, luxury, and finery that elites hoped for. The centro was increasingly one of stark contrasts. The large colonial mansions left behind by elites had deteriorated into tenements where working-class families lived in extremely close quarters, adding to the sense of encroachment from the east into the center. Newly paved streets, grand new buildings, and street traffic appeared as tangible successes of Porfirian attempts at modernization, but the presence of the poor on these streets amid this modern decor painted a different picture: "nude and hungry alcoholics" lay about, sleeping "street people" fell victim to the new trolleys, and the destitute used their *petate* (traditional woven mat) in public as a bed at night or table by day, while their blankets served to cover sleep and sex alike.[12]

Even more demonstrative of these contrasts were the *barrios populares* (lower-class neighborhoods) on the city's northeast edge, where poverty, disease, and disorder reigned. The east side bore the brunt of the newcomers who had been forced into the city from the *campo* (countryside) as well as displaced laborers who were forced to leave the city's west side to make way for elite new neighborhoods. Most of the inhabitants of the east side suffered from poor sanitation, crowded streets, and a lack of basic services. Unlike Roma, with its careful planning and regard for refined aesthetics, the working-class barrios north and east of the Zócalo, such as La Bolsa and Tepito, represented the hazards of *autoconstrucción* (haphazard, unplanned construction), as most lacked basic facilities such as water, sewers, and paved streets.[13] Most of the east side was notorious for filth, disease, and especially crime, characteristics that, in the Porfirian imagination, were less a product of poverty than the result of the moral inferiority of its population. Many new colonias in the east grew out of the indigenous *parcialdades* (segregated areas determined during colonial era), which, even when absorbed by the growing city, retained their "traditional character" and attracted newly arrived rural migrants because of the convenient location and fairly low cost of living. These colonias in the east, finds James Garza, "lay outside . . . cultural modernity, informally belonging to the countryside."[14] These "rural" barrios thus clashed with the Porfirian dream of the ideal and modern city, a showcase of progress and civilization that was both clean and aesthetically pleasing.[15]

The tensions between rich and poor, east and west, and modern urbanity and "uncivilized" campo in many ways worsened and took on different meanings during the armed phase of the revolution, when the city experienced a drastic influx of rural female migrants. Because the capital had been spared the devastation and violence that typified the armed struggle in the countryside, it attracted women who hoped to escape the ravages of war and sought refuge after losing male protection due to death and abandonment. Many parents also sent their daughters to the capital because they believed that the city was safer than the war-torn campo.[16] Life in the city, however, was not as stable as anticipated. In the face of food and housing shortages complicated by sporadic incursions of revolutionary warfare, poor female migrants arriving in the city found opportunities of survival slim.[17] While some women turned to factory work, most survived as street vendors, prostitutes, or servants for the remnant of the Porfirian middle-class society and the emerging revolutionary elite.[18]

The effects of the revolution in the capital city proved important in the formation of female urban working-class identity and struggle and in the visibility of female activism. As John Lear has noted, working-class communities living in squalor relied heavily on female support and organization. Lower-class women's militancy expressed itself in protests and neighborhood actions, such as food riots in reaction to the poor distribution of staple items.[19] Male revolutionaries, journalists, and union leaders condemned these protests as anarchistic and even anti-revolutionary, although rioting women justified their actions as mothers. Conservative politicians questioned these women's morals, referring to them as *mujerzuelas* (loose women) and *populacho* (rabble), and positioned the virtues of *señoras decentes* (respectable upper-class women) against female rioters, who (like prostitutes) were seen as lazy and promiscuous women who transgressed traditional gender boundaries. Considered out of place and out of control, they were even thought to pose a threat to the revolution itself.[20]

Upon securing victory, revolutionary leaders initially dealt with urbanization in a reactive and haphazard manner. This was especially true in their attempts to accommodate the enormous influx of female migrants from the war-torn countryside. In the early years of his presidency, Álvaro Obregón ordered the Departamento de Salubridad Pública (Department of Public Health) to conduct an investigation into the city's problems, especially housing conditions. The dismal state of the vecindades that were home to rural migrants, especially in the central working-class colonias such as La Bolsa, Tepito, and Hidalgo (now Doctores), required immediate attention. The investigation found that tenement residents not only lived in squalid conditions (often in extremely cramped quarters without basic facilities) but also cohabited with domesticated animals and built annexes in the streets to use as workshops or food stalls, behavior that elites associated with the less-than-desirable aspects that migrants brought from the campo. Obregón issued legislation that led to two decrees in the early 1920s that aimed to address rent increases and the growing demand for apartments for the middle and working classes. He also facilitated the construction for a fair share of schools and clinics to serve these overcrowded neighborhoods.[21]

The president's efforts at solving urban problems, however, did not meet with unqualified support; moreover, they had two unintended outcomes. First, the majority of property owners used the decrees to build houses in zones with the highest demand, such as the upscale areas of Juárez and Roma, which did little to benefit the public at large. Second, rent increases continued while congestion persisted.[22] Patrice Olsen has argued that the focus of urban development during the tenure of Sonoran leaders such as Obregón and Calles was not on fulfillment of the revolution's call to social justice but on the "reconstruction of legitimate government itself."[23] Urbanization programs concentrated on the modern colonias of the west side, such as Juárez, Roma, and the new Condesa, where vast resources were committed toward upscale residential zones. Large public works such as the construction of the Valley of Mexico's Drainage Canal benefited colonia Roma and Condesa but ignored poor barrio residents.[24] Despite revolutionary efforts at urban reform, the capital faced a worsening situation by the late 1920s brought on by rapid urbanization, private business interests, lack of proper city planning, and poor enforcement of building regulations.

Part of the failure of governmental plans at controlling urban growth sprang from changing political conditions in the Federal District during and after the armed phase of the revolution. Mexico City's municipal authority reemerged from 1910 to 1928, when the city returned to the democratic *ayuntamiento* system of separate municipal governments. Discontent over absent or inadequate basic services and control over public space gave rise to intensifying battles over jurisdiction and the responsibility of administration between the central government of the city and its separate and distinct ayuntamientos. Legislation often favored the political power of the governor's office, while municipal governments shouldered most of the burden for the upkeep and development of the city.[25] Municipal governments accused federal powers of suppressing the *municipio libre*, the cherished freedom of local authority that had been at the heart of the revolutionary struggle and was enshrined in the 1917 Constitution.[26] Yet, despite the municipal governments' more favorable political climate for the participation of lower-class groups and their sizable budgets for pavement and public sanitation works, they did not furnish the poor colonias with potable water, sewage, and waste collection.[27] Regardless of Obregón's recommendations, municipal leaders preferred fixing the city's infrastructure at the expense of housing and basic services in the name of modernization.[28] Whether unable or unwilling, the ayuntamientos failed to deal effectively with urban growth and remedy the abuses of construction companies and the dreadful conditions of hygiene that prevailed in the lower-class colonias.[29]

As a disjointed set of municipal governments, the city did little to alleviate the problems that accompanied urban growth. The slow pace in the execution of large public-works projects radically changed after 1929, when the federal government did away with the ayuntamientos in favor of the new Departamento del Distrito Federal (DDF, Department of the Federal District). In doing so, it gained exclusive rights to determine the future of the city. By bringing the zone that encompassed the capital under federal control, the national government literally paved the way for the city's expansion as urban boundaries now reflected those of the much larger Federal District. During the period 1930 and 1934, both the federal government and the DDF authorities provided the impetus to solve urban problems. The majority of large public-works projects began during the tenure of President Abelardo Rodríguez and were the result of the 1933 Ley de Planificación y Zonificación del Distrito Federal y Territorios de Baja California (Planning and Zoning Law for the Federal District and the Territories of Baja California). Rodríguez also founded the Architecture Council, which was to review proposals for new buildings, regulate construction licenses, and generally control the form cityscape should take.[30] He appointed Aarón Sáenz as the head of the Distrito Federal in 1932, and Sáenz initiated a vast building program that included the creation of 250 primary and secondary schools (including the gigantic Centro Escolar Revolucionario), low-income housing for workers in colonias Balbuena and San Jacinto, enormous infrastructure projects, several important monuments (such as the Monument to the Revolution), and the subjects of the last two chapters of this book, the Mercado Abelardo Rodríguez and the completion of the Palacio de Bellas Artes.[31]

MODERNITY, REVOLUTION, AND GENDER

When U.S. journalist Carleton Beals returned to the Mexican capital in 1930 after a ten-year absence, he found that what had been a "sleepy little world" had made way for a bustling metropolis. If in 1920 Mexico City had appeared a monotonous, provincial town without *gran vías*, grand aspirations, and even fewer dramatic occurrences, by 1930 the city exhibited all the allure and anxieties of a truly modern metropolis. From 1918 to 1930 the city's surface had tripled and the population almost doubled.[32] The horse-drawn carriages that had been commonplace on the city's streets had made way for cars, and the characteristic cobblestones had been traded in for asphalt. A near invasion of U.S. products and advertisements following on the heels of famous movie stars, and the arrival of the first tourists from the United States changed the feel of the city. As U.S. writer and traveler Anita Brenner noted, neon signs almost made one forget the existence of the vecindades. Beals wondered if the city was still Mexican in the face of this rapid pace of modernization.[33]

What was it exactly that made Mexico City modern?[34] While this is a seemingly straightforward question, it is a highly complex one that forms a major source of inquiry and guideline of this book. As a concept, modernity appears quite intangible and, as an always moving target and ideal, never quite complete. However, we recognize modernity by the markers that render it visible. If it appeared to U.S. travelers and journalists that Mexico City had become "modern" by the early 1930s, this was because particular visible cues signaled that it had. Urbanization often functions as either a measuring stick or a platform for modernity's inroads. Moreover, modifications in the urban landscape not only provide a visible record of the pace of modernization through technological, architectural, and commercial innovations but also function as a means to inculcate desired, "modern" behavior. Michel Foucault taught us that the development of modernity went hand-in-hand with ever-tightening definitions of normality, greater state control over human minds and bodies through what he referred to as "biopower," and, consequently, the production of deviance. The modernity championed by bourgeois liberalism produced discourses that normalized society, creating marginal groups and individuals in the process. Modernity, especially when tied to statecraft and governance, as James Scott has demonstrated, also hinged on a desire for simplification that drives projects of internal colonization as a "civilizing mission." Walter Mignolo agrees that, in order to understand ongoing colonial practices in Latin America, we have to explore modernity as coloniality's "historical counterpart."[35]

The development of Mexico City from 1900 to 1940, an era of rapid modernization in the face of persistent colonial legacies, has much to teach us about the processes in which gender and race relations interfaced with early-twentieth-century modernity. Seen as facilitating the implementation of "civilizing missions" to newly arrived migrants and other marginalized groups, the built environment, in the form of architecture, public art, and urban reform, had the ability to modify the cityscape, influence human activities, and symbolize desired behavior.[36] As early as the Porfiriato, especially Díaz's emphasis on economic and technological modernity, urban modernization plans had an unmistakably cultural component. Urban environments, Mexico City in particular, were seen or used as stages to demonstrate and teach Mexicans—especially the illiterate ones—the trappings of civilization, respect for the regime, and more generally, appropriate ways of acting, dressing, and appearing modern.[37] Indeed, residents of the capital city learned, as Carlos Monsiváis described, an *"irresponsible love of modernity"* that reverberates in the built environment of Mexico City today.[38]

Upon securing national power, the Constitutionalists sought to remake society not only economically and politically but also culturally. The cultural project of the revolutionary leadership, namely, molding the "hearts and minds" of the citizenry through education, popular culture, and new technological means such as radio and film, was as extensive as the scholarship documenting the phenomenon.[39] It was in these efforts that the onset of an overtly transnational, capitalist modernity and revolutionary reforms intersected and found expression in Mexico City's urban landscape.

In addition to governmental efforts to shape the built environment through new, often modern architecture in large public-works and urban-reform efforts of the 1930s, the infiltration of U.S. advertisements and other commercial imagery was, as Beals and Brenner noted, palpable. The sheer proliferation of images and urban reform projects signaled to *capitalinos* and *capitalinas* not only what the city was becoming but even more how it could be imagined.[40] Mexico City's cultural transformation was the culmination of long-term developments, including an increase in economic growth, literacy rates, and advertising, which by the 1930s had left their marks on the urban landscape. New forms of visual culture were indicative of a new age of seeing, influenced by the advent of cinema, technological developments in photography, and advances in print culture.

This book takes as a central premise that ideas about gender played a large role in the processes to modernize and civilize Mexico's citizenry as well as the way the capital city was altered as a principal machine in inculcating modernity. Of course, the revolution (the armed phase and its institutionalization) affected women and men differently, and this shaped how leaders planned the reform phase of the revolution, including urban development. The quest for modernity in 1920s and 1930s Mexico City was articulated through notions of gender, and especially through changing ideas of femininity. The tension between modernity—usually predicated on U.S. and European values—and tradition found some its greatest expressions in concern over changing gender norms. The influx of women, especially those without male protection, into the capital city, coupled with a new visibility of female mobility, coincided with the first sustained efforts at urban reform.

Early gender scholarship on the Mexican Revolution argued that women who had actively participated in the war or whose lives had been strongly affected by it did not receive the advantages that revolutionary programs promised all citizens. According to Elizabeth Salas, the turbulent political situation actually hampered the fight for women's rights, and despite early gains, the women's movement suffered from the effects of warfare.[41] More-recent studies have shown that the revolutionary cultural project itself, rather than political instability and structural forces, greatly hindered the feminist cause. By redirecting women to the private sphere as mothers with governmental incorporation of women's groups in a top-down manner, new leaders hampered progress. Despite large cross-class alliances, mobilization, and activism, women did not achieve either gender parity or the right to vote; thus the current state of the historiography suggests that women were unable to significantly challenge the structures of patriarchy.[42]

Modernity complicated the revolutionary agenda with respect to women. As in Europe and the United States after World War I, women in revolutionary Mexico occupied more-visible roles in society after the war. The revolution initially appeared to open spaces for women to reformulate gender roles and provided a platform to demand political rights and economic possibilities. Not only did women have a greater opportunity to enter the public sphere as workers, teachers, consumers, and activists, but they also began to look and act differently. The chica moderna, inspired by changing gender roles in Europe and the United States, challenged both traditional expectations and revolutionary reform movements. Many urban women admired or attempted to transform themselves into these "modern girls" who cut their braids, danced to new music, and seemed to defy the stereotypical abnegating wife and mother championed by revolutionary reform efforts.[43]

Anxieties over a change in gender roles was one problem of modernity, albeit a persistent one, as ideas of female honor structured the sanctity of both the middle-class home and the nation. Hence the articulation of revolutionary modernity required particular contributions from women. If revolutionaries envisioned a traditional role for the revolutionary woman that relegated her back to the private sphere as mother and wife,[44] they did so out of a sense of what Mary Kay Vaughan has called "modernized patriarchy,"[45] focusing on scientific motherhood and the image of the New Woman as a productive mother and wife. The new state also embarked on large-scale efforts to civilize the popular classes through gender-specific programs. In their attempts to contain prostitutes, reform market women, modernize young *indígena* (indigenous) migrants, and censor adult theater, state officials privileged women over men as stand-ins for their class and race.

Despite protests, governmental reforms resulted in reinforcing traditional spaces for women. Revolutionary reform perpetuated traditional gender roles and devalued women's bid for public power as agents in control of their own destinies. However, these setbacks would not manifest themselves until the mid- to late 1930s, and the early revolutionary period appeared to hold many promises for female advancement. Through the rise of mass media, Mexico became increasingly connected with the outside world. Despite the nationalist—and masculine—nature of the institutionalized revolution, modern ideas of how men and women should (or could) behave pervaded films, the lyrics of songs heard on the radio, and advertising in magazines. In its budding cosmopolitanism, or desire for it, the city itself became a theater in which women and men could imagine themselves playing different roles.

Mexico City's changing cityscape was tracked and articulated through a gendered framework that posited women in public as spectacles. In addition to imagery that came from abroad, a plethora of revolutionary art and film, both government-sponsored and commercial, flooded the Mexican national consciousness. Through this new visual discourse, women's identity emerged as a social problem. More than simply associated with "modern women," the city came to be embodied by the female form in a variety of iterations.[46] Traveler Stuart Chase, visiting in 1931, described the changes in the capital city's urban landscape: "The talkies are all over town, the flappers have their fine black eyes unswervingly on Fifth Avenue."[47] However, the visibility of women in public who appeared unattached and independent, poor, and recently arrived from the campo lent the modernizing cityscape an unheimish feeling.

Deco Body, Deco City envisions the development of Mexico City through the lens of spectacle as a two-pronged approach: the visibility of women's social and physical mobility in the city, and the entertainment industry as helping to facilitate these changes. In his 1967 treatise, *The Society of the Spectacle*, Guy Debord outlined the perils of advanced capitalism in a society informed by "spectacle." Tracing the inception of this type of society to the modernism of the 1920s, Debord found that spectacle amounted to more than "a deliberate distortion of the visual world or as a product of the technology of the mass dissemination of images." Rather, spectacle itself became an "actualized," material worldview, a way of being.[48] In Mexico City, this spectacle, the hypervisibility of transnational capitalism and modernity, was largely seen as embodied by women; that is, women's mobility in urban, public spaces appeared a requisite for modernity.

While primarily examining gender performances in theater as a barometer of change in attitudes toward masculine and feminine behavior, I follow Judith Butler's understanding of performativity as everyday practice reaching far beyond the stage. Butler uses performance as a metaphor to understand that "nature" does not exist, and thus that biologically equivalent bodies may "perform" different genders and forms of embodiment. All identities are performances, yet only certain performances are discernible within the larger constructs of normality.[49] Taking Butler's insights into consideration, spectacle, or the power of seeing and being seen and its attendant media—radio, advertising, modern magazines, photography, and the "theater of the screen," film—facilitated the construction of the new modern, and especially newly gendered, subject. The spectacle driving these new culture industries taught women to perform modern identities through makeup, clothes, posture, mannerisms, and attitude.

During the early decades of the twentieth century the modern metropolis offered greater opportunities for female mobility, sociability, and independence through the rise of entertainment, other leisure activities, and new forms of consumption. Many working, and other financially independent, women used their money with the distinct aim to engage in fashionable entertainments. Inspired by "world cities" such as London and New York, post-revolutionary Mexico City formed a nexus of urban modernity, consumer outlets, and rapid changes in the gender order. Its markets, department stores, theaters, cinemas, dance halls, and zonas libres were places that women, including middle-class women, increasingly frequented. In this transnational environment, changing ideas of body, beauty, and femininity reached Mexico City largely by way of the entertainment industry.[50] As the highly visible markers occupying the centers of modernity, actresses, models, and pinup girls left their imprints on the city's urban landscape. Large *espectáculos* (as variety shows are known in Mexico) had a tremendous influence on ideas about how to appear modern in public. These shows invited Mexican women of different classes and ethnicities to freely move around the modern metropolis and engage in the daily performance of gender.

It was through the entertainment industry, especially spectacular phenomena such as the Deco body, that *capitalinas* learned how to act and appear modern. The Deco body marked a shift from the nineteenth-century aesthetic embodied by the theater diva to the new beauty ideal characterized by the movie star. The voluptuous hourglass figure of the Victorian era, enhanced by restrictive corsets, gave way to the long, sleek physique of well-toned female bodies still celebrated today as the reigning beauty ideal. Lean and slender like the elongated lines of Art Deco, the Deco body literally embodied the aesthetics of the machine age. Whether the serial body parts in theater productions such as the Ziegfeld Follies that resembled the assembly line of a factory, the female android in Fritz Lang's *Metropolis*, or the spectacular stars of the 1925 hit variety show *Voilá la ba-ta-clán*, Deco bodies projected geometric, abstract shapes that dazzled audiences. By the mid-1920s, beauty contestants and experts on physical health considered the body "physical machinery" that reflected modern ideas of health, hygiene, and perfection, all of which were intimately related to the cultivation of physical beauty.

Even if the appearance of the Deco body was a transnational phenomenon that had originated in Europe and the United States, film and theater spectacles functioned as a catalyst in transforming female beauty and cosmopolitan living in Mexico. The Deco body proved highly adaptable to local conditions. Despite its less-than-patriotic qualities, the Deco body reminded both indigenous and mestizo Mexicans that race was no longer as much about color as it was about form. The mestizo modernity propagated by Deco bodies exemplified an accommodation of Western affluence and *mexicanidad* (Mexicanness) as it offered a solution to neutralize the tension between *indigenismo* and *mestizaje*.[51] The conception of the female form as a set of minimal, long lines became a global ideal that reached Mexico, influencing not only female audiences but also architects. U.S. and European cultural influence altered not only the dress and demeanor of its inhabitants but also the built environment, especially because of the conceptualization of women's appearance and modern architecture as mutually constitutive. As Elizabeth Grosz notes, in terms of "cultural saturation" the city "reconstitutes" the body as much as the body "absorbs" the city.[52] A new understanding of female beauty articulated by Deco bodies onstage, whether in the theater or the shop window, called for new definitions of beauty, race, and embodiment.

Ideas about female space in the capital city also hinged on historical and ideological formulations of rural Mexico. In adapting European discourses of modernity and aesthetics, Mexican elites of the 1920s and 1930s developed what I call *camposcape*, a distinctive form of orientalism that equated exotic landscapes of the countryside with indígenas, the past, and national identity. Because of the campo's perceived ties to an eternal and unchanging nature, camposcape represented a constellation of spatial imaginaries imbued with pastoral qualities rendered as timeless, static in geographic, physical, and human features.[53] As a place outside time, it represented a glorified but unspecified past, what Guillermo Bonfil Batalla calls "deep Mexico," a timeless, edenic site of mexicanidad. What made camposcape quintessentially Mexican were its links to indigenous people, lending camposcape particular qualities of internal exoticism.[54] Camposcape fit well, and was in many ways a perfect aesthetic accompaniment to, post-revolutionary indigenismo. If revolutionary cultural politics differed little from its Porfirian predecessors in terms of gender, the post-revolutionary emphasis on race, especially the focus on indigenismo and the creation of a mestizo nation, constituted a palpable difference. Revolutionary modernity was to be a "mestizo modernity." Reforms centered heavily on the elevation of the *campesino* as the authentic hallmark of *lo mexicano* (Mexicanness), and championed indigenismo as best representing mestizo national identity, especially in the visual arts, capturing the imagination of Mexicans and foreigners alike.[55]

The imagined oppositional relationship between the campo and the city, or between periphery and metropolis, structured Mexican discourses of modernity in the decades following the revolution. The romanticized version of the campo contrasted sharply with elite views of rural female migrants who had made their way to the capital in such great numbers. It was not merely these impoverished ex-campesinas but also the romantic qualities ascribed to them, especially in contrast with their ethnic and class counterparts in the city, that lent Mexican modernity a chaotic feel.[56] As the primary representatives of camposcape, market women and female vendors in the city were now visible at the margins of modernity. Moreover, as they transgressed social and gender boundaries, these women took on (or were co-opted by) the tenets of spectacle, albeit as a negative mirror image of their orientalist counterparts.

Camposcape informed urban reform in Mexico City, especially its indigenous and feminine connotations. By representing existing urban markets as places of danger and filth, reformers enacted plans to construct new markets, parks, and theaters as versions of camposcape. These reformist discourses were instrumental in strengthening popular perceptions among the ruling and emerging middle classes that street vending and outdoor markets posed a threat to civilized society as well as an obstacle to the development of the city as an attractive, healthy, and affluent capital. Indeed, the dramatic increase in urban-reform efforts spoke to a new perception of the city as a set of zones of containment and areas of mobility that were predicated on gendered understanding of public space, which in turn were tied to class and ethnicity.

With high levels of urbanization, the "spectacles" that mixed sex, class, and gender proved difficult to contain. Like other early-twentieth-century cities that experienced an influx of heterogeneous population and a growing amount of leisure activities, Mexico City became a theater of female physical and, at times, social mobility. By exploring visual culture (art, architecture, photography, and theater) as emerging culture industries that grappled with the promise and problem of modernity, this book demonstrates that recurrent visual tropes situating the metropolis through female vendors as rural anachronisms, as well as Deco-bodied actresses as modern liberated women, suited the agendas of revolutionary leaders and urban reformers who sought to remove market activity from the city streets, create productive citizens, contain female spectacle, safeguard national patrimony, and stimulate the development of a modern city.

≶ ≶ ≶

Sketching the shifting social and cultural geography from the dictatorship of Porfirio Díaz until the end of the armed phase of the revolution, chapter 1, "Performance: A City of Spectacles," provides an overview of the role of theater, especially famous actresses, in altering gender norms and urban life in the capital city. Framed by the debut of two great theater divas, Esperanza Iris and María Conesa, on the one hand, and the opening of the Teatro Iris, on the other, the chapter explores the influence of female theater performances on men's and women's changing perceptions of femininity and masculinity. These notions were articulated through discourses of the city, especially the understanding of public and private spheres and the positioning of urban life against the campo. Chapter 2, "*Bataclanismo*: From Divas to Deco Bodies," explores the theater as a social space and theater genres as both normative and transformative discourses in analyzing the transition of these changing ideals of femininity in the 1920s. By mapping the change from Porfirian divas to post-revolutionary Deco bodies, this chapter demonstrates how gender ideals influenced the creation of a distinct urban modernity in Mexico City. Using the phenomenon of *bataclanismo* as a barometer of this change, I argue that Deco bodies paved the way for a new, mestizo modernity. Not only did bataclanismo drastically alter the daily performance of gender and race, but it also changed the way the city was imagined. In the barrage of visual materials propagating the new Deco beauty ideal for women, Deco bodies and the city were often intertwined, demonstrating that modern women embodied the urban environment.

Chapter 3, "*Camposcape*: Naturalizing Nudity," examines how the visual arts were instrumental in furthering an exoticism that could be used to measure and fix metropolitan identities against (largely imagined) rural ones. As a distinctive Mexican form of internal exoticism predicated on European examples, camposcape equated the exotic with the feminine and articulated the desirability of healthy, and often nude, indigenous female bodies with nostalgic longings for a lost "Mexican Eden," the roots of the country's true nature. Ironically, however, it would be the Deco bodies of the stage that best performed camposcape in the city, demonstrating how gender and race were reinscribed on the city and on women's bodies through ostensibly competing discourses. The preoccupation with female nudity and sexuality in the wake of bataclanismo led to a new perception of the city as a set of zones of containment and areas of mobility. Chapter 4,

"Promis-ciudad: Projecting Pornography and Mapping Modernity," considers the ways in which nudity and the visibility of female sexuality serve as markers of modernity. Using popular periodicals such as the men's magazine *Vea* (1934–37) as an indicator of the revolutionary leadership's growing concern about public decency, pornography, and the definition of "appropriate" womanhood, the chapter explores the relationship between the growing visibility of female sexuality and ideas about the modern city.

After an overview of the gendered nature of public works executed by city planners in chapter 5, "Planning the Deco City: Urban Reform," which explains how the ideal of the Deco body influenced the re-shaping of the city through architecture, two case studies function as prisms through which to explore the development of gendered public spaces in the city center. As spatially and stylistically enantiomorphic constructions, one a market with a theater (the Mercado Abelardo Rodríguez in chapter 6), the other a theater with a market (Palacio de Bellas Artes in chapter 7), these building projects show how sites of entertainment and performed camposcape received top priority in revolutionary urban reforms. In addition to their practical functions in facilitating urban growth, markets were conceptualized as public theaters that animated and interwove a modernist nostalgia for traditional gender roles, an imagined campo, and revolutionary nationalism, while theaters showcased Deco bodies and female performances as markers of progress, cosmopolitanism, and transnational modernity.

The concern over poor women, public space, and private issues in the capital city was at the core of gendering the revolution and determined what direction that revolution would take. Market women, vendors, street performers, and prostitutes occupied an ever more important but highly ambiguous space on the cusp of public and private spheres, formal and informal economies, race and class identities, modernity and tradition. It is these spaces of the "Deco city" that this book explores and explains.

1

Performance

A CITY OF SPECTACLES

Esperanza Iris, the grand dame of Mexican operetta and the theater's namesake (fig. 1), felt nervous as she looked out over her audience while stagehands made the final preparations. On the night of its inauguration, the elegant theater was filled to the brim with the beau monde of Mexico City. The finest of families, celebrities, bon vivants, foreign dignitaries, reporters, and the top cadres of revolutionary leadership sat in the midst of the theater's refined grandeur. Velvet seats in the boxes, gold and marble ornamentation on the walls, sweeping staircases, and a sumptuous sculpted and warmly lit ceiling all added to the feel of a real *coliseo* befitting the capital city. The excitement of the public was palpable in the throng of voices. The theater was alive with socialites gossiping, families showing off debutantes, the new military elite displaying their stately finery, and young couples exchanging heated glances—a public engrossed in its own performance and spectacle. The revolution was over, and it was time for La Iris, who had but recently returned to Mexico, to conquer the hearts of the capitalinos once again.

The inauguration of the Teatro Esperanza Iris on May 25, 1818, was a crowning achievement for the diva. It was a festive occasion covered extensively by the press, with every last seat filled. Perhaps a full house was all but guaranteed due to publicity that had engulfed the theater since construction began. The commander of the revolutionary forces, Primer Jefe Don Venustiano Carranza—who sat in the best box in the house—attended along with high-ranking military officers, members of the diplomatic corps, and other well-known *políticos*. They listened to the national anthem and several acts of *La Duquesa del Bal-Tabarín*,

FIG. 1. Teatro Esperanza Iris, Donceles Street 36, Centro Histórico. Photo by the author.

the operetta that defined the career of the diva and earned her the title "La Emperatriz de Opereta." The ceremony ended with a concert sponsored by *teatro cronistas* (columnists) from the city's most important newspapers.[1]

This performance in 1918 marked a crowning moment for Iris. In 1899 she had stepped onto the stage as fourteen-year-old María Rosalía Esperanza Bofill Ferrer from the state of Tabasco in her first role as a newspaper boy. From there she embarked on a long career as a stage and film actress, impresario, and celebrity. In 1919, a mere twenty years later, she and her adopted city had changed significantly. Iris had exchanged her provincial origins for the status of a mature, wealthy metropolitan actress who owned her own theater company and had built her own theater. With this she inserted herself into the built environment of the city, and was thus emblematic of larger changes in the city itself. Her rise from newspaper boy to Porfirian diva exemplifies the changes brought about in the social and cultural geography from 1900 to 1920 (from the late Porfiriato until the end of the armed phase of the revolution), especially in terms of the way gender norms connected perceptions of modernity and urban life. Theater performances—as well as the public lives of divas like La Iris—influenced ideas of femininity and masculinity that were articulated through discourses of the city.

The theater world informed the "daily performances of gender" that capitalinos both saw and enacted upon the city streets. How they perceived the gendered nature and class segregation of their city and cityscapes was an extension of the performances they attended. Theater (especially before the advent of mass communication such as film) was the premier visual discourse that used the entanglement of city and gender to set the stage for new, modern sensibilities and subjectivities.

PERFORMATIVITY IN THE PORFIRIAN CITY

Esperanza Iris's debut in a small role on the stage of Mexico City's grand theater El Principal linked her public life of performance to that of the capital city. The play *La cuarta plana* (The fourth page), a spoof on current events in the city, featured adolescent Esperanza as a lovable but tough street kid hawking newspapers. Nineteen years later, La Iris was a diva of great renown in many Latin American countries who captured the hearts of theatergoers as "La Emperatriz de Opereta." But as she cemented her place in the city with the opening of the city's grandest theater, she could add another title to her repertoire: "La Hija Predelicta de Cuidad de México," Mexico City's favorite daughter.

Like Esperanza, Mexico City also had experienced great changes in its transition from Porfirian showcase to revolutionary city. In 1899, counting but 344,721 inhabitants, Mexico's capital was rather small.[2] Despite having undergone drastic changes during the early Porfiriato, the city still bore distinct traces of its colonial past, such as its division into eight districts.[3] The center consisted of the remainder of the old traza, ten to fifteen blocks around the Zócalo that had been set aside for elite peninsulares during early colonization. This central plaza, dominated by mansions, government buildings, and churches, including the Palacio Nacional and the Catedral Metropolitana built with the red tezontle stones recycled from Aztec temples, had functioned as the city's center of gravity since pre-Columbian times. The massive colonial mansions of this area (now known as the centro histórico) propelled Alexander von Humboldt to dub Mexico City the "City of Palaces" upon touring Spain's crown jewel in the early 1800s.[4] Despite colonial attempts to segregate urban space by safeguarding the traza for those of European descent, the centro was a place where classes mingled; and despite efforts to keep physical boundaries of social divisions in place during the Porfiriato, capitalinos did so more avidly than ever at the end of the nineteenth century.

From the turn of the century onward, modernization projects reflective of the changing economic, social, and political conditions of the late Porfiriato were mapped onto this colonial urban structure. Like rapidly growing cities elsewhere in Latin America, Mexico City absorbed a continual stream of displaced rural migrants.[5] During the 1890s, at the height of Porfirian economic power, the city experienced an enormous influx of destitute campesinos who had been displaced by the encroachment of haciendas in rural areas. They came to the city looking for work, and most ended up living in the tenement belt east of the Zócalo. This east side doubled in size from 1880 to 1900, and more than a third of the city's population lived in an area that composed less than 15 percent of the overall urban landmass. Moreover, the migrants proved difficult to contain. If the Porfirian city should exemplify order and progress, with an ample police force on the streets to bar "disorderly elements" from places of affluence and political governance, the migrants who occupied the streets of the centro defied that ideal. As many scholars of Porfirian Mexico City have demonstrated, the culturally (and often ethnically) different ex-campesinos caused "apprehension and fear" on the part of the urban Porfirian elite.[6] This influx of population, as well as what was perceived to be its gendered nature, informed the formation of both symbolic and structural demarcations of an affluent, "feminine" west side positioned against an impoverished, male east.

In positioning and contrasting the poor against the rich, especially in spatial terms, much emphasis was placed on material spectacle, the visual and performative nature of class distinctions that were easily visible on the city streets. Pablo Piccato describes Porfirian society as divided into three segments based on the visibility of class distinctions perceptible in urban space: "Individuals wearing plain shirts comprised the poorest class, people with jackets were members of the middle class, and, at the top of the scale, the upper class donned frock coats."[7] Moreover, this division had gendered dimensions, as it was rendered most visible by women. Gender ideals of the era stipulated that señoras decentes remain indoors or take carefully prescribed steps outside the home. As the population of the metropolis grew, however, women increasingly gained access to work and education. Piccato and Robert Buffington link "unsettled" gender roles with the rapid growth of the city during the Porfiriato, as "women in ever greater numbers left the family hearth for salaried jobs in the public sphere; and streets, restaurants, dance halls, bars and brothels took on an aura of uncontrolled and dangerous popular sociability."[8]

Male intellectuals and social commentators took this opportunity to elaborate on the influence of feminism and to articulate normative behavior for women that centered on discourses of domesticity.

Porfirian *científicos* (as members of Díaz's circle of trusted advisers were referred to) defined class distinctions based on sexuality, sexual difference, and gender characteristics. They "constructed the natural order according to sex and gender," placing the middle- and upper-class woman, the señora decente, "sum of all moral virtues," at the pinnacle of social classification.[9] In many respects, this Porfirian *grande dame* was the epitome of the performative role of a "gracious woman," expressing middle-class status as well as morals. Dressed in European finery, she commanded the admiration of onlookers while leaving or entering public buildings or private residences on the city's posh west side. As fashion was of the utmost importance in maintaining class boundaries, elite women in Latin American cities were identified by their hairstyles and haute couture designed for their public appearances on streets, in parks, and at the theater.[10]

Considering the visible importance of women as embodied markers of class, positivists warned against women's changing roles. Porfirian intellectual Gabino Barreda, for example, wrote a seven-part "Estudio sobre 'El feminismo'" in 1909 in which he concluded that women were inferior to men and hence that feminism, in seeking equality with men (especially in the public sphere), could only result in the unfortunate creation of "public women." Even the famed criminologist Carlos Roumagnac concluded that many of the violent crimes linked to the working class resulted from "sexual rivalry" based on clear gender distinctions. In detailing the sexual identity and practices of criminals he studied at the Belem prison, Roumagnac placed sex and gender at the heart of his criminology.[11] In this, Mexican elites reacted to changing gender norms not unlike their counterparts in Europe. Many European intellectuals and writers also openly attacked the "New Woman" as unfit for modernity, which, they argued, made women prone to hysteria (a nervous condition thought to afflict only women), morphine addiction, and excessive libidinous instincts.[12]

The gendering of space, positioning not only the public sphere against the private sphere but also the affluent areas of the city against the poor ones, colored the perception of Mexico City's changing cityscapes. Tepito's and La Bolsa's numerous *pulquerías*, where the popular classes whiled away their time imbibing agave-derived beverages (*pulque*), were seen as places that fueled crimes of passion associated with the area. This idea became more prevalent after 1890 when a string of murders of prostitutes and other lower-class women branded the area as synonymous with violence, sex, and dangerous women. Crime and alcoholism in these parts of the city upset traditional gender roles, as alcohol was believed to attack "the central traits of femininity."[13]

Prostitution facilitated the sexualization and masculinization of the city's east side, chronicled in novels that captured the imagination of well-to-do Porfirians. Like Zola's *Nana* in France, Frederico Gamboa's *Santa* (1903) became a classic of this new genre. Telling the story of a young woman's descent into prostitution after arriving in the capital city from the countryside, *Santa* demonstrated the corrupting influences of urban space. In addition to prostitution, however, the east side harbored *casas de cita* (houses of assignation) that were used by women and men, including those of the middle class, who sought private or secret meeting places to be able to be sexually intimate, away from prying eyes of family members, servants, or husbands and wives. Historian James Garza states that these spaces existed outside of the sanctions of elite society, "sanctuaries where Porfirian rules of propriety did not apply."[14]

Not surprisingly, científicos hoped to demonstrate that lower-class urban space constituted an "enclosed environment of contagion." By drawing innocents into the orbit of pulque, crime, and vice, this militated against the lofty ideals of the científico Gabino Barreda, who hoped education would further modernity among the masses. Fear of social contagion, the spread of degeneration to the rest of the country, left Porfirians to imagine "Mexican criminals returning to the barbarous ways of the Aztecs."[15] Thus, for modernity to be visible, the modernizing city needed counterpoints, mirrors through which to recognize and differentiate itself. These mirrors were made up not only of crime and moral insanity but also of spectacle, a performativity of norms and behavior that looked to the "actual world" of art, aesthetics, and espectáculos for its inspiration.

Theater has played an important role in shaping Mexico City's cultural and social landscape for a large part of the city's history. As historian Juan Pedro Viquiera Albán has shown, theater had functioned as an educational tool going back to the period of the conquest. It then took center stage during the Bourbon Reforms, when theaters served as laboratories of modernity in which measures dreamed up in Spain were tested in the colonies. Yet the Bourbon Reforms ultimately did little to control spectacle. Instead, the newly built theaters, bullrings, and *pelota* arenas resulted in entertainment infused with plebeian norms. As in early modern Europe, even if plays in Bourbon Mexico City were harnessed as a civilizing agent and educational tool, the theater as a social space remained a site of spectacle, sociability, and leisure for a diverse public.

Bourbon-era theater featured specific gendered tactics to educate audiences, particularly in its attempt to model proper behavior for women. Interestingly, Spanish theater companies—unlike their northern European counterparts—hired women as actresses and, at times, even as directors.[16] Due to the highly public nature of their work, these women were both celebrated and cause for concern. Frivolous plays would be followed by indecent interludes replete with licentious and provocative dances involving female dancers showing off their physiques to please male members of the lower classes. Concerned authorities feared for the corruption of their daughters and wives.[17] In their efforts to regulate theater, administrators not only initiated measures to censor the content of plays but also increased official scrutiny of actresses. Denoting the importance of women's performances offstage as well as on, officials threatened actresses by policing their "immoral" private lives.[18]

Not surprisingly, the popularity of these daring actresses persisted into the nineteenth century. In fact, popular theater, especially the *género chico*—as the genre of comedies, operettas, *zarzuelas*, and *revistas* was known—increasingly played a major role in forging Mexico City's sexual and social attitudes during the Porfiriato. By the 1870s, drama and opera, referred to as the *género grande*, had been replaced in popularity by the zarzuela, a picaresque comedy that became increasingly affordable and popular among the middle classes. Dating to the Spanish two-act court plays of the seventeenth century, *zarzuelas* were dramatic comedies developed along a unified plot and combined dialogue, song, and dance. With a resurgence in Spain in the mid-nineteenth century, zarzuelas became popular with the broader Mexican public and split into two distinct types of shows defined by length and subject matter. The *zarzuela grande*, structurally related to the Viennese operetta (the genre that made Esperanza Iris a star), contained three acts and focused on serious subjects. Its shorter, popular counterpart, the género chico, consisted of one-act zarzuelas and began in 1867 when a weak Spanish economy prompted empresarios to offer cheaper entertainment to low-income audiences. Later popular genres, such as the *revistas* (revues), were closely related to the latter type of zarzuela.[19]

While Spanish in origin, the género chico became most popular in Latin America. What most seemed to attract large, cross-class Latin American audiences to the género chico was its focus on visual elements. Audiences raved about the sheer splendor of the shows, which emphasized song, dance, and stage design rather than language and plot development. These shows also prominently displayed female bodies.[20] Due to growing popularity of the género chico, the *tandas* (as Mexicans called these shows) took more liberties in showing dancers in shorter skirts. The female stars of the tandas were not well schooled in acting or vocal ability, but they became famous for their appearance and stage personas. Despite their centrality as visual attractions, the stars of the tandas were nonetheless thought of as "gracious women." This helped to facilitate links, while still harboring tensions, between the señora decente and the popular stage actress.[21]

As the premier incarnation of the gracious woman, divas dominated the entertainment world of the late Porfirian and early revolutionary periods. Divas made their entry into Mexican theater as early as the 1860s when Angela Peralta, Mexico's first true opera diva (she was simply referred to as "The Star"), rose to prominence. Actresses held high positions and enjoyed great popularity. By midcentury some women, such as Carlota Contreras and Isabel Prieto de Landázuri, even wrote plays. Despite being popular public figures, nineteenth-century actresses were not yet the specialists they would become in the twentieth century, but were required to sing and dance. The great actresses of the early twentieth century, such as Elena Ureña and Virginia Fábregas, made their appearance on the Mexican stage in the 1890s. La Fábregas in particular, considered the first modern actress in Mexico, indelibly imprinted her vision on Mexican theater.[22]

The regard for actresses in Mexico was different from what elite Mexicans considered the more civilized nations of Europe, France in particular. As acting was refigured into a reputable career, actresses—such as the French Sarah Bernhardt—developed close links with feminism.[23] Bernhardt was the quintessential diva of her age, and many Mexican actresses looked to her for inspiration. Her dramatic life off-stage captured the public's attention within, and certainly also outside, France. By acting the New Woman both on and off the stage, divas like Bernhardt inspired women to become assertive in demanding political rights. As urbanites charting their own course through the metropolis, these actresses had a unique, central place in helping multi-class and multi-ethnic female audiences envision larger public roles.

The rise of spectacle was situated in the new urban culture of metropolitan life, in which female performance and urbanization went hand-in-hand. Historians of this process in the United States have studied the links between leisure, entertainment, and consumption as they related to changes in ideas about gender.[24] Modern womanhood in many ways was performed, quite literally, in the theater before it occurred on streets and in stores, offices, cafés, and teahouses. Consequently, women's roles and representations in theater contributed to changing gender norms and influenced the development of modern sexuality.

Unlike other modern women and early feminists, actresses were expected to transgress social boundaries in both their public and private lives. Vaudeville actresses, for instance, created an image of women in charge of their sexuality and instrumental in forging their own subjectivities, not only vis-à-vis men but also with respect to other women. While actresses were assertive offstage, theater traditions made them into far more passive women onstage. This created frictions between women's desire to achieve more autonomy, on the one hand, and female spectacle as a symbol of subordination to men, on the other. Yet in embodying the tension between "active" and "passive spectacle" that informed opposing concepts of modern femininity, the transgressive aspects of actresses' performances were considered scandalous but socially condoned.

Tensions like these found expression in the emergence of comediennes who pushed gender boundaries by questioning the social norms of acceptable female sexual desire, while at same time reveling in the excessive focus on female beauty in theater. "Salomania," the modernist imagining of the Orient that became the entertainment fad of the 1910s, provides a perfect example. Following the original play *Salomé*, by Oscar Wilde, the phenomenon encompassed several stage productions, including operas. Due to its exotic imaginations of the biblical story, female sensuality expressed in the "Dance of the Seven Veils," and shock value (Salomé kisses the severed head of John the Baptist in the final scene), these performances created a theatrical craze. Not merely a sexualized spectacle for men, the many productions featuring Salomé functioned equally as a venue of self-expression for women. From opera to vaudeville, Salomé became a character that taught audiences that overt female sexuality and female autonomy were linked.[25]

Beloved Mexican divas such as María Conesa and Esperanza Iris, influenced by French stars like Sarah Bernhardt and theater phenomena like Salomania, were part of the Porfirian diversions imported from Europe but adapted to Mexican settings (see figs. 2 and 3). Conesa, born in Valencia, Spain, made her Mexican debut in the Teatro Principal during 1901 when she was but a girl, and like Iris, she played a boy in an act she put on with her older sister Teresa. In a tragic crime, the boyfriend of their archrival murdered Teresa while the sisters relaxed in a theater box watching the rest of the show. María was not more than twelve years old at the time of Teresa's death, and an outraged public demanded that minors be banned from working in theaters and other venues. Traumatized by the event, María returned to Spain

FIG. 2. María Conesa, publicity photo, Teatro Principal, ca. 1916.

FIG. 3. Esperanza Iris, publicity photo, "Pay-Pay," 1914.

Pay-Pay

Esperanza Iris
que actúa en Albisu

5¢   Año II Abril 16 - 1914 - Nº 37.

and stopped acting, but she made her comeback four years later in Cuba. Known as La Parisina (the Parisienne), María gained notoriety due to "her provocative and voluptuous movements." Journalists raved about *El Congreso Conesa*, as they renamed *El Congreso Feminista*, the original title of the play that featured the reborn star.[26] At the tender age of sixteen, Conesa had all of Havana at her feet.

The young actress equally came to enjoy fame and notoriety in Mexico due to her scandalous persona on and off the stage. Eclipsing her early successes in Cuba, Conesa's greatest triumph was her interpretation of La Gatita Blanca (The White Kitten) in 1906. Although this was an adaptation of a preexisting production, María's performance became so legendary that it defined the rest of her career. Audiences alternately loved or hated the young diva. Opponents saw her as the incarnation of the devil, and some critics petitioned the city government to prohibit her act, which "filled both fathers and sons with bad thoughts." With sold-out shows María became the highest-paid artist in Mexico, now her adopted home country. According to the cultural critic Carlos Monsiváis, Conesa worked miracles as she single-handedly revived the dying zarzuela genre in Mexico. During the festivities of the hundred-year anniversary of the War for Independence in 1910, she performed for Don Porfirio and his wife, socialite Carmen Romero Rubio, who reportedly attended a show in the Teatro Principal because of the gossip that surrounded the star. María, a Spanish citizen, caused a stir by dressing in a *china poblana* (iconic Mexican traditional figure) outfit, then the quintessential national female costume. But she provoked the audience even more by embroidering the emblem of the eagle, typically reserved only for the Mexican flag, on her dress.[27]

Esperanza Iris, born in 1881 in Villahermosa, in the state of Tabasco, managed to climb to international stardom, touring relentlessly early on in her career. This paid off later, when she used her contacts—a veritable Hispanic transatlantic entertainment network of agents, theaters, and actors stretching from Mexico and Cuba to Brazil, Argentina, and Spain—to amass a small fortune with which she built her own theater.[28] Iris performed operetta classics such as *The Merry Widow*, *Poupeé*, *Eva*, and *Enchantment of a Waltz*. At fifteen she married a theater impresario and director of the legendary Teatro Principal, and after his death she tried her hand at theater management. She acquired the Teatro Ideal after her first European tour but lost it due to poor administration. After joining artistic, business, and personal ventures with the Cuban singer Juan Palmer, then a married man, she made another attempt at running a theater, which resulted in the construction of the highly successful Teatro Esperanza Iris. With the motto of bringing "novelties, art, and luxury" to Mexico City, she worked tirelessly to succeed and became a strong figure, both as an artist and a businesswoman in charge of her own company and theater.[29]

The successful performance of actresses as divas within and outside the theater hinged on the celebration of a number of dichotomies and tensions regarding sexuality in late Porfirian society. Although Conesa and Iris lived their lives in the public eye, they escaped the scorn that most women in public faced. Iris, a young widow and mother of two sons, maintained relationships with married men (on one occasion a man almost fifteen years her junior), yet she seemed capable of holding on to a certain amount of Porfirian respectability. Conesa, despite her professed innocence onstage, continuously faced scandals in her very public private life. When not fined for performing lascivious songs, Conesa was implicated in dealings with high-ranking military officials and diplomats; even more scandalously, she was linked to the capitalino underworld, including La Banda de Automovil Gris (The Gray Car Gang). Both women were respected, however, because they understood the power of the stage as a place where social anxieties and desires could be evoked, celebrated, and neutralized. The success of La Gatita Blanca made Conesa understand the power of picaresque performances in a sexually repressed environment of elite and middle-class society, where, in Monsiváis's words, "comic references to sex are convenient mise-en-scènes of collective orgasms."[30]

Elite Porfirian capitalinos accepted entertainment that hailed from France as elevated, modern, and deliciously indecent. Porfirian society considered the coquette, a sexually risqué role, as a completely acceptable stage character for actresses. Conesa's Gatita had been preceded by diva Ana Judic, whose onstage behavior—according to contemporary critic Manuel Gutiérrez Nájera—exemplified the high art of false innocence. Judic, he wrote, celebrated "this delicious shame with which she says the most shameful things."[31] The beauty of actresses, along with their love lives, became the topic of conversation not only in newspapers but also on the street. The marriage of one of the Moriones sisters, for instance, then an actress and later part of the important impresario duo, caused quite a stir in the city in 1883. Gutiérrez Nájera's literary alter ego, El Duque Job, reflecting on the importance of the press in forging modern society, assigned journalism a large role in influencing public behavior and distinguishing female beauty. "Before, if a woman was pretty," he wrote, "her mirror, her friends and her boyfriends told her so. Today all the *gacetilleros* [gossip columnists] of the capital city say it."[32]

Like Judic and other Mexican incarnations of the French coquette, María Conesa evoked the qualities that characterized the popularity of all great divas: sex and scandal. Her success hinged on her ability to present a girlish innocence onstage as an actress who only acted sexual, all the while blurring the lines between her identity as La Gatita onstage and La Conesa offstage. Consequently, divas such as Conesa and Iris who played (with) the role of the "gracious woman" destabilized gender normativity and extended their performances far into the city. At a time when the city was small, "understandable and traversable," the divas of the género chico transgressed class boundaries that were expressed not only in the realm of gender norms but also in terms of space.[33]

Elite Porfirians were accustomed to enacting their lives in public spaces, but the behavior of the diva pushed the boundaries of how señoras decentes were expected to behave outside the private realm. El Principal, one of the city's most important theaters since the early colonial period, now celebrated divas showing their stocking-clad legs and singing suggestive songs. In reaction, state officials attempted to undo the worst damage: they required El Principal to label the shows "For Men Only. Minors Not Allowed."[34] Divas blurred the lines between their acts in the theater and their performance of their private lives.

Divas and their new performances of gender could "reorient space" in the Porfirian city, because of the close links between theater and a larger visual culture of art and architecture. Divas such as Conesa and Iris had a profound effect on women of all social classes in Mexico City, but their performances fit with a new urban modernity, a new cosmopolitanism to which elites aspired. This echoed and informed larger visual topoi of their day that equally engaged with the effects of modernity, especially those that reflected urban space. The positioning of theaters and other theatrical spectacles in the city and their spatial organization reflected concerns over gender as well as class.

SPATIAL UNDERSTANDINGS OF *ESPECTÁCULOS*

By the end of the Porfiriato, the city counted two distinct entertainment districts: the areas situated around the markets to the east and north of the Zócalo, and the elite theaters of the west. The zone around the Zócalo included an assortment of spectacles—theaters, *carpas* (tent theaters that moved around largely working-class neighborhoods), street performances, salons, and cantinas—that catered to the tastes of the popular classes. The west side, as we saw above, was dominated by divas who performed in renowned theaters that functioned as the gravitational space of the elite theater world.[35]

These elite theaters, including their physical structures, were conceived of as class- and gender-segregated spaces, and architects designed them with class distinctions in mind. Lower-class audiences could attend theater performances on the west side, but they did not sit with their "social betters." Most theaters had separate entrances and stairways leading to specialized areas, such as common areas and box seats. Differentiated ticket prices underwrote the theater's social geography, which further separated the classes. The *abono* system of season ticket subscriptions allowed elite families to buy the best seats, had a similar effect. Class distinctions were further emphasized in architectural designs that resulted in gendered spaces such as the *paraíso* (heaven) or the *cazuela* (casserole). As the best seats in the house, the paraíso was reserved exclusively for men. The next-best seats went to accompanied elite women, who sat in the upscale boxes. Lower-class women viewed plays from the cazuela, a design that went back to the late eighteenth century. In Mexico City's famous Coliseo, the cazuela counted 236 seats, and only older men could serve as ushers for this section.[36]

Seating arrangements for women enhanced class distinctions and further coded the theater as a space of female spectacle, even offstage. Historian Kristin McCleary relates that in Buenos Aires, elite women sat in front of men in the boxes, not only to grant women the better view but also to allow families to show off their unmarried daughters, deemed ready for courtship and marriage, in a respectable manner.[37] In Mexico City the boxes functioned equally as alternative stages for female display and as spaces for spectators. Porfirian elites deemed the display of upper-class, accompanied women in expensive boxes tasteful. Conversely, the cazuela had a reputation as a lowbrow spectacle in itself. Women in the cazuela applauded and commented on plays with such abandon that they attracted the attention of the rest of theater patrons. Some even thought that cazuela women were the female counterpart of the *claque*, men hired to cheer or boo on the impresario's command. Yet the cazuela constituted a more ambiguous space than elite spectators' perspectives would suggest. On one hand, the cazuela did not release women from the courtship scene altogether, as men would crowd the entrances to the section.[38] On the other hand, it freed women from the social constrictions of the box seats, where one had to dress the part of the rich socialite and act demurely. Thus, those who opted for cazuela seats had the opportunity to enjoy the freedom of direct contact with suitors unmediated by family members, as well as the increased opportunity for cross-class female interactions.

In addition to the elite theaters of the west side, female spectacle also characterized the other entertainment district in the Porfirian city, situated in the barrios east and north of the Zócalo. On the east side, espectáculos such as the great circus of the Orrin Brothers entertained the masses on plaza Santo Domingo. Carpas drew colorful and boisterous crowds, while the *jacalones* (makeshift theaters; literally, "shacks") offered short comedies at affordable prices. Often set up around marketplaces, east-end leisure spots were steeped in a carnivalesque focus on the body, especially the female one. Even the area's drinking establishments, such as the notorious pulquerías with names like Delirio (Delirium), La Seductora (The seductress), and El Nido de Amor" (The love nest), evoked sensual pleasures. Not surprisingly, journalists defined these areas as immoral places and equated immorality with poor female inhabitants. Women who dressed in "blouses full of holes that show off too much flesh" appeared promiscuous and were presented as embodying the depravity and decrepitude of their surrounding neighborhood.[39]

Despite the stress on clearly delineated spaces of entertainment and class segregation in urban space, the rise of commercial entertainment broke down these divisions. East-side entertainment, especially street spectacles, increasingly invaded the west side of the centro. Pedestrians stopping to take in jugglers, organ grinders, street vendors, and even women passing by annoyed the more well-to-do and city administrators. Despite their protests, public space belonged to whoever claimed it first, whether a street corner, a right-of-way, or walls used illegally for advertising materials.[40] Journalists also strongly criticized various forms of street performance, especially the circus. Describing how pickpockets stole watches and wallets from unsuspecting spectators, columnists wondered why the municipal government allowed such lowly distractions. The circus, and with it an ensemble of "foul-smelling shacks," converted the stately Zócalo into a mere space for street performances. Puppets, inflated balloons, and other sundries mingling with *aguas* (fruit drinks; literally, "waters") vendors in ramshackle stalls, congested the streets, and hampered the flow of traffic close to the atrium of the Catedral Metropolitana. The circus so irked elites that it seemed to outweigh blood sports in its plebeian character. Why should anyone prohibit the barbarous bullfights, asked one commentator, if the "imbecile monstrosity called the circus is tolerated?"[41] Reporters found that street performance reduced the destitute and sick to a "spectacle of savages."[42] Children asking for alms after a small performance inspired both revulsion and pity.[43]

The simultaneous fascination with and fear of street performances engaged with the patrolling of gender norms as well as class movement. Circus "freaks" and carpa performers presented the unsuspecting passerby with spectacles that played on and crossed gender norms. One journalist lamented the fate of a young *hija del aire* (trapeze artist; literally, "daughter of the air") whom he saw as motherless, street-bred among freaks, and prostituted by her callous father, forming part of a legion of girls whom no one cared about. The circus, a lowly Yankee invention, created nothing more than mutants that defied gender and, hence, human classification: "Not a man, a woman, but a thing." Elite observers decried the proximity of near-nude female bodies contorting as "snakes in the air" and women lifting weights like men as constituting nothing less than human abjection.[44] However, the performers' transgression of street decorum provided women with alternative ideas of how to act in public.

Consequently, even if clear class and ethnic distinctions underlay divisions of space in the urban landscape and in theaters themselves, spectacle invited frequent crossings of these boundaries. Even if posh theaters were usually attended by elite more than lower-class audiences, they generally functioned as a place of sociability for all classes. By the turn of the century, Mexican theaters desperately needed the patronage of lower-class audiences, and advertisements called out to all social groups.[45] Moreover, as more elements from street spectacles found their way into the género chico, theaters were able to attract larger lower-class audiences, much to the dismay of elite theatergoers. The neocolonial facades of upscale venues in the west did little to hide the degradation of tastes inside, according to Mexico City's first modernist author, Manuel Gutiérrez Nájera, whose vitriolic pieces appeared under the nom de plume of the cavalier El Duque Job.

Gutiérrez Nájera, theater critic, Porfirian flaneur, and capitalino cronista, agonized about elite audiences and the deterioration of their sense of taste. While lowbrow theater such as the zarzuelas was fine for lower-class audiences who frequented jacalones on the east end, such fare was deemed below the more affluent—and, he hoped, more discriminating—spectators.[46] Condemning zarzuelas as stupid and obscene, Gutiérrez Nájera ridiculed the clerks and shopkeepers who heartily laughed at the jokes and the actress who lifted her skirt to show her stockings. All zarzuela entailed, according to the cronista, was cheap entertainment for the crowds of the "common hats and cheap rebozos."[47] Hence, for Gutiérrez Nájera, not merely the quality of shows but, more importantly, the performance of the public left much to be desired. In the second-class boxes, people shuffled chairs, kept their hats on during the show, and generally displayed "shameful behavior." Those in the first-class box seats did little better. While dressed in more fashionable clothes, Gutiérrez Nájera observed, they too kept their hats on. Moreover, they simply laughed at everything, like "men who only go to the theater when paying a *real.*" "The theater smelled of the common folk," complained the cronista, adding that this affected the nerves of their betters, including his own.[48]

In addition, El Duque blamed the male audience for "female spectacle," or the lewdness of theater performances. Ashamed to witness sexually explicit scenes in which actresses showed their legs in front of a foreign visitor, the cronista noted with much dismay that the male spectators were "screaming like pigs." Moreover, he complained, this behavior happened not in the carpas but in the city's finest theaters and "in full view of all the society ladies." Interestingly, Gutiérrez Nájera blamed not the actors but the male spectators who applauded "intended innocence with scandalous intent," underlining that how audiences constructed meaning was more important than what playwrights and actors intended their work to be. Even when faced with a simple dance, he reported in *El Cronista de México*, the audience hoped to provoke a can-can. "Is this a public or a herd? A theater or a pigsty?" he asked his distinguished readers.[49]

What was worse, according to the cronista, ruthless impresarios manipulated audiences and used the confusion over what constituted true theater to line their pockets. In an exposé on one such businessman, a certain Sr. Naverrete, Gutiérrez Nájera wrote that the man had understood, like all "geniuses," that Mexicans did not expect greatness, but only female spectacle: "A bit of can-can, a little spice, lots of cheap fare, this is only what we as spectators demand." If the *tiple* (main female star) had a pretty face, her vocal deficiencies would easily be overlooked. The ballerina, on the other hand, could be old and ugly.

As long as the tickets and entertainment were cheap, the tandas were a great success and everyone was satisfied, so reasoned the gran cronista.[50]

Nonetheless, El Duque Job's exasperation over the deterioration of the city's theatrical performances was as much feigned to please the conventions of his age and his readership as it was the product of a contradictory consciousness that betrayed the thinly veiled desires of the nineteenth-century flaneur. Even if Gutiérrez Nájera belonged to a group of respectable newspapermen of class who commented on daily life in the city and condemned the actions of elite men who went slumming, El Duque himself easily fell prey to the same pleasures and desires as the frivolous dandies he readily criticized. He—or any other man—could always indulge in the joy of scoping out the opposite sex in the city's theaters. Armed with binoculars and his assumed identity, El Duque could spy on the wonderful "physiques of unknown girls." Any man would note, continued El Duque lyrically, the beautiful faces that made up "the pearls of the dirty shells called the houses of the *vecindad*." In comparison, ballerinas, dressed in long dresses might resemble statues in their fine artistry, were far less provocative. For Gutiérrez Nájera, positioning himself as an upper-class gentleman of taste who was able to gracefully capitulate to female spectacle, it was not so much actual female nudity that led to perversion but the perception of female bodies on the part of the male viewer: "For an artist, a nude woman is always dressed with the shame of marble. For a man of libido, each dressed woman is always nude."[51]

Consequently, as the género chico became infused with lower-class tastes and incorporated elements from street performances, it grew in popularity with larger segments of the city's population, traversing class boundaries and invading middle- and upper-class spaces. The insertion of popular theater and sexuality that upset Porfirian ideals of decorum highlighted preexisting tensions over women's boundary crossings between public and private realms. Fortified by the daily musings of cronistas such as Gutiérrez Nájera, the zarzuelas of the género chico set up a binary of female performers and a male audience. The star, always a woman, not only enticed men sexually but also invited them to join a world outside Porfirian protocol and propriety. In this she functioned as the vehicle to the city's underworld, legible to capitalinos as the representation of the east side, while the stage functioned as a portal to a realm of unfulfilled wishes and desires. As these actresses catered to a largely male audience, having female spectators attend the increasingly sexualized spectacle of the género chico provoked unease. Men who attended lowbrow theaters stood to lose their health and money, Gutiérrez Nájera dryly remarked, yet women frequenting these places had already "lost everything . . . even honor!"[52]

Hence these performances contributed to the mingling of audiences, tastes, and ultimately class and gender identities that elite Porfirians hoped to keep separate. The fact that thieves could pass as "honest people, being well-dressed and having good manners" was as confounding and "irritating" as the sons of the well-to-do who "frequented Plateros Street" yet turned out to be "pederasts" dressed like women during the infamous "Baile de los Cuarenta y Uno" (Dance of the forty-one, a scandal involving cross-dressing men that became slang for homosexuality).[53] Similarly, prostitutes passed as señoras decentes on the upscale west-side streets. In the shadow of the great Jockey Club at the legendary Casa de los Azulejos, a young José Vasconcelos (secretary of education from 1920 to 1924 and author of *La raza cósmica*) and a group of his fellow students deliriously watched the comings and goings of a well-dressed but suspicious woman named Pepa. She traversed Plateros Street and entered the club with different men at different times, dressed as a Porfirian lady, even if she didn't act like one.[54] Likewise, in José de Cuéllar's *Baile y cochino y la noche buena* (translated into English as *The Magic Lantern: Having a Ball and Christmas Eve*), a series of modernist literary vignettes that chronicled the follies of Porfirian nouveau riche, women are able to pass as their class betters through fashion and deception. The insecurity inherent in "passing" and the fear of the destabilization of identity points to the importance of performance in Porfirian society in terms of class, race, and gender, as well as the relationships between these categories. In a world of clearly demarcated lines of class, respectability, and propriety, the idea of deception bothered elites the most, and acting—especially in its theatrical form—stood at the very center of this "deception." Due to the complex entanglements of acting onstage and acting as passing, as well as notions of spatial differences in the theater and beyond in the city, theaters were mobilized in an attempt to fix race, class, and gender boundaries.

REVISTA AND REVOLUTION

Theater reflected and informed the impressions of travelers and capitalinos alike when viewing gendered behavior on the city streets. As a barometer of social opinion, discontent, hopes, dreams, and desires, theater grappled with the advent of modernity. Although Porfirians looked to Europe, especially France, as the height of civilization, they favored modernization over modernity. In the face of rapid modernization and the accompanying pressures of urbanization, they opted to revel in nostalgia rather than enjoy modern plays. This trend changed drastically with the introduction of *El gran vía*, the first Latin American revista blockbuster.

Although zarzuela had formed the mainstay of theater offerings in the late nineteenth century, national comedies and dramas in the form of revistas, as revue shows were known in Mexico, eclipsed them by the early twentieth century. The first imitations of European revue shows appeared in Mexico as early as 1870, after the French Intervention established vaudeville and the can-can, even if the genre did not dominate the theatrical landscape until 1904.[55] Unlike the Spanish- and French-oriented zarzuelas, the Mexican revista as a genre was able to reflect local realities, including those of a rapidly changing urban and social landscape.[56] Instead of following a unified narrative and plot development, revistas echoed the conventions of print journalism, most notably newspapers and, like their namesakes, magazines.[57] Revistas generally offered a showcase of events taking place in a big city from the perspective of a pedestrian or a tourist. The genre relied heavily on stock characters that had become an entrenched part of a visual economy of rural characters, yet it began to include a variety of urban ones as well—the lottery-ticket seller, the drunk girl, the grotesque foreigner, the fat politician, the policeman, the stool pigeon, the half-breed, the *pelado* (urbanized country bumpkin), the pickpocket, and the talkative barber—who belonged to the new urban landscape of a growing metropolis.[58]

Revistas used national authors, actors, and actresses in regional costumes and played typical music to introduce urban audiences to regional Mexico: *zandugas* from Oaxaca, *sarapes* from Saltillo, *china poblanas* from Puebla, and *jarabe tapías* from Jalisco. Mexico City writers frequently adapted and stylized these regional songs and dances from the campo to please urban audiences.[59] Idealized types, such as the *tehuana* (a woman from the Isthmus of Tehuantepec in the state of Oaxaca; also known for her distinctive dress), effectively solidified the notion of rural, indígena women as symbols of mexicanidad, while the debased (and usually male) pelado became the archetype of the impoverished and degenerate rural migrant in the city. In addition to this cartographic creation of rural and urban personae, revistas incorporated humor and popular music to comment on current events, political debacles, the latest fads, and urban life. Being an adaptable genre, revista quickly paved the way for the advent of national comedies that became popular during the early twentieth century, especially in revolutionary Mexico.

Even if Spanish in origin, the landmark revista *La gran vía* became a truly Latin American urban phenomenon, adapted to local realities in Latin American cities stretching from Buenos Aires to Mexico City. Besides featuring streets as the play's main protagonists, mise-en-scènes highlighted the classic spaces of the metropolis: a theater, a hotel, and a market. In it, the streets of the capital city appeared as characters that complained about the state of urban reform, which centered on bypassing smaller streets in favor of the large thoroughfare, that is, *la gran vía*. Further, the play had a clear class character, as members of the popular classes in the play complained about the destruction of their spaces of leisure, such as dance halls and parks. After *La gran vía* premiered on July 2, 1866, in Madrid, its success inspired companies in New York and London to perform the play. In Buenos Aires the play was adapted to reflect the typical character of the city and was renamed *La gran avenida* to reflect the city's own reality. The revista was eventually banned in Argentina due to its bitingly satirical portrayals of the city's well-known políticos. If the play made it to the stage at all, it did so only for short periods of time.[60]

Revista theater poked fun at the inability of elites to discern between reality and the public performance of wealth, status, gender, and class. For instance, the landmark revista *Chin-Chun-Chan*, starring Esperanza Iris, mocked a wealthy couple from the provinces visiting Mexico City who mistook ostentation and bad taste in clothing for current fashion and misidentified prostitutes as real ladies. This mistake may have made more sense than revista writers or audiences were willing to admit. Some of the best seats in the Teatro Nacional belonged to high-class madams who showed off their new girls and "scanned for clients." Far from circumspect, they flaunted their bodies and expensive imported fineries in the city's best theaters and restaurants.[61]

As revista theater became the vehicle for popular national theater in Mexico, especially during and after the revolution, its gendered nature continued to connect it with transnational currents. As 1920s theater critic and playwright Rudolfo Usigli commented, women's legs in revista, vaudeville, and follies shows became part of an international language. This emphasis on bodies and body language had ambiguous consequences for actresses within Mexican theater. While this emphasis served to democratize theater and popularize it, as more women could aspire to stardom, critics perceived it as a lower, base form of entertainment precisely because revista required little training and relied heavily on showing off women's bodies. Usigli concluded that the quality of revista shows suffered as "its attraction descended from the throat to the legs" in concession to public tastes.[62] Yet the sexual aspect also helped female actresses gain a strong voice of opposition. The star of the revista, always a woman, not only enticed men sexually but also invited them to join her in protest of the status quo.[63]

With its social commentary, metropolitan modernity, overt female sexuality, and outspoken actresses, revista theater set up a new standard of female behavior. This inspired lower- and middle-class women in Mexico to take on a greater role in public life and resist the status quo at a time of social and political upheaval. The enormous success of revistas such as *La gran vía*, which featured the importance of city life and the city as the stage for accelerated modernization and modernity, interestingly intersected with a period in Mexico's history that forever altered not only the country but the capital city as well: the revolution. With its emphasis on current events and daily life, revista theater came to reflect revolutionary upheaval and influenced public opinion about the difficulties that lower-class women faced in Mexico City. As in other Latin American cities, the popularity of theater was seen as contributing to urban unrest as transformation in theater informed larger political, social, and demographic changes in the capital.[64] Throughout the revolution, revista theater, now the staple of the género chico, became influential in shaping popular consciousness.[65]

During the 1920s and 1930s the revista continued to dominate the city's theaters, yet its content, reach, inclusiveness, and potential in staging transformative performance changed markedly. By targeting not only specific groups based on age and gender but also mixed audiences, revista entertained increasingly connected audiences across a wide social spectrum. Families went to see operetta revistas on Sundays, married men attended sexually explicit shows in the notorious Teatro Lírico during the week, and wives took other female family members to see "decent shows" in theaters such as Fábregas and Ideal.[66] Primarily, however, revista theater produced a new audience by connecting disparate social groups and bridging class, race, and gender distinctions.

Revista grew into a hybrid theatrical art form during the revolution, mixing dance acts, comedic skits, suggestive humor, and political commentary. Its continued popularity during the 1920s changed understandings of what theater was and how it should be perceived. Revista theater's ability to change attitudes of its audiences about crucial political developments, not in the least revolutionaries' extensive agenda of cultural reforms intended to "mold hearts and minds," attracted the revolutionary state.

In the wake of the social havoc caused by the revolution, the emerging genre of revista theater proved a platform for actresses whose performances were deemed instrumental in destabilizing gender roles. María Conesa, for instance, was able to hold on to fame during the revolutionary period because of her roles in political revistas. Unlike

Esperanza Iris, who toured outside of troubled Mexico for much of the revolution, Conesa stayed in Mexico City and performed uninterrupted from 1915 until 1923. Although the revolution influenced the content of theater productions, shows were rarely suspended, mostly because officials favored a climate of normality. Moreover, soldiers who arrived in the city sought out places where they could enjoy themselves and relax after the tensions of battle, with many seeking out Conesa's shows. Francisco "Pancho" Villa so fell in love with the artiste, the story goes, that she had to hide from his advances in the stage equipment. La Gatita even had the nerve to cut one side of General Almazan's handlebar mustache during a risqué act, upon which he requested that she cut the other side as well. Álvaro Obregón came to see her perform nearly every night while he was in the city, and he advised playwrights on rewriting lyrics to the songs Conesa sang so as to satirize the actions of his enemies.[67]

However, once the armed phase of the revolution had drawn to a close, revista actresses such as Conesa commanded less-than-enthusiastic acclaim from the city's theater inspectors, who viewed their performances as acts of transgression. The new state employed these inspectors, an overseeing body to monitor plays, theaters, performances, and audiences alike. In the early 1920s, the Departamento de Diversiones Públicas (Department of Public Diversions) was in charge of supervising theaters, carpas, and cinemas.[68] This department, in many ways a leftover from the Porfirian period, worked in concert with the Department of Public Health and city police to ensure that the *salones de espectáculos* (entertainment halls) conformed to the appropriate health standards and safety regulations. It was the duty of theater inspectors not only to "regulate spectacles," including mundane tasks like making sure that shows took place on time, but also to ensure that transgressions were avoided, and register them when they did occur.[69] In addition, the department employed inspectors to monitor the moral content of plays. These *inspectores cronistas*, men with illustrious names such as Hipólite Amor, reviewed plays on a weekly basis, commenting on quality, morality, and audience reception. Concern over the deterioration of moral standards, which was often linked to sanitary conditions and the language used by the actors, focused in particular on the role of spectacle in destabilizing gender and class hierarchies and formed a central theme of inspectors' reports.

Following years of triumph during the armed phase of the revolution, La Conesa received terrible reviews when starring in Teatro Colón's *La mujer modelo* (The model woman) because of the play's depiction of women's independence. It told the story of an audacious and beautiful wife who, in order to reignite the affections of her husband, takes acting lessons that lead her to a life of independence and adventure. Out alone in public, she encounters and challenges her unfaithful husband.[70] Screenplays alone, even ones as daring as *La mujer modelo*, did not alone warrant the inspectors' concern, as it was more often the acted text that produced outrage, not the written word.

It was precisely the articulation of political satire through the use of up-front and open female sexuality that worried inspectors. For instance, the impact of writer Antonio Guzmán Aguilera's (also known as Guz Águila) popular vocabulary, fashionable jokes, and well-ingrained stereotypes that satirized public officials was far worse—found inspector cronista Carlos Samper—when performed in conjunction with suggestive dance acts. The inspector lamented that the female dancers of Teatro Lírico's *El país de las quiebras* (The land of bankruptcies) flaunted their posteriors "in a lewd manner" while performing the "shimmy." Reminiscent of El Duque Job, Samper especially objected to the reaction of the audience, who interpreted "the spasmodic convulsion of the flesh" not as art but as sensuality. He noted that because the dance was situated in a political comedy, it appealed to "the collective" and was reduced to lower-class tastes.[71]

Frequently, the inspectors' indictment of popular theater was less about the content of the plays than about the reaction of the audience, or rather, the synergy between the two. Revista theaters' political plays attracted lower-class audiences, and this worried inspectors. Teatro Colón ran into trouble for mounting the play *El diablo mundo* (The devil's world), which satirized the municipal president.[72] After being fined, Colón's management decided to acquiesce to the authorities, and inspector Samper was given the task of scrapping the offending lines. However, subsequent performances of the revised work did little to alter the initial effect, and in the end it was the audience, not the actors or writers, that was deemed most responsible for the untimely cancellation of performances. Annoyed at the changes made to the play, spectators threw stones at the stage and the actors, prompting the police to step in to restore order.[73] Audiences such as these were held responsible for ruining even "good plays" such as *Los hombres feos* (Ugly men), according to inspector Samper. Although he lauded the play as well written with intelligent jokes, Samper found that its public misconstrued the work to fit "the humor and corruptions of the language of the lowest barrios."[74]

In the end, it was the confusion of categories that most vexed the inspectors. Critics considered El Iris's *La niña Lupe* (The girl named Lupe), which showed *tehuanas* dancing traditional *zandugas*, an important national operetta, yet they vehemently condemned "the *indígenas* and even *criollas*" who spoke as if they were "urban proletarians." Guz Águila's *Pierrot mexicano* (Mexican Pierrot), billed as a *revista nacionalista*, examined "political vices" and civil struggles that inspectors found distasteful. Samper did not care for the music of the "Tacos de Jazz" orchestra and cringed at the emphasis on the hybrid character of *colombina* (a character in the Italian commedia dell'arte) as a china poblana: "I want to note the observation that for certain writers the Mexican types cannot come to life other than moving between a patriotic sentimentalism, and the brutishness of the lepers and pelados of the street and the pulquería." The inspector cronista wondered why revista plays did not conform to proper Spanish grammar and decent forms of the género chico; he condemned most of the city theaters' attempts to innovate Mexican theater after the revolution as "hybridity contrary to art."[75]

If "true national theater"—as defined by the inspectors—was lacking in the city's most prestigious theaters, it was because of the increasing popularity of the hybrid forms of theater in other parts of the city. These performances altered the roles that actors, writers, and even audiences should play, challenging social and new revolutionary norms. Nowhere was this more visible in the city than in the street theater of the carpas.

Carpa actors' improvisational performances used basic revista formulas but radicalized the genre by championing a carnivalesque humor that depended on a continual dialogue between actors and an ever more varied audience with little regard for social standing. Middle-class housewives would take their seats next to waitresses, Spanish shop owners, truck drivers, plumbers, and other working-class folks on the old benches of the numerous carpas. Together, everyone laughed at the ventriloquist, was moved by the fat lady with the excellent voice, and entranced by the tortured rebels.[76]

In their embrace of female stars, carpa actors and owners looked to famous actresses who performed in "highbrow" theaters to make their mark in the city. For instance, while La Iris might have had her own upscale theater, María Conesa's fame earned her a carpa. Conesa was not in any way involved with it, and certainly never performed there, but the fact that the street performers picked her name to grace the little tent theater in Tepito, a working-class neighborhood that enjoyed notoriety as the most dangerous area in the city, showed their affinity for the great star and the importance of female stage personae. The invocation of the famous diva did little to warm the hearts of the city entertainment inspectors, however, who found the tent and its crew to be in "a frightful state." With the roof torn in more than three places, water poured onto the poor spectators during the incessant rains that washed over the city in August 1922. The inspector suspended the shows, but actors asked the audience to attend anyway, setting off, in their words, "a true row." As no police officers were present to enforce his orders (a common complaint of the inspectors), the inspector had no choice but to let the show go on. What was worse, the audience refused to leave after the function.[77]

Incidents such as the one at the Carpa María Conesa typified the tensions between carpa workers and city inspectors, indicating municipal concern over the shifting social geography of performance, which became increasingly difficult to police. As the carpas moved around the city with varying degrees of mobility, they provided a larger public with greater access to radical political revista shows. After the armed phase of the revolution, carpas emerged as highly innovative

and democratic places of sociability where actors, actresses, and spectators came together to express political discontent while reinterpreting
social norms and values. The carpas subverted notions of gender and
place, due to their easy accessibility in critical nodes of the city, an essential relationship with the street, and interactive shows that featured
independent and feisty actresses. Legendary carpa performers such
as Amelia Wilhelmy and Delia Magaña often played *pícaras* (female
thieves) who played pranks on their suitors.[78]

Inspectors and city authorities, bent on regulating both the spectacle on the stage and the spectacle of public immorality, looked to
discourses of social hygiene to articulate their dismay over the city's
changing gender and class norms. Makeshift theaters had appeared
in Mexico by 1870 as provisional theaters set up for the holiday season. With the introduction of permits during the Porfiriato, however,
popular street diversions such as circuses, jacalones, and variety salons
opened with greater frequency. By the early 1920s, popular theaters took
on the name of carpas and lined the streets and plazas of working-class
barrios such as Santa María Redonda, Tepito, and Plaza Garibaldi and
of markets like Lagunilla and La Merced, as well as outlying areas as
far as Tacubaya and Azcapotzalco. City inspectors condoned licensed
street spectacles but expressed frequent concern over the deplorable
conditions of the carpas. Most were makeshift theaters under tent
covers strung up over anything that served the purpose, even electri-
cal wires. Dangerous lighting situations, fire hazards, and a lack of
bathroom facilities characterized the ramshackle nature of the carpas.
Most lacked proper floorboards, so rain flooded the tents after heavy
storms. Lacking fire extinguishers, electricity boxes, or toilets, carpas
frequently exposed audiences to hazardous and unsanitary conditions.
For instance, Carpa Cardenti, situated under a power plant, posed a real
threat to its audience. "Electric sparks fall onto the roof," complained
an inspector after a performance.[79]

City administrators frequently cited unsanitary conditions as the
main reason to clamp down on street performances, even when inappropriate behavior was clearly the issue. Carpa María Conesa eventually was closed down due to its terrible state of disrepair, unsanitary

conditions, and subsequent health concerns. "To get even close to the carpa in question," complained one inspector, "one deals with having to breathe in an intolerable stench; the area is full of fecal matter." Yet, Carpa Minerva was closed after a drunken worker insulted a city official with obscenities.[80] Carpa Mímí was closed on the grounds that its owner had not made the necessary repairs, most importantly, adding proper artist quarters for its actresses so that the public did not have indecent views of the female performers. Due to the lower-class nature, the visibility of female sexuality, and market environment of the carpas, inspectors identified problems of street performances as public-health concerns. They articulated contagion as part of larger social issues, equating a lack of hygiene with a lack of morality, especially in the case of female performers. Even if city officials closed Carpa María Conesa because of its "frightful condition" and the danger it presented to the public, it was primarily the carpa's location that made inspectors nervous. Tepito, a "dirty barrio," represented the worst place to have shows, especially the comedies that celebrated female transgressions and subverted gender norms that drew large crowds.[81]

Even more so than in theaters, a focus of concern for city inspectors in the carpas was the interplay between audience and actors and the insecurity over whether they would perform their proper roles as distinct and separate entities. Both the public and performers from the carpas were *obreros y trabajadores* (workers and laborers), members of the urban working class, and their shared identity as workers significantly blurred the division between the two groups. Performers worked for more than fifteen hours a day. They spent eight hours performing from late afternoon until the wee hours in the morning, and the remainder of the time rehearsing. Shows were reworked almost daily to reflect current events in the city. Audiences paid to stay about two to three hours in the carpa, where they drank and took in politically charged messages, a volatile combination that might have alarming consequences. It was the kind of public event that grabbed the attention of state officials.[82]

Nonetheless, city officials never managed to control life in the carpas or the political content of their shows. Moreover, theaters and street performances were not as neatly divided as inspectors would have wished. While Carpa Ideal's boxing matches often ended in a breakdown of public order that once nearly burned down the little tent, the respectable Arbeu theater supplemented its offerings of plays with similar *luchas* (boxing matches and forerunners of freestyle wrestling fights). One such fight in Arbeu similarly got out of hand when one fighter went to the floor after an "indecent blow." The theater inspector sought help, but his authority was eclipsed by a city official who proclaimed that as a direct representative of the municipal president he would take full control of the situation. Amid the confusion of competing authorities, the public attacked the offender and a large-scale melee ensued.[83]

In their mission to keep plays, actors, and audiences in their "proper places," inspectors grew increasingly convinced that revistas, regardless of where they were performed, were a main source of the problem. To their thinking, revistas catered to the lowest element and used political concerns to "exhibit chinas, vagrants, 'apaches' and other such stock characters, all without the tiniest bit of originality, with vulgar dancers, bad music, and grotesque dance."[84] In its embrace of revista shows, El Iris fared slightly better in the inspectors' reports than "lesser theaters" such as Arbeu. If they considered carpas lowbrow theater, inspectors voiced the same concerns in assessing the hybridity that now typified the theatrical landscape of the revolutionary city at large. Informed by nineteenth-century notions of high theater, they severely disliked the idea of political and even nationalist theater. They believed that these forms diminished Mexico's grandeur, especially when performed in the city's foremost theater.

LA IRIS AND EL IRIS

If revista theater in post-revolutionary Mexico was a vehicle for new ideas about femininity, corporeality, and urbanity, the roles of both El Iris and La Iris exemplified this changing theatrical landscape. From 1918 until 1934, during which the new National Theater of Bellas Artes was left incomplete (see chapter 7), Teatro Esperanza Iris was the most important theater in the city.[85] Even though the theater was a brand-new structure, it appeared to fit better with older, Porfirian sensibilities than with revolutionary promises of cultural reform. El Iris's appearance, if not deceiving, at least hid complex shifts in the theater world in which it participated fully.

In the absence of a true national theater and theater company, El Iris represented the most upscale and significant venue in the city. Before becoming El Iris, the site on Donceles 36–8 had been Teatro Xicoténcatl, which opened its doors in 1912 with the opera *Aida*. Xicoténcatl, while lit properly and able to seat fifteen hundred people, suffered from poor ventilation. Upon buying the plot, Iris decided to tear it down. She contracted architect Federico Mariscal, who later would finish the Palacio de Bellas Artes (Palace of Fine Arts), to carry out the project of building her own theater. The theater was large by anyone's standards, with a seating capacity of twenty-four hundred. Moreover, Iris and her partners bought extremely expensive building materials, such as Brazilian hardwood and Italian marble, and invested grand sums in outfitting the theater with the best lighting available at the time, as they believed light was "the life of a theater." It is remarkable that such a place of luxury and riches had been built between 1914 and 1916, the period of greatest political and social upheaval during the armed phase of the revolution. The entire building was fashioned in a neoclassical style, replete with a frieze. Groups of medallions, sculpted flowers, and allegorical figures that surrounded images of the great diva herself graced the facade, venerating Iris's regal dress and demeanor.[86] La Iris, the diva, had permanently secured a physical presence of herself, El Iris, in the heart of the city.

Even if its construction and its grand opening coincided with the height of revolutionary turmoil and victory, El Iris at first showed no sign of the progressive and nationalist fervor that soon would dominate the visual arts. El Iris, a dream of marble, hardwoods, and velvet, was in many respects a leftover of the elite entertainment world that had epitomized the Porfirian city. Located on the posh west side, it continued the tradition of upscale venues that had made the area the foremost entertainment district in the city.

In its adherence to neoclassical architecture, its segregation of spaces by class, its celebration of turn-of-the-century Art Nouveau style, and its stage, which showcased Viennese operetta and celebrities such as Anna Pavlova and Enrico Caruso, El Iris appeared to continue the type of Eurocentric entertainment Porfirians had previously enjoyed. Appearances, however, proved deceiving. Although El Iris's repertoire stayed close to elite expectations and its theater predominantly celebrated European culture, more Mexican forms of entertainment were gradually included in an attempt to adapt to changing times and revolutionary expectations. For instance, the production of *La mazorca azul* (The blue ear of corn), despite its classic conventions of operetta that celebrated "great pleasures, women, [and] fiery kisses," was but one of many nationalistically tinged operettas that premiered at El Iris. Moreover, Iris and company never stayed long in her own theater or the city. The diva and her partners intelligently harnessed earnings from both the theater and the company by continuing to tour nationally and internationally while renting out El Iris in their absence to an array of companies and productions, the majority of which embraced new theater forms.[87]

El Iris was innovative in its use of space, demonstrating that factors other than content of performances were important in determining its role in the city's changing entertainment offerings. Spatially and architecturally, even if adhering to old-world respectability and ostentatious glamour, El Iris had been designed and built as a multi-use space that could accommodate a variety of performance genres. Furniture could be removed easily, transforming the theater into an ample dance hall. This not only opened theater space to a variety of artists, genres, and plays but also allowed the audience direct participation in large espectáculos, as would a true *centro de farandula* (large street theater). Due to its large range of productions, combining European operetta and avant-garde shows with revista theater, comedians, circus, dance-hall events, and even fashion shows that attracted actors and spectators of all social backgrounds, El Iris embraced a cultural hybridity that came to characterize Mexican theater performances during the 1920s. In this it mirrored the popularity of street theater. The mingling of men and women from different classes who shared the latest gossip about fashion and politics made theatergoing an important activity in holding up appearances and fomenting opportunities for social cohesion.[88] El Iris, a multi-use space between private and public, illusion and reality, the stage and the street, reflected a larger spectacle and the mixture of audiences that played itself out in the city at large.

In contrast to the critiques inspectors bestowed on the revistas performed in El Iris, La Iris still received great reviews, even if her time as a diva seemed to be drawing to a close. Iris first announced her retirement in the early 1920s after showcasing her great successes *Princesa de dólar* and *La cuarta plana*, in which she appeared in her special costume. She surprised and delighted the audience, so wrote grateful inspectors, by singing "Paloma blanca" (White dove) by none other than Maestro Lerdo de Tejada, the head of the Departamento de Diversiones Públicas. Throughout the later 1920s, Iris's continuing cycles of farewells and comebacks would provoke much hilarity in the press. However, by the mid-1920s it appeared that with the retirement of such illustrious theater stars as La Iris, Mimí Derba, and comedian Leopoldo Beristáin, a great epoch of Mexican theater had come to an end.[89]

Unlike Conesa, Iris ultimately traded her status as a worldly femme fatale for the role of a devoted, doting mother and, by extension, a woman who cared for "the people." Her assumption of this more traditional role garnered her the respect of Mexican audiences far into the new century. This drastic change in image echoed the acts of earlier European actresses who returned to self-sacrifice and devotion to the common good as the hallmark of proper femininity.[90] Throughout her long career, Iris acted as the true "Hija Predelicta de Ciudad de México," the title bestowed upon her by the city in 1921. She staged benefit concerts to aid the victims of natural disasters, organized free puppet shows for poor children, and opened her theater to governmental functions.

Moreover, her growing status as a tragic figure who endured her misfortunes as a prescribed part of womanhood but returned as *La tiple de hierro* (The iron lady of the stage) earned her enormous popular support. Esperanza, the fountain of hope, managed to rise above the difficulties of early widowhood, the loss of her two children, failed marriages and business ventures, and the incarceration of her third husband, Paco Sierra.[91] Despite the many announcements of her retirement, Iris became a national mother figure who always returned, caring for her audience and fans, extending her loving embrace once more.[92] Her famous "Charlas para mujeres" (Talks for women), which she conducted in her theater and as crowd pleasers on tour, must be understood in both this context as well as an impetus for female empowerment.

In 1934, Iris received great acclaim for her part as a suffering mother in the blockbuster movie *Mater noster*, followed by a slew of similar roles later in life.[93] On and off the stage, Iris now successfully played a humble woman, honored daughter of Mexico City, and mother to all. For this, the public forgave her relationships with younger men, her wealth, her business cunning, and—as we will see in the next chapter—her *Ba-ta-clán*.

CONCLUSION

In 1899, fourteen-year-old María Rosalía Esperanza Bofill Ferrer from the state of Tabasco embarked on what would become a long career as a stage and film actress, impresario, and celebrity. Twenty years later, she and her adopted Mexico City had changed significantly. She had gone from playing newspaper boy in the revista *La cuarta plana*, a *tipo* (type) emblematic of a modernizing city, to a mature, wealthy actress who owned her own theater company and had built her own theater.

Between 1900 and 1918, Mexico City's social geography underwent drastic changes. Although the city had been spared most of the ravages of warfare that befell the countryside and cities in the north of the country, the capital did see its share of malaise, such as workers' strikes, riots, and severe food shortages. Moreover, even while engaged in a revolution of its own, Mexico did not escape the other revolutionary effects of a rapidly advancing modernity that was taking place in the rest of the world. Esperanza Iris's theater encapsulates the experience of these changes in Mexico.

The theater's outward performance—like that of its owner—as a gracious lady, a señora decente, was deceptive—or more precisely, one of passing. The diva's performances of femininity on and off the stage complicated distinctions between fiction and reality and allowed the fantasy of the stage to spill into the world outside the theater. Judith Butler has demonstrated how normative gender roles come into being through discourses of performativity, where identities are performances, even if they might not be understood as such. Only certain performances, however, are discernible within the larger constructs of normality, and these are then the only ones that "matter."[94] The diva's historical importance, then, was her ability to normalize what was understood as performance (onstage) as a daily performance of gender that Butler recognizes as the main frame underpinning gender identities.

Through her scandals, her love-struck admirers, and her play with conventions, the diva plotted a new path of female sexuality and autonomy in the metropolitan city. Consequently, divas proved ambiguous figures in their incarnation of gracious women. As femmes fatales, sexual objects, and feminists, famous actresses such as María Conesa and Esperanza Iris altered the image of women in public life. As stars of the stage and celebrities, the divas had a profound effect on women of all social classes in Mexico City.[95] Iris, as we will see, would soon change Mexico City's sense of what was feminine, desirable, and beautiful, and, with it, would take the first steps toward creating a new vision of the city.

Bataclanismo

FROM DIVAS TO DECO BODIES

Voilá Paris: La ba-ta-clán, a grand variety spectacle from the French capital, premiered in Teatro Iris in Mexico City on February 12, 1925. Featuring nude and seminude French actresses who performed dances and acts that appeared to be a mix of classical ballet, Ziegfeld Follies chorus lines, and tableaux vivants, the show instantly sent shock waves throughout the Mexican entertainment world and the larger metropolis. Within weeks, Mexican copycat productions capitalized on the show's enormous success, triggering a new entertainment phenomenon named after the original production: *bataclanismo*. It also launched a new kind of female star, the *bataclana*, who came to represent the erotic and more dangerous attributes of the flapper for Mexican audiences. Moreover, the shows represented a new body type, the Deco body, which became the site of contested and divergent notions of modernity.

Bataclanismo, in conjunction with Deco bodies, became a transformative discourse that reached far beyond the theater into the practice of everyday life. As a larger phenomenon, it played a major role in changing gender norms in the wake of the Mexican Revolution and the advent of twentieth-century global capitalism. Analyzing the relationship between bodies and space from Judith Butler's perspective of gender performance, we see how the new transnational aesthetic of feminine embodiment celebrated in *Voilá Paris: La ba-ta-clán* (hereafter, bataclán) influenced a distinct urban modernity and sociability in Mexico City.[1] The show postulated a radically different idea of femininity that included a new way of discerning physical beauty. While it was a transnational phenomenon that had originated in Europe and the United States in the wake of World War I, the Deco body embedded in bataclanismo functioned locally as a catalyst transforming the idea of female beauty and cosmopolitan living in Mexico. The new ideal female physique of the Deco body, which stressed length, height, and androgyny, helped to reconfigure Mexico City in terms of gender, space, and race. By mapping the change from voluptuous divas to this new type of embodiment, the changing gender norms inherent in "transnational acting" on and off the stage influenced the creation of a distinct urban modernity in Mexico City. The Deco body ushered in new gender ideals, helped visualize urban modernity, and facilitated bridging the gap between two divergent racial discourses that accompanied revolutionary reform, indigenismo and mestizaje, paving the way for a "mestizo modernity."[2]

VOILÁ!

In 1925, La Iris used the growing potential of Teatro Iris as a space for innovative theater to introduce the capital city and the nation to a new type of theater, the bataclán, and inadvertently a new female beauty ideal. In contracting the Parisian company of Mme Berthe Rasimi for El Iris, she certainly made good on her promise to use the theater as a venue to bring "novelties, art, and luxury" to Mexico City.[3]

Before arriving in Mexico, the bataclán had enjoyed great success in Europe as well as Argentina and Brazil. In 1922, Mme Rasimi, a great entrepreneur and owner of the Ba-ta-clán Vaudeville Theater in the Bastille quarter of Paris, had taken the ensemble on a South American tour, where the show proved both controversial and extremely successful. The day before the bataclán was to premiere in Rio de Janeiro, the press reported that diplomats who had seen the spectacle in Paris felt it contained scenes insulting the Brazilian national character. Indeed, in August 1922 the show first garnered mixed reactions, and the Brazilian press was initially far from supportive. The day after the premiere, Mme Rasimi issued a public statement in the national newspaper *Gazeta de Notícias* to counter the idea that the show ridiculed Brazilians, an impression that she "had never intended." Rasimi aimed to head off any doubt that the show was offensive: "We French have much respect for our allies in days of pain and glory, and particularly because we adore this marvelous country of incomparable beauty." She continued that the diplomats might have misinterpreted the "ultra-modernist pantomime *Le Boeuf sur le Toit*, in which my theater shows the irony of the prohibition laws in the US." She closed with the hope that this performance in Rio would be one of the best in her long career, befitting the beauty of the city.[4]

Despite, or perhaps because of, the initial brouhaha and rumors of critics, the bataclán was "an indisputable success" in Rio de Janeiro. The cariocas, in anticipation of this "new spectacle in Rio," filled the Teatro Lyrico to the last seat for the opening of *Paris chic* (and the three successive bataclán revues: *Pour vous plaire*, *Voilá Paris*, and *Au revoir*) that Rasimi staged during August. This is most likely where, and how, Esperanza Iris first encountered the show, as she was in Rio for *Phi-Phi*, a production with Brazilian actors and singers she directed. *Phi-Phi* had originally been staged by Estavan Amerante, and even though Iris changed the play only slightly, it was transformed from a "simple" Portuguese version to a "Mexican sumptuous splurge," something both "ingenious and dangerous."[5]

The bataclán proved enormously popular with Mexican audiences as well. Adapted in part from Milhaud's ballet *Le boeuf sur le toit* (*The Ox on the Roof: The Nothing Doing Bar*), the bataclán consisted of an array of dance acts without a single unifying theme. Performed by lanky, scantily dressed Parisian girls, it culminated in a grand spectacle of female flesh that eclipsed anything earlier divas had dared to exhibit. The central theme of seductive female beauty was certainly not new to Mexican theater, but the bataclán was innovative in terms of the spatial relationship of actresses and audience vis-à-vis the stage, the lack of a discernible narrative, and the degree of nudity.[6] While no extant evidence can tell us precisely what the show entailed in Mexico, we do know that the performance of *Voilá Paris* included thirty-one fast-paced scenes with titles such as "Homage to the Rose," "Offering to the Sphinx," "The Day of the Sun," and "Modern Idol." The use of extravagant costumes and stage sets, dynamic dance movements, and female near-nudity was "a true parade of gran gala, an example of divine chic and feminine caprice."[7] Most importantly, the bataclán marked a shift away from a single female star. Instead, a line of chorus girls paraded their bodies with choreographed uniformity that foreshadowed Busby Berkeley's films of the 1930s as well as today's fashion shows. With its extraordinary success in Mexico, the bataclán quickly metamorphosed into a phenomenon, bataclanismo, that would alter how many Mexican men and women came to understand female bodies and feminine behavior.

Not surprisingly, *Voilá Paris* caused a good deal of controversy, which was more and more a crucial ingredient for successful shows. Critics were divided and debated its validity and meaning. Repeatedly advertised and labeled as "the newest spectacle," the bataclán was destined to upset old customs and shock provincial morals. Some critics questioned the virtuousness of the eight dancers, described as "living Greek columns" proudly displaying their naked bodies adorned only with some exotic feathers. Other members of the press, however, expressed admiration. As one theater critic remarked:

> As if they were golden heralds of spring, the pretty little French girls have made our Valley erupt. The sinful happiness of Montmartre has stretched over the metropolis like a radiant fire. The burden of our ancestral melancholy has become lighter, only at hearing their boulevardesque laughter. We marvel at the Venusian parade of the modern goddesses of Paris, who move about the stage as living statues.[8]

If the dancers looked like "goddesses" and "living statues," they certainly evoked human desires and showed off their bodies in shameless fashion.[9] Iris had struck gold. The triumph of *Voilá Paris* inspired two more presentations by the ensemble within the same month: *Cachez-Ça* and *Oh La La!* The performances included fashion shows, where the dancers-turned-models got even closer to the public through the innovative use of catwalks.

Despite its apparent superficiality, the bataclán revolutionized Mexican theater by infusing a new, overt female sexuality into the revista genre, which, due to its embrace of hybridity, innovation, and political satire, was quick to adapt to the success of the bataclán. *Voilá Mexique: El Rataplan* (Here is Mexico: The rat manifesto), a satire by producer José Campillo and actor Roberto Soto, debuted in El Lírico just a month later and became an instant classic. Thanks to fierce promotion that promised "neither an old one, nor an ugly one" in the cast of Mexican girls, it met with even greater success than its Parisian original. Some Mexican historians have explained *El Rataplan*'s success as a nationalistic impulse to demonstrate that Mexico refused to stay behind the European avant-garde and, as such, that it was indicative of the era's rather superficial exuberance. According to these scholars, the phenomenon was born of modern ennui and indifference, of excess and fraud, of a desire to forget the hardships of the revolution.[10] *El Rataplan*, however, did not consist of mere mimicry. Unlike its French counterpart, the work mixed female sexuality with political satire much as carpa theater did, questioning social conditions in the city's poorest barrios. Due to their association with sex and political scandal, these new revistas and their stars remained profitable business material well into the 1930s, as evidenced by biographies of famous bataclanas.[11]

Bataclanesque shows such as *El Rataplan* thus fused eroticized female nudity with social commentary, a combination that quickly became an essential feature of Mexican revistas. In bataclán-infused revista, nudity was deemed modern, and therefore was not censored by the theater inspectors of the Department of Public Diversions. The fact that families now attended revistas was considered the best proof that the genre consisted of "moral entertainment." Political content, on the other hand, was more likely to catch the attention of censors. Under the auspices of the municipal government and the theater inspectors, censorship was most heavily leveled against the political revistas critical of the revolutionary leadership, such as "Don Adolfo's Orchard Sister Water," "National Bargain Sale," and "Obregón's Garden."[12]

Due to the influence of the bataclán, the codified cast of revista theater made up of nineteenth-century regional tipos that had evolved into twentieth-century stock urban characters now mingled with naked, statuesque bodies and positioned mexicanidad against the "exquisite feathers and delicious veils" of Parisian-like chorus girls. Moreover, *El Rataplan* turned revista theater into a truly cosmopolitan performance, rallying new energies in the face of the caudillo showmanship of national leaders. While bataclanismo might have offended middle-class sentiments in the "elite" Iris, it quickly spread throughout theaters across the city, including in lower-class barrios and their carpas that integrated bataclanismo into their larger repertoire of satire and social commentary. "Lo bataclanesco," speaking to revista's potential in combining sex and politics, quickly became fashionable beyond its initial bourgeois audience, fueling a wave of theatrical works characterized by lack of clothing, including *La fiebre del ba-ta-clán* (The fever of the bataclán), with María Conesa; *No lo tapes!* (Don't cover it!), which saw the debut of Lupe Vélez as bataclanismo's first real star; and, eventually, *Desnudos para familias* (Nudes for families).[13] Even if this stark contrast reflected the contradictions that marked Mexican society's search for modernity, the presence of bataclanesque figures in revistas also suggested that Deco bodies represented a desirable femininity that could be integrated into a proudly nationalist society.

DECO BODY: SEEING AND BEING SEEN

Despite the allure of bataclanismo, the promise of the bataclán—bringing Paris to Mexico City—was not a novel idea. Porfirian entertainment relied heavily on French constructs and imports, creating a world dominated by divas. From their association, even if implicit, with the emerging identity of the New Woman at the end of the nineteenth century, divas had much in common with bataclanismo's chica moderna, who would ascend the stage in the 1920s. However, while there were certainly continuities between the two in terms of female stardom, fomenting new ideas of female sexuality, feminine gender roles, and notoriety, there were also marked differences. These are most apparent in ideas of corporeal beauty and desirable body type, as well as how these came to bear on the gendered nature of cityscape.

Divas, through their central role in opera, had created a center of gravity onstage that reflected their personal power, expressed in charisma as well as body type. The hourglass figure of the diva, accentuated by her opulent dress, jewels, and aristocratic demeanor, earned her honorable titles such as Iris's nickname, "La Emperatriz de Opereta." Although the diva was certainly perceived as a sex symbol, her power resided in her personality, which—even if she was still young—projected the identity of a strong and mature woman who reveled in riches, commanded a large following of fans, and appeared in charge of her own destiny. Often described as gentle, sympathetic, and gracious, the diva was a woman whose charms, appeal, and independence were neatly interwoven with an image of strong femininity that, while exciting, did not offend her many male admirers.[14] The woman who came to inhabit the new Deco body, however, was connected to a distinctly different phenomenon. Far more modern, this incarnation of the New Woman was an androgynous emblem of the machine age.

On the global stage, the ideal of the New Woman emerged in the post–World War I era, a period that facilitated women's claims to new forms of both political and social mobility. This ideology was articulated through a radically different idea of femininity that postulated a new way of discerning physical beauty. The Deco body marked a shift from the nineteenth-century aesthetic embodied by the theater diva to the new beauty ideal characterized by movie stars such as Clara Bow, Louise Brooks, and Lillian Gish.

As early as 1913, Gabrielle "Coco" Chanel sold her first collection of radically novel clothing that freed the waist and legs through new fashions that "blurred the line between masculine and feminine" and reconstituted the architecture of the female body by making breasts, waist, and hips disappear in simple lines.[15] The loose-fitting, comfortable clothing left much room for movement, allowing women to engage in work and play with much greater ease. This coincided with a new visibility of middle-class women in the wake of World War I, both in the workforce and in visual representations.[16] As scholars of gender and modernity have argued, the crucial element within the construction of the New Woman and new ideas of corporeality was how she and her Deco body came to be seen. The historian Liz

Conor uses the concept of the "appearing woman" to explain how modern visual technologies changed female visibility in public and how people thought about what women were supposed to be, that is, a "woman-object." This, however, did not entail victimization and loss of agency; instead, it gave women a way to take an active part in "appearing."[17] Consequently, the fact that women became images, and came to accept and look at themselves as images, would be central in forging the modern femininity of the 1920s.

Not surprisingly, as "appearing women," the more of the body that bataclanas revealed, the more public exposure they enjoyed and the more they modeled a new, modern feminine visibility. Bataclanesco imagery inundated Mexico City's press starting in 1925, ranging from refined aestheticization to sultry satire. The press informed the way female spectacle was to be seen and helped to consolidate bataclanismo as a distinct discourse. It was this discourse, rather than the original show, that took the Deco body beyond its theatrical limits and promoted its performance as part of everyday metropolitan modernity.

In addition to the photos of actresses that adorned newspapers, weeklies, and magazines, the drawings of artist and cartoonist Ernesto García Cabral captured bataclán's Deco bodies to unparalleled perfection.[18] His many covers for the immensely popular *Revista de Revistas*, a high-circulation weekly owned by the national newspaper *Excélsior*, stood out owing to their innovation in style, layout, and color in an era of largely black-and-white imagery. Cabral also connected the Deco bodies of the stage with the New Women in the city by showing both as sophisticated, independent, and stylish. In many ways, these women, who appeared in many guises yet inhabited shared physiques and flaunted similar attitudes, were stand-ins for the modern metropolis.[19] Through their color, their brazen style, and their Deco bodies, Cabral's women mapped the future of a new femininity onto the developing metropolis.

Cabral, nicknamed "El Chango" (The monkey), was described by contemporaries as a bohemian, a nonconformist, and a genius. In his work he connected an incipient Mexican metropolitanism to female bodies like no other Mexican visual artist of his time.[20] The internationally renowned muralists Diego Rivera and José Clemente Orozco considered him the greatest sketch artist of their generation, while other contemporaries—always happy to nationalize greatness— praised him as a true Mexican artist due to his use of vibrant colors. So influential were Cabral's *portadas* (covers) that fashion designers eagerly awaited each issue of *Revista de Revistas* before designing new collections. According to a retrospective, Cabral "specialized in painting women ingénues and sophisticates who seemed to languish in a constant state of elegance."[21] Cabral always rendered the Deco bodies of these New Women as long and languid, confident, and relaxed, even when he placed them in the midst of frenetic and exciting modern scenes.

Similar in effect to the mannequin as a crucial icon of new 1920s femininity, Cabral's women were a focal point in the turbulent vortex of cosmopolitan modernity: "fixed before the fleeting, distracted gaze of the metropolis, while reinforcing the sense of anonymity in city presence as spectacle without identity."[22] While Cabral is best remembered in Mexico for his political caricatures, his art outlining a new type of femininity was prolific and powerful. Even his unsigned movie posters from the 1940s were easily recognizable to collectors as "Cabrals" due to his signature style in representing the female form.[23] Cabral's women were as essential to his art as they were to the vision of the city.

Cabral started illustrating portadas for *Revista de Revistas* in 1920, upon his return from Europe and Buenos Aires. Like many of his predecessors in Paris, Cabral was drawn to the glamour of the demimonde, expressed in the interplay of the bright lights and dark shadows of the bustling metropolis. Inspired by his recollections of bohemian Paris, Cabral's early drawings drew on the tenets of Art Nouveau and transposed such stock urban characters as society women, prostitutes, and pimps into the landscape of Mexico City. By 1925, however, when he captured the essence of the bataclán for the cover of

FIG. 4. Ernesto García Cabral, cover, *Revista de Revistas*, December 6, 1925.

Revista de Revistas, his style had changed markedly, and the frills and embellishment characteristic of Art Nouveau had made way for the simple, elongated lines of Art Deco.[24] In this bataclán portada, Cabral contrasted a well-lit, graceful dancer against a dark, circumspect audience of upscale male spectators (fig. 4). Reducing the stage to a single line and rendering the dancer in both profile and straight on, Cabral's

EN EL BA-TA-CLAN   101647

Como se deleitan nuestros hombres "serios" con el novedoso espectáculo parisiense.

Por García Cabral.

FIG. 5. Ernesto García Cabral, *En el ba-ta-clan*, *Jueves de Excélsior*, February 26, 1925.

use of space is ingenious; he captures the intricate movements of the dancer's body while revealing only a slight glimpse of her face and eyes. Slender but strong, elegant but indifferent, and sexy yet androgynous, she appears to be walking a tightrope, harmonizing feminine fragility and sexual boldness. The men, stirred but baffled, take in the spectacle.

Cabral's black-and-white drawing *En el ba-ta-clan* (fig. 5), a composite of the performances on both sides of the stage, gets closer to the totality of the spectacle. The elongated dancers, statuesque while in full movement, are alternated with caricatures of the audience. Cabral's unforgiving close-ups of gawking, lustful, and incredulous older upper-class "gentlemen" and one indignant wife (portrayed as an older, unattractive woman) invoke ingrained stereotypes of gendered behavior that pitched newly empowered young flappers against older women, especially in their competition to attract the affections of older, economically established men.

In the city as drawn by Cabral, even mestizo and indigenous Mexican women could aspire to the new beauty ideal. Week after week, the portadas of *Revista de Revistas* revealed that the celebration of the new female ideal, while predicated on white bodies, relied on form, not skin color. This echoed, perhaps inadvertently, the ideas of José Vasconcelos in *La raza cósmica*, which appeared in the same year. Vasconcelos's embrace of the mestizo as "a bridge to the future" required "the development of a new aesthetic that would not privilege whiteness at the cost of bronzeness."[25] Cabral's representations of Art Deco mestizas in various shades of "bronze," like the "national" beauties of *El Rataplan* and other bataclanesque revistas, demonstrated that an authentic mexicana performed modernity just as well as any other Deco girl when fitted into the right shape and equipped with the appropriate attitude (fig. 6).

Cabral's portadas spoke not only to a large audience but also to the budding mass media of modern journalism and mass marketing of which his work was an integral part. Historian Joanne Hershfield argues that due to Mexico's high illiteracy rates, modernization and development in Mexico were in large part "dependent on the circulation of a global visual culture."[26] Cabral's distinct way of seeing reverberated in news photography, journalistic reports, and advertisements, constituting a visual economy that permeated the capitalinos' collective consciousness. By the mid-1920s, Hollywood had effectively demonstrated that entertainment was big business, both in terms of ticket sales and the role it played in creating new consumer markets.[27] Similarly, by the 1920s publishers had hit upon a successful formula of

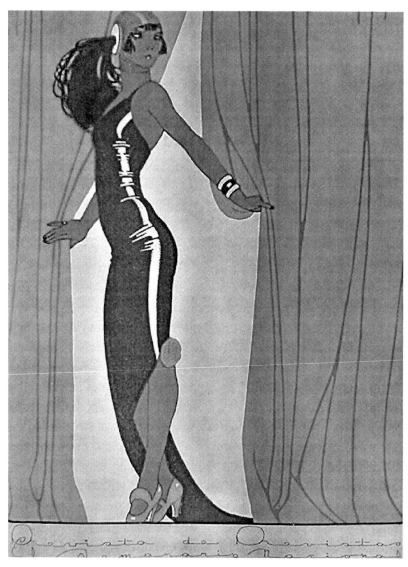

FIG. 6. Ernesto García Cabral, cover, *Revista de Revistas*, July 4, 1926.

selling magazines below production cost in order to boost circulation
and attract advertising revenues. Intersecting historically with the rise
of modern journalism as well as the mass production and consumption of beauty products, the Deco body provided transnational beauty
industries with a new tool for selling merchandise in Mexico.

Commercial culture industries, the beauty business in particular, were quick to appropriate the Deco body as their main vehicle in marketing an array of affordable luxury products to middle- and lower-class women. In the United States the image of the flapper was fashioned in large part by writers such as F. Scott Fitzgerald, who proclaimed that the flapper's identity stemmed not only from the "shape of her body and placement of her curves" but also from the products she consumed. Although advertising had mainly featured men out of consideration for female modesty at the turn of the century, by the 1920s consumption was conceived of as a feminine activity. While production continued to be associated with men, shopping promised women freedom from patriarchal constraints. This consumption did not necessarily destabilize traditional gender relations or result in a comprehensive independence for women, but the advertising industry found eager consumers in young women who sought to express their independence. They looked to theater and film for cues about products in order to realize the image and style that symbolized the freedom of the modern woman. While the flapper communicated individuality, she expressed this in consumer conformity.[28] In Mexico, the *flapperista* sold an array of products (fashion, cigarettes, creams, automobiles) but associated the modern woman with rebellion, controversy, and self-determination, thus liberating as well as commodifying feminine independence.[29]

Although this incipient form of transnational gendered capitalism might have not been empowering in a feminist sense, the world of leisure and shopping did afford working-class and middle-class women a valid reason to be in public and move through public space. This provided them with a sense of mobility, freedom, and female sociability. In the United States, entertainment and leisure became important strategies in working women's construction of self, definition of their autonomy, and access to the public sphere. Most young women in New York City at the turn of the century sought out employment that would facilitate their access to cinemas, theaters, clubs, and dance halls.

Shopping also served as entertainment. Working women's mobility in large cities in both the Unites States and Mexico provided them with ways to "enact public subjectivities" based on their identity as consumers.[30] Working women now looked around with an "active" gaze on the street and within and outside the theater. This consumer gaze was part of a larger cultural fabric of wishes and expectations, yet one that legitimized women's presence in public and made them active participants in the construction of their own desires.

Changing ideas of beauty, especially tied to consumerism, also reached Mexico by way of the entertainment industry. Historians Mary Kay Vaughan and Rubén Gallo suggest that in Mexico, emerging consumer culture revolved in large part around "public spectatorship" produced by new urban spaces such as department stores, parks, dance halls, theaters, trams, boulevards, and stadiums.[31] Advertisements for U.S. makeup, French perfumes, and Mexican facial creams frequently appeared in popular publications and highlighted their growing presence in the city's pharmacies, clothing outlets, and smaller retail stores.[32] Advances in photography added to and reflected this spectatorship and mediated its relationship with the modern metropolis, advertisements, and new venues of commercial culture. Journalist, writer, and social commentator Salvador Novo argued that it was not until the 1920s that Mexican women had the equipment and spaces at their disposal to perfect their looks, even if this entailed a standardization of beauty he largely blamed on the popularity of cinema.[33] As fashion and ready-to-wear clothes increasingly became available to lower-class women, class lines were blurred by an advertising industry that marketed products to a primarily female audience "regardless of class."[34] Buying garments on installment plans made it easy for most Mexican girls to dress like Joan Crawford and other Hollywood stars. Fashion provided Mexican women with an acquisitive gaze—a consumerist "erotics of looking."[35]

A new understanding of female beauty articulated by Deco bodies onstage, whether in the theater or in a shop window, called for a new aesthetic of seeing and female visibility. Emerging advertising discourses selling a new corporeal beauty that was lengthy, thin, lithe, and—above all—statuesque clearly echoed bataclán reviews. Theater critics described in detail the "physically suggestive and most harmonious lines" of the "modern goddesses of Paris, who move[d] about the stage as living statues." Photos of bataclán stars such as "the beautiful Dydienne, whose physique has provoked great admiration of those who frequent the bataclán show," added to the new visual aesthetic.[36] Advertisements and retail fashion displays began to deploy this vision of femininity, especially with the new "realistic" mannequin, who, not incidentally, made her debut at the Paris Exhibition of Decorative Art in 1925. A favorite object in advertising, "the feminine appeared as a replica mannequin … in visual designs on billboard and in print" and taught women—in Mexico, too—to appear as statues: "*mannequins vivants*—living mannequins."[37] In many variety and entertainment magazines of the late 1920s and early 1930s, when women were deemed and described as beautiful, the adjective *escultura* (sculptural) was used frequently as a superlative. Hence the statuesque beauties of the theater found their way into the public spaces of the city, where female consumers learned to identify with models and to desire inhabiting their Deco bodies.[38]

Consequently, beyond selling products and inspiring consumerism, commodification of the Deco body changed the way women perceived their own bodies and the possibility of transformation.[39] While some advertisers simply inserted Deco bodies into campaigns for preexisting goods, new products promising consumers the opportunity to attain the Deco body through their use also proliferated. In the late 1920s and early 1930s, the number of advertisements for beauty products that accompanied opinion and editorial articles warning women to *guardar la linea* (save their lines) through weight loss and exercise increased dramatically. Moreover, advertisements with a focus on enhancing the female form through the use of products such as stockings, shoes, and dresses to create the appearance of increased height, or those that guaranteed female readers "breasts like a statue" proliferated, while announcements for skin-whitening cream that had been so popular during the Porfiriato significantly decreased.[40] Mexican women, stated Novo, now embarked on weekly—and lengthy—visits to beauty parlors to dye their hair, have their eyebrows plucked, undergo facial clay mask treatments, and receive manicures, all in an effort to emulate "the statuesque beauty of Venus de Milo."[41] Indeed, the emphasis in these visual discourses on becoming "like a statue" was later understood by Simone de Beauvoir to cast a woman's objectified body as a "glorious double." When a woman beholds herself in the mirror, Beauvoir noted, "she is a work of art, *a living statue*, she shapes it, adorns it, puts it on show."[42]

Through its connection to the world of entertainment, the Deco body outlined a feminine form that mapped the desirable emblems of a new, statuesque "Deco aesthetic" onto feminine embodiment. Literary scholars similarly have noted the importance of a changing conceptualization of the body as a visual marker of modernism and modernity. Mark Seltzer, in *Bodies and Machines*, finds that with the birth of advertising, bodies became more geometric, abstract, and typical, a "working model" for a new conceptualization of realism. Lucy Fischer argues that Art Deco "compressed," "streamlined," and simplified women's corporeality. Although the female form featured heavily in Art Deco, it represented the female body as a silhouette, a mere outline. Anne Anlin Cheng takes this even further when she states that modernist aesthetics imagined the female form as "pure surface" that was to be molded at will by artists, performers, and consumers. The results of the Industrial Revolution, including advances in mechanical reproduction, encouraged new technologies "to forge a fantasy about a modern, renewed, and disciplined body."[43]

Sleek, thin, and long, the Deco body was reflective of the machine age of the 1920s. The repetition of homogeneous, streamlined forms became a hallmark of modernism, where bodies were configured to aestheticize both harmonious collectives of sameness and desired qualities such as precision, productivity, and discipline. These aesthetics infiltrated female spectacle, both through transnational entertainment and beauty industries. Beauty contestants and health experts considered the body "physical machinery" that reflected modern ideas about health, hygiene, and perfection. The silver screen and theater stage represented bodily perfection as either the repetition of female form (or female body parts) or the single, machine-like Deco body. Critics such as Siegfried Kracauer were quick to remark that the representation of legs in series, as seen in productions such as the Ziegfeld Follies or other revue theater, resembled the workings of a factory; female dancers were "a machine of girls" that "epitomiz[ed] the optimism of American capitalism and mechanical success."[44]

Popular films demonstrating both the allure and the danger of the modern woman, such as Fritz Lang's *Metropolis*, dazzled audiences. The perfect Deco body of the female android that controls "the engine-city Metropolis" becomes a stand-in for modern urbanity. Modeling the ideal female proportions and shape, the robot is the ultimate modern woman in her mechanistic perfection: seductive, sexually brazen, and smart. Yet in her rebellion against her maker she is shown to be cold, cunning, soulless, and thus evil. As a mannequin come to life, she is not "authentic," but a mere copy, "a mask masquerading as femininity."[45] The Deco body was to be like a machine, a moving statue: steeled, gleaming, impenetrable, invulnerable. This fascination with technology inspired people of the early twentieth century to try to possess a body of "machine-like perfection," a "Taylorized body" whose "lines" had to be carefully maintained. Conor's insights are particularly apt: "What changed with modern standards was not only form, but form as a technique and a practice of bodily regulation and containment."[46]

The quest to realize the ideal of statuesque beauty through a regimen of diet, exercise, and products to discipline the body had become a mainstay of the popular press in Mexico by the late 1920s and early 1930s. Popular magazines and even newspapers in the capital city increasingly published photo essays on the quest for bodily perfection where step-by-step preparation of engineering beauty could be captured and shown. Articles stressed the need to *ciudar sus líneas* (save one's lines) through diets that would produce rapid weight loss, along with daily exercise to tone and lengthen the body (fig. 7). These articles appeared frequently as part of, or followed by, stories on Hollywood and Mexican stars and starlets. In these stories, the Deco bodies of movie stars functioned as the highest, but attainable, goal to stay slim and to engineer good skin.

∼Para Conservar la Línea∼

Cosas que se Deben Tener ∼Presentes∼

E L aire y el sol son los más poderosos reconstituyentes.

Los distintos ejercicios gimnásticos, que de por sí reportan innumerables beneficios al organismo, cobran singular importancia cuando se ejecutan al aire libre.

Si usted agrega a su programa diario unos breves minutos de gimnasia metodizada, al cabo de algunos días constituirá su pasatiempo favorito, contribuyendo a mantener o conseguir su belleza, cimentando su salud.

El sol y el aire del mar dan a la piel ese color bronceado que tanto hermosea los encantos femeninos.

La agilidad y desenvoltura física y la lucidez mental son consecuencias de la educación física.

Levantándose temprano gozará de los incomparables beneficios del aire puro.

Los ejercicios respiratorios están considerados como un natural y eficientísimo tratamiento para las afecciones del pecho.

El aire inspirado a orillas del mar o en lugares sanos en que el oxígeno se renueva constantemente, regulariza los cambios gaseosos y mantiene la perfecta permeabilidad de los bronquios.

La gimnasia respiratoria llega a obrar favorablemente en males gravísimos, como ser: casos de pleuresía con derrame y compresión, evitando de esta manera la inminente atrofia.

EL EJERCICIO DE ESTA SEMANA

Es éste un ejercicio de simple ejecución y que reúne múltiples beneficios en su acción. Pone en actividad numerosos músculos, especialmente los de las regiones abdominal, pectoral, etc., desalojando o impidiendo el avance del tejido adiposo. Es, pues, de interés a aquellas personas que ven peligrar la belleza de su línea ante la amenaza de la obesidad. Consta de dos tiempos:

TIEMPO No. 1.—El atleta aparece en la segunda posición de gimnasia elemental, es decir: los talones juntos, las puntas de los pies ligeramente separadas, las piernas rígidas, el cuerpo derecho, el busto erguido, las manos levemente apoyadas en la cintura, la cabeza alta, la barbilla recogida y la vista al frente. Inicia el ejercicio con un movimiento simultáneo de los brazos y el busto. Este último ejecuta una flexión de cintura al tiempo que los brazos se elevan sobre la cabeza hasta conseguir que las puntas de los dedos de las manos se toquen. Tal es la figura de esta página.

TIEMPO No. 2.—El atleta vuelve a la posición anterior o sea a la segunda de gimnasia elemental, hallándose en disposición de repetir el ejercicio.

Las personas que lo practiquen con el fin de adelgazar, deben hacerlo con ropa de abrigo.

CONSULTORIO

Kin Kan Kun, Mixcoac.—Envíeme sus medidas antropométricas y me será grato contestarle.

Titina, Veracruz.—La natación es la que puede contribuir a su mejor desarrollo físico.

Lociela, Ciudad.—La gimnasia respiratoria le facilitará lo que ansia. El cigarrillo no solamente mancha los dientes, sino que ocasiona desórdenes gástricos. Abandónelo.

Don Jean, Ciudad.—No debe usted temer el desaire, pues sus medidas antropométricas son correlativas. Como comprenderá, esta índole de consultas no nos es posible contestarlas desde esta página.

FIG. 7. "Para conservar la línea," *Universal Ilustrado*, July 23, 1931.

In addition to its direct links to the world of entertainment and the machine age, the Deco body's modern allure resulted from its implicit ties to athleticism and its attendant aesthetics. Mexican audiences had become aware of female athletes by the 1920s, yet the 1930s saw a marked increase in women's participation in sports. Revolutionary leaders held that athletics benefited women in moderation but that exercise should in no way interfere with traditional feminine behavior. As other political parties in Europe embraced eugenics as the vehicle to engineer public health, the Partido Nacional Revolucionario (PNR; National Revolutionary Party) promoted male and female participation in sports as an interactive "spectacle" that would combat lower-class vice and function as the road to creating a stronger race. Physical education for women entailed, however, that a woman never lose her femininity. Whether belonging to the PNR, Christian youth groups, or socialist sports associations, female athletes appeared on the pages of the Mexican press as "graceful young ladies" who practiced gymnastics or formed dance groups.[47]

An emphasis on health within the articulation of beauty that disciplined and streamlined bodies according to the Deco body ideal elevated sports as "physical culture." But this also had to sidestep what Judith Butler has referred to as "gender trouble." Bodies, even if engaged in what was considered non-gender-appropriate behaviors, should retain their legibility as part of a well-accepted, well-rehearsed, and well-performed binary: either male or female, but not both. Hence, if Deco bodies facilitated women's entry into male practices such as sports, they remained deployed as female sexed and sexual bodies so as to not upstage the accepted gender binary. Consequently, athleticism was encouraged, even desirable, so long as it enhanced but ultimately retained the female form. Obtaining a Deco body, touted by popular media and advertisers as women's work, consequently helped feminize female athleticism and enhance its rather austere aesthetic.

To help women mimic the graceful movements of the Deco bodies of film and theater, popular publications taught them to move like mannequins: "walking very slowly ... keeping the upper body immobile, while moving with 'correct poise' from the hips."[48] In Mexican magazines, beauty advisers to the stars and other experts frequently revealed their "trade secrets" that taught female readers to subject themselves to "the rules of health in order not to lose their lines." They also instructed them to walk elegantly like models and famous stars (who, used to the ever-present camera, learned to have better posture) and offered strategies for losing thigh and belly fat.[49] This movement of the Deco body, moreover, served an additional aim. Unlike the flaneur, who could wander through the modern metropolis aimlessly, women should walk in public space with a direct purpose. Mannequins helped women by modeling how they should inhabit cityscape, "accept the inevitability of being looked at," and become a spectacle in order to "truly exist in the city."[50]

Hence, while promising greater freedoms and playing with traditional gender norms through androgynous, angular forms and short hair, the Deco body ideal also presented women with an intense routine of "discipline and punish." Cheng finds that "the sleek, the understated, and the unadorned" that became "tasteful" in the 1920s was of crucial importance in "civilizing" women and teaching them "the pleasure of self-management." Even if it lent women greater physical mobility, sleek "flapper" clothing required the cultivation of a body that would suit its emphasis on length and slenderness. Liberated from restrictive clothing, the body itself now became "a muscular corset," women's own means of restraining themselves. As Susan Bordo remarks, women might have felt attracted by the freedom and independence that this "boyish body ideal" promised, but "as a feminist protest, the obsession with slenderness is hopelessly counterproductive."[51] To Bordo, the transnational Deco bodies of the 1920s were nothing more than an illusion that hid what Michel Foucault saw as the intensifying trend of disciplining bodies in the name of modernity.[52]

According to this Foucauldian view, Deco bodies were, above all, docile bodies. Representing the co-optation of women's push for greater political and socioeconomic rights unleashed by their greater participation in society, Deco bodies heralded what Bordo has called "the most powerful normalizing mechanisms" of the twentieth century. Or as Cheng finds, even more aptly, the desire to inhabit a Deco body was intertwined with the preoccupation to discipline the body through diet, exercise, and fashion regimens, or the "pleasure of self-management." This ensured that women remained engaged with beauty ideals rather than social advancement.[53]

However, changing ideas about feminine beauty implicitly tied slenderness with social strategies and advantages for women. Conor notes that in Australia, feminine beauty was an important requisite for romantic heterosexual relationships. Women were thought to be "entitled to beauty as insurance against desertion and infidelity," and they construed their right to beauty as part "the modern dictums of romance and health." During the 1920s, popular media increasingly postulated transnational discourses that associated beauty with health. In these discourses, beauty became a manifestation of health and in turn a logical extension of the self, an idea that helped combat the notion that "modern beauty involved trickery, imitation, and techniques of camouflage."[54] In Mexico, even in conservative magazines such as *El Hogar*, housewives were told to maintain and "save" the health of their skin as "a treasure." Skin, the author of the article "Belleza feminina" warned, lasts until death, and "a woman's ugliness is worse than that death."[55] Statements like these were designed to make women understand that they were their bodies, reflecting Conor's insight that the "imperative that they appear beautiful" led women to regard their appearance as "the real meaning of self."[56]

The belief that beauty equated health was greatly facilitated by the appearance of "new experts" with seeming "scientific authority" who taught women to "watch themselves."[57] Government validation, albeit indirect, of beauty-enhancing products such as pharmaceutical and medicinal items played a significant role in this process. If the mass media propagated new beauty ideals through a visual economy of Deco bodies, the revolutionary state largely determined the extent to which women would have access to the new beauty products. Public-health officials, however, differed little in their assessments of what constituted beauty from those who developed, marketed, and sold an ever-growing array of beauty products. The classification, production, and sale of beauty products in Mexico was regulated by the Department of Public Health, which in 1928 drew up a new ordinance that considered both drugs and beauty products as part of the same category of pharmaceuticals. Hence, *abortivas* (abortifacients), which could be obtained in drugstores with a doctor's prescription, were mentioned in the same legislative article that regulated hair products. By articulating regulations in terms of health through beauty, government officials followed the beauty industry in viewing beauty products as an extension of the search for health. This also meant that beauty products largely were sold at pharmacies, which conferred additional scientific and medicinal legitimacy on beauty regimens and aesthetic products.[58]

Engineering beauty was presented as a scientific enterprise that could be taught and learned, with or without products. Dispatches from Hollywood and New York City showed Mexican women how U.S.-style beauty was merely a matter of education. Articles translated from English stressed that a healthy lifestyle that would lead one to beauty. A routine of nine hours of sleep, sports, and a clean face underscored that the investment of time and discipline, as much as the use of beauty products, was crucial in attaining a Deco body. One certainly was advised to use creams to enhance the contours of one's face, but ultimately the emphasis in engineering good skin was on facial exercises to stimulate "the circulation of blood." A photo essay about beauty schools in the United States, "En los templos de la belleza" (Inside the temples of beauty), conceived of the classroom as a scientific stage where girls performed: applying masks, massaging the scalp to shampoo hair properly, using the correct makeup, and slapping their chins to fight sagging facial muscles. The photographs captured the end result of the transformation, a series of nearly homogenized faces and Deco bodies.[59] This homogenization, as well as the repetition of homogeneous and streamlined forms, was the hallmark of modernism and part of the allure of the machine age. Mass-produced ready-to-wear clothing that "replaced personalized fittings" greatly standardized fashion and conceptualized women's shapes and sizes as fitting predetermined patterns. Homogeneity made female bodies appear as "copies" and inspired women to desire being a copy, but it also meant that women of all classes and races could copy the ideal.

The idea that Mexican women might become like all other women in their quest for universal beauty caused concern among some male readers and commentators. The new emphasis on acquiring modern beauty certainly had its detractors, who especially seemed to worry about its power in blurring class lines and gender norms. According to Novo, the superficiality of the beauty regimen eclipsed a woman's greater charms, such as her intelligence and personality. Even if a woman had good skin, she could be *malcriada* (badly raised) and *brusca* (rude). Moreover, mimicry, Novo wryly commented, did not result in perfection: "Between beauty and makeup—it seems childish to emphasize it—there is the vast difference that separates life from the theater."[60]

If female bodies signaled that health constituted beauty, and beauty health, they could only function as proper markers of nation and modernity when confined to their proper place.[61] Deco bodies informed the modern city. Although they were packaged and marketed by Hollywood for the rest of the world and imagined as white, Deco bodies spoke to Mexicans because of their essential emphasis on a new form that connected them with modernity. Form, not race, became the dominant feature of this new ideal. As such, the Deco body formed a bridge connecting indigenismo to mestizaje. Also, women who embraced the new look did so for a variety of reasons. By looking at the nameless stars of the bataclán, and soon thereafter the Mexican *El Rataplan*, Mexican women of all ethnic backgrounds could imagine themselves as modern beauties. All they had to do was slim down, grow tall (i.e., wear heels and waist-less dresses), use makeup accentuating the eyes and the mouth, and act the part, or as Conor would say, make themselves "appear."[62]

MEDIATING IDENTITIES

The ideal of the transnational Deco body clashed with the image of womanhood that many in Mexico treasured as the quintessential embodiment of mexicanidad, where ideas of beauty, national identity, and femininity intersected with constructions about place and space. Tensions between the female beauty ideal presented by modern, urban, androgynous-looking Deco bodies and the idealized feminine embodied in indigenismo found their clearest expression within debates over a suitable national identity. Male readers of *Mujeres y Deportes* complained about this weekly magazine's heavy emphasis on Hollywood beauties at the expense of the charms of Mexican women. The editorial staff remedied the situation by including a page of "typical Mexican ladies" with photos and captions that invoked a gendered classification of race and place reminiscent of colonial *casta* (classification of different groupings of race mixing) paintings. "From Guadalajara, Latina, cultured and Indian," reads the caption below a photo of a young mestiza, followed by photos with captions such as "from a Spanish father and Indian mother, the result is," "product of a Spanish father and French mother equals a true Mexican woman," and, finally, the modern capitalina as the "representative type of youth in today's Mexico."[63]

Thus, the fear of homogenized beauty centered not so much on the condemnation of the outward appearance of Deco bodies in favor of inner beauty, charm, and personality, as cronistas such as Novo first seemed to suggest, but rather on the danger of compromising the markers of class and mexicanidad. The "ugliness of beauty pageants," Novo reasoned, was that they did not take into account regional and ethnic variance. In describing this difference, however, he resorted to the ingrained habit of casting racial difference as a gendered landscape. "Today," he wrote in 1929, "we can distinguish principally between the following types of Mexican women: white, corn-colored, and dark; from those again we can distinguish those who live in the tropical valleys and those who have been born in the fresh and romantic mountains." In contrast to those in the countryside, Novo wrote, women from Mexico City were elegant, slender, and Latina. However unnecessary it might be, according to the cronista, the capitalina used cosmetics quite liberally, and this enhanced the bodily difference that set her apart from rural mexicanas. Yet the capital city also counted a vast and ever-growing number of rural women, removed from the campo, whom Novo labeled as "Indio." These "unwashed masses," he stated matter-of-factly, generally did not make "the slightest effort to hide their bronzed color with help of powders and other cosmetics."[64]

In the wake of the bataclán, women aspiring to modern gender norms did appear to enjoy greater mobility in Mexico City. The success of bataclanesque shows and the allure of the Deco body created a discourse of a new femininity that helped women take firm steps outside of preconceived roles. As the bataclán glorified Deco bodies with short hair, it validated the struggles of the *pelonas* a year earlier, in 1924, when young women with short hair had endured physical attacks by men.[65] Not only did bataclanismo make it easier for Mexican women to cut their long *trenzas* (braids)[66] and wear high-heeled shoes, but the acts of Deco icons such as Lupe Vélez, with her outlandish behavior, independence, and devotion to dancing the Charleston, propelled them out of their class and ethnic boundaries and their usual areas of town, joining the ranks of "modern girls around the globe" who equally enjoyed a greater presence on city streets. In the early 1920s, elite Mexican women did not frequent drinking establishments other than Café Colón, the epicenter of refined society, and Sanborns. Here, elegant ladies would meet between 5 and 7 p.m. to partake of refreshments and ice cream while German operetta played in the background. At the end of the decade, many upper- and middle-class Mexican women in search of their own adventures and bohemian nightlife had begun to explore the carpas and dance salons near Plaza Garibaldi, an area that had been officially set aside for legalized prostitution since 1918.[67]

Crossing over to "the dark side"—slumming, even—became more acceptable and enticing to these women by the end of the 1920s. Not only did actresses have greater independence in deciding where to perform, but female spectators were increasingly attracted to the fashionable spectacle of street theater, even in small alleyways. Moreover, a visible segment of middle-class women now stayed out all night drinking in cabarets. These women, according to Novo, made up the female half of the nouveau riche, who self-identified as "modern," bought Fords on installment, and slept in on Sundays, rising only in time to attend a movie. In promoting female social and physical mobility, bataclanismo was not simply a mirror to changing gender norms in Mexico; it facilitated that change.[68]

Still, in order for women to claim that modernity, one had to act the part. The role of the quintessential modern girl was difficult to perform, as the chica moderna seemed to be an enigmatic "hybrid creature." On the one hand, her Deco body appeared androgynous; on the other, she exuded a bold, feminine sexuality. In owning her money and her body, the modern girl seemed to own modernity. Looking young and boyish, and acting as a deviant girl, the chica moderna certainly did not appear innocent. Her behavior was practical, even manipulative, but no longer in the dramatic style of the diva. By dressing, dancing, and smoking in a provocative manner, she embodied the new liberated woman, a transnational emblem of the ascendancy of global capital and Western modernity. Yet with images of the chica moderna circulating within nationalist discourses, finds Hershfield, "the modern Mexican woman was not merely a carbon copy of her U.S., British and German sisters, a 'flapper' who spoke Spanish."[69]

Cube Bonifant, a young female columnist, appeared to be such a rebellious chica moderna. Writing short articles for mainstream national publications such as *El Universal Ilustrado* and *El Mundo* (and later producing copy for major radio stations), she created poignant pieces about modern city life from a "female" vantage point. Her vignettes of urban life of 1920s Mexico City encompassed *crónica* (in-depth reporting on mostly cultural phenomena) mainstays such as reports on entertainment, notable events, and people, all delivered with humor and wit. But her work also featured caustic criticism on the *gente decente*—the "Sonoran class" that had secured the revolution—and countered empty moralizing about what women should and should not do. Moreover, accompanying Bonifant's columns were numerous, often changing, photos of her as the consummate modern girl: short hair, stylish makeup, and pouting lips.

Cube exemplified the new post-revolutionary female subject not only in terms of her youthful, exuberant, and above all modern appearance but also in her physical and social mobility. A defiant, spirited young woman from the provinces, she was emblematic of the roughly 60 percent of women that made up the wave of rural-to-urban migration that reached the capital city during and directly after the armed phase of the revolution. Born Antonia Bonifant López in Sinaloa in 1904, she and her mother and sisters escaped the revolution in the countryside and arrived in the Federal District in 1920. Largely because her father had not joined them, Bonifant needed money to support herself as well as her family.[70] In 1921 she landed a job writing columns for *El Universal Ilustrado*. Handpicked by its publisher, Carlos Noriega Hope, at the tender age of seventeen, Bonifant would write regular columns from the position of the "modern girl." Cube was largely self-taught, and the displacement of her family informed much of her criticism and sharp pen when describing and analyzing elites in post-revolutionary Mexico.

As a cronista, Cube reflected on a changing urban landscape, especially the characteristics of people and cultures "left out of official versions of national modernity."[71] In her chronicles of the city she professed her love for soccer and bullfights, described plays and literary events, offered critiques of fashion, performances, and jazz music, reported on hanging out in cabarets, and frequently commented on the crime section of newspapers—in other words, many topics not usually discussed by female writers. While obviously celebrating the excitement of advancing modernity in the city, Bonifant—like Novo and other cronistas—equally criticized modern life. The bon vivants she encountered and overheard in fashionable public spots often felt the wrath of her sharp pen as she condemned them as a homogeneous, pseudo-intellectual lot "full of various forms of stupidity and insipidness."[72]

A perfect modern girl, Bonifant was a rebel who set out to shock her audience, stating explicitly that she preferred risqué erotica to predictable women's literature. She "anointed herself with the memorable title of 'little Marquise de Sade'" and spoke out with unpatriotic verve against the governmentally prescribed role of mother. In her columns, Bonifant was, as her biographer Viviane Mahieux notes, "aggressively confrontational" and brought a "willfully modern approach to women's journalism." In her irreverence and rebelliousness, Bonifant was not representative of most women writers in Mexico. In fact, she made many uncomfortable, especially in using her subject position as female writer to "interrupt literary ambitions" and what she perceived to be the vapid intellectual masquerading of other authors and other women who enjoyed increasing visibility in the public eye.[73]

Bonifant was so aggressive, in fact, that she was thought "to write *against* women rather than *for* them." For instance, in her column for *El Universal Ilustrado*, she condemned feminists as "ugly, nearly ancient, corny and solemn" women with wrinkly frowns who forced Bonifant, listening to their speeches, to "look at [her] nails" in discomfort. Invited to speak at a feminist conference, she denied being a feminist, because "women need to be feminine, friendly and worthy of our home, if we want to reign." Yet, despite this uncharacteristic call to a docile, domestic femininity, Bonifant condemned self-proclaimed female intellectuals as women of "long hair and short ideas" during a women's writing event and described grabbing for her cigarettes and smoking "like a man" to relieve her boredom.[74]

Bonifant cultivated her image of rebel carefully, not only in written statements but also in being—as Conor would say—an "appearing" woman. Mahieux agrees that Bonifant used her column as a stage from which to project a "recognizable public identity" at a time when female writers were primarily linked to the world of theater and performance culture. In creating a recognizable public persona and resorting to the nickname "Cube," Bonifant tapped into a "theatrical manipulation of an image." Cube's persona was amplified by visual appearances in the press, such as the gossip and "socialite" columns of others, as well in the many photographs that graced the top or side bar of her own columns.[75] Bonifant liked to be photographed—so much, in fact, that she received letters in which male readers expressed their dismay over her apparent fondness for her own image. She answered one of these letters in her column, stating that having her "photos taken is premeditated, out of treachery and advantage," as well as for "the simple reason of liking" it.

Not surprisingly, Bonifant attracted a lot of criticism. Many "serious" writers openly disapproved of her work and used traditional ideas about femininity to put her in her place. Her most aggressive critic was none other than Ernesto García Cabral, whose series of caricatures of the irreverent Cube appeared in *Excélsior* in 1923. Attacking the cronista for her "intellectual ambitions, her selfish and headstrong modernity, and her personal life," Cabral set off a number of heated prose-versus-cartoon exchanges with the dogmatic Cube, who—in her own attempt at outwitting the artist—accused him of pretense, feigned aggression, and lack of masculinity.[76]

Cube's counterattack reveals much about how gendered these public taunts were, both in terms of the initial attack and her response. Cabral's first cartoon featured Cube as one of his famous modern girls in an exchange with a man, using Schopenhauer's idea that "woman is an animal of long hair and short ideas" to address the woman, now with short hair, who says, "That is why I have cut mine." With the trope of hair as her object of gendered derision, Bonifant embarked on a series of daily columns where a hairy Cabral ("cute as a monkey") is rendered as a tempestuous artist. His hair is indicative of both his anger and danger as well as of a feminine nature that, in the end, makes him inferior to the women he taunts and terrorizes.[77] As a fictitious female friend comments after Bonifant feigns a fear of dying at the artist's deadly sharp pencil (like a Florentine dagger): "Bah. He has done something worse than you; instead of using scissors to cut one's hair, he has used them to lop off ideas, and in that, he has, like women, long hair and short ideas." In the end, in a clear attack on his masculinity, Cabral is, as her friend concludes, one of those unfortunate men who makes women "feel a little bit like men, right?" instead of a man with whom they feel like "real women."[78] To Mahieux, the critiques leveled against Bonifant were not due solely to her gender rebellion but also showed how much these writers, all producing as journalists, had in common in terms of class and how the revolution had formed their fates. Bonifant was from the provinces, young, self-taught, had fallen from middle-class wealth to lower-class poverty, and, like so many others, her artistic sense was informed by international currents, even if she had never traveled abroad.[79]

Bonifant was able to break into the male world of journalism largely because she was hired to write exclusively for a female audience. Publishers, desiring a larger market of readers and understanding the need for a new approach to articles for women, started hiring female writers. More than mere economic incentives, the 1920s and 1930s represented a time when culture industries in most of Latin America were young and still flexible and spontaneous enough to result in a "creative effervescence." Despite Cube's rebelliousness and appearance indicative of a new age, roles, and ideas, female cronistas might not have been as risqué considering that (especially when contrasted with serious literature) writing about "aesthetic, frivolous, and cosmopolitan matters" was perceived as "effeminate."[80]

Perhaps in an effort to escape this verdict, and in defiance of having being hired to write "women-only" columns, Bonifant demonstrated an "overt irreverence" toward the very columns she wrote. Yet her political position and her actual views on matters of women and gender were hard to pin down. Even if appearing as a perfect flapper herself, smoking cigarettes and wearing her hair short, she was "against the 'flapperization' of her contemporaries" and in her critiques actually affirmed the stereotype of women as passive consumers. It thus appears that while she disowned the flapper fashion, she seemed emblematic of the flapper persona. Yet, as the passage above indicates, she was also "highly critical of feminist activism" and equated flappers and feminists in that they were slaves to fashion, whether in clothing or in "intellectual mores." Yet despite these loud protestations against feminism, Bonifant claimed to be "neither a feminist, nor an anti-feminist," calling herself instead "the place (or point) between the bulls and the opera." Moreover, her overt rebelliousness and public criticism of Sonoran elites did not stop her from writing with poise and respect about her "ten minute" interview with the then first lady, Doña María Tapia de Obregón. All of these moves and positions were further complicated by the fact that Bonifant undermined, perhaps tongue-in-cheek, her own assertions. Referring to herself as "a little liar," she appeared to reject truth, saying it was "like some men: agreeable but not interesting."[81]

Bonifant's crónicas, no matter how aggressive and sharp in their criticism of Bohemian figures like Cabral and women of various ideological stripes and subject positions, never quite revealed who she was and where she stood. Despite her caustic rejection of modern femininity (while embracing other aspects), Cube exuded every bit the modern girl who both inhabited a Deco body and acted irreverently. Modern, outspoken, discordant, and simultaneously interested in brash self-representation, Bonifant was both an example and a complication of the chica moderna who occupied a Mexican Deco body.[82] Her aggression not only hid her true feelings but perhaps also led to confusion as to where she, as a modern girl, belonged in revolutionary society. While Bonifant was able to shape the preconceived notion of the female chronicler to her advantage, she could not escape the doubly "feminine and hence frivolous" nature of either her gender or the commercial genre for which she wrote.[83] In what might have been a futile attempt to "outperform" male cronistas and escape feminine "frivolity," Bonifant appropriated the "virile" and masculinist discourse that dominated the revolution in her efforts to condemn women (especially feminists as old, ugly, and unfashionable) as well as outdo male adversaries such as Cabral.

While fairly unique as a female journalist, Cube Bonifant was a female and, above all, modern answer to nineteenth-century Porfirian cronistas such as Gutierrez Nájera who illustrated the discontinuities (and continuities) between the appearing and acting of the modern girl; she showed how difficult it was to act like a chica moderna, even if one chose to look like one. Similarly, the irony of Cabral's public condemnation of Bonifant demonstrates that no matter how much he adored the look of modern girls, he did not quite accept them when they acted independently.

TRANSNATIONAL ACTING

The movement of chicas modernas and their appropriation of the Deco body with its multiple positionalities ran directly counter to revolutionary ideas of acceptable feminine roles and clashed with the mainstay of revolutionary programs for women, which allowed women a measure of power only as mothers. If the chica moderna was anything, she certainly was not a traditional, abnegating mother. In the late 1920s and early 1930s, the general perception of women's social mobility became intrinsically tied to their financial and sexual independence. In this construction of autonomy, female agency in marriage choices structured much of the public debate over what constituted femininity, especially as the revolutionary leadership passed liberal divorce laws that earned Mexico the dubious reputation of "divorce Mecca" abroad, and this undermined the plans to incorporate women into the revolutionary project as a domestic, unpaid workforce in the social reproduction of revolutionary citizenry.[84]

If the choice to forgo marriage or opt for divorce was at the center of women's independence and the road to female liberation, working-class chicas modernas appeared to be well on their way to freedom. In her weekly advice column, "Para ellas" (in *Mujeres y Deportes*), Carmina explained that working women in the city found matrimony highly problematic, largely for economic reasons. As a flaneuse on her self-proclaimed *gira periodista* (journalistic tour) through the city, Carmina interviewed women about marriage and concluded that most working-class women believed that financially stable men did not want to marry. Instead of making what Carmina called the "double sacrifice" of marrying a poor man and still having to work, these women opted to live alone. In concluding her tour, Carmina described the capital as a city of women taking to the streets in forging their own destinies.[85]

While marriage appeared less and less alluring, the city's popular press treated divorce as a hallmark of modernity. Often discussed as part of the commentary on the behavior of female entertainers, divorce was a dangerous but not altogether undesirable consequence of Mexico's entry into the modern world. Rising divorce rates were thought to be the result of "the growing waywardness of women," but in the weekly gossip mills of sensationalist entertainment magazines, both Mexican celebrities and Hollywood stars discussed divorce as a glamorous affair. In a 1934 interview in Hollywood, the Mexican actress Dolores del Río "warned" Mexican audiences, tongue-in-cheek, about conjugal problems resulting from the abundance of temptations by "enchanting, adventurous people" that modern women such as herself faced. While divorces of female celebrities such as del Rio and Lupe Vélez enticed readers and sold magazines on the premise that the overt sexuality of modern women led to divorce, the problem of divorce was largely pinned on the perception of what Judith Jack Halberstam calls "female masculinity."[86] For many, the rising popularity of Deco bodies that led women to adopt outward appearances traditionally associated with masculinity—such as dress, haircuts, and athleticism—constituted visible and insurmountable evidence of a drastic upset in gender norms and an imminent threat to the heteronormative family.

The lure and danger of female masculinity that threatened the sanctity of marriage, and by extension the Mexican family, expressed itself in "transnational acting" in the city. Young women claimed independence and mobility less by acting like men than by behaving like famous actresses who claimed masculine traits. In the early 1930s, entertainment magazines frequently featured articles on European stars such as Greta Garbo and Marlene Dietrich as masculine women who defied traditional gender roles and refused to marry. Garbo and Dietrich earned fame and fortune as new-style icons who performed as women yet took up masculine dress, deviance, and desire. In sensationalist stories such as "Marlene without Pants," the popular press both celebrated and criticized actresses like Dietrich for cross-dressing. More than any other actress of her time, Garbo was used by magazines to exemplify the mysterious, masculine woman. An anomaly, Garbo embodied a cold, admired, and distanced "dominating force" not comparable to anyone, yet she was the woman whom every other woman aspired to be. In her strength and superiority as well as through her Deco body of broad shoulders and slender hips, Garbo was deemed the quintessential woman of the future, "a symbol of women's emancipation."

These same articles were quick to point out, however, that such a woman suffered from mental disorders as part of larger sociological phenomena inherent in modernity. Psychologists explained that Garbo engaged in masculine behavior and adopted masculine dress to claim "the father's superiority" and hence was a result of persisting inequality between men and women. As a warning to female readers that masculine women such as Garbo were not empowered, they explained that women like Garbo were "victims of male protest" who ultimately would reject matrimony to their own peril.[87]

The fear of the independent, and hence masculine, woman who threatened the institution of marriage and family also haunted the advice columns of many women's magazines. *La Familia* offered "Consejas a las casadas" (Advice to married women) on how to avoid divorce through a set of lengthy directives that emphasized the need for wives' docility, ignorance, and comely appearance while warding off female sociability: "Never deny your husband when he asks you to go out with him"; "Make sure that he thinks you admire him and that he has always something to teach you"; "Wear your best and most attractive clothing for him"; "Don't talk with others about your husband or your intimate life"; and "Don't become accustomed to spending all your time with your female friends."[88]

Although the chica moderna's "disagreeable" appearance alienated traditional society, it was deemed necessary in order for women to truly emancipate themselves from the prison of the traditional family. In the pursuit of equal status before the law and functioning as the architect of her own destiny, a woman should be free to exercise, cut her hair short, claim physical and social mobility, and manage her own life. However, the boyish girl, rather than Garbo's more threatening masculine femme fatale, needed to retain her innocence in order to fulfill the final goal of her independence: to be a true compañera to her man. Modern women, warned Carmina, who confused "drinks, cigarettes, and acting like a flapper" with actual modernity, who "lamentably confused liberty with libertinage," and whose only interest appeared to be to traverse the city in search of worldly pleasures, amounted to nothing. Considering the apparent flexibility and occasional confusion as to what it meant for women to not only appear modern but also act modern, the idea of the modern girl was often stretched to entail a number of traits that some chicas modernas might not have recognized. For instance, "La muchacha moderna," a typical serial fiction piece that appeared in the women's magazine *El Hogar*, told the story of a rich girl who was about to finish her doctorate but suddenly had to deal with her mother's illness. The "muchacha moderna" finds solace in marriage to a "friend of the family" in the face a distant, uncaring father who has an affair with an American actress who is lacking in all morals. Although there appears to be little that was modern about the story, its main character, Arleta, is described as possessing "a modern soul" because she can accept her lot and her pain.[89] Stories like these and columns like Carmina's thus instructed female readers that marriage should be modernized through partnership, rather than forsaken. Moreover, one was allowed—motivated, even—to look like a chica moderna and cultivate a Deco body as long as one did not behave like a wayward flapper.

Similar to the aestheticization of female athleticism through new delineations of health, the articulation of gender through youth and the eroticized allure of androgyny did much to appease the threatening behavior of the masculine woman. Columnists like Carmina commented that because of exercise and other means to achieve Deco bodies, modern women did not look like men, but rather resembled adolescent boys. Waxing eloquent about boys who lived adventurous lives, thrived on imagination, and lost their innocence in manhood, Carmina explained that boyish enthusiasm characterized modern women who "propelled themselves toward the unknown" in search of self-expression, new experiences, and new ambitions. As men grew circumspect with age and skeptical of *grandes aventuras*, women grew bold. Norma Shearer's remark that "life begins at thirty" and Carmina's insight that feminism had prolonged women's youth did much to underscore that youth, or at least the impermanence of age, redeemed the modern and even masculine woman.[90]

CONCLUSION

Bataclanismo—the vast number of copycat theater productions, art, advertisements, and media coverage in the wake of *Voilá Paris: La bataclán*—not only drastically altered daily performances and perceptions of gender and race but also changed the way the city was imagined. As it intersected with the rise of mass media and advertising (radio, photojournalism, fashion, and mass marketing of beauty products), its grasp on society relied heavily on visual means. Deco bodies and the city were often intertwined in this barrage of visual materials that propagated a new beauty ideal for women, illustrating that metropolitan modernity was mutually constitutive with the physical and behavioral aspects of a new femininity. If, as Peter Stallybrass and Allon

White have suggested, identity formation is a process that centers on associations between place, class, and body, the bataclán provided the vocabulary to articulate entirely new female subjectivities.[91]

Through new cultural forms in the 1920s, the rise of the mass media in particular, Mexico became increasingly connected with the rest of the world. Despite the nationalist and masculine nature of the institutional revolution, modern ideas of how men and particularly women could behave pervaded revista theater, films, the lyrics of songs heard on the radio, and advertising in magazines. In the 1920s and early 1930s, these culture industries were for the most part in their infancy. Nonetheless, many urban women admired or made attempts to transform themselves into chicas modernas—they cut their braids, danced to new music, and seemed to defy the stereotypical abnegating wife and mother championed by state programs for women. Through visual media, Mexican women, like their counterparts elsewhere, learned to dress, use makeup, slim down, and even consider plastic surgery as they gazed at female entertainment stars. Hershfield posits that through a Mexicanization of the transnational flapper, the chica moderna was able to modernize a number of female roles available to Mexican women in the 1920s and 1930s: the working, exotic, and even domestic woman.[92] Yet, I would argue that it was through the transnational vehicle of the Deco body that these various types of femininity were able to coexist and map onto each other and the city.

The desirability of the Deco body—white, thin, and tall—might have appeared to run counter to the aesthetics inherent in indigenismo, which revolutionary leaders embraced as the answer to forge a national culture that would be uniquely Mexican. Yet the Deco body of the modern metropolis reminded indígena and mestiza alike that being Mexican and modern was no longer so much about color as it was about form. Thus, unlike places such as Australia, where—as Conor tells us—women of different ages, weights, looks, and races who wanted to appear modern found it increasingly more difficult to "make spectacles of themselves" and quickly reached the limits of their "new-found visibility" due to the homogeneity of the Deco body ideal,[93] women of color in Mexico were told to aspire to a "mestizo modernity" that privileged form over color, making the spectacular woman available to mestizo girls, "truly" Mexican women.

Through the use of Deco bodies, indigenous and mestizo women could perform modernity as much as white women could perform indigenismo.[94] Hence, indigenismo of the 1920s was not as incompatible with modernity as the revolutionaries made it out to be. Unlike the denunciation of nineteenth-century ideals of femininity, in part symbolized by the white-powdered, hourglass-shaped divas and the frills of French Art Nouveau of the feminized Porfirian elite, the Deco body did not entail a rejection of color. Shaping Deco bodies was not a matter of whitening in the strictest sense, but about engineering form. *La raza*, used so often in revolutionary discourse as a stand-in for all inhabitants of the Mexican nation but referring largely to indigenous people, was invited to grow tall and slender, without the excess of historic circumstance weighing them down. *Indias*, too, were beautiful once they had lost their roundness and learned to wear heels, long and languid as the indígenas celebrated in muralism or the mestizaje of the *india bonita*. The Deco body thus facilitated the integration of indigenismo and mestizaje discourses.

In doing so, the Deco body helped to define as well as to erase differences of its "exotic others" of modernism's twin discourse: primitivism. Cheng, in reflecting upon the enormous success and popularity of Josephine Baker in Europe as an icon of both primitivism and modernism, underscores the importance of the infatuation with the surface of new forms, the desire for what she calls "a second skin" in the articulation of race. "For a brief period in the early twentieth century," she suggests, "there was this tensile and delicate moment when these flirtations with the surface led to profound engagements with and reimaginings of the relationship between interiority and exteriority, between essence and covering." Hence, theater, the art of performance and "the circularity of the specular exchange that in fact informs those performances," especially in their reproducibility through new industrial and technological inventions, played a defining role not only in changing ideas about gender norms but also in the actual embodiment of modernity.[95]

Yet while Deco bodies became more acceptable, the corresponding behavior of the modern girl was more problematic. The chica moderna proved an unstable signifier at the crossroads of revolutionary reform and national development. On the one hand, in modeling herself after flappers from the United States and Europe, her metropolitan identity fit well with revolutionary dictums of economic modernization through industrialization, urbanization, and the fomentation of tourism. Ascendant middle-class leaders from the outward-looking state of Sonora pitched the revolution as a young, modern, and innovative movement, bent on fashioning real social equality. Its cultural programs attracted artists and bohemians with radical sentiments and lent the revolution a progressive, irreverent allure.[96] On the other hand, however, the chica moderna seemed at odds with revolutionary nationalism, especially—as we will see in the following chapter—in comparison with the *camposcape* of indigenous women who took center stage in many government-commissioned murals, often depicted as humble indígena and campesina, as enduring symbols of the nation that communicated the authenticity of the revolution.

3

Camposcape

NATURALIZING NUDITY

In the spring of 1925, Santa Anita's Festival of Flowers seemed to follow its tranquil trend of previous years. The large displays of flowers, the selection of *indias bonitas*,[1] and the boat rides on the Viga Canal all communicated what residents of neighboring Mexico City had come to expect of the small pueblo in the Federal District since the Porfiriato: the respite of a peaceful pastoral, the link to a colorful past, and the promise that mexicanidad was alive and well in the campo.[2] Unfortunately, wrote Manuel Rámirez Cárdenas of *El Globo* the next day, this idyllic tradition was rudely interrupted by a group of audacious, scantily clad women. The culprits, actresses of Mexico City's Teatro Lírico, walked through Santa Anita's streets in "picaresque clothing" (stage outfits that left little to the imagination, particularly in broad daylight), upsetting visitors and campesinos alike. According to Cárdenas, *mamas* and *abuelitas* were shocked by the display, averting their eyes from the female spectacle in fear of "el pecado mortal."[3] Thankfully for the mothers and grandmothers in the audience, the festival continued in predictable fashion after the initial uproar. Organizers continued with the traditional dances, and judges selected an india bonita from a pool of "decent" young mestizas to represent the pueblo and the festival.

Unbeknownst to the residents of rural Santa Anita, the daring actresses of El Lírico were part of bataclanismo, the new craze that had swept through Mexico City like wildfire, turning the entertainment world upside down and pushing many to reconsider what constituted female beauty, decency, and modernity. If Deco bodies informed metropolitan identities and tied particular understandings of embodiment to the city, they—as well as the modern city—did not represent what was thought to be authentically Mexican. Instead, the campo, an undifferentiated reference to Mexico's many-faceted countryside, symbolized national essence. In particular, artistic and popular understandings of this space, what I refer to as *camposcape*, romanticized this idealized countryside as a site of national authenticity, origin, and beauty.

Originating in the nineteenth century, camposcape was a visual vocabulary of an anachronistic, and often feminized and racialized, countryside tied to ideas of national "authenticity." Depictions of rural Mexico became more consciously indigenous after the revolution, when the nationalist qualities of camposcape accrued multiple meanings, many of them wedded to indigenismo as both aesthetic and scientific project. The visual arts in particular were instrumental in furthering an exoticism that could be used to measure metropolitan identities against (largely imagined) rural ones. As a distinctive Mexican form of internal orientalism predicated on European examples, camposcape equated the exotic with the feminine and articulated the desirability of healthy and often nude indigenous female bodies with nostalgic longings for a lost, Mexican Eden: its roots and true nature. Within discourses of female nudity, sexuality, and ideas about their proper places, camposcape functioned as a frame that established acceptable forms of visual nudity.

High art depicted indigenous spaces as camposcape, colorful, exotic places replete with tehuanas that provided Mexicans with an enduring link to the countryside. However, open-air markets in the city often represented places of filth, degradation, and vice. Not surprisingly, the construction of the tehuana as a national symbol left little room for the living and breathing indigenous women from ethnically diverse groups struggling to survive in the capital city. Unlike Diego Rivera's romanticized murals of pre-Columbian markets, photojournalists rendered contemporary indigenous open-air markets in the city in problematic terms. Due to the constraints of the medium, photography deprived markets of color, offering instead grays and blacks that added to the fashionable black-and-white contrast of Art Deco modernity but tended to represent indigenous people as undifferentiated and drab. The lack of color, moreover, stripped photos of unnecessary embellishment, lent them an aura of fact, and also homogenized subjects. Yet the lure of camposcape, even if difficult to reconcile with the bleak realities of market women in the city, informed much of the city's news photography in the 1920s. However, it would be the Deco bodies of the stage that best performed camposcape in the city.

The presence of camposcape in the city was performed not by indígenas per se but by modern women inhabiting Deco bodies. Impoverished campesinos—even the romantic qualities ascribed to them that contrasted sharply with their ethnic and class counterparts in the city— lent Mexican modernity an incomplete and chaotic feel. Downtrodden pelados, later immortalized by the comedian Cantinflas, who emerged from the carpas and rose to national fame, signaled that revolutionary reform would have to contend with lower-class cultural resistance, especially in the cities.[4] Thus, while the revolutionaries promoted a national identity based on an indigenous countryside, tensions with a desired modernity abounded in the 1920s and 1930s, which coincided with, and was captured by, the rise of mass media such as radio, film, advertising, and comic books. Ultimately performed by women regardless of race and class, camposcape invaded visual representations from high art to popular culture, commercial representations to murals commissioned by the revolutionary government, news photography to news reports. With its emphasis on mexicanidad, authenticity, and indigenismo, camposcape taught Mexicans that artistic nudity, bodily integrity, and health belonged to the countryside.

NOSTALGIC TEMPORALITIES

Even if camposcape was not endowed with particular indigenous characteristics until the cultural phase of the Mexican Revolution, its emergence dates to early colonialist visual and textual narratives. Discourses of discovery linked the exploration of the virgin territory of the New World with sexual conquest and depicted expeditions for economic and political gain as an archetypal journey to a new land both anachronistic and female. Early European images of the "New

World" depicted male conquistadores and explorers taking possession of an America symbolized by indigenous women.[5] Some of the
earliest scientific or pseudo-scientific voyagers of the eighteenth and
nineteenth centuries, such as Alexander von Humboldt, ostensibly
the first non-Spaniard whom the Crown allowed to travel the colonies and conduct scientific research, and the Italian artist Claudio
Linati, who visited and documented newly independent Mexico in
the late 1820s, along with adventurers such as John Lloyd Stephens
and proto-ethnographers and archaeologists like Frederick Star and
Désiré Charnay, all echoed earlier colonial constructions of indigene-
ity. Star and Charnay, who traveled in southern Mexico during the
late nineteenth century, studied and classified Mexico's indigenous
people, often by situating them in romantic depictions of Mexico's
untamed wilderness as well as the ruins of archaeological sites and
other such "discoveries."

During the nineteenth century, and in part influenced by the work
of these outsiders, camposcape developed into a distinctive form of
self-definition for the Mexican elite that looked to Europe for inspiration. While Mexico in this sense had a long-standing tradition
of using female figures to symbolize the nation, equating women
with nature,[6] late-nineteenth-century Art Nouveau marked an un-
precedented period of artists depicting females and the feminine as
symbolic of a dreamy, highly irrational, and erotic nature.[7] With its
pomp and circumstance, upper-class Porfirian society reveled in an
aesthetic that was considered largely feminine. Porfirian cityscapes
hoped to invoke, if not mimic, the florid and decadent aesthetic of
fin de siècle Art Nouveau of French modernity, which elaborated the
exotic, the ethereal, and the natural—the very qualities believed to
invoke femininity.

An infatuation with exotic locales far from urban centers was another convention of Art Nouveau, especially in the longing for unspoiled
nature and unspoiled gender identities. In its search for purity, novelty,
and adventure, Art Nouveau and other modernist art championed
sensual femininity as a vehicle to a better life. As a prime example,
Paul Gauguin's paintings of Tahiti were steeped in the promise of

escaping from a bourgeois life to a tropical paradise that fulfilled the painter's search for plenitude, pleasure, and female bodies. As a flight from modern, urban Paris and its darker realities brought about by capitalism and industrialization, the art of Gauguin showcased the artist as Promethean hero and constructed a fantasy of female geography.[8] While symbolizing an ever-outward voyage to the periphery and margins, the "primitivism" of the Tahiti paintings constructed male power predicated on racial and sexual fantasies.

Similar to Gauguin's native women of Tahiti, indigenous women took center stage for artists, travelers, and urban elites fascinated with a primitive, exotic, and "authentic" Mexico. If the prostitute was the archetype of female danger in the Porfirian city (as her presence lent the city a distinct flavor of European modernity), the tehuana was the exotic figure that most haunted the Porfirian imagination of the campo. In many travel accounts and visual texts from the nineteenth century through the early decades of the twentieth, the tehuana emerged as an enigma, an ambiguous figure who embodied seduction, unbridled female sexuality, independence, beauty, and strength but also represented the soul of southern, indígena Mexico.

Writers and artists conflated the idealized tehuana with the land, the exotic beauty of Oaxaca's jungles. The tehuana did not merely represent a particular place, the Isthmus of Tehuantepec; she actually embodied the landscape. Starting with Linati's lithographs in the early years following independence, artistic depictions of tehuanas rendered them as camposcape, idealized landscapes outside of time where indigenous women represented a romanticization of nature, tradition, and rural life. Linati made Mexican culture visible for European audiences as a series of stock types, so-called *tipos mexicanos*, folkloric images of lower-class occupations. Linati's collection resembled contemporary botanical and zoological plates and created a veritable taxonomy of social and cultural classifications.[9] Moreover, his depictions of "Mexican customs and costumes" indexed people by occupation but also featured regional tipos such as the tehuana.[10] Placed in easily recognizable rural areas, the tehuana's traditional dress identified her as symbol of a regional Mexico on the brink of nationhood. Depicted as bound by tradition and yet freed from the sexual restriction of the gente decente, the tehuana's traditional garb signaled convention while forming a clear tension with the overt sexuality of her barely covered breasts (fig. 8).

The tehuana increasingly became a stand-in for the region she symbolized. Travel accounts, photographs, and paintings remind one of popular fairy tales of the time in which men, captured by the mesmerizing beauty and ethereal allure of magical tehuanas, lead dreamy lives in a fantasyland outside of time.[11] In 1909, travel writer Robert Terry underscored the transnational nature of the tehuana as largely an imperialist, orientalist construct. If the Isthmus of Tehuantepec was indeed a place of wonder, he reasoned, this was solely due to its "oriental" nature, which he portrayed as undeniably feminine:

> The traveler is surprised into admiration of the superb symmetry and oftentimes striking beauty of the women, who form the bulk of the population. The racial and facial characteristics of the women are more noticeable. . . . They bear a stronger resemblance to Burmese than Mexicans, and their custom and dress bear out the comparison. . . . [T]he skirt is a replica of the Malay or Burmese sarong, silk kerchiefs wound coquettishly around the head, turbanwise, complete a very piquant costume. They are true Orientals in their fondness for brilliant colors.[12]

Terry thus privileged race as an expression of female essence and subsequently mapped a transnational discourse of the sensual Orient onto indigenous Mexico.

The French novelist Charles Brasseur also placed tehuanas in mythic time, remaking them into oriental goddesses and queens by likening women he met from the isthmus to historical and mythic figures like Cleopatra and Isis.[13] Foreign writers in search of "piquant costumes" were not alone in constructing the tehuana as orientalized indígena. Not only were tehuanas equated with the Orient in the sense that they symbolized the colonialized other, but in order to be desirable they were more than merely Mexican. Due to the transnational qualities of

Pl. II.

XIX. Siècle

COSTUMES MEXICAINS.
Jeune femme de Tehuantepec
Capuche de gaze brodée. Jupon collant, de cotonnade bleue.

Lith. Régnier.

FIG. 8. Claudio Linati, *Jeune femme de Tehuantepec*, from *Costumes et mœurs de Mexique par Linati: Une collection de trente trois planches* (London: Engelmann, Graf Coindet, & Cie, 1830). Courtesy of Madrid Museo de America.

orientalism, the tehuana connected urban Mexico with cosmopolitan currents in the arts and culture of Europe and the United States. Not surprisingly, the orientalized tehuana was in keeping with conventions of Art Nouveau and European fin de siècle culture like the femmes fatales Medusa and Salomé.[14]

As historian Francie Chassen-Lopez shows, much of what rendered the tehuana as "typically Mexican" came into being in the 1890s and early 1900s, a time when the isthmus saw great economic development, primarily through early efforts at oil production for foreign markets. Self-styled businesswoman Juana Catalina Romero, popularly known as Juana Cata, crafted much of the tehuana's image. She was the principal force behind popularizing and commercializing the tehuana *traje* (costume) as she de-indigenized it by adding European lace, ruffles, petticoats, and velvet and redesigned it according to the dictates of Porfirian (and Victorian) fashion sensibilities. This example of "cultural mestizaje" shows how the tehuana became a perfect vehicle of modernity through what Chassen-Lopez fittingly labels "Zapotec ingenuity."[15]

However, the shadow side of this exoticism was present in discourses of indigenous people in Mexico that revealed the poverty, disease, and destruction of indigenous cultures. Samuel Ramos, describing the orientalization of indigenous people in Mexico in less romantic terms, found that due to "Egypticism," modernization in Mexico was hampered by "the weight of its culture."[16] Ethnographic photography during the Porfirian period started as positivist cataloging of exotic objects with a museum-oriented intention, but it produced what Roger Bartra poetically labels "an aesthetic of melancholy." Camposcape, however, countered and displaced this misery. Presented in the form of desirable female landscapes, camposcape increasingly came to embody an "authentic" national essence that surpassed, or bypassed, the "Indian's misery" en route to its arrival at full modernity.[17] Ramos's idea of "cultural weight," a factor that was seen as detrimental to modernization, was exactly the type of exotic primitivism that lent Mexico an aura of authenticity in the modernizing world. This camposcape not only informed the imagination of urban elites as to what the campo should look like but also influenced their perception of raced and gendered spaces in the city itself. The Porfirian city's segregation of urban spaces based on class and race bore distinct gendered characteristics. If the elite urge to segregate cityscapes proved difficult to realize in concrete terms, the apparently clear ideological distinction between town and country—with its enduring traditions, timeless nature, and clear-cut gender difference—promised a stable binary in confusing times.

As landscape, camposcape provided urban audiences with "an intensely visual idea," a scene or frame with which to imagine an anachronistic space from which they, as viewers, were safely absent. Geographer Tim Creswell finds that, although we live in places, "we do not live in landscapes—we look at them."[18] I would add that landscapes also allow viewers to romanticize racial and gendered others in it by assigning them segregated spaces outside of their daily realms. Camposcape represented a tableau vivant of timeless indigenous women where nudity was innocent, pure, and artistic and where, subsequently, matters of race were elided by aesthetics of gender. When reporters, as we will see, referred to sunburned skin as "a type of fabric covering the body," they inferred that non-white bodies were not really naked and that skin color could be assigned a temporary position.[19]

As a frame in which to contain and place women's naked bodies in the name of aesthetics and health, camposcape represented a means to neutralize or disavow the political ramifications of the desire of elite Mexicans for nude indigenous or mestiza women and a place where pressing social problems of indigenous people receded into a pacified, aestheticized female landscape. The modern city dweller could escape to either the isthmus for a dose of authenticity or—more likely—to the camposcape constructed through art, theater, popular culture, and the media.

IMAGING CAMPOSCAPE IN THE CITY

If the nineteenth-century fascination with tehuanas had created a discourse through which exotic indígenas embodied rural landscapes, the tehuana tipo crystallized into a gendered national identity in the turbulent decades following the armed phase of the revolution. As many cultural historians have shown, the cultural project of the revolutionary leadership involved molding the "hearts and minds" of the citizenry through education, popular culture, and new mass media such as radio and film.[20] By the 1920s the tehuana presented culture brokers with an unstable but attractive signifier in a long chain of mimetic capital from high art (paintings, murals, and photos) to popular culture (film, radio, advertisements, and theater) that transformed the tehuana from a particular regional tipo to a general national symbol.

The cultural phase of the revolution produced a renaissance in the arts, and most of this artistic production looked to revolutionary indigenismo that valorized Mexico's indigenous past and elevated indigenous cultures as national patrimony. In the didactic art of Mexican muralism in particular, archetypal indígenas represented Mexico's enduring links to its past as well as its outlying rural regions. Even if Mexican art was in step with the dictates of the cultural revolution as highly nationalist, it also adhered to the tenets of modernism. In many ways, indigenismo could be classified as a modernist movement, especially as it shared the preoccupation with primitivism, exotic others, and essentialist notions tying femininity and indigenous peoples to ideas about human origins. Much of the art representing women of the Isthmus of Tehuantepec contrasted a mysterious, native, timeless, and sensual femininity with the construction of the artist—objective, scientific, contemporary, civilized, and male—as the outsider traveling from the city back in time to observe nature. Tehuantepec was a place of unbridled fantasy and desire symbolized by exotic women constructed to serve a nationalist role in the work of painters such as Rivera, who, like Gauguin's paintings of Tahiti, communicated a desire to escape bourgeois life. As the primary *grande* of Mexican muralism, Rivera used the indígena as a visual trope of revolutionary nationalism. Rivera, who had lived in Europe during the armed phase of the revolution, frequently portrayed indigenous areas in the tropics as a return to paradise of plenitude, pleasure, and female bodies much like Gauguin's Tahiti half a century earlier: exotic locales filled with innocent native women free from bourgeois social and sexual constraint.

In the bohemian circles of Mexico City, indigenous southern states such as Oaxaca were celebrated as places that celebrated free love, where one could imagine oneself leading an unconventional lifestyle.[21] Depicted as both a place of stasis outside of time and a space of female origins, camposcape linked exotic locales to "timeless women," places from which indigenous men were conspicuously absent.[22] Travel guides of the early 1930s echoed these artistic understandings of the tehuana as camposcape. Moreover, the tehuana-as-landcape construct had reached a point of culmination: "Whatever virtues Tehuantepec may have, it is chiefly known for its beautiful women, the Tehuanas," wrote Frances Toor in her 1936 guide. Carleton Beals solidified this notion by positing that the tehuana and the isthmus had become one and the same.[23]

Apart from ideas about her indigenous beauty, her sensuous nature echoing Oaxaca's luscious environments, and her exotic appearance, much of the tehuana's revolutionary or post-revolutionary allure resulted from discourses about her economic power. It was in the marketplace that the tehuana came into being as spectacle and cultural phenomenon. An interesting tension marked tehuana discourses in this respect, because the market functioned as a site of economic independence of women, female sociability, and exotic museum. Toor complimented the tehuanas for their modern, almost Western, work ethic, but she did not hesitate to juxtapose this with the real tourist attraction: the daily festival of the market as a premodern event.[24] The campo tehuanas were described as beautiful, healthy, and clean. Authors from Mexico and United States indicated that the real spectacle was not so much the sights, sounds, and smells of the market but the fact that women ran the show. Their descriptions of tehuanas meeting every morning and evening to sell their wares, gossip, show off their colorful dresses, and see and be seen cast the markets of Oaxaca as a particular female place of power and pleasure, where work and leisure met.[25] Markets in the campo were thus rendered in romantic terms, and although these markets were seemingly chaotic, strong and attractive women were in control. Admiration coupled with a longing for an edenic escape from the bleak realities of the homogenizing modernity in the city marked the tone of these 1930s market narratives.

By the late 1930s and early and 1940s, Rivera, then working on the murals adorning the stairwell of the Palacio Nacional, executed *Gran Tenochtitlan* (1945), a vibrant scene of the famous Tlatelolco tianguis of the Aztec capital. A fine, albeit no longer innovative, example of his signature style of indigenismo, the mural called upon the iconography of markets established since the conquest yet employed an interesting shift in perspective. Incorporating a split diorama to show the market at eye level as well as a grand aerial view of Tenochtitlán to the south that highlighted the causeway and the Templo Mayor, Rivera invoked the sense of wonder similar to that of conquistador Bernal Díaz del Castillo as he first beheld the great city:

> These great towns and *cues* and buildings rising from the water, all made of stone, seemed like an enchanted vision from the tale of Amadis. Indeed, some of our soldiers asked whether it was not all a dream. . . . Some of our soldiers that have been in many part of the world, in Constantinople, in Rome, and all over Italy, said that they have never seen a market (plaza) so well laid out, so large, so orderly, and so filled with people.[26]

Indeed, Rivera's mural (perhaps inadvertently) echoed early conquest discourses about the grandeur of Tenochtitlán, especially the scale and exotic nature of its markets.[27]

Even if informed by early conquistador narratives, Rivera's market scene was a modern one, showcasing a pre-Columbian cornucopia of goods and people from the far reaches of the Aztec empire. Within this feast of color and form in which the sounds and smells of the market reverberate, a beautiful woman takes center stage. Unlike the other women in the market, who are tending to their wares, this woman commands the attention from the men surrounding her. Young and alluring with long, free-flowing hair crowned by a bouquet of calla lilies, she lifts her dress to reveal the jewelry and paint as symbols that mark her body as a "public woman." The sexual tension she provokes hints at her identity as a prostitute, yet above all, Rivera's use of contemporary symbols signal that this woman, painted in the likeness of his wife, Frida Kahlo, is strong, never fully available, and free. The men to the left might debate whether to procure her services, but she has diverted her gaze away to the distance. By the 1930s, Rivera, as the official artist of the revolutionary regime, envisioned the ideal market as an homage to indigenismo. Here the glory of indigenous women resided in an idealized past and a mythical space, rooted in conquest narratives. The urban discourses that had created the myth of the tehuana now invoked her for an artistic voyage to the glory of Mexico's pre-Cortesian past.

Through the camposcape that she represented, the tehuana was consolidated into a clearly recognizable tipo, especially when placed in the setting of the city.[28] The tipos, and especially their visual and theatrical evocations, had belied Porifirian efforts to come to terms with the alienation produced by rapid urbanization. Nostalgia for an imagined past and a longing for the clarity of premodern identities played a significant part in the desire to fix a range of subjectivities into clearly recognizable tipos. As art historian Olivier Debroise has shown, tipo imagery helped to legitimize the political exclusion of working-class men and women without whose services the city could not function properly. Tipos served as an attempt to render lower-class rural migrants, who lacked a fixed place or clear individuality, legible to urban audiences.[29]

Camposcape emerged as a central theme in maintaining a "natural order" in the post-revolutionary metropolis. Not only was camposcape instrumental in linking gender identity to Mexicanness, but it also influenced how Porfirians perceived the configuration of urban space in terms of race and class. Mexican elites managed to transform plebeian places into entertainment and spectacle in much the same way that, as Peter Stallybrass and Allon White explain, markets in early modern Europe cast vendors as main actors in literary and artistic productions. Plays, photographs, and paintings (as Rivera's *Gran Tenochtitlan* illustrated) glorified markets and market types as edenic romance that centered on elite imaginations of the countryside.[30] The literal orientalizing of the early 1900s had morphed into a more general romance of the tehuana, whose oriental and sensual qualities no longer needed a specific geographical point of reference.

The image of the orientalized tehuana, consolidated as a tipo that pervaded ideals of the campo, had real-life consequences for rural women in search of work in the Porfirian, revolutionary, and post-revolutionary city. As representatives of the campo in the city, indigenous women dominated petty trade. Despite being romanticized and sexualized, the newly arrived rural and largely indigenous migrants baffled elites and aspiring elites when they encountered real-life campesinos in urban settings.[31] In keeping with Anne McClintock's assessment of elite slumming in East End London at the turn of the nineteenth century, James Garza finds that Porfirians similarly regarded poor, marginalized campo-like neighborhoods such as La Bolsa with both trepidation and excitement. News media sent reporters to these areas of town as if they had mounted a "safari-like expedition," hiring guides to provide access to the dismal state of affairs in which the poor lived and the strange, nearly exotic nature of their existence.[32]

Places in the city where the campo punctuated the facade of order and progress held great fascination for elite Mexicans and foreign visitors alike. Characterized by officials as centers of crime where small-time thieves dealt in stolen goods, markets and street vending areas inspired social commentators and travelers to designate them as sites of horror, mystique, and pleasure. As a columnist for *El Mundo* wrote in 1899:

> Everyone who encounters the market of Baratillo for the first time staggers before being able to penetrate such an ant hill bristling with nauseating huts made of blackened wood. And if one enters, he can be sure that he will come upon surprise after surprise, both in its entirety and in its details, and it will appear a dream that all of this population of rottenness and ugliness exists in the core of our city.[33]

If markets such Baratillo and El Volador were dens of thieves, they were also areas that promised strange delights. The market, written as a site of filth and crime, equally remained a place of wonder, a place, our *El Mundo* columnist promised, "between kaleidoscope and the macabre."[34] Moving through it, however nauseating, produced a dreamlike state of surprise, color, and morbid excitement. One of the first travel guides on Mexico published for U.S. readers, *Terry's Mexico* (1909), extolled the same reverie when describing the city's markets. While denouncing El Volador as a hoax and "a bazaar where tawdry and microbic refuse is sold to the credulous and the indigent," Terry waxed eloquently about the adjacent flower market, with its "tropical song-birds in native-made bamboo cages . . . the fresh, fragrant flowers brought by Indians from the surrounding country."[35]

For elites, then, the Porfirian market represented a contact zone, a space both sublime and liminal, between horror and agitation, fear and pleasure. In stark contrast to Porfirian objectives to separate the classes, female vendors acted as go-betweens of the market as a contact zone. They inhabited a place of excitement where dominant and subordinate classes met and exchanged glances, news, and money for goods. Journalists advised women where to shop, how to shop, and how to avoid what they deemed useless conversation, revealing that markets were not only places to buy goods but also sites of sociability where women transcended class lines to catch up on gossip and exchange views. Markets were potentially dangerous places of female activity, where class boundaries and gender-appropriate behavior could easily be transgressed.[36]

Due to the tensions between romanticized depictions of tehuanas and newspaper accounts of market dangers, female street vendors signaled both desire and deviance, which consequently provoked Porfirian upper-class anxiety over female propriety. The street and the market were places of sexual ambiguity, as women working in retail trades were perceived as indistinguishable from prostitutes in the same areas of the city. Lower-class women who did not take precautions when entering public places proscribed for the señora decente suggested immorality to Porfirian capitalinos, who believed that poor women, in their struggle for survival, would succumb to what they deemed immoral work with greater ease. However, for many poor women, selling food, pulque, or small household items in the streets was the alternative to destitution. Furthermore, to vendors, the street was home. What the middle class considered their public space was in fact a private place for women vendors.

While these Porfirian attitudes toward poor, female vendors did not change significantly in the revolutionary and post-revolutionary periods, descriptions of urban markets took on the romantic tenets of camposcape, even if at times succumbing to representations of "picturesque poverty." In the descriptions of the oppositional extremes that informed the city in the 1930s, contemporary open-air markets took on an ancient, pre-Columbian identity. Foreign observers and city officials alike typified the markets as indigenous sites in the city, "buzzing with Indian chatter," which they readily contrasted with the modern metropolis of department stores, limousines, and airplanes. It was this contrast between the timeless indigenous past within the modern present that captured the imagination of foreign visitors and lured tourists. Travel writers from the United States such as Beals, Toor, and Anita Brenner marveled at the exiting spectacle of exotic beauty and picturesque poverty of city markets. "Beauty and poverty, color and squalor jostle. Meat and flies, soap and beggars, laces and rags cascade in indiscriminate confusion," found Beals. "Around the markets are interesting Indian types, often in regional dress; quaint old churches, with funny but beloved saints. . . . [B]y riding slowly, one can see much even from an automobile," advised Toor.[37] Their narratives were accompanied by colorful paintings, drawings, or lithographs invoking luscious fruits, pretty chinas poblanas, or stunning tehuanas, such as the calendar for the Mexican Tourism Association in 1937 (see fig. 9).

Despite its promises for radical social action, new leadership, and a bold constitution, the revolution did little to change, and perhaps even accentuated, popular perceptions of the campo in the city. While an "incomplete modernity" had certainly arrived in Mexico City, observers such as Beals maintained that its cityscape remained one of contrasts:

FIG. 9. A. K. Preta, *Indígena con flores*, Mexican Tourism Association Calendar, 1937.

rich and poor, rural and urban, modern and tradition. Like the revista plays of the Mexican stage, the capital cityscape harbored a hodgepodge of types and styles, the pelado and tehuana, Art Deco modernism and neocolonial nostalgia, flappers and indígenas, department stores and street vendors. In this sea of clashing cultural forms, markets, even city markets, appeared to link the hustling and bustling metropolis to an easier, purer, better past. Markets remained an exemplary space of rural pastoral, a picturesque camposcape, where the campo could be discursively performed in the city.

PHOTOGRAPHING URBAN CAMPOSCAPES

In her sensual and exotic otherness, the tehuana did not relocate so easily to the city. Although in Mexican high art and letters the tehuana communicated a glorified camposcape, the presence of actual indigenous women on the city streets and in city markets, especially as captured by the new medium of news photography, produced anxiety rather than pleasure. Early "street" photography illustrates how the staging of indigenous vendors in the city attempted to neutralize Porfirian preoccupations with gender and space. In *Selling Gorditas at Guadalupe*, a photograph taken by Charles Waite at the turn of the century, the serialization of the sunshades and campesinas retains the picturesque nature of the campo without upsetting the Porfirian dictum of order and progress (fig. 10). The tortilla vendors, each nearly identical to the next, sit immobilized, isolated from each other in a long row parallel to the contours of street and sidewalk, across from the Basilica of Guadalupe, home to the patron saint of Mexico, the Virgin of Guadelupe. While the women are spaced in an orderly fashion, they emerge as an anomaly in the ideal Porfirian city, as they are juxtaposed with European finesse of the lady's dress and noblesse oblige of her manners. The Porfirian "gracious woman" is the only person whom Waite shows as an individual with a distinct appearance and capable of movement.

Waite, a U.S. photographer residing in Mexico City, brought the campo to the city, translating camposcape to an urban context. He began by producing studio shots and postcards and traveled to the Isthmus of Tehuantepec to photograph tehuanas engaged in various domestic tasks, such as washing clothes in rivers, feeding animals, and selling wares in the market. His most famous portraits featured actresses posing as tehuanas in his Mexico City studio. *Selling Gorditas at Guadalupe*, however, portrays indigenous women not as market women but as street vendors placed on a cobblestone street, rather than on the immaculate sidewalk or park benches behind them, and

FIG. 10. Charles Waite, *Selling Gorditas at Guadalupe, Mex.*, gelatin silver print, ca. 1900. 996-003-0020, C. B. Waite Mexico Photograph Album, Center for Southwest Research, University Libraries, University of New Mexico.

renders them out of place. Although the indigenous women seem to be aware of being seen by the camera, the urbanite remains oblivious of the public attention. The uneasy meeting between merchandise and money, campo and city, poor and rich, and brown and white hands takes place dead center in the photograph, demonstrating what Luce Irigaray has referred to as "women's work of cultural exchange."[38]

Ultimately, camposcapes in the city brought elites and aspiring elites face-to-face with the contradictions of modernity. As sites of female spectacle, open-air markets and market-like streets functioned both as spaces of commercial exchange and as contact zones, places where the romantic camposcape informed the negotiation of gender and class identities in the modern metropolis. These contradictions of modernity required—as Waite demonstrated—the civilizing hand of a refined female aesthetic that would save the "brutalized" and masculinized (female) masses from themselves and prevent the deterioration of camposcape. In short, in order to maintain differentiations of class and race, between cityscape and camposcape, visual imagery depicting camposcape in the city relied on the performance of white or mestiza women. The enacted camposcape of Waite's photo studio, where actresses posed as tehuanas, soon would have a larger following on Mexico City's streets.

By the 1920s, popular magazines and even newspapers in the capital city increasingly published photo essays, not only on the quest for bodily perfection (as we saw in the previous chapter) but also to capture changes in the city, such as female mobility. The turn to the photo essay represented an effort to render the city and its current events legible to an ever larger, and perhaps illiterate, public. The photo essay, where the pictures themselves told most of the story (accompanied by a caption of no more than two to three sentences), helped to visualize and serialize the news and the urban landscape of the capital city.

Due to photography's centrality in reporting on developments during the armed phase of the revolution, news photography occupied an ever more present and important role in the dissemination of information in Mexico. While the layout, content, and quality of photos did not change significantly from the mid-1920s to the late 1930s, the perception of photography, especially photojournalism, as the harbinger of modernity, visibility, truth, and democracy did. It is evident from the emphasis on the camera as a separate discourse, the focus on imagery over words, and the many articles on amateur photography that photojournalism had come into its own as a valid, even desirable, way to view the world.

The press instructed capitalinos in the art of seeing based on its own photojournalism aesthetic. Even before the 1920s, the influential photographer Agustín Víctor Casasola had made a decisive contribution to how the revolution and the countryside, where the majority of battles were fought, were perceived in the capital. Originally a photographer for the Porfirian regime, Casasola gained fame as a visual chronicler of the revolution. In 1912 or 1914, depending on the sources, Casasola founded the Agencia de Información Fotográfica with the objective of collecting photographs taken by a range of photographers and selling them to the Mexican and the foreign press.[39] In many ways, the Casasola images made the revolution both visible and understandable to city audiences. In addition, to many of the urban poor got their information about revolutionary developments from the Casasola agency shop window, where crowds of curious pedestrians followed the latest news by looking at images to check up on the state of the revolution. Moreover, the Casasola photographs of the revolution constructed a particularly ideologically charged image of the campo for consumption by capitalinos, who, despite being shielded from most of the battles, had not visited other places in the country and had no way to visualize them.[40]

The Casasola agency also significantly affected how capitalinos came to see and imagine their own city. While the majority of art photographers portrayed Mexican culture in a positive light, photojournalists covered the more negative aspects of the revolution, such as conflict, poverty, corruption, and the hazards of modern life that were experienced in an urban setting closer to home.[41] Even if Casasola himself did not venture much outside of Mexico City, his vivid images of the growing metropolis as a place of social unrest where people took to the streets to demonstrate and confront the military redefined the capital as an increasingly modern urban space.[42]

Casasola's imagery of what were considered the more negative rural aspects of the revolution in the city, such as the incursions by the "campesino" armies of Emiliano Zapata and Francisco Villa, represented a counterpoint to camposcape. John Ross finds that rural revolutionaries like Zapata, reviled in the Mexico City press as Atilla the Hun, "hated the city and the city hated him." Thus, where virtual— and, more, importantly, female—indígenas in high and popular art became camposcape, male zapatistas taking the city were the "Indiada," bloodthirsty savages who at their worst would rape innocent women and at best constituted the unwashed country bumpkins in Sanborns, photographed by Casasola, who certainly did not belong in the city.[43]

Photojournalists increasingly were influenced by the modernist tendencies of Mexican art photography, which was rapidly coming into its own. Modernist practice, in Mexico as elsewhere, was marked by ambivalence toward urban space, a tension that formed a fertile basis for both "modernism's utopian formalism and its dystopian view of the human condition."[44] In modern photography, and increasingly in photojournalism as well, the urban landscape—including the people who moved in it—did not merely function as a backdrop; it became the principal actor.

The urban environment provided the opportunity to capture moments of spontaneity that made for modern, unposed, and candid photos. "Today's photography," read the text of a how-to article, "shows life in motion and in flight" when the photographed subject does not suspect the presence of the photographer. "The camera observes what the eye can't without being observed itself," states the author, who suggests that one use a friend as a foil to distract potential subjects.[45] Instructing amateur photographers on how to capture the city, reporters on the medium advised that "busy street corners are great locations," where the traffic police, fruit vendors, and a doubled-over shoeshine boy all made excellent subjects. Considering news photography's infatuation with modernist art, its aim in arresting the hustle and bustle of city life "in flight," and its search for contrasts, it is not surprising that markets were thought to make for an especially picturesque subject and a "beautiful study in photography."[46] Photojournalism offered new ways of seeing place and time and added to the "picturesque" tensions between tradition and modernity. In the well-ingrained binary of past-campo and future-city, city markets formed places where the countryside punctured modernity.

A Casasola photo from 1925 depicting a market space demonstrates such tensions. In the image, a market stall is foregrounded by an array of female regional tipos that were quickly gathering momentum as national icons.[47] Probably shot for a special assignment during a particular festival where regional tipos increasingly surfaced as visual mnemonic devices of national unity, the photo depicts an *artesanía* (handicrafts) stand where urban mestizas dressed as indígenas pose in a straight line. Two make-believe tehuanas and a china poblana, among others, model traditional pots and trays, yet all wear fashionable, modern shoes. Even though the photograph depicts a fiesta, the women look serious, and the hilarity that usually accompanies dress-up events is absent. Even if the city does not appear in the photo, the women's bodies, makeup, and shoes signal urban space. Here, the modern *urbe* resides not only in buildings and technology but also in the mestizo modernity of Deco bodies that functioned as a stand-in for the metropolis. Through the use of Deco bodies, the photographer is able to solve the contradictions between the genre of rural tipos and the urban scenery in an effort to document "authenticity" and modern cityscape. The photographer seems to indicate that the campo flourishes in the city, provided modern mestizas perform it.

Other Casasola images from this period presented viewers with similar re-creations of the countryside in the city center. Faux indígenas wearing prefabricated costumes and sporting bobbed hair, headbands, and dark lipstick often appeared in these photographs alongside tents and stalls adorned with flora and fauna of the country's southern regions. Yet these images also contained markers of the city, such as the facades of colonial and neoclassical buildings, completing the illusion of a sanitized countryside that can only enter the city's public places through performance. Staged images such as these passed as news photography and consequently sought to duplicate the indigenismo of revolutionary art production, while photos of actual market women and vendors remained conspicuously absent from newspapers. Even though aesthetic considerations probably formed the main reason for the omission of photographs, government officials also restricted the use of cameras. In 1934 the federal government, concerned with the country's international image, tightened its regulations over what foreigners and citizens could and could not photograph. The new rules stipulated that photos and film not create any detrimental impression. The U.S. consul warned that tourists should abstain from photographing "burro carts, beggars, and shacks," indicating that the once picturesque market scenes had deteriorated in representations of persistent poverty that embarrassed the revolutionary state.[48]

Although photography depicting city markets appeared to contrast sharply with post-revolutionary art steeped in indigenismo, such as muralism, it shared in the construction of a highly nationalist camposcape and further tied this to performed marketplaces. Moreover, it contributed to the notion that even if this market-camposcape could be performed across race and class, it was largely women who engaged in its performance. The trope of the female indígena—now regardless of ethnicity—presented culture industries with a movable camposcape that traveled across imagery yet signified both Mexican authenticity and modernity. From middle-class mestizas who frequented photo studios posing as indigenous women to Frida Kahlo's appropriation of the tehuana costume, from Dolores Del Rio's performance in Emilio Fernández's film *María Candelaria* to the mestizas competing in india bonita beauty contests and dancing the *zandunga* (traditional music and dance from Oaxaca) in the national Ballet Folklórico, white and mestiza women often acted out indigenismo on and off the stage.[49] Photo-illustrated searches for the most beautiful woman in Mexico in popular magazines, as we saw in the previous chapter, where female beauty was mapped onto various iconic locales of campo (mountain highlands, tropical lowlands, or colonial pueblos), equated women with landscapes much in the way that colonial representations had indexed race and place through a gendered classification.[50] Mexicanidad came to reflect a camposcape populated with female archetypes where, as Julia Tuñon notes, "the nation acquire[d] a gendered character: essential Mexico is indigenous, ergo it is feminine."[51] The lure of this camposcape was that of the idyllic national garden, a place of unbridled fantasy and desire symbolized by exotic indigenous women, which was performed not only in art, letters, and the theater but—through markets—in the city streets as well.

NATURALIZING NUDITY

The performance of camposcape in the service of the nation, and for consumption in the city, encompassed an array of art forms, popular culture, and "news" photography. Women, regardless of class and race, engaged in this performance, and in an effort to elide the tensions between the realities of life in the city for rural female migrants and their romantic, artistic counterparts, Deco bodies were thought to best animate photographic camposcape in the city. However, the androgynous and sexual allure of Deco bodies complicated this venture. Modern Deco bodies performed camposcape appropriately when dressed in the rural costumes of the tehuana and other regional tipos, but they could not embody camposcape in the city while nude. Artistic camposcape, in contrast, championed indigenous—and at times mestiza—nudity as aesthetically refined, pure, healthy, and authentically Mexican. It is not surprising that nudism, a new, budding, modern phenomenon in the 1920s and 1930s, would appropriate the discourse of artistic camposcape to legitimate its existence and allow for naked Deco bodies in the countryside.

By the 1920s, across the globe, representations of female nudity were deemed acceptable, even aesthetically refined, when tied to the world of art and contemporary practices pertaining to the cultivation of physical health. In order to maintain respectability, however, artistic and athletic nude bodies had to be contained in their proper place. For art, athleticism, and nudism, this place necessarily was located outside the ideological, if not physical, realm of the city. As many artists and revolutionary ideologues proposed that mexicanidad resided in camposcape, the naked modern, urban, androgynous-looking female Deco bodies formed a stark contrast to the idealized, traditional female nudity represented by "authentically Mexican" indigenous women embedded in camposcape.

Because much of the revolutionary didacticism of Rivera's work drew on a modernist nostalgia that equated the female nude with a tropical, indigenous, and paradisiacal campo, his nude mestizas and indígenas became central tropes within a new nationalist iconography that reinforced the stereotype of women as timeless nature. Symbolizing death and renewal of life in his mural series *Subterranean Forces, The Virgin Earth, Germination and The Flowering,* (Universidad Autónoma Chapingo, 1924–27), Rivera repeatedly equates the female nude indígena with the campo.[52] This allegorical depiction of women culminates in his 1926 mural *The Liberated Earth with the Natural Forces Controlled by Man* (fig. 11), which showcases a nude mestiza whose bodily outlines vaguely correspond to those of Mexico's territory, "ingeniously" representing the nation as a space where "Woman" and the Earth become one.[53] At the center, Lupe Marín, just having given birth to Rivera's child, reclines within the soil embodying the fertilized (and hence "liberated"?) Earth, the archetypal mother who gives birth

FIG. 11. Diego Rivera, *The Liberated Earth with the Natural Forces Controlled by Man*, Autonomous University at Chapingo, 1926. © 2014 Banco de México Diego Rivera Frida Kahlo Museums Trust, Mexico, DF / Artists Rights Society (ARS) New York.

to life itself. Marín was River's principal model at that time, and her nudity had become part of the imaginary that connected woman to the new revolutionary nation-state. She embodied what Salvador Oropesa calls "la encuerada nacional," that is, the most ubiquitous naked body in Mexico, a "representative of the new and strong Mexican woman."[54]

In contrast, a male figure bequeathing the Promethean gift of fire is climbing out of an ancient volcano, ready to hand the torch of knowledge to an indigenous man who eagerly anticipates operating the elaborate machinery that controls the forces of the Earth. While he too is naked, he is rendered active: he stands upright, muscles flexed, his muscular back defined by the bright light of the sun. Right of center, the Earth's vagina appears penetrated by a hydroelectric, silver tube, which elicits its life-giving waters. Demarcated by long braids, indigenous women are passive spectators to this scene; they remain seated amidst tropical fruit, gazing upon the scene from dark places. Men, even indigenous ones, are the rightful heirs wielding modernity's tools to dominate the female Earth and make it productive. Rivera himself explained the image as follows: "On the bottom of the wall is the fertilized soil. The wind is behind her like a maternal force, like water and fire, that produces energy: almighty electricity at the service of humankind."[55] The scene is suggestive of a new origin myth. Modernist ideas glorifying the machine, which replaces female generative power with male technology, surface in Rivera's work where the man-machine dominating female camposcape clashes with the dark powers of the woman-machine, or the metropolis.[56]

The camposcape of nude indígenas represented a difficult touchstone for the chica moderna, who could try to either perform camposcape or differentiate herself against it. In her first crónica, "Una fuga a la provincia" (Escape to the provinces), chica moderna and "enfant terrible" Cube Bonifant describes her visit to Ameca, a small pueblo in Jalisco. Though in her first report she is shocked and subsequently bored by the absence of the trappings of modernity, intellectual life, newspapers, and modern literature,[57] in the next she glorifies camposcape in all its abundance. She is impressed by the return of spring in Earth's greenery and flowers, the opening of windows to the freshness of the *madreselva* (literally, "mother jungle"), the "flowering of the peaches," and "the brilliant eyes and flushed cheeks of girls." In a passage that evokes Linati's tehuana, Cube reports that the girls' "dark skin, fresh and throbbing under clear silks and pale ribbons, [is] showing through their white transparent trajes." At this sight, Bonifant seems to feel out of place as a city girl, so she "arranges her short and curly hair" in the hope "she won't attract attention." Resorting to the uncharacteristic defense of having "cultivated modesty," the "little Marquesa de Sade" struggles at the sight of the piquant campo beauties in see-through clothing.[58]

Despite Bonifant's apparent unease at women of the campo appearing (somewhat) nude in transparent dresses in 1921, by the early 1930s the topic of nudism started to interest Mexico City's public, or at the very least, the city's mainstream press. While Mexican journalists did not clearly define nudism, their reports showed that they understood the practice to include sunbathing, conducting physical exercise, and generally taking in the "restorative effects" of nature, all while nude. Various early articles described nudism as a modern, cosmopolitan, and above all healthy middle-to-upper-class practice with origins in northern Europe and the United States. In keeping with perceived ties to new understandings about physical culture and its credibility as a scientifically sound practice that was recognized in modern countries such as Germany and the United States, Mexican press reports also treated nudism as a serious phenomenon, writing extensively about the history, location, and developments of various nudist camps in Europe. These early stories, while cautious in tone, portrayed nudism in a positive light, emphasizing its health benefits and the high moral character and physical and spiritual beauty of its practitioners. Reporters assured readers that while sunbathing in the nude might represent a "horrible thought" for many Mexicans, the requirements for joining nudist colonies were strict. The "horrible thought," a remark left unexplained by a journalist reporting on nudism in the Mexican press, clearly communicated a fear of sexual danger posed by the combination of unattached men and public exposure of nude women.[59]

Ideals of beauty that shifted the emphasis away from being naked did much to legitimize the moral value of nudism. Reporters describing the strange quality of sunburned skin as "a type of fabric covering the body" appeared to reduce the importance of skin color by assigning it a temporary position, suggesting it was environmentally contingent, and communicated that nude—and, by inference, colored—bodies were not really naked. Nudism elevated the beauty and harmony of the human form when positioned in nature against "the yellow of the sand, the blue of the water, and the green of the pines." Moreover, this beauty, even if physical, conformed to the aesthetics of classical art, and nude bodies became, in effect, statues devoid of sensuality: "I can attest that a prolonged gaze at the nude human body eliminates any sensual response," a reporter confessed.[60] Journalists proposed that, stripped from eroticism, nudity was the vehicle to perfect physical and mental health and the only way to combat the onslaught of prohibitions, complexes, and clothes that were understood to deform the body.[61] Instead of an unhealthy, sinful, and pornographic desire for naked bodies, man was to "regard his nudity with the same indifference as do the animals."[62]

According to popular portrayals, this pure, harmonious state of nudity could only be achieved in the countryside. By the mid-1930s, reports in major Mexican newspapers invoked discourses of a pastoral utopia reminiscent of the Garden of Eden when describing nudist colonies in Mexico. Being nude, in "Adam's suit," certainly echoed the innocence of an earthly paradise.[63] The success of the nudist camp, tellingly referred to as campo in Spanish (the same word for "countryside"), depended upon its distance from the pollutants of modern life in the city. Echoing transnational discourses on the cultivation of health that prescribed an "abundance of fresh air, and clear sunshine" for "bringing perfection of the human form and loveliness to the face,"[64] reporters in Mexico told readers that nudists adhered to a strict vegetarian diet and, by bathing not only in the sun but also in the "open air," fortified their bodies and their souls.[65] Nudists told the press that the movement represented an absolute return to nature in order to free the body of the ailments that plagued modern society.

As a result, a disciplining of the body through sports—as was practiced on a large scale in the city—was not necessary; all one needed was the curative workings of nature and "unlimited space to move in, free from society with its sophistication and decadence, its dark houses, tight clothes, and pessimistic and cowardly people, who fear their bodies."[66] Instead, nudist quarters contained stylish facilities allowing one to sleep in the open air.[67] Mostly because nudism was restricted to the campo, social commentators cautiously supported the movement in Mexico. Reassuring readers that nudists did not advocate going to the theater and the cinema or traveling on streetcars in the nude, Salvador Novo found the impetus to sunbathe and be closer to nature an understandable and even noble pursuit and viewed nudism's focus on "physical culture" as unquestionably ethical. Mexico, with its sun and its high moral standards, reasoned the cronista, was a perfect country for the practice of nudism as a "festival for body and mind."[68]

From these exposés, the spread of nudist practices in Mexico—as part of an advancing modernity—seemed inevitable.[69] By 1938, Mexican nudists, under the leadership of José Paramo, the "patriarch of Mexican nudism," organized large conferences to advance their cause, which had grown from a search for health to also touting a sense of national pride. Prominent Mexican nudists such as Paramo argued that even if the movement had originated abroad, nudism was a practice in keeping with nationalist values and revolutionary indigenismo. Stating that the *indios* of Mexico were "natural nudists," they echoed the nationalist tenets of mexicanidad, which equated indígenas with "the most perfect moral and physical entity of our population."[70] After all, these nudists concluded, in contrast to "the patron and the worker who go about covered from head to toe, the indígena works naked, or almost naked."[71] Nudity contained in camposcape was rendered gender-neutral, healthy, traditional, and productive, and it could easily be reconciled with nationalist sentiments.

By the late 1930s, however, nudism had lost most of its aura of innocence in the mainstream Mexican press as it moved closer to the capital, its female citizens, and the watchful eye of the national government, which was headed by a president bent on establishing moral order through morality campaigns and censorship.[72] More-conservative Mexican newspapers emphasized and probably exaggerated the speed with which the movement had grown around the world as well as in Mexico, treating it as an alarming phenomenon.[73] While nudism might have seemed the most natural thing in the world in countries such as the United States, where "*desnudismo* was practiced out in public," stated one Don Catrino, a columnist for *Gráfico*, Mexicans could not but condemn the practice as immoral.[74] Major newspapers reported that nudist colonies had been established in the smaller pueblos of the Federal District, such as San Angel, Mixcoac, and San Rafael, facilitating the congregation of capitalinos to partake in nudist activities on the weekends. Journalists started to question the desirability of nudism so close to Mexico City, especially as women from the capital were described as eager to join the movement, which clearly undercut the relatively gender-neutral reporting that had characterized earlier stories.[75] With the active participation of women, the movement appeared to have grown dramatically, or so reported the Mexican press.

"The fair sex" increasingly was reported to liberally attend nudist congresses, indicating either a growing interest in the movement among women or the conservative press's equation of women's liberation with female nudity.[76] In San Rafael, female nudists—almost all of them single women—were said to greatly outnumber male nudists, much to the surprise of a visiting reporter.[77] Largely filtered through discourses of urban dangers, doubts remained as to whether the practice of nudism was morally sound. Accounts describing nudism as the pursuit of the rich and famous and other denizens of the urban *beau monde* raised eyebrows among Mexican conservatives, who condemned nudism not only as immoral and dangerous but also as cosmopolitan snobbery.[78] Moreover, the dark world of the Mexico City weekly *Detectives: Policía, Teatros, Deportes* and men's magazines such as *Mujeres y Deportes* asserted, as we will see in more detail in the next chapter, that the boundaries separating urban-like violent crime from nudism and nudism from libertinage were weak. Reporting on a suicide case involving three nudists in a camp close to Los Angeles, California, reporters stated that the incident had launched a police investigation into nudist colonies and concluded that they were places where "members engaged in orgies, heavy drinking, gambling and free love."[79] Articles accompanied by photos of bare-breasted women sought to debunk the contention that nudism was healthy and devoid of sexual desire. To illustrate the danger, reports increased in which women complained of unwanted sexual attention in the camps.[80]

Tellingly, when the Mexican press wondered if it was really healthy to be a nudist, their concerns were often articulated through the lens of female beauty.[81] According to its detractors, nudism was less than aesthetically pleasing, considering the fact that only a few human bodies were naturally as healthy and "beautiful as statues," while the vast majority suffered from defects.[82] Even worse, the popular press now posited that nudism caused the demise of feminine charms, as female practitioners revealed that they had aged tremendously from sunbathing nude.[83] The confusion over the health benefits of nudism, what the practice actually entailed, and, as detractors pointed out, its unstable relationship with crime, disease, and sexual desire was complicated by the use of the word *desnudez*, which reputable journalists as well as sensationalists used to reveal and unveil anything deemed debased, degenerate, or dangerous.

Yet, despite these critiques, the popular press generally portrayed nudism—especially when clearly confined to the countryside—in a favorable light and connected nudism, camposcape, and essentialized notions of indigenismo in positive ways. Whether through art or the physical culture of nudism, camposcape provided an ideological realm where female nudity was acceptable and healthy, even aesthetically refined. In camposcape, nudism represented the quest for a faultless, classical body cast as a set of perfect lines, no longer encumbered by its color. The sanitized, rather than the sexualized, Deco body might be able to represent camposcape if healthy. Yet the quest for a healthy Deco body could be conceptualized, imagined, and engineered differently depending on where it was to be in place. In the artistic and athletic realm of camposcape, modern bodies could move freely, unhampered by the clothes and restrictions of urban society, and even bathe nude in the sun, activities deemed inappropriate for urban consumption.

CONCLUSION

On April 3, 1936, the DDF's Civic Action Committee organized a public celebration in the pueblo of Santa Anita around the beauty pageant "La Flor Más Bella de Ejido."[84] Representatives of all delegations of the Federal District competed for the honor to represent camposcape, which now entailed a national essence articulated through the accomplishments of the revolution. The selection of the "most beautiful ejidal flower" was accompanied by public talks and lectures on the female emancipation that the revolution had brought.[85] It had been more than a decade since the urban Deco bodies of the *Rataplan* had invaded the pastoral idyll of the village, with near-nude actresses from the city upstaging the pretty "Indian" girls during the pueblo's traditional Easter celebration. Contrary to what the villagers might have thought, the outrageous Rataplanistas did not invade the pueblo in an attempt to shock provincial mores and force campesinos to confront metropolitan modernity. In fact, the National Authors Association had awarded the show with that year's first prize in stage writing, and the ensemble had been invited to accept the award during the Santa Anita festivities. That the cast decided to show up in full (or rather less) regalia remained somewhat surprising, but journalist Manuel Rámirez Cárdenas's sensationalistic, hurried tone and reliance on bataclanismo's stock characters (pretty, modern girls versus jealous, indignant older women) indicated that the scandal owed more to the efforts of our cronista than to the presence of sexy actresses. What appeared more disturbing to the journalist was that the near-nude Deco bodies, out of place in camposcape, had ruptured the rhetoric of idealized and nationalized "indígena" beauty. Bataclanismo certainly had caused a stir, but the fact that the focal point of the production—the semi-nude Deco body of the chorus girl—was readily accepted in the world of Mexican entertainment as an emblem of modernity was in and of itself shocking. The Deco bodies of Lírico's actresses were not dressed, or even undressed, to be in camposcape.

After the armed phase of the revolution, the popularity of the tehuana tipo as timeless, edenic, and above all authentically Mexican, easily gave way to a more overt nationalist interpretation in which the tehuana transcended her regional identity and no longer needed a particular point of reference on a map. As a now pure icon of revolutionary and indigenista Mexico, she not only trumped other folkloric female figures (such as the china poblana) but also tied modern understandings of beauty, health, and sensual nudity to the idealized countryside. Through camposcape, the countryside represented a safe space that could accommodate indigenous nudity as nationalist art as well as nudism as a middle-class search for health.

If female bodies signaled that health constituted beauty, and beauty health, they could only function as proper markers of nation and modernity when confined to their proper place. Within the discussions of the possible dangers of nudism, journalists not only invoked the loss of female beauty as one of its primary concerns but also used female bodies as spatial vectors on which to plot the desirability of nudity on an idyllic pastoral camposcape. Moreover, the desirability of the Deco body—which appeared primarily as white, thin, and tall—complicated the aesthetics inherent in indigenismo, which revolutionary leaders embraced as the answer to forging a uniquely Mexican national culture.

The discourse of the tehuana took an interesting turn after the 1930s, when writers began to construe the economic independence of the rural tehuana as antisocial and arrogant behavior aimed a disrupting the proper gender order. In the 1946 update of her travel guide, Frances Toor's opinion of the tehuanas had changed considerably. They no longer embodied an exotic and benign cultural trait; and even if Toor still found the region and its women beautiful, she now judged them as proud and conceited women who monopolized markets and dominated their men.[86] Despite their beauty, their confidence was out of place. Toor replaced the tehuana photos, with captions describing them as "graceful goddesses," in the 1936 guide with pictures of other exotic, but humbler, women, such as the unassuming "Zoque girl." Alternately, other artists and intellectuals attempted to rehabilitate the tehuana's market activities as nurturing and family oriented. Sergei Eisenstein, in Mexico filming *Que viva México*, described the markets of Tehuantepec as an investment in marriage and family. Novelist Augustín Yáñez waxed eloquently about the tenderness of a young tehuana vendor who sold fruit out of a maternal duty to alleviate the hunger of her people.[87]

Whether depicted in a positive or negative light, the rural market emerged from travel narratives and artistic discourses as central to a female indígena identity, a camposcape where economic, social, and physical freedom coincided. The market was the cornerstone of tehuana power, a place of sociability, money, and wares. Like the "contact zones" described by Mary Louise Pratt where incongruent cultures struggle with each other, the market allowed for the meeting of inhabitants of different worlds and subsequent self-differentiation of the tehuana vis-à-vis her visitors and vice versa.[88] The market was the quintessential site where the tehuana performed her identity, a show of senses, sounds, smells, and colors that mirrored the spectacle of her alluring femininity. While properly in place, the tehuana's performance—albeit nontraditional in terms of gender hierarchy—was considered desirable, somehow proper and pure. The Isthmus of Tehuantepec was the place in the popular imagination with a timeless past, magic, and wonder, which inscribed the female indígena with status. Moreover, the tehuana's sensuality and at times overt sexuality was a large part of the attraction to this Arcadian countryside. Her nudity, or near-nudity, was pure, Mexican, and artistic when in place in the jungles, mountains, and rivers or lakes of camposcape.

Camposcapes in the city were not without concerns, as they brought elites and aspiring elites face-to-face with the contradictions of modernity. As sites of female spectacle, open-air markets and market-like streets functioned both as spaces of commercial exchange and as contact zones where romanticized camposcape informed the negotiation of gender and class identities in the modern metropolis. Yet camposcape further proliferated female spectacle in Mexico City, rather than curtail it. Modernity and tradition, which Anne Rubenstein views as coexistent discourses used by different groups for different purposes, coalesced primarily around the representation of women. Thus, she argues, "the discourse of tradition did not require a return to the imagined past," but instead offered a moral counterweight to modernity.[89] Similarly, indigenismo, glorifying Mexico's indigenous past and displacing indigenous people from the present, helped to articulate a mestizo modernity. Here, indigenous "traditions" served to place Mexico as unique among modern nations as well as a living museum that formed an identity which, in order to achieve modernity, should be overcome. In this sense, the camposcape of indígenas represented a nostalgia against which the chica moderna could differentiate herself.

Promis-ciudad

PROJECTING PORNOGRAPHY
AND MAPPING MODERNITY

In 1934, *Vea: Semanario Moderno* (Look: The modern weekly) started its tenure as one of Mexico City's most risqué adult magazines.[1] In stories such as such as "La cita" (The date), little was left to the imagination:

> I would kiss her mouth; and then, traveling to her throat, her firm, throbbing breasts; then our mouths would rejoin, gasping, wet, eager; our feverish kisses multiplying; our hands would run luxuriously over each other's fleshy contours, and finally, vanquished by our voluptuousness, we would surrender ourselves to each other in unparalleled ecstasy. . . . However, when I felt her drop to her knees by my side, offering me her honeyed lips, I could do no more than take her, howling like a beast.[2]

In addition to these sexually explicit narratives, each edition of *Vea* also contained a variety of photographs of scantily clad and nude girls. These female bodies took up many pages in the magazine and were suggestively inserted into cityscape, usually transposed onto important architectural markers of Mexico City. Photos of young women in sexy undergarments or fully disrobed were superimposed on the capital's important landmarks, such as Castillo de Chapultepec and the Palacio de Bellas Artes (figs. 12 and 13). These images of white and mestiza girls on Mexico City's streets invite few, if any, contemporary comparisons. They seem out of place, especially when compared to the familiar and much celebrated contemporary imagery of camposcape such as Diego Rivera's murals glorifying indígenas. *Vea*'s depiction of urban female nudity differed strongly from the modernist visual discourses, discussed in the previous chapters, that are inherent in Mexico's cultural revolution.

Considered in the light of bataclanismo, however, the young women of *Vea* and their placement on the daytime streets of the capital city told a larger story about the visibility of female mobility, sexuality, and embodiment and their ties to changing gender roles in Mexico. *Voilá Paris: La ba-ta-clán*, with its novel use of stage design, unapologetic use of nudity, and Deco bodies, had altered the theatrical landscape of the Mexican stage as well as that of the city. Esperanza Iris and Mme Rasimi had introduced the latest ideas of a new, brazen, and highly sexual femininity to Mexico; many women in Mexico City used the bataclán and its Deco bodies to contest the revalorization of male authority that typified revolutionary reform. In doing so, they ran up against new political elites and their ideas of revolutionary womanhood, even if these elites (reformers from the outward-looking northern state of Sonora) also hoped for a more metropolitan Mexico City that could join the ranks of Paris, Berlin, or New York City.

Vea's depiction of female mobility in the capital city clashed with this revolutionary nationalism, the new state's project for women, and feminist aspirations. Like other magazines of its kind, *Vea* faced tenacious resistance from Mexico City's morally minded inhabitants. During the mid-1930s the capital saw a veritable wave of new publications that thrived due to the display of partially dressed bodies. Because *Vea* and other weeklies, such as *Forma*, *Malhora*, and *Detectives*, openly sold seduction and sexuality, they provoked serious opposition from concerned citizens.

Vea linked female sexuality and civic space—especially Mexico City's monuments invested with ideas about Mexican national identity and state power—and subverted ideas about the public sphere and urban governance. The preoccupation with female nudity and sexuality in the wake of bataclanismo led to a new perception of the city as a set of zones of containment versus areas of mobility. These places were

FIG. 12. From *Vea: Semanario Moderno*, November 2, 1934.

predicated on earlier understandings of the gendered nature of public
space that, in turn, were tied to class and ethnicity. The movement of
chicas modernas and their appropriation of the Deco body with its
multiple positionalities ran directly counter to modernist longings
for a feminized countryside.

FIG. 13. From *Vea: Semanario Moderno*, August 9, 1935.

PROJECTING PORNOGRAPHY

From the standpoint of twenty-first-century sensibilities, and perhaps even those of some of its contemporary audience, *Vea* would hardly qualify as pornographic. Featuring short articles on sports, celebrities, theater, cinema, lifestyle, and other aspects of popular culture, it was presented as an entertainment magazine. *Vea*'s editors explained in their inaugural editorial statement that what the city needed was a humorous publication that would free its readers from the "habit of reading serious newspapers." Despite *Vea*'s emphasis on frivolity, however, its humor would remain within the bounds of "discretion."[3] While this at times involved satire and caricatures of political figures, *Vea*'s humor mostly consisted of cartoons that revolved around sexy young women, generally actresses, and played on sexual double entendres. Even if serious descriptions of steamy sexual encounters like "La cita" made up much of *Vea*'s written material, its overarching aim, and indeed the reason for its existence, was playful innocence.

Considering the tension between *Vea*'s explicitly sexual narratives and its focus on frivolous entertainment, how did its readers interpret the images that often physically connected the two on the magazine's pages? Representative of transnational distribution networks showing "sexy" women, it relied on stock images largely imported from the United States that were meant to titillate through the power of suggestion rather than expose the public to shocking material. Indeed, *Vea*'s visual "pornographic" content could scarcely compete with the anonymous photos of prostitutes that had circulated during the Porfiriato.[4] Its allure often consisted more of what remained hidden and untold than what was actually revealed. Like the U.S. men's magazine *Playboy* less than a quarter century later, its editors pandered to (what they assumed to be) an all-male audience by showing an array of nude or semi-nude young women whose looks conformed to a new transnational beauty ideal and whose attitude expressed a youthful, mischievous, and above all healthy interest in heterosexual encounters. Like its 1950s counterpart in the United States, *Vea* maintained a remarkable uniformity in its choice of female bodies. But, unlike the shared project in cultivating heteronormative sexual desire through homogeneous female bodies, the magazines deviated in their choice of which female form most evoked male desire. *Playboy* excelled at creating mature, voluptuous, and buxom blonds, even if their bodies were made up of oppositional components: "On top is the face of Shirley Temple; below is the body of Jayne Mansfield."[5] *Vea*, on the other hand, focused on the 1920s transnational beauty ideal of the white, lean, and small-breasted Deco body in representing its object of desire. Unlike the Playmates, *Vea*'s girls, while young, were in their early twenties and had age-proportionate, intact bodies. Moreover, *Vea* showed little variety in the models' portrayed occupations: all were showgirls.

Given the popularity of the French grand variety spectacle *Voilá Paris* nearly a decade earlier, the infatuation with showgirls was hardly a surprise. Bataclanismo had launched a new kind of female star, the bataclana, who came to represent the more dangerous, overt sexual aspect of the flapperista in Mexico. Her Deco body, like that of superstar Josephine Baker, who embraced her androgyny "as much as she played up her ultra-femininity," became the site of contested and divergent notions of modernity.[6] Thus, *Vea*'s choice of showgirls and actresses as markers of both healthy sexual desire and modernity made good sense in both a Mexican and a transnational context. Early films in the United States and Europe celebrated the idea of "selling" actresses for the price of a ticket, through which viewers had access to onscreen female bodies, if only fleetingly. Sharon Ullman argues that "actresses became, in effect, stand-in prostitutes." These early cinematic constructions of female bodies around the trope of the prostitute helped to create "commercialized public sexuality" and represented a tool to inculcate "healthy" heterosexuality.[7] *Vea*, with its tagline of a modern magazine, similarly connected desirable female bodies to modern capitalism.

As classic bataclanas, *Vea*'s nude showgirls foreshadowed the popularity of the 1940s pinups and 1950s Playmates. While their nipples and behinds were clearly visible, their pubic hair was conspicuously absent: their pelvic area remained hidden from view through the strategic use of covering, shadow, or particular angling of the hips. In addition to photographs of showgirls clearly borrowed from U.S. publications, *Vea* introduced Mexican nudes as "artistic studies" by actual and aspiring art photographers. More than once, *Vea* showcased work by the well-known contemporary art photographer Augustín Jiménez y Ortega, who produced photos that closely resembled the images generated by *Vea*'s house photographer, "César" (fig. 14). The rendition of these nudes was safely anchored within the confines of classical aesthetic considerations of beauty and art.

Unlike the transnational versions, *Vea* both envisioned and produced female nudity in urban settings, depicting most women in fairly active positions—sitting, standing upright, or otherwise in motion (dancing, walking, strutting). The November 2, 1934, and August 9, 1935, editions show that *Vea*'s editors conceptualized the built environment of Mexico City in terms of feminized landscapes that adorned the "City of Palaces" (figs. 12 and 13). In these images, the city becomes a stage where girls in suggestive underwear strike streetwalker poses and fully nude women dance energetically in front of famous landmarks such as the Palacio de Bellas Artes. The representation, according to the caption, invites readers to "contemplate the sumptuous Palacio de Bellas Artes in admiration of the sculpted body of Irma," not only suggesting an intimate relationship between female bodies and buildings but also attempting to insert (com)motion into a rather static cityscape. Elizabeth Grosz states that "different forms of lived spatiality (the verticality of the city, as opposed to the horizontality of the landscape) must have effects on the ways we live space and thus on our corporeal alignment, comportment, and orientations."[8] Unlike the "passive" female bodies that dominated much nineteenth-century art, such as the classic erotic figures of reclining Mayas and Odalisques or contemporary art photography by the likes of Manuel Álvarez Bravo, *Vea*'s Deco bodies were those of the chicas modernas.

In addition to the irony implicit in positioning transgressive female nudes on the nation's foremost theater, which staged the nationalistic Ballet Folklórico, *Vea*'s editors also proposed a modern aesthetic of movement in embracing new visual techniques. The use of montage in what editors referred to as "graphic representations," sandwiching multiple images of the same woman onto a postcard-like bird's-eye view of the theater and adjacent streets, lends the image a cinematic allure that adds to the sense of movement and modernity. In embracing photomontage, an innovative technique championed by art photographers (such as Lola Álvarez Bravo) and political vanguard publications alike, *Vea*'s editors placed their nude girls squarely within the political and artistic landscape of modernity.[9] Thus, *Vea*'s girls were in movement in more ways than one. It was this movement that was

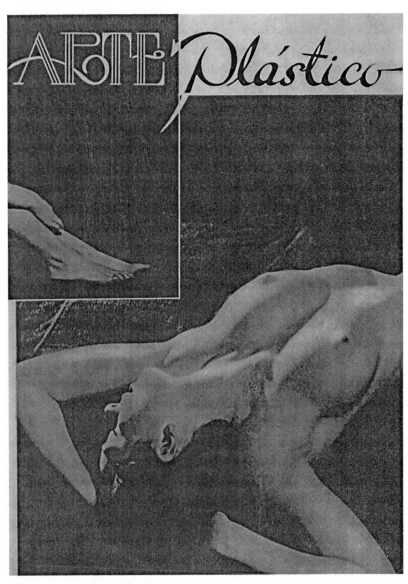

FIG. 14. César, "Arte plástico," *Vea: Semanario Moderno*, February 12, 1937.

understood, or that editors tried to communicate to its audience, as modern, positive, lighthearted, and, most importantly, nonthreatening.

Despite *Vea*'s focus on innocuous entertainment and desired modernity, it (like *Forma*, *Malhora*, and *Detectives*) faced resistance from conservative social sectors. Catholics were the most vocal and visible opponents of these racy magazines. Needless to say, the Catholic formulation of the ideal woman as an obedient, humble wife and mother who suffered for the good of her husband, her children, and her faith contrasted sharply with the progressive, and in their estimation immoral, aspects of the chica moderna. For Catholics, a woman who defied tradition, postponed or gave up on marriage, or rejected motherhood was anything but humble and subservient. Patience Shell notes: "Catholics, in particular, feared for the morals of young women who bobbed their hair, raised their skirts, and took up the tango."[10]

Labeling even comics as pornographic, the Catholic Church used traditionalist discourses to turn its attention to cities and launch national campaigns against pornography. Magazines that displayed naked female bodies and women in "daring clothing" or that included articles about divorce and "inappropriate dancing" were suspect in the eyes of Catholic censure. Thus, while most capitalinos believed that reading publications such as *Vea* provided "evidence of [their] participation in modernity," conservatives feared the impact of these publications on the innocent, especially children. Even more telling, as Anne Rubenstein indicates, conservatives considered the mere *appearance* of the chica moderna on the pages of these periodicals pornographic.[11]

Not only did the church have a complex and far-reaching role in the lives of Catholic women in (post)revolutionary Mexico, but the issue of women's changing roles deeply affected the tenuous relationship and power struggle between the church and the state. As groundbreaking scholarship by Kristina Boylan, Patience Shell, Anne Rubenstein, and others has shown, in maintaining control over civil society both the church and the state found women to be of the utmost importance, and each targeted women as its principal agent in a civilizing or modernizing mission.[12] Sexual mores frequently formed the pretext for battles between church and state in the fight for women's support and loyalty.

Even before the state directly promoted sex education in the 1920s, teachers used Margaret Sanger's pamphlets in civics classes in girls' vocational schools. Government also blamed the high rates of venereal diseases among Mexico City's population (between 1916 and 1920 syphilis had become the major reason for miscarriages) on the church for its having "promoted secrecy regarding matters of sexuality."[13]

The church, however, was not the only one to condemn *Vea*, as women's groups across a broad ideological spectrum were among the most vocal opponents of "pornographic magazines." Not only the powerful Damas Católicas but also women with vastly different ideological convictions deemed *Vea* indecent and offensive. In the winter of 1936, the conservative Unión de Sociedades Femeniles Cristianas (Federation of Christian Women's Societies), along with the Unión Feminina Mexicanista (Mexican Women's Unity) and the Unión de Mujeres Mexicanas (Federation of Mexican Women), wrote President Cárdenas to object to the accessibility of *Vea* and *Malhora*, which were sold "everywhere in broad daylight." Because the publication or distribution of pornographic materials constituted a crime, the president ordered the DDF to enforce the law, and the judicial police removed several publications from the street in February 1936. In June, however, renewed complaints about leaflets advertising "obscene films" and new copies of *Vea* and *Forma* inundating the streets and plazas of the centro indicated that the president's ordinances were difficult to enforce.[14]

By the late 1930s, revolutionary nationalism was often invoked in the fight against the depiction of uncovered female bodies.[15] The ruling party's newspaper, *El Nacional*, started its own morality campaign, which implicated foreign agitators and "socialists" in the perversion of children, especially through publications that dealt openly with sex. In March 1939, a subcommittee of the Frente Único Pro Derecho de la Mujer (Women's Rights United Front), the largest women's association in Mexico at that time, asked President Cárdenas for the cessation of the entertainment weekly *Mujeres y Deportes* and the family comic *Paquín* on grounds that they were funded by "German and Italian fascists." The Frente Único de Padres de Familia (Parents United Front) even cited article 33 of the 1917 Mexican Constitution in order to blame foreigners for the spread of moral decay in the capital. Other concerned citizens opined that having such Mexican magazines circulate in other countries would tarnish Mexico's international image.[16] By analyzing *Vea* imagery, which suggestively placed foreign-looking starlets in front of state monuments such as Castillo de Chapultepec (then the presidential residence and an enduring symbol of Mexico's struggle against U.S. imperialism) (fig. 12), we are better able to grasp the political consequences of *Vea*'s "frivolity" and the nationalist sentiments it generated in the protest against "pornographic" magazines. By the end of 1937, at the federal district attorney's office, the Legión Mexicana de la Decencia (Mexican Decency League) denounced *Vea* on "obscenity" charges due to its "photographic nudes." President Cárdenas banned *Vea*, and its editor in chief was imprisoned briefly.[17] While precise information is lacking on why Cárdenas banned *Vea*, his reconciliation with the Catholic Church might have had an influence. Stephen Andes mentions that an "amelioration of Church-state relations under Lázaro Cárdenas in 1938" facilitated greater influence for Acción Católica (Catholic Action) in social matters.[18] The revolutionary state deemed nude Deco bodies pornographic and unsuitable for public viewing, even though these bodies had signaled the advent of global modernity a decade earlier.

Mexico was hardly alone among nation-states in either its governmental concerns over public morality, order, and decency or in its attempts to address these concerns through the containment of "deviant sexuality." Over the course of the 1930s, an international trend of strengthening pornography laws developed. In 1930, the U.S. Motion Picture Production Code "banished sexual themes and imagery from the silver screen" and sought to curb "sexual deviance," even though early film had been the medium par excellence in the unbridled exploration of sexual desire, including erotic films that featured vibrators.[19] In Europe, efforts to arrest the accessibility of pornography ran up against freedom of expression in the arts, literature in particular. Relying on an analysis of the opposition and censorship that faced James Joyce's *Ulysses* due to its explicit treatment of sexuality, Walter Kendrick has shown that the range of what constituted pornography readily shrank throughout the twentieth century due to "literary value." In 1929, Virginia Woolf weighed in on the *Ulysses* debate by stating that there were two kinds of indecencies: one that aimed to cause pleasure or corruption, and one where indecency was a mere by-product of what otherwise was a "scientific, social, *aesthetic*" work.[20] The "I know it when I see it" argument came to structure most definitions and subsequent legislation of pornography in Europe and the United States, as pornography came to be categorized as that which was obscene by the standards of the average person. Considering that the Mexican postrevolutionary elite of the 1920s concentrated their efforts on reform that would both nationalize and "modernize" Mexico's economy (and society) in keeping with "Western" models, the tightening of pornography laws in the name of civilization—and what Michel Foucault called the production of deviance—clearly affected Mexico as well.[21]

The connection between sexuality and art on which *Vea* drew was certainly not new, as an ongoing conflation of the two had long facilitated the legitimacy of erotic imagery and text in Europe and the United States. Anne Anlin Cheng concludes that assigned difference between high art and pornography is deceptive, as they are "preconditions" for each other in their mutual preoccupation with female sexuality. Hence, intentional slippages between these categories led to a tacit acceptance and mainstreaming of soft porn and also added to the enduring allure of art.[22] *Vea*'s deliberate deployment of these slippages was no different. Editors claimed that the magazine subscribed to common notions of decency from its inception, maintaining that its portrayal of female nudity constituted art and that the explicit short stories had literary merit. In keeping with "good taste" and creative conventions, *Vea*'s nudes were labeled and introduced as subjects of artistic studies. In contrast, high-art photography of the day, such as the striking images of the French photographer Henri Cartier-Bresson, who visited Mexico in 1934, revealed far more about the real lives of "public women" (mainly prostitutes), showcased "deviant" female sexuality, and lacked the "tasteful" aesthetics and erotic allure of *Vea*'s nudes and showgirls.

While the reasons for the government's censorship of *Vea* are multiple and complex, the crossing of gender and class lines represented symbolically and physically in the cityscape constituted a crucial element in what earned *Vea* its pornographic label.[23] Its identification with that which was in "good taste," decent, artistic, and of value in terms of bourgeois acceptance was meant to resonate with an upper- and middle-class, well-educated, white or mestizo male readership in the capital city who would consume the stories and images in the privacy of home offices. Yet the fairly low price of fifteen centavos an issue and the sale of copies on busy street corners in the city center (as the protest of concerned capitalinas informed us) suggests that *Vea* was readily visible, if not available, to a larger audience, without discrimination on the basis of class, age, ethnicity, or gender.[24] Hence it was the ease of acquiring *Vea* in the city that led to the need to define it as pornographic.

When placed in a larger historical context of Western modernity, we see that the connections between sexuality, knowledge, and politics proved both attractive and problematic as sexual materials became more accessible to a larger public made up of women and the lower classes due to print culture. For instance, the rise of pornography in Europe was closely linked to the realm of "forbidden knowledge," whether contained in Enlightenment philosophy, secret museums, annals of prostitution, or medical manuals.[25] The birth of pornography as literary and visual expression was an integral part of the emergence of Western modernity precisely because it functioned as a category of understanding of human behavior, and hence as a tool in the production of knowledge. Pornography was linked to heresy, philosophy, science, and a search for individual freedom, especially in its political character when criticizing absolutism, such as the case of the infamous Marquis de Sade. In Mexico, political satire was interwoven with eroticism through bataclanesque theater, which familiarized audiences with the idea that social criticism went hand-in-glove with female nudity. With its ties to dissent and iconoclasm, knowledge of sex was thought to be dangerous to the established order and hence was off-limits to the general public, especially the lower classes and women.[26] These notions clashed with revolutionary discourses that constructed traditional forms of femininity, including feminized landscapes, as a part of an appropriate national identity, with the result that modernity based on women's sexual liberation became harder to trace.

PROMIS-CIUDAD: THE LURE OF PORNOTOPIA

Manuel Álvarez Bravo, arguably Mexico's most influential art photographer of the twentieth century, composed an image titled *Parábola óptica* (Optical parable) in 1931 (fig. 15). In this unconventional rendition of a storefront on a street in Mexico City's centro, Álvarez Bravo offered a close-up of the capital that captures the symbols of modernity through modernist techniques. The photograph depicts an advertising sign and its multiple refractions in glass panels, alluding to fragmentation of experiences that that characterizes life in a modern city. At first glance a mundane scene of an ordinary optometry store, the multiple sets of disembodied eyes emerging from a shadowy hall of mirrors gradually transform the store window into a haunting example of urban alienation. The photographer, who is understood to control the act of seeing, shows the viewer that the city looks back. The many fragments and reflections of the eyes intensify the gaze of the city, which encompasses an infinite sadness as well as a terrifying non-human mechanics. In their penetrating silence, the eyes unnerve and question the viewer. The shop owner's name, E. Spirito (*espíritu*), emphasizes what the viewer already knows: the eyes function as portals for the spirit.

At this point in his career, Álvarez Bravo was exploring the city through storefronts, shop windows, and the fragmentation of the female body. Two earlier images, *Covered Dummy* and *Dummy*, both from 1930, marked the shop window as female space, where the mannequin represents the iconized homogeneous woman, white and middle class, object of consumer desire and double of the female consumer herself, a stage where consumption originates. In *Parábola óptica*, the eyes that beckon the consumer appear to be female, and even though they are painted on the window, Álvarez Bravo made them appear to recede back in space due to the optical effects of light and reflection. The eyes haunt viewers because they are locked inside, held captive

FIG. 15. Manuel Álvarez-Bravo, *Parábola óptica*, gelatin silver print, 1931. © Colette Urbajtel/Archivo Manuel Álvarez Bravo, SC.

by glass and steel. Despite the sunshine outside, the darkness within from which the eyes stare at the viewer further indicates a sense of bondage and despair. Floating uneasily in enclosed space, without a voice to speak or body to move, these eyes seem to belong to women held in dark structures, unable to enter the public realm of day. Yet it is these particular eyes, the sign informs the viewer, that are the guardians of modern spectacles. This, Álvarez Bravo concludes, constitutes an optical illusion as well as parable, a matter of envisioning a modern space where women led a shadowy existence. Capturing the eyes of the city enclosed in dark space, *Parábola óptica* reminds one of the dark alienation of late-nineteenth-century life rather than the liberating light of the "swinging 1920s." With its haunting Victorian spirit devoid of a human body, this image makes for a stark contrast with *Vea*'s ultra-visible Deco bodies. However, Álvarez Bravo crafted this image not in the late nineteenth century but at nearly the same time *Vea* depicted a sexualized female presence in the modern city as healthy, happy, and innocent. Soon, Álvarez Bravo left his city meanderings to roam the countryside photographing nude indigenous women as high art camposcape. Yet, as a closer look at Mexico City's popular press bears out, imagery linking the city's dark spaces with women's haunting spirits was more common than either *Vea* or Álvarez Bravo seemed to suggest.

As *Vea*'s ban demonstrated, by the late 1930s theatrical Deco bodies had become closely tied to Mexican understandings of pornography. New medical discourses such as psychoanalysis also contributed to these understandings. Early psychiatrists such as Richard von Krafft-Ebing and Sigmund Freud appeared to make knowledge about sex respectable. Freud argued for a liberation from the "prudery and prurience which governs the attitude of most 'civilized people' in matters of sexuality."[27] Although changes in sexual attitudes began before the Roaring Twenties, young people who came of age at this time constituted the first generation that embraced the idea that women could be equal to men in expressing desire and engaging in sexual activities.[28] Popularized notions of Freudian theories became commonplace in both European and U.S. scientific and popular discourses in the 1920s, which reached Mexico as well. *Vea*, *Detectives*, and *Mujeres y Deportes* frequently ran translated articles from the United States that referenced and discussed Freudian ideas and framed women's sexual liberation within a Freudian framework. However, talk about sex was acceptable only if the sex in question, such as that of heterosexual married couple, was "healthy" and served procreative purposes.[29] The "popular pathology of pornography" associated porn (and the implied link to masturbation) with "mental retardation," an idea championed by Freud, who linked sexual deviance to arrested development and held "monogamous genital heterosexuality" as the highest expression of human sexual desire.[30]

These notions also linked deviant sexuality to urban space. According to Lawrence Knopp, urban life was thought to foster the "eroticization of many of the characteristic experiences of modern life: anonymity, voyeurism, exhibitionism, consumption, authority (and challenges to it), tactility, motion, danger, power, navigation and restlessness."[31] The Mexican popular press readily expressed these sentiments, albeit in a negative light. Pornography, reporters found, was difficult to resist when living in the modern city. In the notorious burlesque Teatro Lírico, men came to see what they could not possess, Salvador Novo commented, "like those who frequent the cinema to see a beautiful house in which they cannot live."[32] Equating the desire for sexually provocative women with a consumerist urge to own real estate, spatial assessments of pornography foreshadowed a similar bourgeois condemnation of midcentury youth in Europe (thought to be lower-class males) who "had no taste for art, literature, or anything of social importance" but instead chose to "dwell in the never-never land ... of pornotopia."[33]

Mexico City's ultimate "never-never land" of illegitimate eroticism in the 1930s was Plaza Garibaldi, in the northeast of the city's historic district around the Zócalo. Known for its burlesque theater celebrated in the neighboring zona libre, Plaza Garibaldi used eroticized Deco bodies to sell sex. Started in the lower-class Teatro María Guerrero and followed quickly by the burlesque spectacles in the Teatro Principal, "men-only" shows turned to titillating adult entertainment that stripped Deco bodies of their last vestiges of artful and artistic nudity.[34] While these productions, theaters, and areas of town were considered pornographic, they nonetheless invoked or continued the conventions that the bataclán had put in motion. Bataclanismo remained profitable theater material long after its allure as a high art from Paris had faded from the minds of the middle classes and theater critics. Revista songs such as "Las racionistas" made it clear that bataclanesque theater simply served female exhibitionism and indicated that its performers were "third-rate actresses" ready to drop their parasols (the only item standing between their nude bodies and their male audience) as they were en route to prostitution:

> We are girls on an allowance [also "third-rate actresses"], in train-
> ing to enter the theater in a bataclán costume....
>   So, gentlemen, you'd like to see our forms? Well, up with the
> parasols and ... behold our womanhood.[35]

The production from which these lyrics are taken, *De México a Cuba*, apparently fit a growing trend that equated the pornification of the Mexican entertainment world with perfidious foreign influences (particularly from Cuba). Theater critics for major publications lamented the lack of decent Mexican national theater, arguing that Mexican theater was near death because of the pervasiveness of erotic Cuban theater: "daughters of slime, tropical obscenities, Afro-Cuban foolishness."[36]

Due to their popularity, burlesque shows provoked some citizens to petition President Cárdenas to protect public decency. As in Europe and the United States, marginalized areas of the city associated with poverty and a failure on the part of the state to establish "the dominant order" were labeled erotic, especially in comparison to more affluent, desexualized areas.[37] Throughout the 1930s, popular theaters such as Lírico and Apolo, situated in the lower-class barrios of Tepito and Lagunilla close to Garibaldi, faced increasing government censorship and outright suppression of shows due to charges of pornography. Complaints in the popular press and from citizen groups pressured the municipal government to enforce theater regulations and close "men-only" theaters. In 1932, *Diversiones* criticized the head of the DDF, Don Vicente Estrada Cajigal, for looking the other way and tolerating the "lepers of Garibaldi" and "the filth of the 'for men only' shows."[38] In 1939, pro-family organizations demanded the closure of Apolo, where they believed morals were compromised by "filthy and squalid ways."[39]

The theater was closed on numerous occasions between 1937 and 1942 despite the management's best efforts to stage magic shows for families as a wholesome break from its adult entertainment. Continued complaints, condemning both shows and audiences as immoral, led to its permanent closure in 1942 by Mexico City's Oficina de Espectáculos (Office of Entertainment).[40]

Most theater critics, however, believed that denying men access to eroticized Deco bodies, or the places inscribed by them, would not eliminate the problem of pornography. Novo warned that closing all the men-only theaters would be an ineffective way to repress the male libido.[41] He urged officials to run these theaters out of business, not by closing them, but by creating alternative options for "true recreation." In 1929, Novo suggested that the municipal government strengthen the city's cultural offerings with good ballet companies, sports, and a symphony orchestra with a particular focus on reaching out to the lower-class neighborhoods.[42] Perhaps heeding Novo's advice, the city government started "Public Recreation" programs, open-air comedies, and its own revista productions.[43] The Cardinista state, however, opted for a more repressive stance in dealing with entertainment centered on female nudity, hoping to intervene in the underworld and curtail the activities of its denizens. Like *Vea*'s efforts to index the city's desire for modernity by transposing healthy, attractive Deco bodies onto its most revered public spaces as if they were in camposcape, mapping mexicanidad onto the female spectacle of the underworld proved extremely problematic.

Linking pornography to the vice and violence of the underworld had a venerable tradition, not only through prostitution but also through common understandings of urban topography that linked sex and dirt with both bodily infection and society's "underbelly." D. H. Lawrence wrote in his 1929 essay, "Pornography and Obscenity," that while neither could be properly defined, "genuine pornography is almost always underworld, it doesn't come into the open." Linking sex and commerce, Lawrence found that pornography sold "by the underworld" was an "insult to the human body" and made human nudity cheap and ugly, the sex act "trivial and nasty."[44] It was this world, however, that publications like *Vea* and *Detectives* introduced as metropolitan modernity to Mexican readers. Yet, while *Vea* projected its "pornography" as healthy, artistic, and beautiful, *Detectives* celebrated the vice, scandal, and sexual libertinage of the underworld. Both publications, however, taught capitalino aficionados of pulp fiction that despite its lack of skyscrapers, Mexico City could be counted among the world's great modern capitals, even as it struggled with the shadow side of modernity.

Unlike its noir counterparts, *Vea* did not equate sexual freedom with the vices of the underworld. Instead of the disembodied eyes of *Parábola óptica* or the disemboweled bodies in *Detectives*, it showed pretty young women who were healthy, fun-loving, light-skinned, and ready to "act transnational." With their poses captured on the city's principal thoroughfares and between its most distinguished buildings in broad daylight, the October 1934 edition illustrates that *Vea* conceptualized the built environment of Mexico City in terms of feminized landscape (fig. 12). Here, eroticized bodies of the stage connected the Castillo de Chapultepec (then the presidential residence), the soon-to-be-completed Palacio de Bellas Artes, and the first landmark Art Deco high-rise, La Nacional, named for the insurance company that was to occupy the city's first skyscraper. The magazine positioned cut-and-pasted publicity shots of nude to semi-nude starlets, usually imported from Hollywood but sometimes mexicanas, onto the capital's national landmarks such as the Zócalo, Bosque de Chapultepec (Chapultepec Park), the Palacio Nacional, and even the Catedral Metropolitana.

As noted earlier, these depictions of nudity were meant to be both "frivolous" and artistic. Indeed, like most 1930s portrait photography imported from the United States and Europe, *Vea*'s images display an "electroplated lighting" that lent a "finish" to skin and naked bodies. In their "promise of erotic materiality that is self-consciously inorganic," writes Anlin Cheng, *Vea*'s girls connected female nudes to the machine age. Instead of bodily residue of sweat, recalling the messiness of sex, *Vea*'s Deco bodies had the clean look of "metallurgical, plastic and other synthetic materials." According to feminist film theorist Laura Mulvey, this "reassuringly luminous garment of beauty" constitutes a "mask of femininity" that "covers over the problematic aspects of the female body." *Vea*'s girls reflected, as Liz Conor posits, the feminization of public space due to women's increased participation in public life, offset discursively by an "inventory" of female tipos in an attempt to "contain and order the increasingly 'unfixed' and mutable meanings of modern femininity."[45]

In their attempt to capitalize on bataclanismo's associations with high art, frivolity, and eroticism, *Vea*'s editors clearly aimed at light "adult entertainment." Indexing the city's desire for modernity by photographically inserting attractive Deco bodies into its most revered public spaces as if they were in artistic and nudist camposcape, the magazine appropriated discourses of health, beauty, and mexicanidad associated with the countryside. The use of healthy bodies as symbols of modernity, however, was in tension with imagery that marked naked urban female bodies as dangerous and was used to discourage morally minded citizens from straying into "dirty" lower-class neighborhoods. *Vea*'s nude girls consequently marked a reversal of symbolic systems of representation that linked body and space. Henri Lefebvre argues that while the relations of reproduction are spatially produced through sexual symbols,

> this is a symbolism that conceals more than it reveals, the more so since the relations of reproduction are divided into frontal, public, overt—and hence coded—relations on the one hand, and on the other covert, clandestine and repressed relations, which precisely because they are so repressed, characterize transgressions related not so much to sex per se as to sexual pleasure, its preconditions and consequences.[46]

Vea's editors inadvertently used the symbols of "covert, clandestine and repressed relations" to signal accepted spaces that were "frontal, public, overt." This representation clashed with perceived notions of space, where the countryside represented a safe space that could accommodate both indigenous nudity (as nationalist art) and nudism (as a middle-class search for health), but the naked bodies of women in the city (including the undressed stars of revue and burlesque theater and "girls" in *Vea*) were coded as pornography.

The treatment of nudism in the Mexican popular press functioned as a parallel discourse to pornography that established acceptable forms of visual nakedness which *Vea*'s editors believed they could safely draw on. Yet unlike the nudity contained in camposcape, which was rendered healthy, traditional, and productive, *Vea*'s titillating urban female nudity was deemed dirty and un-Mexican by its detractors. As such, Mexico City's popular press played out the tensions between the nude physique of camposcape as natural bodies that bathed in sun and air, placed in an idyllic pastoral place outside of time, and the sexualized Deco bodies of pornotopia, spaces of the city that represented the embodiment of deviant desires.

THROUGH THE PORTALS OF THE UNDERWORLD

If *Vea* hoped to demonstrate that female nudity in the city was healthy and modern, *Detectives* and *Mujeres y Deportes* showcased a city captive to the perils of urban modernity. They placed a heterotopic domain dominated by darkness, danger, and especially deception at the heart of the capital city. Sensationalistic articles portrayed cantinas and brothels as portals to the underworld and revealed how even dance schools and similar sites of daytime respectability changed with the onset of darkness. Restaurants in the centro, where the "humble folk" broke bread during the day, hid their true identity as venues of crime and sex advertised by neon lights and "cheap music" after "decent folk" had gone home. Inconspicuous cafés might sell coffee in the morning, but they offered large quantities of marijuana for sale at night. Launderettes where Chinese men appeared to dedicate their time to washing clothes were nothing but cheap facades for opium dens.[47] After nightfall, the innocuous daytime roads of the centro shrank to dark alleys where whores and other double-crossing women worked the streets.[48]

In *Mujeres y Deportes*, articles such as "Mientras México duerme" (While Mexico City sleeps) took the reader into this nocturnal world of excitement, danger, and sexual deviance. The article included a large photo of dark, deserted streets framed by head shots of criminal types. Positing that the underworld manifested itself after sundown, it elevated the fearless police detectives of the Federal District who risked their lives to protect the unsuspecting populace. In this world of darkness and deception, detectives' eyes scanned the city's places of illicit pleasure for signs of menace. Photos of groups of men loitering around the door of a cantina at night, with the caption, "The metropolitan world of crime chooses cantinas and brothels as its meeting places, and gets confused with churchgoers and workers," left much to the imagination, as did the magazine's descriptions of the women who occupied this world.[49]

Indeed, it was often the presence of suspicious women that alerted authorities to criminal endeavors and pinpointed places of ill repute in the vast urban landscape of nighttime activity and entertainment. For instance, when agents of the judicial division of the Department of Public Health labeled businessmen Henry Helfland and Isaac Sevilla as suspicious persons, they noted that, beyond their notoriety as *toxicomanos* (drug addicts), Helfland and Sevilla were regularly seen at various theaters with "elegantly dressed women of the night." Even though the two men, who owned a retail store in women's clothing, were undoubtedly involved in smuggling heroin, their classification as shady characters of Mexico City's ever more visible underworld depended equally on their association with prostitutes and adult entertainment.[50]

The underworld's female denizens, all of them "suspicious" female characters, were sexualized women—prostitutes, "degenerates," and the recently deflowered (rendered either as victims or as villains of deception). *Mujeres y Deportes* writers revealed that the elegantly dressed women (such as those seen with Helfland and Sevilla) who wore artfully applied makeup and embraced, entertained, and made love to thieves and even murderers were undoubtedly the lowest class of traitors to society. Performing as elegant ladies, these prostitutes seduced unsuspecting men while paying homage and money to the *hampa*, as the group of hard-core professional criminals was known. In addition to these agents of deception, the underworld sketched by these magazines was filled with fallen women who had been deceived, victimized, and corrupted, much like the protagonists in Arcady Boytler's 1934 landmark film, *La mujer del puerto*, and Federico Gamboa's famous 1903 novel, *Santa*. "Girls without experience and money think they can make an honest living there [in dance halls]," revealed reporter Armando Salinas, but after charging a few centavos for a dance and falling in love with the wrong men, they too joined the ranks of the "sad caravan of delinquency."[51]

To the contrary, the masculine woman was not the sad young victim or the pawn of her pimp but rather the tough, independent woman who in these magazines inhabited the stereotype of either the money-hungry opportunist or the sex-crazed degenerate. As Mark Seltzer observes, "the counterpart stories of the fallen girl" dominated discussions of class tensions that were cast in terms of gender and appeared to equate the masculine woman with economic opportunism, coldheartedness, and overt, exhibitionist sexuality.[52] With weekly columns such as "En casa de Venus" (In the house of Venus), in which reporters-cum-flaneurs explored the underbelly of the city, *Detectives* opened the doors of *casas públicas* (brothels) to showcase the "private lives" of prostitutes living and working in the zonas libres. Touring the zonas, reporters likened brothels to theaters where "dispassionate spectators" like themselves witnessed scenes close to those performed in burlesque theaters: "a picturesque and dramatic row of forms [women], diverse as they are distinct." Moreover, brazen prostitutes confided in interviews that—much as *Vea*'s starlets feigned innocence in the face of their tantalizing sexuality—they experienced great pleasure in using the window as a stage to show themselves nude to hundreds of men out on the street below.[53]

The rise of a different kind of prostitution, one in which women were seen to be taking control of their lives and sexuality, troubled these journalists. Prostitution that allowed women economic and social independence instead of mere victimhood, opined writers for *Detectives*, was due to an "excessive inclination for freedom," a break with established gender roles. The "Venus" columnist explained that upon marrying, men feared the loss of their virility, mostly because modern women such as the chicas modernas had become too "manly" and no longer knew how to offer "the enchantment of being a submissive and homely wife." The prototypical woman of the underworld did not fit the mold of submissive housewife. The new prostitute turned to sex work not only because of financial incentives and the troubling economy. Instead, *Detectives* depicted prostitutes as all-too-liberated women who acted like men in their search for sexual pleasure: "Yolanda tells me that she is happy she left her boring and rude husband and is in charge of her own exciting life."[54]

Detectives showed that by the mid-1930s the enjoyment of perverse pleasures of the flesh certainly was on the rise, and not only in the zonas libres. Elegant brothels catering to the sons of the rich and famous operated freely in upscale neighborhoods such as Roma, Juárez, and Condesa. More scandalous, not only sons but also emboldened daughters of the gente decente frequented these establishments, wrote a "Venus" columnist. Taking his readers on a tour of colonia Del Valle, the reporter described meeting a female employee of a former president in the process of "offering herself" to three men at the same time— not because of need for money, he assured readers, but solely for the "pleasure of disgracing herself." The gallant journalist offered to take her away, but high-ranking military men intervened, he stated, now ignoring his previous suggestion that she had freely embarked on her course of action.[55] Indeed, "scandalous stories" such as these in *Detectives* and other popular magazines detailed "the tendency of daughters of the city elites to spend their free afternoons in discreet brothels in the metropolis' most exclusive neighborhoods."[56] In addition to "discreet" brothels, cabaret shows showcased exclusive and expensive "erotic lesbian shows" for "masculine consumption," on which men spent hundreds of pesos.[57]

Female exhibitionism and sexual agency not merely for the sake of money but as part of a new female desire were deemed problematic and pornographic. Unlike the classic striptease, where the theatrical act of removing her clothes rendered a woman the object of "the masculine, medical and hygienic gaze," the flapper was deemed masculine in her exhibitionism, which turned her into an object and fetish. These modern women of the 1920s were portrayed as reveling in exhibiting themselves and turning themselves into sexual spectacles as part of modernity.[58] Consequently, in their displays of overt sexuality, their embrace of object status, and their appropriation of daring behavior, women who populated the underworld shared critical characteristics with the chicas modernas. As a transnational icon of modernity, the Modern Girl, especially in her incarnation of the irreverent and sexually overt flapper, was seen by many as wearing multiple masks. Like Louise Brooks's quintessential character Lulu in *Pandora's Box*, even when considered "frank" and "open" the flapper was seen as "deceitful in her appearance, a figure of trickery and illusion, whose real hair color, complexion, age, and moral nature could not be visually ascertained." In her ability and desire of self-making, her "mistake in personifying … the character she has seen imitated," the flapper appeared akin to the prostitute in her violation of the natural order, "the normative link between 'the female' and 'the natural.'"[59] It was this "shape-shifting," especially in terms of the reversal of gender roles, that made the flapper something she was not, or was not supposed to be, and which undeniably tied her to the realm of the underworld.

The underworld represented a place where post-revolutionary concerns not only about feminine but also appropriate masculine behavior came into sharp focus. In 1920s and 1930s Mexico, new norms of masculine behavior had their roots in the revolutionary struggle against an aging patriarch that subsequently took on an additional sense of urgency and violence.[60] The revolutionary general as well as the young city criminal equally drew on this new, combative masculinity. While city detectives projected the prototype of the modern, urban New Man as the embodiment of a dynamic, young, revolutionary, and male state, the underworld, made up of tricky pelados and violent machos, formed its nocturnal, dangerous shadow. Hidden behind a concern over women on the part of the state and the general public was the matter of controlling wayward men, an issue that took on a feverish tone at a time when the armed phase of the revolution had supposedly ended yet sporadic rebellions threatened the still fragile new order. Like governments in other epochs and places engaged in postwar reconstruction, the Mexican state looked to women in rehabilitating and domesticating rebellious young men. A preoccupation with the underworld thus reflected the heady, insecure years after the revolution.

From this perspective, it is not surprising that *Detectives*—along with most of Mexico City's popular press—depicted the presence of women other than prostitutes in this urban landscape of pleasure and sin as the actual transgressors. Not prostitutes, but female visitors, who, like men, came looking for adventure, were considered the most dangerous women making their way into the underworld. Unlike the heterosexual man, who inhabited the accepted role as customer, and the (conceivably) heterosexual prostitute, who sold her services, women outside of sex work could not be accommodated within this legitimized world of monetary transactions. Motivated by a desire to get to know "lowly venues" and their own "unknown emotions," reported columnist Armando Salinas, these women set out on adventures without realizing the "frightful consequences." One such woman, *Detectives* warned, was cheated out of three thousand pesos, while another fared far worse. Instead of money, criminals took her womb in an act of atrocious slaughter reminiscent of the bloody deeds of Jack the Ripper and his Mexican counterpart, the Porfirian Chalequero.[61] It was the mobile woman without a distinct identity, not the classified and contained woman of the prostitution zones, who appeared to transgress real and imagined borders and cause problems.

Detectives thus mapped onto the city a heterotopic space where private transgression translated into public pleasure. Similar to its depiction of burlesque theater, the underworld served to titillate its audience with the spectacle of sensationalism, sex, and scandal even while condemning it as immoral. In the underworld's pornotopia, "normal" men could express the very wishes that they had to repress in polite society. In the capitalino version of noir press, the portals to pornotopia— cabarets, cantinas, and *casas de cita* (houses of assignation)—established an urban iconography that formed the backdrop against which a new modernist male subject could come into being. This development was not different from the ascendancy of "junior men" elsewhere around the world, nor were prostitutes and other lower-class women a novelty in serving as conduits to the exploration of the city and the urban socialization of these men.[62] In many Latin American locales, prostitution zones functioned as places of male socialization where middle- and upper-class clientele learned the ways of the city through commercial sexual transactions. By positioning sexual spectacle against the virtues of "normal women," centers of prostitution functioned as important cultural urban spaces that formed modern ideas of male sociability and masculinity.[63] Hence, the medical-political establishment was not preoccupied with prostitution as social evil in and of itself but rather as a threat to the existing gender order at a time when many women were seeking greater entry into public life.

Like Álvarez Bravo's *Parábola óptica*, the underworld in *Detectives* was depicted as a parallel city occupying the nether regions of metropolitan modernity, its geography a dark mirror that reflected what could not be shown and repressed that which could not be discussed in broad daylight. As a mental construct and nineteenth-century invention, the underworld not only embraced the nocturnal world of vice and violence but also functioned as a map to the subconscious, the central locus of Freudian theory, which constituted an equally shady site of modern atavism. It was a place where dark secrets hid, forbidden knowledge lived, and the dangers of female sexuality ran rampant. Banned in polite society, the "wishful impulses" of sexual desire freely roamed the underworld, and as such it served as a place of escape from repressive bourgeois morality. Buried within its modern cosmopolitanism, the city thus appeared to have an *umbral ombligo*, a secret origin, an underworld that both hid and facilitated sexual encounters (in theaters, hotels, or cafés), recalling Elizabeth Wilson's description of the modern city as "a magic set of boxes, with, inside each box, a yet smaller and more secret one."[64]

MAPPING MODERNITY: FEMALE ZONES

Like *Vea*'s Deco girls striking theatrical poses in the capital's urban landscape, *Conflicto en el tráfico* (Traffic incident), another of Ernesto García Cabral's covers for *Revista de Revistas*, communicates the importance of beholding the modern woman as an emblem and incarnation of the modern city (fig. 16). In full technicolor *avant la lettre*, the woman in hot pink holds up traffic; she (in many ways very similar to Cabral's rendition of the actresses of the bataclán)[65] appears to be an exhibitionist who makes a spectacle of herself by creating a commotion in front of a large audience. Unlike her bold move forward, the male spectators with unmarked features and gray suits recede into a nondescript cityscape. Indeed, Cabral's "city woman" so resembles her Deco-bodied counterpart of the stage that her performance is essentially that of an actress acting out the city, giving shape to what became a well-worn symbol of modernity: the female disturbance of traffic.

Cabral's image not only identifies and celebrates the cosmopolitan woman as a crucial ingredient in the recipe for modernity but also draws attention to its problematic. Outside of Mexico, the "holding up traffic" scene became a classic trope in the representation of modern city girls, clearly indicating that these representations both sexualized public urban space and led to ambivalence about the political ramifications of modern girls' newfound visibility. *Conflicto en el tráfico* aptly illustrated new venues of seeing that separated the need for personal contact from looking at (women's) bodies. Movement through the city, such as by public transportation, meant that people were put into the position of prolonged and repeated looking at each other without the need for speaking. The modern city, with its rapid pace of "commodity exchange, traffic, movement, contemplation, and visual distraction," created fresh modes of gendered interaction. Imagery of the chicas modernas qualifying cityscape, such as that by Cabral and in *Vea*, signaled not only how the city transformed women but also the power of women to sexualize public space.[66]

Enabled by new public transportation networks such as buses, trolleys, and cars to discover new physical places and explore new social territories of the capital city, young women—in search of employment, new fashions, and fun—increased their mobility throughout the city. Historians Katherine Bliss and Ann Blum have used representations of traffic, the new phenomenon of the "motorcar" in particular, as a way to understand changing gender roles, sexuality, and their relationship to

FIG. 16. Ernesto García Cabral, *Conflicto en el tráfico*, *Revista de Revistas*, August 9, 1925.

public space in Mexico. In many ways, they illustrate that the motorcar represented the era's "rapid cultural and demographic transformation of the capital." Cars especially could offer women protection, yet they also made "a public street the intimate site of a willing sexual tryst" and provided young women with new means to transgress traditional boundaries that delineated the social and class geography of Mexico City. Similar to the "pervasive sexualization of steam technologies and trains in nineteenth-century discourse," the motorcar, whether driving it or stopping in it, became the vehicle of choice to map women's physical and social mobility onto an increasingly sexualized urban landscape.[67]

Thus the condemnation of the authorities in the light of prostitution was not confined to the opinions of journalists, but entailed a larger public concern over the perceived threats of female mobility, sexual danger, and the growing phenomenon of "female zones" in Mexico City's urban landscape. Due to unceasing reports in *Detectives* and similar weeklies that decried the growing presence of a shadowy underworld and its undeniable ties to pornotopia, concerned capitalinos criticized what they perceived to be contradictory governmental policies in fighting crime and sexual vices. Ostensibly, the Mexican state's attempts to exert control over the city's pornotopic underworld were quite extensive. Although it allowed legalized prostitution as the lesser evil, it equally sought to curtail and contain these activities. Sanctioning prostitution in what they euphemistically and ironically called *zonas de tolerancia* or *zonas libres* (zones of toleration or free zones), officials envisioned order in the city by keeping bodies, especially female, in their right and proper places.

The inception of these zones dated to 1912, the early years of the armed phase of the revolution, when city officials created the first zone to combat the overwhelming presence of prostitutes in the Zócalo who used the then extant gardens of the illustrious plaza to conduct their business.[68] This zone comprised the then largely undeveloped area around Cuauhtemotzín Street in the lower-class colonia Obrera, where several madams had already established brothels. The second zone was established in the area framed by Santa María Redonda,

Comonfort, República de Ecuador, and Juan Alvarez Streets, close to Tepito. Although the zonas libres were confirmed by legislation in 1926, their boundaries were still not properly fixed in 1929, as "the issue was more tricky than a first visit to the area indicated," according to a study carried out by investigators of both the Health Department and the DDF. An elementary school on Panama Street inadvertently ended up in the second zone, and mounting traffic problems around the districts caused great alarm for neighboring residents. Even if the investigators believed that one zone, with a policed periphery, should suffice to contain sexual commerce, they understood this to be an unrealistic ideal. The study concluded that it would be best to keep the zonas de tolerancia exactly the way they were, rather than consolidate the areas, augment patrols, and keep cars, factories, and schools outside of the zones, and thus proposed little to no change. Plans for the unfortunate school on Panama Street entailed moving the students out of the zone as quickly as possible and converting the building into a social service office to perform inspections of minors and mentally disabled handicapped girls working as prostitutes.[69]

Consequently, current problems notwithstanding, investigators advised the departments in question to maintain the zones as they then operated, as they were *consagradas por el uso*, (blessed by use) and accepted by the larger public. They reasoned that "honest citizens" living in proximity to the zones were accustomed to the inconvenience and only protested in minimal ways, while prostitutes always resisted being moved due to economic reasons. Because brothels had to conform to Health Department sanitary standards, which presented owners with heavy costs, investigators wrote that it would not be entirely fair to move them. Most importantly, the authors of the report feared that the sex workers would resort to drastic and vocal forms of protest in their attacks against the authorities. They were especially worried about the possibility of press campaigns such as those recently directed at the DDF when they opened Netzahualcoyotl Street in the zone to traffic and public access. In response, the prostitutes had resorted to boycotting the dreaded *control sanitario* (mandatory doctor examinations).[70]

By the early 1930s, however, public concern mounted over the contradictory governmental policies in designing and maintaining the zones. The "honest citizens" who lived close by were not as content as the investigators indicated. Members of the Junta de Obreros, Industriales, Propretarios y Vecinos de las Calles de Cuauhtemotzín y Adyacentes (Assembly of Workers, Industrialists, Property Owners and Neighbors of Cuauhtemotzín and Adjacent Streets) in the centro complained bitterly to the federal government. Although they had protested against the existence and growth of the zone for years, they felt that the DDF's extensive work in paving and improving "little used and little known" streets to open them to motorized traffic was the last straw. Appealing to officials' concern for the public image of the city and constant quest for the tourist dollar, they used the Comisión Mixta Pro-Turismo (Joint Pro-Tourism Committee) to petition the Secretaría de Gobernación (Department of the Interior) to remove the zone altogether. Now that these streets had become major thoroughfares and "an obligatory road" to the airport, they said, tourists had no other choice but to gaze on "the spectacle of immorality" that would form their first impression of the city and, by extension, the entire nation. They suggested that the zone be moved to an area of town without churches, schools, factories, or people having to traverse the area by car, bus, or trolley, where police could exercise more vigilance.[71]

While these pleas appeared to fall on deaf ears, revolutionary reformers were intent on "limiting the lure of the brothel" by separating entertainment activities such as cabaret, cantina, and hotel business from paid sex and brothel pursuits. The city's 1926 ordinance called for the separation of brothels and entertainment centers in an effort to keep prostitution transparent to police. New health laws banned the sale of alcohol and set hours for musical entertainment in brothels, while owners of dance halls, cantinas, and hotels faced closure if they allowed prostitutes to frequent their establishments. Yet, these governmental policies met with little success. Even if article 151 of the Codigo Sanatario (Health Code) barred brothels from serving alcohol, judging from the many reports from the judicial division of the Health Department on fines levied against the brothel owners, the beer and tequila continued to flow quite liberally.[72] Even at the risk of losing their license, cantina owners such as Cecilia Soto knowingly allowed prostitutes to conduct business in these establishments night after night and to enter and leave brothels through their adjacent cantinas. Some, like Arsenio Heria, even converted their cantinas into dance halls without proper permits.[73] Moreover, the strict alcohol and entertainment ordinances caused the patrons of prostitutes to visit cabarets instead, which in turn increasingly became sexualized spaces. Claimed by the underworld and pornotopia, these places of entertainment changed in character, especially as registered prostitutes used them illegally.[74]

Yet the instability of the zones' spatial boundaries was not the only reason for officials' efforts to keep everything, and especially every body, in its proper place. In fact, women's increased physical and social mobility caused the most concern, as it compromised gender-segregated urban space. Here the confusion of spatial and female identities often led to the collapsing of categories; that is, the misidentification of who counted as a prostitute and the confusion over what constituted a designated space for commercial sex became increasingly problematic and intertwined. Health Department officials advised city authorities to close *casas de cita* and hotels that did not conform to the standards of decency and public order. They found, however, that despite sanctions, reputable hotels outside the zones, "honorable establishments by outward appearance," continued to open their doors to prostitutes and their clientele.[75] In 1929, Manuel Ruiz, manager of the Hotel Independencia, was called in by the judicial branch of the Health Department for allowing a prostitute and her client to take a room in his hotel. Hotel owners objected to the stricter laws that held them accountable for identifying and refusing prostitutes, and in his defense Ruiz stated that they had registered as a married couple. The hotel had no way, he said, of "distinguishing an honest woman from a prostitute, let alone a *clandestina* (unregistered sex worker)."[76] The movement of women into sexualized spaces, as well as their elusive identities, confounded officials, who noted in their reports that prostitutes used tricks and "oriental entrances" (reminiscent of popular literature's linking of prostitutes and opium dens) as portals to the underworld to pass between salons, cantinas, and brothels.[77]

City officials, even with cooperation from the police, were never able to enforce the measures that would aid them in mapping order onto the nocturnal city and keeping capitalinas in their proper place. In 1934, the year of *Vea*'s inception, the judicial division of the Health Department (in an effort to amend 1933 legislation that allowed prostitutes to use registered hotels for sexual commerce) reminded hotel owners that it was now absolutely forbidden for them to rent out rooms to unregistered prostitutes, "women whose conduct is notoriously immoral," even if they had done so occasionally or by accident. If Fransisco Vázquez Pérez, head of the judicial division, hoped to curb clandestine prostitution, he conflated changing gender norms with women's *mala conducta* (bad behavior), and then this with prostitution.[78] The fear of mistaken identities that had marked the Porfiriato still haunted post-revolutionary authorities, especially when faced with the women's freer movement throughout the city coupled with female behavior and appearances that they could no longer read.

Depictions of sexy girls on the streets of the capital by the likes of Cabral or *Vea* indicated a trend of female mobility and a spread of overt female sexuality that contrasted sharply with governmental efforts to keep illicit sexual activity confined to particular zones. Even if the Deco bodies of sexy chicas modernas sketched by Cabral might have represented the desirability of a piquant interlude in traffic or the "frivolous element" hinted at by *Vea*'s editors, these images must have been understood within the context of changing gender roles and women's liberation. *Vea*'s years of existence coincided with a tumultuous time in women's activism. The 1930s saw enormous fervor in women's organizing and the visibility of women's political activities in the capital. During this decade, Mexico City hosted three feminist congresses with the overarching goal of female suffrage. Sponsored by the PNR, these congresses attracted an array of often-conflicting factions representing a wide political spectrum. In general, women were divided among progressive, conservative, and communist camps.[79] While much has been made of the failure of the Mexican women's movement to secure voting rights at this time owing to factional disagreements, the congresses did produce positive results. Coverage in the press increased the public's familiarity with feminist causes and drew attention to women's problems, helping to dispel the persistent myth that Mexican women were passive and not interested in "matters outside of the home."[80] Although few women joined radical revolutionary causes, as most of them supported the Catholic Church and conservatives, the fervor and visibility of progressive and radical women, especially teachers, journalists, and government employees, helped to establish the image of the "modern woman" in connection to radical politics and her importance in post-revolutionary Mexican society.[81]

However, feminists and other female activists at the congresses, as well as those in support of women's rights in general, had to contend with complicated press coverage and outright ridicule. The largely male press corps played up disagreements between various factions, especially where issues of sexuality were concerned. Rosario Sansores, reporting for the women's weekly *La Familia*, found that "the feminist congresses have ... given pretext to men in qualifying us as inept and ignorant." It was in particular the women's disagreement on how to solve the "thorny problem of prostitution" that provoked jokes, taunts, and jeers by "los señores periodistas." Perhaps for these reasons, Sansores added that the president of the new women's association Liga Nacional Feminina (National Women's League), Elise Gomez Viuda de Florez, announced that the group would proceed carefully in order "to succeed through persuasion and not force." Sansores, reporting for what was undoubtedly not the most liberal magazine, stressed that despite infighting and negative reporting in the press, the congresses had been a "resounding success." Mexican women were finally coming together to organize themselves and address "the numerous problems that face the campesina and *obrera* (female worker)."[82] Hence, *Vea*'s depictions of scantily clad women on the city's streets were conversant with a women's movement that was not only increasingly visible but also increasingly scrutinized.

Considering this political climate and the political rights at stake, it may come as no surprise that many women in the capital city opposed popular depictions of their movements and behaviors such as those that appeared in *Vea* or, as we saw in the case of Cube Bonifant, those sketched by Cabral. When traveling by public transportation, noted an anonymous writer in the women's magazine *El Hogar* (The home), capitalinas who "circulate through the streets and avenues of our metropolis in order to take care of their domestic duties" faced lewd comments from men hanging around on street corners and in public transportation.[83] In a piece that argued for "safety for women," this ostensibly female author singled out sexual harassment, that is, men's inappropriate behavior in approaching women in public as sexual objects, rather than discussing the violent crime that many women in the capital city faced. While the article did not complicate the category of "women," the offending men were readily identified as the lower-class, "always drunk and bad smelling" *peladito vagabundo* (low-life bum). What was worse, these "spectacles" of indecency did not befall only women straying into lower-class neighborhoods but also women on the respectable, bourgeois thoroughfares of the centro.[84]

Moreover, in stressing that women took to the streets not out of a sense of adventure but "to take care of their domestic duties," *El Hogar* argued for a continued respect for women based on their traditional role in the home. Modern life required women to make "efforts and sacrifices" in ways that "no other culture had before," having to leave the house daily to ensure either her own well-being or that of her family, to work in factories, agencies, or retail stores. Consequently, she "mix[ed] herself in the whirlpool of the city" not out of selfish pursuits of leisure but because of "her great, civilizing role." Tellingly, the author based her plea for better treatment of women not on women's deserving equal standing with men but on women's assigned gender difference: "her weakness" and "her difficult condition as a woman." Hence, found the author, women should be entitled to find "a reflection of her private life, and deferential and affectionate treatment" everywhere. According to the philosophy of *El Hogar*, when women went out on the street, they did not go as men, but as domestic beings who needed to take the symbolic protection of the house with them.[85]

Thus, due to naturalized gender difference and sexual danger, the idea that women's growing presence on the city streets and movements in the public realm necessitated greater male protection, whether on the part of the state or from individual men, was touted as much by women themselves as by their male counterparts in the press. The danger of female mobility, especially when linked to ideas of sexual freedom, informed policies of troubled state reformers who feared the degenerative effects of venereal diseases such as syphilis and warned parents as well as young women themselves to guard against "physical adventure."[86] However, as the historian Pablo Piccato has shown, the revolutionary state did little to protect women against sexual violence, placed the burden of proof on the victim, and few prosecutions led to convictions.[87] This was especially the case if sexual crimes took place in the domestic sphere. Ironically, in response to the 1929 penal code's leniency with respect to honor killings, male kin and husbands were expected to protect women from harm. Public opinion held that "despite the claims of feminists" and the "illusion" of women's emancipation, women needed protection.[88]

Consequently, violence against women was seen not only a direct result of urbanization and attendant social change but also as a reflection of a modernity that had allowed women greater sexual license, and therefore greater culpability.[89] In his analysis of rape cases of the 1920s and 1930s, Piccato found that "all victims were suspected of consenting to intercourse" and that officials were confused when distinguishing between instances of rape and incidents where women engaged in "illicit sex" of their own free will.[90] Women who had become too modern and "masculine"—a conceptualization that, in case of the flapper, equated modernity and masculinity in girls with sexual abandon—had forgone their right to protection. Worse, "women should return to the behavior that made them 'the honor and the decorum of Mexican society' in a mythical prerevolutionary past."[91]

With a closer look at city girls of Cabral's illustrations and the magazine *Vea*, and the constructions of female sexuality in public space and sexual danger, it appears that it was collapsing discourses on female modernity that equated any modern girl with a wayward, oversexed flapper. This complicated the discursive terrain in which Mexican women seeking modern subject positions found themselves and in which they had to negotiate new identities. Even for women who considered themselves modern and actively fought for political rights, these collapsing discourses undermined their credibility and political agenda; their opposition to *Vea* and its projection of female sexuality in the city as pornography had less to do with decency and more to do with politics.

CONCLUSION

Women's sexual liberation was a distinct marker of Western modernization in the twentieth century, with liberal capitalist societies measuring gender equality by the barometer of female sexual liberty and sexual availability. In *The Politics of the Veil*, Joan Scott demonstrates that charges of cultural inferiority and political oppression have often been leveled against "non-Western" societies because of differences in sexual attitudes, especially where the visibility of women's sexual oppression and expression is concerned.[92] By "denuding" girls in public space, *Vea*'s editors made Mexican female bodies and sexuality legible and transparent. In keeping with modernist aesthetics, the nudity of female Deco bodies that graced *Vea*'s pages unveiled mysteries but reduced the complexity of the female form. The Deco bodies of the magazine reflected the gleam and sheen of the machine age, a homogenization of perfect bodies as both products and tools in production. The striptease, the taking off of layers, thus functioned as a critical metaphor of modernism's infatuation with legibility, one where skin becomes essence. In Cheng's words, "the new bareness" of the machine age corresponded to essence, which "has been merely displaced from interiority to exteriority."[93] *Vea* transferred the interiority of sexuality to the exterior of a woman's being, her appearance; here, her essence, her sexuality, became legible and her sense of self became modern.

Vea's "pornography" similarly underlines the importance of sexual desire in fomenting new attitudes and subjectivities during the institutional phase of the Mexican Revolution, echoing larger discourses that considered sexual desire an integral part of metropolitan modernity. Like most mainstream pornography of the early twentieth century, *Vea* sought to stimulate heterosexual encounters in order to legitimize its own existence, and as such it underwrote heteronormativity at a time when feminist consciousness and organizing was prevalent and gender identities were in flux, in one part due to the revolution, and in another to transnational trends. *Vea* taught Mexican men and women that the chica moderna was neither odd nor masculine, but rather sexually bold, attractive, and available. As such, *Vea* served to stabilize volatile gender identities by neutralizing and co-opting the chica moderna's more dangerous aspects, including her potential for female masculinity, to serve a heterosexual framework. By sexualizing and feminizing rebellious flappers, *Vea*'s endorsement of "healthy heterosexuality" did little to subvert the status quo. Rather, it helped endorse state discourses that propagated pronatalism and traditional gender roles.

Yet, *Vea*'s creation of desire, its depictions of feminized space, and the dialogue between the two also tell us about the relationship between sex, the city, and gendered revolutionary subjectivities. On the one hand, we find that the placement of women in urban landscapes reveals a fascination with female sexuality as conversant with a sophisticated, urbane femininity. In the production of feminine public space, the sexually active woman served as an emblem of transnational modernity in terms of her participation and visibility within the city's growing networks of circulation and economic exchanges. Much like visual discourses that connected female mobility, beauty, and Deco bodies, *Vea*'s girls made Mexico City into a bright space of transnational modernity, wrapping sites of tension and contestation, government and commerce, tradition and innovation in a seductive, feminine embrace. As such, the magazine signaled an acceptance of middle-class women in public and envisioned female mobility, both physical and social, as desirable. *Vea* showed that female sexuality made Mexico City beautiful, attractive, and above all, modern.

On the other hand, *Vea*'s feminized cityscapes problematized the ideological messages concerning gender and space inherent in revolutionary reform and popular culture, as well as women's bids for political recognition and power. By claiming symbolic access to the male bastions of national importance in the capital city, *Vea*'s chicas modernas appeared to use seduction as a means to subvert patriarchal power. Yet many women's groups who objected to the magazine as immoral did not experience *Vea*'s sexualized female space as either liberatory or empowering. By reducing women's power once again to female sexuality and women's sexuality to "frivolity," *Vea* easily could have been construed as standing in the way of a women's political agenda. While vying for suffrage rights, elite, white, middle-class urban women might not have wanted to be discredited by depictions of women like themselves as superficial girls interested only in posing as pinups, or to have their access to urban space and, by extension, the public sphere hampered by something that they feared might weaken their bid for political power.

Bataclanismo had invited Mexican women of all classes and ethnicities to embody the Deco aesthetic, to freely move around the modern metropolis and engage in the daily performance of transgressing social and gender boundaries. According to Anne McClintock, inversions of the traditional gender order as expressed in dress, work, sex, and boundary crossings are not merely acts of resistance; rather, they constitute ambiguous zones where women and men work out the tensions between social norms, fantasy, and desires. Tellingly, these dangerous zones need to be "secured" and transformed into spectacles through the exchange of money by paying women for their "performance."[94] Mexico City's spatial configuration of desire—Plaza Garibaldi, the carpas, the revista theaters, and the zones of prostitution—all had been secured by capitalist-endorsed spectacle. On the other hand, women who drew on this spectacle in order to enact the lives they envisioned proved difficult to place, both for those who endorsed this liberation and those who hoped to stifle it.

By clearing *Vea*'s feminine sexual frivolity off the streets yet condoning other magazines' sensationalistic portrayals of prostitution and other dangers tied to sexual liberty, the Mexican revolutionary state affirmed its policy to contain female sexuality to either the zonas libres or the conjugal home. The movement of women—especially middle-class women—into lower-class, sexualized parts of the city that had been set aside as areas of containment confounded officials. Female visitors in pornotopia added to the instability of female identities.

No longer was there an easy way to distinguish "decent women" from prostitutes. The magazine's prohibition shows that what is allowed and acceptable is as much about content (nudity) as it is about context (place). In contrast to *Vea*, most of Mexico City's popular press played out the tensions between the nude physiques of camposcape as natural bodies in an idyllic pastoral place outside of time, on the one hand, and the sexualized Deco bodies of the pornotopic underworld that represented the embodiment of deviant desires, on the other. *Vea* projected sexualized female cityscapes as healthy, artistic, and beautiful, whereas other publications condemned the vice, scandal, and sexual libertinage of the underworld. The relationship that *Vea* intimated between female bodies, historic landmarks, and the nation-state was of an urban, subversive nature when compared to the pastoral, idyllic nudity inherent in the ardent nationalism of revolutionary art production.

Consequently, *Vea*'s girls inverted and confused the underworld and the camposcape, reversing representational categories of sexuality, and with it, what constituted women's proper place. Even if *Vea*'s symbolism linking female sexuality and urban space invoked a multitude of readings, ranging from selling or beautifying the city to feminizing or scandalizing it, they all inherently contained the notion that the city was now a public stage for women. *Vea*'s placement of female bodies in the city compromised what was already a highly contested space. An uneasy mix of desire for modernity and progress, monuments and nationalism, and anxiety over women in public underpinned the agenda of revolutionary urban reform in Mexico City. *Vea*'s girls subverted ideas of gendered public space and sexual governance held by officials and reformers, but they also illustrated ideas connecting women, alternate femininities, and modernity. As we will see in the next chapter, these gendered tensions present in the search for cosmopolitan modernity influenced urban reformers and architects as they set out to fashion a revolutionary city.

Planning the Deco City

URBAN REFORM

By the early 1930s, visitors entering the new Parque México were greeted by a statue of a robust indigenous woman. Pouring water from two large urns into a small pool of blue water, the woman beckoned passersby away from the hustle and bustle of the large new thoroughfare of Insurgentes to a place where life was tranquil, easy, and uncorrupted by modern life (fig. 17). What visitors and residents of the surrounding colonia Condesa encountered upon entering the park, however, was more than a shady respite of trails, ponds, and fountains, even though the park counted these treasures among its charms. Directly beyond the fountain, on the grounds that had once housed the upscale horse-racing track Hipódromo, visitors came to a large open-air theater. Bathed in Art Deco, the theater's stage was graced by two slender columns bearing two women significantly distinct from the indígena: tall, angular, and white (fig. 18). Named after the first man to accomplish the feat of transcontinental flight, the Teatro al Aire Libre Lindbergh and its Deco bodies inspired Mexicans to reach for the skies.

The completion of Parque México coincided with the first great push in urban reform since the Porfiriato. From 1929 until 1934 officials concentrated on large public-works projects, including market buildings, parks, and monuments. The planning and building of the upscale, middle-class colonia Condesa, a neighborhood that typified Art Deco architecture, occurred nearly at the same time. While some Deco buildings, such as La Nacional, had been built in the centro, planners of the late 1920s and early 1930s were careful not to insert what they deemed to be aesthetically divergent styles into the city's

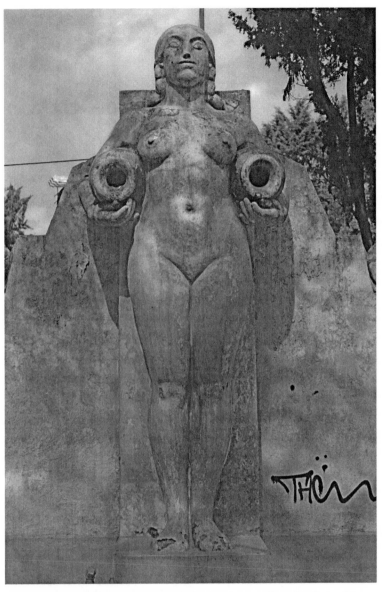

FIG. 17. Statue, Parque México, colonia Condesa, 1927. Photo by the author.

FIG. 18. Teatro Lindbergh stage (detail), constructed in 1927. Photo by the author.

colonial core. They hoped to safeguard not only the centro's colonial mansions, which they viewed as national monuments, but the entire colonial area, which they hoped to preserve as a veritable museum. Colonia Condesa, on the other hand, presented private enterprise with opportunities to turn profits on the upper- and middle-class demand for modern housing in a cosmopolitan setting. The ascending class sought to live in comfort and beauty, and for this they looked to the world of entertainment, a realm where they encountered Deco bodies. Bataclanismo and the magazine *Vea* demonstrated that artistic Deco bodies came to represent health, beauty, and sexual freedom, and they aligned these with a desirable cosmopolitan modernity. Instead of the "pornography" of the underworld, in *Vea* one could gaze on healthy and lighthearted bataclanas placed demonstratively in the cityscape. This practice inadvertently echoed architectural debates that similarly intertwined women and urban space, health and urban reform, and most of all, bodies and buildings. Architects commissioned to design the buildings of the revolutionary era conceived of urban renewal in terms of engineering feminine beauty, where—like *Vea*—the semi-nude Deco bodies of the stage formed an aesthetic blueprint for creating a modern city.

COLONIA CONDESA

Parque México was the front-runner of larger construction efforts in the creation of colonia Condesa (fig. 19), the first and arguably the only Art Deco neighborhood in the city. Despite its promise of futurity and fast-paced sensibilities, the development of the neighborhood took place gradually. For its early history we have to go back to colonia Roma and Circus Orrin, a stroll of a few blocks to the north and east and about twenty-five years back in time, when a circus proprietor secured the rights to develop the district.

The construction of the upscale colonia Roma, the first planned neighborhood in the city, started when the Compañía de Terrenos de la Calzada de Chapultepec, headed by the Briton Edward Walter Orrin of the immensely popular Circus Orrin, secured the building rights in December 1901. Named after the old pueblo of Romito, the new neighborhood would comprise lots of various sizes, ranging from four hundred to five thousand square meters (roughly 0.10 to 1.25 acres), and was envisioned to house stately mansions surrounded by large gardens and other upscale urban residences. The price of lots reached upward to 25 pesos per square meter on the installment plan, while houses built by the company sold at between 14,000 and 18,000 pesos

FIG. 19. Map of colonia Condesa, ca. 1930s. Courtesy of the author.

per structure. The most obvious connection between the entertainment magnate and the new community was its streets, all of which were to bear names of illustrious European cities visited at one time by the famous *circo*.[1] Roma would become an upscale neighborhood for wealthy Porfirians and illustrious divas like María Conesa and Esperanza Iris as well as the architect responsible for the Art Nouveau exterior of the Palacio de Bellas Artes, Adamo Boari.[2]

A year after acquiring the rights to Roma, Orrin and company founded the Compañía Colonia de la Condesa and set about developing the new neighborhood. With 200,000 pesos in capital, the company enjoyed the administrative advice of one Fernando Pimentel y Fagoaga and a list of stockholders that read like a who's who of the Porfirian elite, including José Yves Limantour, Enrique Creel, and Porfirio Díaz Jr. The development company, which also included U.S. investor Cassius Clay Lamm, carefully followed the municipal restrictions that had been put in place in 1903. The new regulations were designed to standardize the city, and to that end they stipulated street widths, naming schemes of streets in the city, paving of streets and sidewalks, construction of sewage and potable water systems, tree planting, and the ceding of land for public amenities such as parks, markets, and schools. Streetcar lines were to connect the area to the city center by 1913. Despite these auspicious beginnings, the company had a relatively short lifespan and was liquidated in 1907, delaying the Condesa's full development until the 1920s.[3]

Even if Roma and Condesa dated to the turn of the century and were conceptualized as middle-class colonias that, according to some urban historians, bore the imprint of Porfirian city planning, they also demonstrated vast differences.[4] Colonia Condesa was named after the seventeenth-century hacienda known for its French and Italian flower gardens, a celebration of excessive wealth. But unlike its ornate, European-style counterpart, this zone was emblematic of the development of the numerous new middle- and upper-class neighborhoods that reflected a conceptualization of modernity based on U.S.-style capitalism and architectural innovations. With its "Art Deco, Moderne and International Style buildings and Anglo-American-inspired garden-city planning" that echoed camposcape, Condesa had become Mexico's most modern, fashionable, and Western neighborhood by the early 1930s.[5]

The development of Condesa was interwoven with the political and economic ambitions of the new revolutionary elite. Many of the new colonias, of which Condesa was to be the exemplar, were developed by real estate developer José de la Lama. In 1925, de la Lama asked permission from the ayuntamiento to "divide the lands originally belonging to the Jockey Club in the former Hipódromo de la Condesa," the open land that housed what was left of the dilapidated Porfirian racetrack that had been abandoned fifteen years earlier. The project was to include "30,000 square meters [roughly 7.5 acres] of land for green spaces, and 20,000 square meters [about 5 acres] for public services, including schools, a church and a market." Although la Lama's earlier proposal for the Condesa had been turned down, a 1924 change in the leadership of the ayuntamiento allowed the new council to approve the Jockey Club deal "on the eve of more stringent laws that would have placed limits on such a subdivision."[6] President Plutarco Elías Calles and national power brokers of his inner circle were directly involved in building the new neighborhood. Arturo de Saracho, former spy and later ambassador to Spain, met with close friend President Calles in August 1926 to finalize the contract for the Compañía Fraccionadora y Constructora del Hipódromo de la Condesa, in which they both appeared to have some financial stake. Moreover, Calles's daughter Hortensia and her husband, Fernando Torreblanca, who happened to be Calles's main secretary, soon moved into a private mansion in Condesa across from the colonia's second park, Parque España.[7]

The start of construction of houses in the new *fraccionamiento* (colonia in the making) Hipódromo-Condesa followed the design and example of its principal park, Parque México, envisioned to function as the heart of the new colonia.[8] Engineer José Luis Cuevas set aside 67,000 square meters (about 16.5 acres) to construct the park and Teatro Lindbergh, named after the aviator who had graced Mexico with a visit earlier that year.[9] With the park's combination of beauty and a focus on the "modern lines" of contemporary architecture, officials of the Departamento de Obras Públicas (Department of Public Works) believed it equaled, if not surpassed, the illustrious Alameda Central in the city center and the enormous Bosque de Chapultepec on the city's west side. Parque México was designed to function as a place with campo-like characteristics, such as a waterfall, lush foliage, an abundance of trees, and a variety of plants to provide the shade and tranquillity that the other new large parks lacked.[10] Parque México was part of a larger project on the part of the revolutionary state to promote sports, outdoor recreation, and the idea that healthy minds reside in healthy bodies. Other new sport parks designed and executed by the DDF planning commission were, they argued, too far away, too vast to be inviting, and so austere that working-class people did not feel comfortable entering them. Centro Deportivo Venustiano Carranza, the largest of these parks, consisted of an enormous terrain once destined to become a prison and was chosen by DDF officials to serve their revolutionary vision as a center of constructive freedom and instructive play.[11]

Juxtapositioned against the largesse and grandeur of these established parks, Parque México's meandering paths, quiet demeanor, and echoes of an idealized campo as embodied by the grand indígena greeting the visitor at its entrance were infused with post-revolutionary discursive assemblages of artistic and indigenista camposcape, reminding urbanites of the proper demarcations of revolutionary mexicanidad. Predating comprehensive urban plans that aimed to augment sanitary and health conditions in the capital city, stipulating that "unbuilt acreage was to be converted into parks and gardens,"[12] the park would both invoke and neutralize what Mark Seltzer calls "the psychotopography of the machine culture." Being able to escape the hustle and bustle of the modern city with its motorized traffic, factories, and mechanized life, visitors to Parque México could imagine themselves transported into a place of timeless aesthetics, where landscapes were converted into "arrested" natural panoramas of a still-life image, scenery such as that of "cinematographic illusionism."[13]

Unlike venues such as the Carranza sports complex, Parque México, which was surrounded by Condesa's Deco architecture and middle-class sensibilities, did not have the appearance of a space created for lower-class recreation. Yet its appeal of camposcape, especially when taken together with didactic spaces to gather significant audiences, served to remind both fashionable urbanites and lower-class visitors of their revolutionary responsibilities. Unlike Bosque de Chapultepec and Alameda Central, Parque México included modern amenities that carried a price tag of 211,000 pesos. On the smaller end of the park, cut in two by Michoacán Street, the city placed a radio tower that also functioned as a clock surrounded by a small plaza with benches for the radio listeners. Instead of commercial radio, public receivers aired governmental programs created by the Secretaría de Educación Publica (Department of Education).[14] Patience Shell finds that "simply being outdoors could not guarantee moral improvement" and hence had to be supervised. Parks were suspect for illicit (sexual) behavior, and Condesa's didactic value extended to its design and carefully placed messages to teach park-goers how to behave properly in green spaces. An abundance of signs dating to the park's inception (and still in existence today) warned visitors against straying off paths, littering, eating in the park, and allowing children to play unsupervised. While the middle class might have embraced such moralization, the real purpose behind this popular attraction was to provide an opportunity to enlighten lower-class people from "less moral parts of the city."[15]

The park's Teatro Lindbergh functioned equally as an educational space and a multi-class nexus. The large, open-air theater was what made the park unique. Positioned near a large pond and fronted by a fountain with "a statue of woman," as the staff casually referred to our formidable indígena, it could hold three hundred artists and about eight thousand spectators, seven thousand in front of the stage and another thousand under the two large, curving pergolas that—above and beyond their function of framing the theater space—were designed as an area to serve as theater boxes.[16] Like the Teatro del Pueblo (discussed in chapter 6), Teatro Lindbergh was part of a wave of national and revolutionary theaters designed to educate the lower classes through entertainment. But here in the upscale Condesa, proletarian theater seemed out of place alongside the emphasis on bourgeois modernity, luxury, and refinement. Little is known regarding what types of performances were scheduled at the open-air venue, but records of one concert in April 1934 indicate that a group of 250 inmates from the Casa de Orientación (a correctional facility) performed a mise-en-scène set to music titled *Fuerza campesina* (Farmer strength). It was aimed at teaching urban audiences about Emiliano Zapata's struggle for land on behalf of the "great masses of rural workers."[17]

While women of the lower classes performed working-class functions in Teatro Lindbergh, the colonia's residents preferred more upscale amusements. Both Roma and the nascent Condesa had traditionally been dominated by bullfighting, evidenced by an enormous ring built in 1907 that dominated Condesa's physical and cultural landscape, along with the aforementioned Jockey Club's racetrack. In the 1920s, bullfighting aficionados relaxed in restaurant Son-Sin at the intersection of Sonora and Sinaloa Streets before and after fights, while enjoying the taste of *carne seca* (a dried-beef dish from northern Mexico) and the sounds of *corridos* (folk songs popularized during the revolution) that immortalized the feats of famous toreadors. The elegant Cine Balmori on Jalisco Street (later the avenida Álvaro Obregón) attracted an elite crowd that also frequented the adjacent Café Globo for baked treats after shows or went out to restaurants such as Eréndira and Donají for regional fare from Oaxaca and Michoacán. The street was home to the Parían, named after the famous great colonial market on the Zócalo, where housewives would shop so as to avoid the crowded, lower-class markets in the center.[18]

Moreover, the colonia's modernity, Art Deco architecture, and penchant for spectacle came to be associated with women of the city's entertainment industry as the most visible element of the ascendant capitalist class with close ties to the national levels of politics. In an apparent spoof on the life of María Conesa, José Vasconcelos's *El banquete de palacio* told the story of "la Condesa," a Spanish actress and chanteuse retired from the theater. Condesa was a slender, white beauty with dark eyes and "nervous flesh," and her famed sensuality caused adolescents' eyes to glaze over and incited políticos' libidos to "show her off like a new car to their trusted friends." After seducing the likes of Francisco Villa and many Carranzista and Obregonista generals, Vasconcelos's Condesa stages her comeback in the late 1920s under direction of President Calles, who installed the Condesa in one of the best palaces of the "colonia Callista." There, according to Vasconcelos, she shared power and wealth with one of the *jefes* (political bosses) of the Calles administration.[19] In the story, Condesa functioned as a stand-in for the newly built neighborhood during the Calles years. The star herself lived in Roma, not far from the new colonia, with a high-level Callista administrator.[20]

Cronista Cube Bonifant equally linked modern, fashionable girls with the colonia. In one of her columns she described such a young woman: "high heels, short skirt, a face that resembles a pattern of colors—red lips, pink cheeks, blue eyelids, black eyelashes, brown eyebrows, the rest purple—blond hair, curled, a lock of hair that covers ... half of the face." As part of this colorful description, Bonifant paints a street scene where this young woman attracts the attention of a group of young men. In a signature Bonifant moment, the cronista describes the girl walking her little dog in front of male admirers as a young starlet enacting her neighborhood: the girl is colonia Roma-Condesa.[21]

If Condesa served Porfirian entrepreneurs and the new revolutionary elite—groups that readily overlapped—Parque México's physical camposcape and performed camposcapes in Teatro Lindbergh served to remind residents of the presence of the new revolutionary state and its commitment to less fortunate citizens. In its attempt to usurp or appropriate ideals of camposcape, now infused with revolutionary rhetoric of health, reform, and mexicanidad, Parque México and the surrounding colonia Condesa could be cynically viewed as the creation of what Guy Debord in *The Society of the Spectacle* called a "pseudo-countryside," the inevitable by-product of capitalist-propelled urbanism of commodified experience that passes as "a moment of authentic life" which simply "turns out to be merely a life more *authentically spectacular*." However, Parque México can also be seen as a means to realize the futuristic vision of architects and planners like Le Corbusier, who believed that modern technology would facilitate the "advantages of the Garden City with those of the traditional city" and create an urban environment of "parklands" where, "instead of the population moving to the suburbs, the suburbs move into the city." Harking back to Thomas More's *Utopia* (1516), where citizens are mandated to live two years in the country so they might constructively inhabit "garden cities," Condesa's modern cosmopolitan living is in keeping with Le Corbusier's notion that while "work and domestic life take place in high-rise structures, cultivation of the spirit and body takes place in the parkland."[22]

Ultimately, Condesa became a showcase of new middle-class wealth and tastes built by the revolutionary elite and provided an "image of modernity, prosperity and a renewed sense of nationalism" for middle-class Mexicans. As Salvador Novo remarked, young, elegant people considered themselves lucky if they could move to the Hipódromo-Condesa. The renowned painter Pedro Friedeberg, who lived on Condesa's calle Amsterdam in the late 1930s and early 1940s as a child, described the family apartment as modern and "enormous," its large walls decorated with mosaics depicting the feats of Don Quixote and Sancho Panza. The building, a "tower of babel" with its array of international inhabitants (mostly Europeans escaping World War II), also counted four gigantic interior patios with concrete fountains tiled with serpent motifs and "geometric, Aztecoid forms that were part of the architectural style used in colonia Condesa-Hipodromo."[23]

Parque México earned lavish praise from landscape architects for being an "elegant and ultra-modern corner of the capital." Indeed, its appeal to melancholic anachronism notwithstanding, visitors were reassured that "traveling" through the park, like the spaces of healthy, artistic, and stylized nudism, was an exercise in revolutionary modernity. Much of Condesa's success hinged on its reputation as a purely Art Deco neighborhood, one that was, Patrice Olsen notes, "without a doubt, one of the most clear and vivid examples of the important aesthetic resources displayed by Deco," and, I would add, one that demonstrated the links between camposcape, modernity, and sultry women, a space where the Deco bodies of *Vea*'s bataclanas could be in place.[24]

ARCHITECTURAL VISIONS: "DECO-TECTURE"

Mexican architecture of the 1920s came into its own at a time when architecture around the globe, especially in Europe and the United States, was undergoing great changes in the wake of World War I. During the Porfiriato, artists and architects had employed Art Nouveau in their beautifications efforts of urban landscapes in an effort to copy European designs. The style exemplified dreaminess, irrationality, and eroticism woven into depictions of nature, women, and buildings.[25] Art Nouveau architecture, consequently, was feminine in conception, and its use of new materials such as glass, textile, and metal expressed the movement's emphasis on decoration and a flowing, organic style that was considered highly feminine. In keeping with the reign of orientalism, new structures were executed in mixtures of Japanese, arabesque, and Gothic styles dripping with ornamentation. For instance, the buildings of the Spanish architect Antoní Gaudí revisited the traditional Mudéjar style by way of a Gothic fantasyland. Most of his work appeared fragmented and kaleidoscopic, without beginning or end. When critics dismissed Gaudí's work or that of other Art Nouveau architects, they labeled it as feminized and decadent, "colonial rather than cosmopolitan."[26]

Despite its critics, Art Nouveau was considered well suited to a newly emerging capitalist world driven by advertising and other expressions of consumerism. Clothing design, a renewed emphasis on stained glass (such as the famous Tiffany Company), and intricate and delicate metalwork used for interiors as well as building facades, railings, entrances, and window frames typified products fashioned for an increasingly feminine consumer market. Art Nouveau enhanced the feminine appeal of the department store, the crystal palace, and the theater as a new way of seeing that undergirded late-nineteenth-century capitalist development.

Mexican architects followed Art Nouveau's celebration of organic design and decoration as the hallmarks of feminine splendor. Female beauty, so often defined by popular stage divas such as Esperanza Iris, also inspired the architectural design of her theater as well as many of the new buildings in the posh area west of the centro. In the Centro Mercantil, the Gran Hotel de México, built in 1896, showcased an elaborate stain-glass ceiling designed by Jaques Gruber and an elevator made of forged iron and glass. The rebuilt Art Nouveau structure originally was designed for the Düsseldorf Industrial Art Exhibition in 1902 (now Chopo Museum) and added a distinct European Jugendstil allure to the western colonia of Santa Maria la Ribera.[27] Most illustrative was the design of Italian architect Adamo Boari's new Palacio de Bellas Artes, which revealed that a focus on Art Nouveau dominated Porfirian architectural aesthetics and that "ornamentation reigned supreme."[28]

Interior spaces, too, bore the hallmarks of Art Nouveau, especially the houses of elite and ascendant middle-class residents. The Mexican surrealist artist Pedro Friedeberg lived with his grandparents in colonia San Rafael (on a street that is now Insurgentes Norte) before moving to the new colonia Condesa. The large, stately Porfirian building that was the family home of his youth looked out on what would become the Monumento a la Revolución. It also housed the Greek embassy on the first floor, while the servants occupied a musty, dark basement. Friedeberg remembers his grandparents' house as a place with lots of "atmosphere," marquees of leaded glass, a roof terrace, large rooms with Jugendstil furniture, oriental rugs, and wallpaper with patterns that hypnotized the young child, who would get trapped tracing and studying the lines of borders, arabesques, and "tarantulas." The Art Nouveau decorations included reproductions of Böcklin paintings that depicted mermaids and druidic rituals.[29]

The reliance on Art Nouveau ceased, however, when the "long nineteenth century" came to a crashing halt. In the effort to turn away from the errors and perceived evils of old regimes, not only politicians but also artists, authors, and architects looked for meaningful new expressions to effect real political and social change. In the United States, the bold and daring skyscrapers that came to dominate the urban landscapes of Chicago and New York City designed by the likes of Louis Sullivan, Daniel Burnham, and John Wellborn Root, as well as the "pure design" Prairie school homes by Frank Lloyd Wright, signaled that architects were ready to break with the "stylistic purity" of the Beaux Arts and erect tall structures based on "fundamental ahistorical principles of composition," ones that reflected stark geometrical shapes.[30] Futurism, functionalism, and their descendant modernism drastically rejected the past as they embraced the machine age and its new technologies to craft a "new culture of the masses," in Europe. Movements such as De Stijl (The Netherlands), Bauhaus (Germany), and L'Esprit Nouveau (France), of which Le Corbusier's work was highly influential, revolved around the concepts of simplicity, objectivity, and collectivism.

In its rejection of the past, the new architecture sought to liberate itself from Art Nouveau's heavy emphasis on ornamentation, its Beaux Arts luxury, and the lack of political commitment to larger social goals. Despite Art Nouveau's claim as a popular movement, its handcrafted products had been available predominantly to a rich minority. Moreover, over time its emphasis on individuality and originality had given way to "repeatable forms based on vernacular and classical."[31] Adolf Loos, the Austro-Hungarian architect whose work predated and influenced many modernists, came out strongly against the frills and eclecticism of Art Nouveau and declared ornamentation a crime. The architectural styles that developed in the wake of World War I stressed practicality over aesthetics, function over form, machine over nature, and, even if idealized and stylized, future over past. As Alan Colquhoun eloquently puts it: "Whereas previous avant-gardes, from Art Nouveau to Expressionism, had sought to rescue tradition by means of the very modernity that threatened to destroy it, Futurism advocated the obliteration of all traces of traditional culture and the creation of a totally new, machine-based culture of the masses."[32] Functionalism and futurism thus marked a strong turn away from "borrowed styles," instead offering the honesty of simple lines, geometric shapes, and plain surfaces to better symbolize the modern era. Stripped of "dishonest" elements such as "false fronts" that "masked the true physical reality of the building," architecture could be born anew.[33]

Yet the functionalist dictum "form follows function," originally championed by Louis Sullivan, resulted in the cultivation of a particular modernist aesthetic rather than a total lack of visual markers. Stressing vertical lines, simplified geometrical patterns, and ordered spaces, the modernist movement that grew out of functionalism and futurism increasingly adopted a "machine aesthetic" that, instead of hiding industrial structures and materials, would reveal them. Le Corbusier might have emphasized functionality and efficiency by conceptual-izing the home as "a machine for living" and "the planned city as a large efficient machine with many closely calibrated parts," but his view still contained a particular aesthetic. He saw in architecture an art form that most effectively "achieves a state of platonic grandeur, mathematical order, speculation, the perception of harmony that lies in emotional relationships." Like many of his contemporaries, he had, finds the historian James Scott, a "love (or mania?) for simple repetitive lines" and held reason to be "an unbroken … straight line."[34]

The influence of functionalism can be seen across Latin America, but most especially in Brazil and Argentina. At the invitation of both governments, Le Corbusier traveled to Latin America in 1929, visiting Montevideo and São Paulo as well as Buenos Aires and Rio de Janeiro, and drafted urban-renewal plans for the last two cities. Taken with the grandeur of the continent and the seemingly limitless possibilities for a modernist future, he saw in South America "a renewed energy capable of doing away with all academic methods." Although Le Corbusier's plans were rejected at the time, parts of them would be taken up and realized many years later during the Vargas years (1930–45 and 1951–54) and the 1960s. His vision for Latin America came to greatest fruition in Brasilia: a completely new, rigorously planned city wrought out of the chaos of the jungle.[35]

Although Le Corbusier never visited Mexico, young Mexican architects of the 1920s were enthusiastic about modernism and the possibilities of adapting functionalist ideas to serve Mexican cityscapes. But the embrace of these new forms was waylaid in the wake of the revolution as Mexican architects searched for a new, national style that would best express the revolutionary objectives and demand for political, economic, and social reform. The development of Mexican architecture was a complex and often contradictory process during this time, as many styles vied for dominance. While no single, unique style emerged, the neocolonial style enjoyed the most favor in the 1920s, when the new revolutionary state became a "facilitator of innovative architecture."[36] For many, neocolonialism best expressed a nationalist architecture during the period of the institutionalized revolution. As early as 1914, Federico Mariscal gave a series of lectures that were "critical to the establishment of new architectural ethos toward the Mexican past," a vision that reached a larger audience with the 1915 publication of his *La patria y la arquitectura nacional* (The fatherland and national architecture). Mariscal outlined a project of mestizaje in overcoming Mexico's dependence on French positivism, which had dominated Mexican architecture as well as education since the onset of the Porfiriato. According to Enrique de Anda Alanís, Mariscal proposed that viceregal architecture, harking back to a colonial style, was "integral to Mexican culture" and national identity. Anda Alanís finds that because of Mariscal's prominent position in the architect guild, his vision provided an "intellectual framework" and ethos that most architects of the period would turn to,[37] as he inspired architects to "awaken that colonial tradition and infuse it with the vigor of the revolution."[38]

In attempting to create a viable distance between the architectural "exotic eclecticism" of the Porfiriato, the neocolonial style served as an expression of nationalism by working with regional materials, including *tezontle* (volcanic rock used in construction since Aztec times and recycled in colonial buildings), *azulejos* (blue ceramic tile), and *chiluca* (gray stone used since pre-Colombian times also recycled in colonial architecture). This allowed for a single approach without alienating either the conservative segments of society, which feared drastic revolutionary change, or the progressives, who looked to the past in order to establish an authentic Mexican identity.[39] Like Mariscal, José Vasconcelos, the writer-philosopher and ardent nationalist who headed the Department of Education from 1920 to 1924, actively promoted the neocolonial style as a "reflection of mexicanidad." Conceptualizing buildings in themselves as an education for both students and educators, he offered big government budgets to architects willing to build in the neocolonial style.[40]

Yet not all architects of the era were in favor of the neocolonial style. As a "primarily a horizontal style," it proved costly in the face of rising land prices and was not appropriate for the significant number of schools, hospitals, housing, and office buildings that the city's growing population needed. There were also ideological motives for rejecting the colonial past as the marker of the present, as questions remained about its suitability as the national style. The more radical young architects who trained at the Academy of San Carlos and felt that the objective of the revolution was to modernize the nation found the neocolonial style "incongruent with the needs of the 'real world' and unable to assimilate the new culture" of revolutionary transformation in both architecture and society at large. This small group, made up of "vocal" intellectuals, architects, and engineers influenced by functionalism—including the architects Juan O'Gorman, Alvaro Aburto, and Juan Legarreta—clamored for a new architecture that would fulfill the promises of the revolution and "what they perceived to be its central objective: to modernize the nation." Le Corbusier, Bauhaus, Loos, and Gropius offered these new architects in search of a socially conscious architecture a style where "form does not determine function, but function determines form."[41]

In their response to revolutionary reform and the surfacing of new architectural forms in Europe and the United States, most of Mexico's architects fell into two camps: those who opted for the neocolonial style, which they thought best fit the city's "historic district," and functionalists like O'Gorman, who believed the revolution would be best served by a stripped-down modernism.[42] Functionalism, however, was "not destined to remake the city quickly." While it eventually made deep inroads in Mexican architecture, facilitated by new materials such as cement (more widely available through new state-backed cement factories), functionalism too met with considerable criticism, especially from those architects who lamented its lack of "Mexican character" and aesthetics. The tension over what best represented Mexico's national identity resulted from colliding viewpoints alternately privileging tradition or modernity, preservation or renewal. In response, moderates such as Mariscal, who designed and built Teatro Iris and finished the Palacio de Bellas Artes (see chapter 7), championed neocolonialism mostly out of aesthetic considerations. Mariscal believed that beauty could not be separated from the totality of architecture and hence that functionalism was too narrow in its objectives.[43] In his framework, architects not only developed a new architecture for the revolutionary period but also were responsible for safeguarding colonial buildings as national patrimony. Hence, concepts of the new went hand-in-glove with the past, like architecture with archaeology. Younger architects, however, believed that functionalism freed them from the past and from a "facile copying of French or other styles," giving them "a freedom that would allow them to assert a Mexican identity in architecture." O'Gorman in particular found in functionalism a style that kept architects from "having to resort to the anachronistic." Antonio Muñoz García, who built the Mercado Abelardo Rodríguez (see chapter 6), found the new neocolonial buildings to be "absurd" in their attempt to "revive a dead architecture" that risked "converting architecture into archeology."[44]

In the debates over which architectural style best suited revolutionary objectives and a national style, Art Deco proved to be a compromise that many Mexican architects could agree on. Named "posthumously" (in the 1960s), Art Deco, which took its name from the 1925 Exposition Internationale des Arts Décoratifs et Industriels Modernes, referred to the style that surfaced between 1910 and 1935 and influenced an array of material culture: fashion, arts, jewelry, housewares, architecture, and interior design. The aim of the exposition, which drew the participation of an array of different designers, among them Le Corbusier, was to "reassert French dominance in the decorative arts." Although the eclecticism of Art Deco (which was known at the time simply as *style moderne*) appeared to share in the exotic and hedonist legacy of Art Nouveau, Deco artists also sought to fashion a new style that would reflect modernity. Rejecting the emphasis on nature and natural form, Art Deco looked to the modern city of the machine age and was referred to by some as the "skyscraper style." In its imagery and graphics, Art Deco celebrated mechanical production, speed, and efficiency, fostering collaboration among industry, mass production, and art.[45] Unlike more radical modernists, however, Deco artists embraced consumerism and rejected leftist idealism. While sharing the sense of an aesthetic modernism with functionalism, it clearly lacked its social concerns.[46]

Art Deco ushered in a "transitional period" in Mexican architecture, providing warring factions with a conciliatory position. However, Art Deco did not dominate Mexico's post-revolutionary architectural landscape; it was but one of what Olsen has described as a jumble of architectural styles that vied for dominance in the post-revolutionary city. Yet in its ready adaptability, Art Deco lent itself well to the revolution's penchant for mestizaje and hybridity. Architects in search of a mestizo modernity believed that Art Deco best expressed a modernist aesthetic that Mexicans could live with.[47] Moreover, Art Deco proposed a familiar concept: female beauty, and more specifically, the female form that constituted a central tenet of this design.

CITY-BODIES: THE SOCIAL
CONSTRUCTION OF FEMALE SPACE

Mexican architects who would execute the majority of urban-reform efforts of the 1920s and early 1930s had learned to think of the built environment as an expression of female beauty. The majority of them had come of age during the Porfiriato and had been trained at the country's most prestigious school of fine arts, the Academy of San Carlos. When receiving commissions to design the buildings of the revolutionary era, they conceived of urban renewal in terms of feminine beauty and enhancing female space.

The *Plan de estudios de la Escuela Nacional de Bellas Artes*, which outlined the study of architecture at the academy, ensured that aspiring architects (the vast majority of whom were men) spent most of their time in the classroom engaged in drawing.[48] The Department of Education stipulated that a thorough knowledge of the proportions of the human body, acquired through drawing, was of principal importance to the study of architecture. Although students copied models from photographs or plaster, they also had ample opportunity to sketch live subjects, which were often nude female models. Students also had to take courses in sculpture, where they again concentrated on the human form. Not until the fourth year of study did students spend most of their time concentrating on the technical facets of architecture, such as architectural theories, topography, building materials, legal codes, and "hygiene"—in other words, the construction of healthy spaces with sanitary facilities and sufficient ventilation. Consequently, their training focused on aesthetics, not the technical aspects of architecture; instead, classes focused on honing students' skills through drawing plants, animals, and other ornamentation centered on the classic female nude.[49] Young architects who came of age during the late Porfiriato and early revolutionary years learned to conceptualize buildings based on their visual interpretation of human bodies, mostly the female body. Not only did architecture students turn to the female nude for inspiration in designing buildings, but they first practiced their art in the realm of entertainment. They took part in competitions to design and decorate the main space and stage of Teatro Arbeu for the city's university graduation ceremony in 1913. Students were instructed to submit designs under a pseudonym, stay close to the architectural style of the theater, and keep to a budget of one thousand pesos.[50] Thus, aspiring architects first practiced designing interiors on theaters, where the conceptualization of space revolved around the nexus of female spectacle and performance.

Even if the Department of Education's program in training architects changed slightly during the revolution, the emphasis on the construction of beauty remained. In 1915, instruction in fine arts underwent a reorganization that seemed indicative of the momentous changes in Mexican society. In one the first programs that directly affected the way education would be conceptualized, Undersecretary Felix Palavicini (incidentally, a childhood friend of Esperanza Iris) underscored the importance of education as a comprehensive project in the creation of new citizens. The main Constitutionalist objective of this mission entailed a nationalization of the country's culture, spearheaded by the new Secretaría de Bellas Artes (Department of Fine Arts), which was instructed to rescue architectural treasures, mostly colonial in origin, as national patrimony. Any foreign influence that had been dominant during the dictatorship, a time of "mediocre spectacles" when art had been but an "imported luxury article," would be eradicated. Instead, the department would encourage national production of the arts by promoting a larger understanding, and diffusion, of aesthetics. For instance, in order to ensure the beauty of public buildings' exteriors, the task of inspecting their construction, which had been under the supervision of the Department of Public Works, came under the domain of the Department of Fine Arts. Architecture itself, however, was removed from the fine arts roster and placed within the school of engineering, which the department's administrators considered "its natural place."[51]

Despite the change in the study of architecture from art to engineering, the architecture curriculum appears to have changed little during and directly after the revolution, with a sense of the centrality of aesthetics remaining. Up until the mid-1920s, at the Academy of San Carlos, "nineteenth-century eclecticism dominated ... the curriculum," and "student projects involved copying the style of the past." In 1925, the arrival of functionalist José Villagrán García at the academy forced a change in the curriculum in providing a chance to study modern architecture. However, in general, professors were more interested in replicating traditional aesthetics than in the workings of engineering and construction.[52] Consequently, architects who came of age during the late Porfiriato and early revolutionary years continued to learn that buildings were based on the visual interpretation of human bodies, the female body in particular.

Mexican architects were not the only ones to connect the building of urban structures with women's bodies and define cityscape in terms of female space; consciously or not, they drew on a long tradition that associated the development of cities with an understanding of the built environment as an expression of female space. From humankind's earliest attempts at creating settlements, finds Lewis Mumford, the move toward permanent residences entailed a process of "domestication." More than envisioning a "natural" gendered division of labor, Mumford believed that women's bodies informed the creation of villages, and eventually cities. For most of its history, the city was associated with women's functions: "a storehouse, a conservator and accumulator," and, because of its role in facilitating leisure time, "a collective expression of love" where female sexuality flourished in new forms of sociability such as theater or in prostitution.[53]

In her essay "*Chora*, Women, Dwelling," the feminist theorist Elizabeth Grosz argues that in the Western tradition, female space has been constructed as "passive." Through the concept of the *chora*, "a site of nothingness, a womb," men harnessed female power to create potentiality, but they also sought to "protect" and control it. Thus, where Mumford sees the female city as a "Neolithic container" and an outgrowth of natural gender differences, Grosz problematizes the process of identifying space with women's biology as determined by social and historical understandings of gender differences. This identification, she asserts, has served to exclude women from what by the nineteenth century was understood as "public space."[54]

Grosz's and Mumford's differences in interpretation do not preclude the detection of a long historical tradition that has equated women's bodies with urbanization that would show up in Mexican discourses of architecture and urban reform. The Roman architect Vitruvius conceived of not only contained spaces of urban potentiality as female but also the outward features of the built environment itself. Columns, to Vitruvius, constituted the most important foundation of his dictum that buildings be solid, useful, and, above all, beautiful.[55] The foundational element of the column was a focal point of ancient architecture, where columns acted as the built versions of human bodies, their proportions symbolizing those of ideal corporeal forms of men and women:

> Doric column came to exhibit the proportion, soundness and attractiveness of the male body, [while the temple in honor of Diana called for the column lengths as well as appearance adapted to female] slenderness [and a more] lofty appearance [that incorporated] for the capital, as for hair, . . . draped volutes on either side to resemble curled locks . . . and they let flutes down the whole trunk of the column to mimic, in matronly manner, the folds of the stola.[56]

As the centerpiece in fashioning the "architectural ornament" of any built structure, columns were envisioned as stylized statues, their elongated lines constituting those of the simplified human form.[57] As such, Vitruvius's columns shed light on the commentary that followed the premiere of the bataclán, explaining how critics could envision nude, spectacular female bodies as "modern goddesses . . . who move[d] about the stage as living statues."[58] Journalists reporting on nudism evoked the aesthetics of classical art to describe nude female bodies as statues devoid of sensuality. Discourses on the female, column-like statues reverberated in the long, female pillars flanking the stage of Teatro Lindbergh in Parque México.

The Vitruvian focus on columns offers an alternative vision for assessing the drive for, and aesthetic project of, verticalization in the urban landscape of the early twentieth century, including in Mexico. Verticalization is often thought to represent the masculinization or masculine nature of the built environment (especially the idea that straight lines, obelisks, and skyscrapers are predicated on "phallic design").[59] Vitruvian columns show the importance of ideal female forms in envisioning a vertical city, and they symbolize the relationship between bodies and cities as well as the historical trajectory—however uneven—from seeing the early city as female space to envisioning buildings as female bodies. Grosz argues for understanding the relationship between cities and bodies as "mutually constitutive," where the urban landscape provides "the context and coordinates for contemporary forms of body" as much as the body "transforms" and "reinscribes" the urban space. This mutually defining relationship, moreover, depends on a gendered ordering in assigning meaning. Thus, Grosz not only complicates the naturalized the spatial gender schema of Mumford, and even LeFebvre; she also finds that space determines gender construction: gender comes into being because of spatial qualities.[60]

BUILDING BODIES: DECO BODY, DECO CITY

The bodies of the lanky, column-like beauties of the bataclán, the form of the "escultura Irma" who graced the pages of *Vea*, and the lines of ideal nudist bodies in camposcape were the "classic" ones predicated on a vision of architecture that went back to Vitruvius. While functionalist architects clamored for "function over form," functionalism's simple and straight lines expressed an aesthetic where the human form was modernized to fit simplified, geometric designs. If Art Nouveau's heavy emphasis on "organicism" and naturalist (albeit dreamlike) decoration had been one of "dissolving structure into ornament," in functionalism the building itself became the ornament. Indeed, the Italian architect Umberto Boccioni "saw the sculptural figure as no longer isolated from its surrounding space," and Le Corbusier held that "Man" represented a "geometric animal."[61] Much of the emphasis in envisioning simplified human forms as representing, as well as forming part of, built structures was articulated through discourses that championed honesty, purity, and integrity in the service of modernity and civilization. In order to reach these goals, modernist architects sought to bare the essence of buildings, making them legible in terms of their function, and this required not only stripping them of excessive clutter and ornamentation but using the stand-in of female bodies to do so. As Anne Anlin Cheng explains:

The discourse of the "pure" modern surface thus produces a nexus of metonymic meanings—purity, cleanliness, simplicity, anonymity, masculinity, civilization, technology, intellectual abstraction, that are set off against notions of excessive adornment, inarticulate sensuality, femininity, backwardness.[62]

Clean, pure, and bare surfaces proved attractive in the confusion and chaos of modern life, especially as expressed in cityscape: mounting signals and signs, increased human physical and social mobility, and rapidly changing class and gender norms. The ability to assess a person's social status, race, gender, and function in society—elements considered the crucial markers of identity expressed in one's appearance—thus became all the more important. Hence, as we saw in the previous chapter, the idea of women's essence, in the legibility of her body and sexuality, became an integral part of liberal modernity.

The "new bareness" characterizing the new architecture corresponded to, as bataclanismo and *Vea* taught us, the denuding of the female form that took place in the contemporaneous world of entertainment. As architects were conceptualizing buildings as extensions or mirrors of the human form, those bodies were "denuded and unveiled everywhere: in particular in the theatrical culture of the striptease in the early twentieth century." Adolf Loos, advocating for the Dress Reform Movement in Vienna, argued for the "shedding of excessive clothing for women," especially the luxurious, heavily ornamented, and extremely restrictive dress of the diva.[63] Le Corbusier also invoked women's fashion when articulating the reasons for his rejection of the grand French architectural styles of the past.[64] Hence, nude bodies, whether those of *Vea*'s showgirls on daylight city streets or those of functionalist buildings in the modern city, signaled that one's essential sense of self—especially for women—no longer was an interior quality but had become an exterior one.[65] In exhibiting that essence, architecture should generate beauty without ornamentation.

Mexican architects who received commissions to design the buildings of the revolutionary era might have been divided in "moderate" and "radical modernist" camps, yet they shared an understanding that buildings were like bodies. Those who had come of age during the Porfiriato and had studied architecture as part of a fine arts roster conceived of urban renewal in terms of engineering feminine beauty. Younger architects, like the European and U.S. modernists they sought to emulate, were not enamored with the past but in search of a Mexican architectural future. They looked for simplification and "honesty" when assessing appropriate styles and building materials: "nothing should be hidden or concealed." Buildings should remain unadorned, "without disguising, covering or changing them, under the pretext of embellishing them."[66] Art Deco offered both groups the familiar concept of generating feminine beauty through the built environment, but it provided new, simplified, elongated designs and sparse ornamentation that characterized the new ideals of feminine embodiment, through, as some architects liked to say, "nude" forms.

As an academic movement, Art Deco offered both scientific principles and an alternative aesthetic to a society not quite ready to "assimilate the nudity of forms" inherent in modernism.[67] Yet the nudity of forms and the sense of engineering beauty predicated on the female form dominated architectural debates of the era and structured some of the critical differences between radical and moderate groups. Radical modernists were seen as functionalists resorting to what more conservative architects thought were the "extreme lines" of Neue Sachlichkeit (New Objectivity), while moderates believed that modernist architecture possessed the ability to generate beauty, even if without ornamentation.

Antonio Muñoz García, the architect who executed several large public-works projects in Mexico City during the early 1930s, underscored the importance of beauty in fashioning the new, nude architecture: "We will undress architecture, but not until we are sure to have found beautiful lines, and beautiful forms so we can show them without offending good judgment and the right intent."[68] He reasoned that the architecture of his day had become simplified, "leaving nude the elemental forms" much in the same way that the bataclán had undressed the Deco bodies of its dancers in the name of tasteful art, ads for beauty products promoted Deco bodies, and nudists were seeking a return to nature.

> Today, in order to undress, a woman first makes sure she has a buena línea [literally—a good line, or a good figure], and if not she seeks it by making sacrifices. To reach the best aspect of youth and health, she uses lotions and cosmetics, because if her nudity will reveal ugliness, it arouses pity, hilarity or repugnance, while showing off beauty produces applause. Ugliness prefers to cover itself at any costs.[69]

In keeping with film scholar Lucy Fischer's insight that "a discourse on sexual difference" informed the Art Deco aesthetic, Mexican architects like Muñoz García conceptualized buildings as female bodies. One could undress them to show their health, their fine lines, and their beauty, or one could torture their natural forms into monstrosities in need of coverage. Muñoz García reasoned that architects had the obligation to construct beauty. Architecture without beauty, he concluded in dramatic fashion, "would cease to be architecture."[70]

The feminine "fine lines" of new buildings that Art Deco offered did not resemble just any female body; rather, it was the bare, slim physique of the bataclana that graced the pages of *Vea* that had become the nudist par excellence. Art Deco was tied not to the domestic sphere but to the world of entertainment: lavish set designs, costumes, and dance postures that influenced designs to transform stars into what Mark Winokur calls "sculpturesque pieces."[71] Silvano Palafox, the architect responsible for the first Deco high-rise, La Nacional (in the centro histórico), which was often showcased flanked by Deco bodies in the pages of *Vea*, placed his architectural philosophies within the context of theatrical performance. Speaking out against functionalism, Palafox argued that an architect should design buildings to satisfy man's "spiritual needs," such as the need to enjoy "a show at Teatro Lírico." As this theater was known for its spicy revistas featuring pretty bataclanas, he equated the search for architectural beauty with female nude spectacle. For Palafox, a building could only be beautiful if it was functional in the broadest sense, that is, if it served man's "aesthetic emotion."[72]

The use of Deco bodies in entertainment mirrored modernist and Deco conventions in art, such as the serialization of objects, the emphasis on functionality, and the simplification of ornamentation, reflecting a modern society dominated by new technologies. Like the homogeneity of mass production exemplified by the conveyor belt, modernist aesthetics promised order in a fairly chaotic world. Even if modernist architects disagreed on the need for beauty, the subject's centrality within their debates and the understanding that the female body formed its suitable blueprint proved influential in Deco architecture. The fact that architectural designs followed closely in the footsteps of the new physiques formulated by the world of show business underlined that spectacle and the "art of seeing" structured contemporary ideals of what form the city should take.

The Deco buildings envisioned by Palafox, Muñoz García, and likeminded architects were slow to materialize, but their projects gathered momentum by the early 1930s. Few or no Deco designs were executed in the 1920s except for Carlos Obregón Santacilia's project for the new building to house the Department of Public Health and Javier Státoli's plan of the open-air theater Teatro Lindbergh in colonia Condesa, which became the most notable Deco example of its time. Art Deco fit nicely with the shift toward a more capitalist and urban revolution during the Calles administration and throughout the Maximato, when most Deco buildings were planned and executed.[73] Indeed, with its ties to the world of entertainment and leisure, further evidenced by the many Art Deco cinema buildings that sprang up in urban environments around the world, Deco-tecture was intimately associated with the capitalist and consumerist "invasion from the North." Stores sported "large plate glass windows, electric advertisements signs flashed up, [and] American trade names became as well known as the names of movie stars." Another Deco structure, the Ermita-Hipódromo building sitting on a triangular lot at the intersection of Revolución, Jalisco, and Tacubaya Streets in the Condesa, contained apartments and commercial space, including a prominent movie theater. Described as "innovative," "ingenious," and, invoking the human form, "agile," the building was wedge-shaped and counted eight stories.[74]

Other than the buildings of colonia Condesa and storefronts, the most famous example of Deco-tecture of the early 1930s, and more readily visible, was Mexico City's first high-rise, La Nacional (completed in 1934). As with other structures dedicated to commerce, such as Palacio del Hierro (1921), Edificio Uruquay (1922), and Edificio High Life, building and planning commissions allowed La Nacional to be built in the centro histórico despite its lack of conformity to the neo-colonial standards set for the zone. As elsewhere, high-rises signaled commercial enterprise and symbolized capitalist success.

The verticalization of Mexico City's built environment did not apply only to new structures. Existing buildings, including not only commercial buildings such as Hotel Regis and Banco de México but also the seat of government, the Palacio Nacional, increased in height in the 1920s. Interestingly, the project of augmenting buildings in the capital, Olsen argues, did not result from a perceived need due to "space constraints" or "high urban land prices" but for "socio-cultural reasons." Even if actual skyscrapers had not appeared in Mexico's cityscape, they were a touchstone of modernity in advertisements and discussions in architectural magazines. The skyscraper symbolized economic progress and success. Thus, both the business sector and the revolutionary government increasingly adhered to commercial and capitalist ideologies in the attendant aesthetic considerations in building the modern city.[75]

Other than the commercial success of their design, Deco buildings like La Nacional represented a revolutionary triumph in terms of construction. Mexican engineers, challenged by the city's unstable subsoil, had solved structural problems and proved that building "vertically as well as horizontally" was now within the realm of architectural possibility.[76] This victory was helped along by the appearance of new building materials that facilitated both verticalization and building Deco buildings. The arrival of cement, as Rubén Gallo has shown, greatly influenced architecture and urban planning. Cement transformed the cityscape, and along with it, Mexico City's inhabitants' ability to move around. Not only buildings but also roadways and public projects such as new schools, office buildings, factories, and markets made from cement radically altered the city, creating what Gallo calls "a completely different spatial logic" in which capitalinos learned "to exist in the new spaces of modernity." In addition to fulfilling practical needs, cement was highly ideological. As a completely novel material, it signaled "a clear break with the past" and provided architects with the means to express their artistic visions and ideological projects. Endorsed by such modernist visionaries as Le Corbusier and Gropius, cement was inexpensive, readily available, but most of all modern.[77]

While cement propelled architects to formulate new building techniques, designs, and blueprints, the material itself equally articulated a new, modernist aesthetic. Mexican architects such as Manuel Ortíz Monasterio proposed that advances in technology and new building materials necessitated a reconceptualization of form. These architects embraced an "aesthetic of cement" and reveled in its physical appearance, which was "unlike any [other] building material."[78] As "the most visible" of the new media, the *polvo mágico* (magic powder) facilitated the new, nude architecture that modernist architects envisioned. The malleability and modernist aesthetics of cement made it possible to build structures that conformed to the bare Deco body. In its sleekness and emphasis on modern surface, the Deco body was above all sculptural.[79] Through the many references to the Deco body–whether onstage during the bataclán or in media advertisements—as being "like a statue," the arrival of this new material underscored the connection between the new body's plasticity and that of this new moldable stone. In their appreciation of cement, artists like Manuel Álvarez Bravo explored the beauty of "an unadorned concrete structure" and the "elegance" that was achieved through "reducing architecture to its barest elements." Cement magnate Sánchez Fogerty advertised his product by stating that "to design is not to disguise."[80] If functionalism's most fundamental precept was that "form follows function," it was both woman's and building's function to be beautiful when bare.

Just as Deco bodies informed the discourse surrounding the birth of the Condesa, the new neighborhood embodied the hybridity inherent in Deco's eclectic architectural styles as well as the cultural landscape of the growing metropolis. Olsen concludes that because the city government proposed few or no guidelines for architects to follow, the creation of urban space mirrored the contradictions of the revolution itself and were demonstrated through incompatible elements "visible in nearly every colonia or neighborhood." Yet it was the hybridity inspired by Art Deco in particular that frustrated the radical modernist architects. Much to the dismay of these architects, residences in the Condesa exhibited a hodgepodge of foreign styles modeled after both Art Deco and what they disdainfully labeled the California-colonial or Hollywood style. Architecture student Mauricio Gómez Mayorga condemned the hybrid styles that between 1926 and 1930 spread "like a cancer all around the Hipódromo suburbs" and showed off the poor tastes of the nouveau riche, who looked to "a colonial style invented by the vulgar and uncultured prosperity of Hollywood."[81]

Indeed, Deco did not please all architects. Even if moderate modernists such as Muñoz Garcia and Palafox readily embraced Art Deco, radical functionalists condemned the Deco aesthetic as a bourgeois ploy. O'Gorman denounced the "beauty" of colonia Condesa as an anarchism of new styles of houses typified by ideals of art without "order, science, or even historical responsibility to any class, only with one excuse: we are artists and we feel." He found the difference between technical architects and artistic architects perfectly clear: the former sought to serve the greater good by designing for the majority of the population, while the latter catered to the taste of "large landowners and industrialists," thinly disguised by the idea that beauty served to satisfy humanity's "spiritual needs."[82]

More conservative architects such as Carlos Obregón Santacilia, "trusted for his candid appraisal of buildings," also found that buildings such as La Nacional and Ermita-Hipódromo did not "fit Mexican needs." Art Deco structures were thought to "distort" their surroundings and form an ill fit with the city's existing built environment. Even if these structures were considered "innovative" by some, planners and architects like Obregón Santacilia believed that they did not reflect authentic "Mexican culture," or what they perceived to be the preferences and needs of rural migrants who were "accustomed to open spaces and to constructions that grow horizontally, where the sun and green spaces predominate; nature and human being are the most important."[83] Instead of the camposcape of Parque México surrounded by vertical Deco structures and constructed for bourgeois consumption, opposing architects sought to create an urban environment that reflected lower-class needs and allowed campesinos to feel at home. The spectacles of modernity remained complicated in accommodating mexicanidad, all the more as they ran counter to the dictum of revolutionary reform to fashion a healthy city for all.

Despite its slow start and persistent detractors, Deco architecture—in its "characteristic abstract, streamlined forms, curved corners, and stylized plant, animal, and human forms"—spread throughout the city during the 1930s. It reverberated in the newly constructed banks, schools, hospitals, and, as we will see in detail in chapters 6 and 7, markets and theaters, as well as in street ornamentations such as fountains, lampposts, and planters.[84] Hence, while Mexico City never became a full-fledged "Deco city" harboring entire Deco districts, such as Miami Beach, its influence was felt broadly and widely, especially for a city (and its administrators) that favored colonial and neocolonial styles. This "broad" application of Deco, especially in the face of structural conditions such as the city's "sponge-like" subsoil, shows the importance of Art Deco's ideological power and the strength of the impetus to cast the city as emblematic of Deco modernity. Even if Mexico City did not become a vertical Deco city such as a Chicago or New York, the fact that architects conceptualized buildings as Deco bodies testifies to the power and contradictions of gender "cosmopolitics," the legacy of female space and female sexuality in the construction of cosmopolitan modernity.

URBAN REFORM

During the very years when bataclanismo reigned supreme as the entertainment par excellence, the city underwent a political reorganization that had tremendous consequences in terms of urban space. With the elimination of the ayuntamientos in 1929 and the shift of democratic municipal power to a central government appointed by the federal executive, Mexico City was primed to occupy the entire Valley of Mexico and become the Federal District. As the city expanded, its citizens faced stricter regulations, especially where "public women" were concerned. Through the newly established Department of the Federal District, the national government promoted the idea of gender-segregated spaces in the city. New city officials directly tied to the national executive sought to enhance the containment of female sexuality in prostitution zones, while its commissioned architects envisioned Deco bodies as blueprints in the quest for revolutionary architecture.

When the DDF inherited the position of sole authority in administering Mexico City, it garnered power to execute reforms in the name of health, modernity, and—above all—the institutional revolution. As a highly centralized power accountable only to the federal executive, the revived DDF inherited a situation of increased demand for services and public-health projects by the popular classes in order for the revolution to have meaning in an urban setting. Revolutionary leadership, such as President Abelardo Rodríguez and DDF regent Aarón Sáenz, believed that in order to make good on some of the promises of the revolution, they had to address long-standing urban problems and focus on large public-works projects such as drainage systems, roads, schools, and market buildings. However, they also wanted to make Mexico City over into a showcase of revolutionary progress, modernity, and power. Both architecture and urban reform proved important practical and ideological tools in achieving the consolidation of the revolution in the capital city.

From the early 1920s, urban development in the capital city reflected an uneven approach. The revolution, especially the prolonged and devastating violence in the countryside, had pushed an inordinate number of rural migrants, mostly women, into a city that was experiencing food shortages, overcrowding, few opportunities for decent employment, and a rise in unsanitary living conditions. Despite some revolutionary efforts at urban reform, such as studies by the Obregón administration on the housing conditions of the urban poor, by the late 1920s the capital faced a worsening situation brought on by rapid urbanization, a government favoring private business interests, lack of proper city planning, and poor enforcement of building regulations. The unabated flood of migrants put financial strains on both local and national governments that made it difficult to meet the ever-growing demand for housing, schools, and infrastructure.[85]

Whether due to incompetence, unwillingness, or uncontrollable structural forces, it was clear to capitalinos by 1929 that urban reform had failed. In the face of worsening urban problems, national leaders' anxiety mounted at the growing political opposition in the municipal governments, the lack of unity among these *municipios*, and the control wielded by a corrupt labor leadership in the capital. In December 1928, Calles eliminated the democratic ayuntamiento system in favor of a centralized and federalized government of the Federal District, leading to the creation of the Partido Nacional Revolucionario (PNR) as the revolution's official party in March 1929. The newly empowered PNR, through the agency of the DDF, rapidly altered the city. With the incorporation of the formerly autonomous outlying municipalities, the Federal District tripled in size, which lent the newly restructured Mexico City ample room to expand. Armed with the newly established federal control over Mexico City, the capital's cityscape under President Plutarco Elías Calles became emblematic of the ascendency of a revolutionary elite and their consolidation of power. Even if the creation of some new structures suggested a concern for "the fulfillment of revolutionary promises," Porfirian real estate moguls retained their wealth, influence, and urban landholdings. It was a public secret that Calles himself was heavily implicated in business dealings, including real estate and urban development companies that were involved in corruption. Calles and Sáenz owned FYUSA (Compañía de Fomento y Urbanización S.A.; Urban Development, Inc.), one of the notorious "construction companies that monopolized the contracting of public works."[86]

However, between 1930 and 1934 the federal government and the DDF authorities also provided the impetus to solve certain urban problems, including housing for the lower classes and workers. The majority of these efforts began during the tenure of President Abelardo Rodríguez. Dubbed the "Country Club President," Rodríguez, an enthusiastic investor when governor of Baja California, was a millionaire upon ascending the presidency. Residing in a posh villa in Chapultepec Heights, Rodríguez also owned a considerable part of Mexico City's nightlife, most notably the upscale Foreign Club.[87] The club, where the then still Mexican Rita Hayward made her debut as part of the "Dancing Cansinas" ensemble, was advertised as the most modern and sumptuous social center in the entire republic, the place where Mexican and international artists delivered the greatest *espectáculos*.[88] As a cunning capitalist entrepreneur connected to the portals of the underworld, Rodríguez was neither a strict moralist who would clean up the city nor a revolutionary reformer addressing the issues of social justice.

Revisionist history has been kinder than contemporary public opinion in assessing Rodríguez's accomplishments. Although he served for only two years, his administration took on considerable and significant urban-reform projects, most of which were the result of the Ley de Planificación y Zonificación del Distrito Federal y Territorios de Baja California (Planning and Zoning Law for the Federal District and the Territories of Baja California), promulgated by Rodríguez in January 1933. That same year, Rodríguez founded the Architecture Council with the objective to review proposals for new buildings, regulate construction licenses, and generally control the form cityscape should take. Based on the provisions of the new planning legislation, the DDF hired architect Carlos Contreras to head the project of developing a master plan for the Federal District and control urban growth. The law allowed Rodríguez to claim property for public use without legislative oversight or approval and to make Contreras's commission central to all major building projects initiated by government agencies. Although its effectiveness was hampered by corruption, budget reductions, and departmental infighting, the commission made significant gains, such as the construction of colonias Balbuena and San Jacinto for workers in 1933 and 1934.[89]

As part of his plan to address social tensions in the capital city, ameliorate the state of public works, and instate effective urban renewal, Rodríguez appointed Sáenz as the head of the Federal District in 1932. Sáenz's arrival ended a turbulent period, under the two-year administration of Pascual Ortiz Rubio, that had seen the arrival and departure of seven jefes. Upon arriving at the helm of the DDF, Sáenz initiated a vast building program that included the creation of 250 primary and secondary schools, including, on the site of the former Belém prison, the gigantic Centro Escolar Revolucionario (Revolutionary School Center), which included a small stadium, a swimming pool, an open-air theater, and playgrounds. The school served one of the most densely populated areas in the city center, and its one hundred classrooms could accommodate about five thousand students. Sáenz also commissioned the construction of housing for low-income workers for the new colonias Balbuena and San Jacinto and launched enormous infrastructure projects that improved sanitation, paved streets, and created powers stations. Finally, under Sáenz's direction, several important monuments were built or completed, such as the Monumento a la Revolución (begun as the Porfirian Legislative Palace) and the funerary monument for Álvaro Obregón.[90]

In executing these plans, Rodríguez and Saénz were some of the first revolutionary administrators to turn almost exclusively to planning commissions. In order to effect a better—if not new, then at least improved—city, architects and planners had more power in controlling cityscape than in the 1920s, when the city seemed to lack urban planning and its growth commenced according to what Patrice Olsen considers a rather haphazard scheme dictated by profit incentives. Or, if not lacking in planning, Mexico City expressed what Mumford labeled an "organic planning" that "moves from need to need, from opportunity to opportunity."[91]

In contrast, Sáenz's vision for the city corresponded to an incipient discourse on the need for urban planning. The first technical journals that addressed urban problems in terms of scientific planning were published in Mexico in the late 1920s and early 1930s (*Planeación* in 1927 and *Casas* in 1935).[92] Moreover, national and international congresses on urban planning started in the 1920s and proliferated in the 1930s. In 1925 some young Mexican architects participated in an international exposition on architecture and planning hosted by the American Institute of Architects, which asked them to ponder the social function of their vocation. Architect and planner Sylvano Palafox, who headed the Society for Mexican Architects, organized Mexico's first national planning conference, which took place in January 1930.[93]

In addition to considering the dictates of economic development, the desire for modernization, and the needs of the lower classes, planners envisioned building a utopian revolutionary city that would be both practical and beautiful. In defining its beauty, however, they oscillated between preserving the city's past and facilitating its future. In charting both modernity and "authenticity," planners, architects, and builders underscored that the city harbored a tension between vertical and horizontal lines. In envisioning the new city, Contreras believed that "planning would seem to be an insurmountable task," not only due to the importance of infrastructure improvements but also because "it was incumbent upon them to plan and achieve 'beautiful places.'" Indeed, some of President Obregón's first steps toward urban planning and renewal had been efforts to beautify the Zócalo alongside renovations to the Palacio Nacional.[94] Like architects in search of blueprints that would express the Deco body aesthetic, planners gravitated toward older ideas of the city as female space. Whether a previous tendency or a sensibility toward "organic planning," especially as expressed in horizontal growth, new scientific planners also required a stress on beautification and a logic of constructing organic beauty such as the camposcape of Parque México in colonia Condesa.

Besides seeking to create urban renditions of female camposcape, leaders such as Sáenz sought to reify the revolution as national patrimony by erecting "male monuments," inserting "los nombres de hombres" into the city's infrastructure, and conserving the centro as a historic district. In serving the goals of maintaining and promoting particular visions of national patrimony, parts of Mexico City were to serve as a theater of history, where the revolutionary past was kept alive through its urban spaces. During Sáenz's tenure as regent, Mexico City received two large monuments, the Monumento a la Revolución and the monument commemorating Álvaro Obregón, each symbolic of revolutionary hero worship. As the revolution was largely commemorated through the glorification of its fallen heroes (even if some of these heroes, such as Emiliano Zapata and Pancho Villa, had diametrically opposed the middle-class victors from the North), membership in the imagined revolutionary family was literally cemented into place. The Monumento a la Revolución incorporated and eventually housed the remains of the great leaders of the different revolutionary factions: Madero, Carranza, Villa, Obregón, Calles, and Cárdenas (with Zapata notably missing). Moreover, in enforcing a state-centered and male city, the nation's "cult of heroes" was embedded in the city's very infrastructure. During the armed phase of the revolution, streets had been renamed for Mexico's, and particularly the revolution's, greatest leaders, a practice that continued well into the 1920s and 1930s.[95] Imbuing central urban features and public spaces with the names of important men connected to the revolutionary state functioned as a way to reinsert male authority in a city that had been deemed unruly, chaotic, and feminine, especially in terms of Porfirian, Art Nouveau legacies.

Increasingly, architects and urban-planning professionals on the city's planning advisory board strongly argued for the protection and restoration of the colonial architecture of the downtown areas. President Emilio Portes Gil's 1930 Ley de Planificación General (General Planning Law) directed that historic buildings and neighborhoods be kept intact to maintain their "typical character." A 1931 decree stipulated that the "urban picturesque," especially the area around the Zócalo, should be conserved through the creation of a historic zone to safeguard what planners saw as the city's authentic character. Contreras, the Architecture Council's chairman, advocated the establishment of a Central Archaeological and Monumental Zone within which the DDF would control all construction to retain the colonial character of the area. Rodríguez, eager to stimulate a budding tourism industry, reinforced these efforts for federal control over historic monuments through legislation ratified in 1934 that stressed not only conservation but also renovation. He entrusted the Department of Education with the protection of patrimony, which facilitated the creation of the Instituto Nacional de Antropología e

Historia (National Institute of Anthropology and History) in 1938. With this, President Lázaro Cárdenas finalized the institutionalization of state control over national patrimony, and with it, the urban landscape.[96]

Legislation to safeguard colonial buildings proved difficult to enforce, however. Even if some decrees protected "certain areas," there was no clear understanding of what a *zona típica* (traditional zone) was, and moreover, what constituted "typically Mexican." Safeguarding national patrimony frequently entailed removing "unwanted elements" from the streets in the centro histórico and motivated legislation that encouraged private investment. Contreras stressed the protection of retail businesses from the "unsightly vendors crowding the downtown streets." Consequently, despite its focus on conservation, legislation accelerated the transformation of the Zócalo and adjacent streets to what was deemed a more orderly yet also more commercial centro marked by styles incongruent with colonial architecture. Unattractive to pedestrians, the revamped Zócalo, from which Porfirian gardens, tramways, and pedestrian spaces had been removed by the mid-1930s, made ample way for automobile traffic.[97]

The planning legislation of the early 1930s harvested mixed results. The laws proved to have a dual purpose: on the one hand, conserving national patrimony based on a revalorized colonial past, and on the other, functional modernity. However, both answered to aesthetic considerations, often before the more practical issues. The DDF's penchant for technocratic solutions reinforced the impression that the city's new administration followed the precepts of high modernism: simplification, utility, and legibility. In order to make good on revolutionary promises, the DDF needed to make urban reform and building construction legible to the citizenry. The DDF's "project of legibility" equally depended on, in James Scott's words, "state simplifications," that is, a technocratic approach that appeared non-political or which glossed over political divisions in the city by staging urban reform as a performance of statecraft that visibly served as well as memorialized the revolution. Such an approach had gravitas especially in countries like Mexico after the revolution, where civil society was weak and where "progressive, revolutionary elites" acted on "a popular mandate to transform" an ailing society.[98]

Like Le Corbusier's idealized "radiant city" (*La ville radieuse*, 1933), a utopia planned around the scientific and technical dictates of "The Plan," Mexico City's previous haphazard growth and its "lack of planning" straddled a series of competing ideologies that could be brought into harmony through ideas about "beauty."[99] Yet unlike the later and futuristic Brasilia, Mexico City's past was not to be an "impediment" but an inspiration, and part of the cultural fabric of "desires," "history," and "traditions" of its inhabitants.[100]

CONCLUSION

The flurry of urban-reform efforts spanning the period from 1929 to 1934 spoke to an understanding of urban development that served a set of divergent agendas, some of which were at odds with one another. On one hand, the conceptualization of the city as female space and the likening of Deco bodies to modern buildings personalized and eroticized the new architectural forms associated with global modernity, such as the planning and building of the upscale, middle-class Art Deco colonia Condesa. On the other hand, revolutionary officials believed that the city, especially the centro histórico, should serve as a mnemonic device where monuments, place-names, and colonial patrimony dedicated to iconic male heroes would keep national history alive. Urban planning not only illustrated the tension between the need to preserve history (and create public memory) and the urge to modernize cityscape, but also demonstrated how these processes were ideologically informed by gender concerns. Attempts to modernize the city resulted in zones of containment and venues for mobility that were inherently gendered.

Art Deco, especially its ideological blueprint of the female Deco body, seemed able to elide the tensions in revolutionary leaders' urban-reform agenda that expressed itself in the capital's cityscape. Art Deco, seen as a transitional phase when architects searched for a national style befitting a true revolutionary Mexican identity, came to occupy an important place in Mexican architecture of the 1920s and 1930s.

Providing warring factions with a conciliatory position, Art Deco—in its celebration of hybridity and adaptability to local motifs—was able to communicate transnational modernity without offending nationalist sentiments. The Deco architecture of colonia Condesa demonstrated that metropolitan modernity of the Roaring Twenties could be framed within the ideals of the revolution and still retain a distinct Mexican national flavor.[101]

Art Deco also offered Mexican architects the familiar concept of generating beauty based on female bodies, even if this now meant the new, simplified, and "nude" elongated forms. Architects looked to the Deco bodies of modernity to build beautiful, healthy, and desirable structures befitting their visions for cosmopolitanism. Muñoz García and Palafox used Art Deco to underscore the importance of female nudity in fashioning a new architecture. Much in the same way that *Vea*'s editors promoted its use of sexy, beautiful, and, most importantly, healthy Deco bodies in the name of tasteful entertainment, they likened buildings to fine lines of beautiful female bodies and placed architectural visions within the context of female theatrical performance. Through these new female forms as well as the built environment, capitalinos learned to conceptualize the appearance of their city no longer as a matter of beautification modeled on an aesthetics loosely associated with femininity, as they had during Porfirian times, but as a particular feminine form of the future.

In the end, Deco bodies and camposcape—or, rather, a Deco-fication of camposcape—functioned as a means to harmonize the city and the campo as distinctive spheres (which sharpened tensions between the rural and the urbane, tradition and modernity, and indigenismo and mestizaje). To return to our water-bearing statue at the entrance of Parque México: although her braids, her full, strong, and indigenous physique, and her nudity appeared to embody camposcape, and identified her as quintessentially Mexican, she also bore an uncanny resemblance to European statues of Salomé, who, as we saw in chapter 1, had become the symbol par excellence of the Orient. Moreover, the indígena introduced visitors to Teatro Lindbergh and colonia Condesa, places of Art Deco spectacle. While the camposcape of Parque México (and, as we will see in chapters 6 and 7, that of Mercado Abelardo Rodríguez and the Palacio de Bellas Artes) sought to neutralize tensions in revolutionary urban reform, the mestizo modernity inherent in Deco bodies exemplified a long-sought-after accommodation of Western affluence and mexicanidad as they offered a way to bridge the gap between indigenismo and mestizaje.

Mercado Abelardo Rodríguez

On November 24, 1934, just a few days after the Revolution Day celebrations in the city, President Abelardo Rodríguez and president-elect
Lázaro Cárdenas joined in a celebration to open a new marketplace on
Venezuela Street, in the heart of Mexico City's colonial center. It was
a joyous occasion; demonstration stands, exhibits, and an orchestra
playing traditional Mexican music drew large crowds and merchants
from all over the city. Residents of the surrounding neighborhoods
on the edge of the notorious tenement district around the Zócalo
poured out to visit the new market, admire the craftsmanship of the
new furniture sets on display from upscale stores on Juárez Street,
and marvel at the exhibits of water-distribution systems and other
public-works projects for which construction was under way. Within
a year, the second generation of muralists would decorate the market
with colorful images of the campo. On the second floor above the
main hall bustling with the many festivities, stands, and exhibits, the
Art Deco Teatro del Pueblo (Theater of the People) stood out as the
structure's crowning achievement.

From the market's first day of operation, urban planners concluded
that it was a resounding success. Aarón Sáenz, head of the Federal
District and the mastermind behind the surge of public works started
under the Rodríguez administration, proudly announced that the DDF
had restored markets to their "primordial quality" by constructing the
Mercado Abelardo Rodríguez (fig. 20). It was singled out especially for
catering to the needs of the poorest sector of the city.[1] Foreign visitors
agreed. Frances Toor, an expatriate from the United States and author
of Mexican travel guides, commented that it was the most beautiful

FIG. 20. Mercado Abelardo Rodríguez, *Informe del Departamento del Distrito Federal*, 1934.

modern market in the city, and Bernard Deutsch, president of the New York Board of Aldermen, exclaimed that it surpassed markets of such quintessential modern cities as New York and Paris.[2]

With the Mercado Abelardo Rodríguez, the DDF indeed appeared to have built an impressive facility. Besides being a modern, efficient, and sanitary structure that would supply the poorer neighborhoods of the centro with affordable, high-quality food, the Mercado housed a civic center, a day-care center, a civil registry, and a theater, as well as a series of didactic murals about the campo. The complex thus addressed revolutionary objectives in terms of education, family, public health, and fair pricing of basic necessities. Even if the market, with its excellent sanitation making great strides toward fighting disease, fit perfectly into the DDF's plans for modernization, it also abided by regulations of national patrimony in keeping the colonial style of the historic district intact.[3] With the completion of the Mercado, the DDF leadership apparently had achieved three important urban-reform objectives that often seemed at odds with each other: saving national patrimony, gearing up for modernity, and fulfilling the promises of the revolution in one structure.

As a multifaceted facility, the Mercado functioned as a microcosm of revolutionary reform, but it also sparked controversies over vendor displacement, vagrancy, and government corruption. These controversies, especially when coupled with the protests by market women, questioned why city officials such as Sáenz favored market improvement over other public projects, such as public housing.[4] If architects conceptualized building healthy and attractive urban landscapes modeled on Deco bodies while revolutionary reformers conceived of the city as alternating areas of gendered zones and monuments, markets addressed seemingly disparate revolutionary aims. Market renovation was planned and executed in the context of a discourse that positioned markets as camposcape, places populated with female archetypes symbolizing mexicanidad. In showing women in camposcape, markets connected the city of female space with the grandeur of new buildings erected in the name of the revolution and its heroes. In short, beyond markets' practical functions in facilitating urban growth by providing city dwellers with adequate food supplies, their performative quality made them public theaters that animated and interwove notions of camposcape, indigenismo, the revolution, and national identity through walls, stalls, and murals.

MARKETS AS CONTACT ZONES

Markets were tied to camposcape, the tehuana, and imaginings of national origins in a precolonial past, but they were also emblematic of poverty, disease, and undesirable rural elements. As we saw in previous chapters, such spaces were representative of both the promise and problems of the presence of the campo in the city. Since the late nineteenth century, disease and contagion had figured prominently in discourses surrounding markets, connecting these to social and moral considerations. Porfirian markets had provided nineteenth-century capitalinos not only with food but also with fear and fascination, which resulted in imagining markets as sites of urban decay. Hence, a vivid reimagining of market spaces affected urban-reform efforts more than contemporaries cared to admit. Moreover, upper- and middle-class Porfirians clamored for gender boundaries within public space, a concept that would come to occupy a central place in the urban imagination of capitalinos in the twentieth century.[5]

The municipal authorities built indoor markets with the understanding that the social classes, and especially women as markers of these classes, should remain separate. Elite Porfirian conceptions held that frequenting markets and lower-class areas where female vendors plied their wares made women vulnerable to prostitution, especially when the señoras decentes were mistaken for prostitutes. Yet the municipal regulation of street vending affected poor women merchants more than their male counterparts, because it pushed women outside of municipal markets. Women began to function as illegal vendors and *ambulantes* (street vendors), while men dominated the area inside the municipal markets. Maintaining a market stall cost more than occupying a place on the street, as stall owners paid license fees and tax to the city government; it was these expenses that female vendors often could not afford.[6] The growing presence of poor, indigenous women living their private lives in public view and bearing a resemblance to "public women" (prostitutes) confused the boundaries of public decency and private sins and provoked fears and tensions among the Porfirian elites.

While city government was working to remove large segments of the lower classes from the streets, including vendors, market improvement remained a low priority on the list of public works. Ayuntamientos enjoyed a significant amount of income from the seventeen large and numerous smaller markets, so municipal authorities were not inclined to invest in improvements.[7] In the late nineteenth century, ayuntamientos built two indoor markets, La Lagunilla and La Merced, which became the largest markets in Mexico City. These markets, however, did little to eliminate food shortages or the disease, crime, and congestion associated with street vending. Although municipal governments constructed these markets and carried the burden of responsibility for their condition, in July 1903 the government of the Federal District stepped in to create the Consejo Superior de Salubridad

(Supreme Health Council) as an office of the advisory board for the Health Department and charged it with market inspection. Despite these measures, "misery and messiness" prevailed, especially in La Merced and in the famous Volador adjacent to the Zócalo. The latter had to be closed due to the abundance of vendors who crowded the neighboring streets in what numerous residents and foreign travelers alike referred to as "repugnant" stalls.[8] In general, the markets suffered from unhygienic conditions due to the absence of paved floors, running water, and drainage systems.

The new Porfirian markets also did not eliminate the existence or need for an informal economy in foodstuffs, which contemporaries saw as the most detrimental result of market inefficiency. Growing commercial activity, especially that of women vendors, spilled over into the streets around the markets and spread from the tianguis (open-air "Indian" markets) in the streets and plazas to the patios of vecindades. Moreover, despite urbanization strategies, the tenement population around La Merced increased.[9] By the end of the Porfiriato, the city counted more than three million small business owners, including many who conducted business on the streets around municipal markets but neglected to pay rent to the authorities.[10]

By the late twentieth century La Merced had grown to occupy 20 percent of the surface area of the centro histórico and 40 percent of its historic monuments. It best illustrates the development of markets in the centro from the late Porfiriato to the start of the institutionalized revolution. Housed in a convent and operated by the order of Our Lady of Mercy during colonial times, La Merced did not become a grand market until well into the nineteenth century, when, empowered by the Reforma Laws, the liberals managed to expropriate church holdings. In an attempt to keep up with the demands of a growing urban population, the municipal government overhauled La Merced in 1903 and 1904. Increased security and improved administration streamlined the market, and it became the eastern gateway for agricultural products from Xochimilco, Mixquic, and Chalco. La Merced experienced its major economic and demographic explosion starting in 1930, which transformed the market to the largest commercial facility in the city and the country. Between 1920 and 1940, La Merced's relentless growth was one of the primary reasons for Mexico City's commercial expansion. Above and beyond the enormous diversity in traditional products sold in both permanent and semi-fixed stalls, the market complex included thirty-seven pulquerías, forty-four cantinas, forty *cervecerías* (beer halls), and ten billiards halls, accounting for a sizable share of the centro's places of leisure.[11]

Even if La Merced was unique in its rise to the city's foremost market complex, its expansion was representative of the development of most markets and, more generally, commercial activity in the core of the rapidly growing city.[12] Despite the increase in market commerce in the mid-1920s, city officials appeared ill-equipped to manage the enormous, haphazard growth in markets. Indoor markets built during the Porfiriato could not contain the ever-growing groups of vendors and their products that inadvertently ended up crowding the streets around the market buildings. Municipal reports called for ways to control food vendors who took over streets, obstructed traffic, and made a mockery of sanitation and social hygiene. Many vendors spread out their wares on the ground and cooked tortillas on makeshift grills, leading city officials to worry about contamination.[13] Inspectors from the Health Department condemned the wooden, rat-infested stalls of city markets such as San Cosme, which could not be properly cleaned. In addition, these officials maintained that unhygienic conditions in markets were complicated by a lack of morals and order. Vendors displayed clothing, newspapers, and *sarapes* (blankets) along with food products, thereby adding to the perception of an overall state of confusion and chaos. Flies and stray cats and dogs feasted on the meat in unattended stalls, and the trash was piled in heaps. Worse, vendors relieved themselves in public parks and streets, reducing adjacent areas to a giant lavatory.[14] In his recollections of accompanying servants to shop at La Merced, painter Pedro Friedeberg describes the market's extended wooden walkways that connected streets because of the black, filthy mud underneath occupied by rats: "Everything was a picturesque dirtiness that nobody worried about too much."[15]

Because of this the lack of vigilance, order, and hygiene, markets exemplified the precarious existence and problematic aspects of the campo in the city. On the one hand, markets were rightly viewed as absolutely necessary in furnishing the majority of the city's population with basic daily necessities. On the other hand, they were seen as places of filth and vice that, depending on the time of day and one's perspective, changed from picturesque camposcape to portal of the underworld. Health Department inspectors warned that in some markets up to two hundred vendors slept in their stalls at night, while others came together in large groups in the adjacent parks and plazas to drink and engage in other "lowly" activities. During the day, inebriated vagrants passed out in streets around the markets after drinking illegal pulque that vendors hid in their stalls, while con artists deceived the innocent through illegal gambling and other prohibited games involving money. Markets had become *focos de escandalo y vicio* (centers of scandal and vice) where duplicitous and dirty women attended to the needs of "people without order."[16]

In the early 1920s, in order to remove the unsightly vendors, federal authorities paved streets and plazas, a project that fit in well in the overall idea of urban renewal. Municipal leaders initially conceptualized urban reform as a matter of infrastructure: paving streets, opening the city to motorized traffic, and increasing public transportation while discouraging the use of animal-drawn carts and warning pedestrians of car-related dangers. Indeed, they held that "congestion and chaos" and the fact that the "City of Palaces had not evolved to accommodate automobile traffic" constituted the city's main problem.[17] Yet this lack of modernity was conceptualized through the lack of health and hygiene of markets whose vendors spilled out onto the city streets. Thus, the unhealthy conditions in large markets such as La Lagunilla, which were filled with "parasites and filthy people," would only be eliminated by providing the adjacent streets and plazas with asphalt.[18] The broadening and "elongation" of streets, a significant concept in Art Deco, was a practical and equally aesthetic project tied to the need for beautifying space.[19] Despite an increase in traffic accidents, paving of the city continued unabated; even Cuauhtemotzín, the heart of the most notorious prostitution zone, received a better street surface in 1926.

Not until 1926, however, did revolutionary leaders start to directly address market problems. Municipal authorities first furnished La Merced with a garbage facility, two large warehouses, and new paint, while Mercado Hidalgo received electricity. They also constructed permanent stalls, a school, bathrooms, and a room with sewing machines for female vendors in Mercado Juárez. Additionally, they set aside the Plaza de Alhondiga as a provisional market for the many vendors who did not fit in the existing buildings and ordered that the many wooden barracks that the vendors used as a trash heap and dormitory be torn down. The Health Department also started an educational program for market inspectors to remind them of their responsibilities and tutor them in the practice of good hygiene. The talks took place twice a month and trained personnel how to interact with vendors as part of their lessons in quality control of perishable foodstuffs such as meat, fish, butter, coffee, and prepared meals.[20]

Despite these measures, the sanitation, control, and vice problems associated with city markets remained. In 1928 vendors still crowded the streets, slept in their stalls, and engaged in unsanitary practices. City officials understood that the existing markets were inadequate to suit the necessities of Mexico City's burgeoning population and that the vendors peddling their wares on the street did so due to the worsening economic situation in the country. Health inspectors found that competing market unions and political intrigue complicated the already difficult situation. Steep hikes in tax rates imposed by municipal governments and lack of membership in the proper union pushed vendors—especially the economically more vulnerable female vendors—out of the markets and onto the streets.[21]

When President Rodríguez took office in 1932, the situation had not improved. The hygiene in the city at large left much to be desired, and doctors advised the new president to prohibit street vending, because the poor air quality resulting from in an increase in motorized traffic polluted the tacos and even candies sold on the street with contaminated dust. Moreover, they urged the construction of market buildings with perfectly straight walls to discourage the vendors from urinating in public.[22] Concerned citizen Alberto Olague Soria petitioned President Rodríguez with a request to establish special police units in each market to supervise hygiene, because markets attracted "a multitude of drunks and dirty people laying half-naked on the sidewalks."[23] Indeed, public-health problems plagued city markets. When several typhus outbreaks were linked to La Lagunilla, the Department of Public Health responded by delousing all individuals found to be infested in the region of the market.[24]

Problems of disease and lack of sanitation in the crowded centro formed the primary motivation in building new markets, yet planners articulated these public-health reforms in terms of the dangers of street vending and the need for social control. With the influx of rural migrants after the revolution and the increased pressures on the city's facilities, revolutionaries started to worry about the impact of the formal and informal markets on public order. In the early 1930s the Health Department surveyed the condition in the city's markets and concluded that drastic improvements were needed, especially in the light of persistent complaints and protests in the barrios from more affluent residents who felt that their rights as property owners were severely compromised. To ameliorate these problems, officials proposed the creation of a large new market within the centro.[25]

MARKETS OF WOMEN

The centro bustled with people, which worried government officials of the Federal District. The revolution had caused the city's population to swell, with rural migrants increasing the population by one-third. During the 1920s the city expanded again, by 58 percent. Prior to 1925, an average of 40 to 160 people per building lived in the blocks adjacent to the future Mercado Abelardo Rodríguez. In the greater vicinity of the market, the vecindades housed between 220 and 250 people per building.[26]

In addition to the increase in numbers, the culture of the campo proved difficult to eradicate. Many unskilled and casual laborers had strong ties to the countryside, and the persistence of rural traditions was crucial to maintaining their identity. Moreover, recent arrivals from the campo sustained and invigorated rural traditions in the city.[27] Residents of crowded tenements in the centro included the dislocated poor who used patios as extensions of their homes, where they dried laundry, raised chickens, and grew flowers and medicinal herbs on their roofs. Newly arrived *chilangos* (slang term for inhabitants of Mexico City) consulted curanderos and in many ways re-created their former rural lives within the barrios of the centro.[28] In time these practices reflected and were informed by circular migration patterns where extended families had members in both rural and urban areas. The revolution thus triggered migration patterns that caused city and countryside to mix, but they did not merge. Rural-to-urban migration and the transformation of the campesino into a full-fledged modern city dweller were not simple, unilinear, or complete processes. The relationship between rural and urban spaces and cultures was a complex dialectic, a process where rural culture informed the city as much as the city's modernity transformed rural migrants.[29] Mexico City was becoming *Chilangolandia*, as Frida Kahlo affectionately named her hometown, a metropolis made up of rural migrants.

Consequently, the campo informed revolutionary Mexico City and influenced urban reform in significant ways. Rural migrants joined the ranks of cheap labor, yet they also greatly increased the number of inhabitants in the capital and thus put new pressures on the city's social and economic infrastructure, especially in furnishing adequate foodstuffs. Despite the fancy department stores that flanked the centro's upscale streets, there were few to no centralized commercial venues at which to purchase food, other than markets. After sending a commission to investigate the housing situation in the capital, officials were alarmed by the staggering problems that the majority of the city's inhabitants faced on a daily basis. The living conditions in tenements, perpetuated by the criminal attitude of slumlords, shocked the commission members. They described the situation as a disaster and agreed with poor inhabitants who complained that "in the heart of the city, the revolution has not arrived." Landlords exploited the poor, who were resigned to living in slums worse than "rooms of death." The commission urged the authorities to save these people, who, they noted, lived in veritable pigsties under conditions worse than those found in the notorious Belém jail.[30]

FIG. 21. From *Detectives*, October 17, 1932.

Competing discourses on what markets were and what they should become in a revolutionary context had been percolating into the capitalinos' collective unconsciousness for some time. Moreover, these discourses hinged on the understanding that markets were public places of female activities, caught between the ideas of camposcape and the danger of the market. On the one hand, markets had been lauded through the theatrical interpretations of romanticized camposcapes in revistas, the visual productions surrounding the tehuana, and the faux indígenas who performed camposcape in Casasola news photography. On the other hand, through government narratives that emphasized filth and squalor, sensationalist weeklies that linked markets with the underworld, and journalists who pointed to the dangers of female space, capitalinos received mixed and contradictory messages on the state of markets, and even more so the women who animated them. Market women emerged from these complex discursive entanglements as both heroic and authentic, as well as uniquely recalcitrant. If, as Lupe Marín related in her 1930s novel, *La Única*, market women were admired as outspoken and spirited,[31] *Detectives* covers and feature articles illustrated that they were above all dangerous women, who served tamales made from children's flesh, were addicted to drugs and alcohol, and belonged to the vice-ridden world of organized crime (see fig. 21). Indeed, these "markets of women" invoked an established iconography of urban noir space in which women were the principal actors who performed danger and despair. Sites of modernity such as cabarets, brothels, and deserted streets, and now markets frequently functioned as the backdrop for female danger as they linked sex, crime, and violence. By the early 1930s, markets and market women—urban campesinas—came to represent a particular portal to the capitalino underworld in the Mexican imagination.

Moreover, during the early 1930s market workers became the most militant of all working-class groups in the city's center, adding to their reputation as troublemakers. They complained bitterly against the blatant corruption of DDF inspectors and market administrators who pressured the small owners into paying large bribes, usually in an effort to stave off the closure of their market stalls.[32] In petitioning President Rodríguez, booth owners in Mercado Hidalgo asked that the former administrator Sr. Hurtado be punished for letting his brother, a member of an advisory board to the DDF, buy goods at better prices.[33] Vendors on Tacuba Street in the centro complained about a market administrator who assigned the vendors marginal spots in a dirty alley under the pretext of traffic problems, when they preferred to remain in Tacuba Street. They also accused him of extortion. Market vendors in colonia Tacubaya faced similar harassment from another bad administrator, who, under the guise of order, moved their stalls to a closed-off street, with the result that they lost a great deal of business. DDF's Jefe de Mercados (Head of Markets) and other groups met to address these problems, but the DDF ultimately told vendors that it was simply a matter of reorganization and "proper order."[34]

Above and beyond these concerns, stall owners opposed street vendors, who sold their wares "illegally," that is, without paying the heavy taxes that the city and federal governments levied in the markets.[35] Market workers, especially those housed in La Lagunilla, complained about governmental negligence, corruption, and the poor hygiene of the market, noting that this was largely brought about by a corrupt administrator who allowed street vendors to set up shop near or in the market. According to the *locutarios* (stall owners), the street vendors did not abide by the regulations set forth by the Health Department, the DDF, and the Ministry of the Interior. The economic crisis of 1929 to 1932 had a severe impact on the rural segments of the Federal District, such as the farmers of Nativas and Itzapalapa, who tried to subsist by selling their products in urban markets.[36] These so-called *golondrinas* (swallows) sold their staple foods directly to the people of Mexico City from makeshift stalls outside La Merced and similar market complexes, or from their small trucks driving through various neighborhoods in the city.[37]

However, the vast majority of the ambulantes were not golondrinas, but poor Mexican women. The enormous growth of street vending followed in the wake of the economic crisis of 1929–32, when many factory workers, service industry employees, and lower-level government employees lost their jobs. Street vendors furnished the poorest barrios of the city with substandard, cheap food and were the ones most damaged by the actions of the DDF, the federal government, and organized commerce. The DDF passed a new commerce code in 1928 in an attempt to restrict street vending, yet it did not enforce its regulations until 1930, when the problem had reached epic proportions. The ordinance stipulated stall size and prohibited a vendor from owning more than one stall or selling products sold in neighboring shops. Besides facing more stringent restrictions, the ambulantes were more vulnerable to the relentless corruption of the DDF and Health Department representatives than the market vendors, as they had little protection or official recourse. Female vendors especially received rough treatment and suffered abuse at the hands of police, inspectors, and other representatives of the state, who inspired fear by regularly detaining female vendors in jail for one to two days, leaving their children without means for survival. These ambulantes scored a victory in March 1932, when new regulations allowed them to operate in the centro and sell cigarettes, matches, fruits, candy, and "typical Mexican products."[38]

Despite the ongoing intimidation by governmental officials, union-organized female street vendors staged highly visible protests and petitioned successive presidents to secure their livelihood and be given equal rights. The first labor organizations representing market vendors, including women's unions such as the Federación de Ambulantes and the Union Feminina de Comerciantes y Madres de la Familia, appeared in the late 1920s and early 1930s.[39] An organization called Feminista de Mercados actively participated during at least one of the three feminist congresses organized by the PNR in the early 1930s.[40] Market women also petitioned the president to serve on the board of the Consejo Consultivo (Advisory Board) of the DDF, its premier planning commission, but they were turned down.[41]

Female ambulantes also constituted a significant segment of petitioners who in March 1933 opposed the move of their stalls from Honduras Street, where they resided, to La Lagunilla. Later that year, fifty female vendors pleaded with President Rodríguez for protections against groups interested in removing their stalls from the streets adjacent to La Merced market, stating they were the sole breadwinners for their families. Aarón Sáenz answered that the streets had been reclaimed at the request of public transportation workers and firemen, who needed to use the street to attend to emergencies. In response, the union representative of the Sindicato de Commerciantes en Pequeño del Exterior e Interior del Mercado de la Merced y Calles Adyacentes (Union of Retailers of the Exterior and Interior of the Merced Market and Adjacent Streets) maintained that the president should resolve the matter and halt inter-union conflicts.[42]

Probably due to their feisty independence and ability to organize themselves through labor unions, these female vendors did not demonstrate the pastoral purity and pleasures of camposcape, even if they were representatives of the campo in the city. Instead, they were seen as embodying places of poverty and moral decay. A *New York Times* correspondent noted that Mexico City's markets were sites of squalor, where old women went from stall to stall to beg for food.[43] Reminiscent of Porfirian sentiments, post-revolutionary market women provoked anxiety as they appeared to live their private lives in public space. As public mothers, these women's apparent inability or unwillingness to conform to appropriate gender norms inspired both pity and unease. Urban planners felt that women who raised their children in the same stalls where they sold goods made their customers "uncomfortable."[44]

The discursive entanglements that tied markets to camposcape as well as the perfidious underworld would have direct consequences for the urban-reform efforts that commenced during the Rodríguez and Cárdenas administrations. If, as Lewis Mumford stated, the city itself was a "container" of *"surplus women"* that stood in need of male protection, market women stood in need of protection, containment, and transformation, all the more so to function as exemplars in revolutionary socialization of a larger citizenry.[45] In their occupations and protests, these women had to work for, not against, the revolution. For revolutionary leaders, this meant that the open-air markets and vendors who lined the streets of the historic district had to go. Here the plans of the federal government and the DDF coincided, and both governing bodies decided it was time to clean up the city streets. If, as they believed, the vast majority of street vendors were women, the creation of a public market in the center was all the more necessary.

BUILDING CAMPOSCAPE

On July 15, 1934, a *New York Times* reporter enthusiastically announced: "Mexico City goes modern! Not until the arrival of Cortes in 1500 [*sic*] have there been initiated such radical changes and improvements." The author detailed the enormous public-works projects under construction: sewage systems, parks and gardens, the educational complex replacing the notorious Belém prison, the "city's first skyscraper" (La Nacional), and the Palacio de Bellas Artes, which would house a new national theater. Mexico City would finally embrace a full-fledged modernity. The reporter noted that the Mexican government had spent nearly $3 million in 1933 and would double that amount for building projects in 1934. The reporter praised the new DDF jefe, Aarón Sáenz, the former governor of Nuevo León, as "a leader in city up-building and modernity."[46]

Given the multiplicity of challenges that urban planners of the DDF faced in the early 1930s and the vast resources committed to public-works projects, it seems odd that the creation of new public spaces was a priority. Even if urban planners, reformers, and architects of the DDF commissions envisioned the construction of new markets as a public-works venture, they also had other reasons for altering the built environment of the inner city. In building new markets, they created new public spaces, especially for women, with the goal of forming exemplary revolutionary citizens. Underlying this project were a number of cultural assumptions about relations among place, gender, and identity that frequently proved to be at odds with one another.

As a consequence, deciding what the new markets should look like was not easy. In late 1932, for instance, developer Antonio Chavez asked President Rodríguez for a nineteen-year contract to construct a market on the site of the former Volador market adjacent to the Zócalo. The DDF Obras Públicas (Public Works Commission) advised the president against it. The value of the lot was $311.40 per square meter, and the commissioners were concerned that Chavez would exploit the building for profit and that the city would lose control over commerce in the market. Moreover, the commission believed that the structure would not help to beautify the city, an issue they considered of the utmost importance, especially as the building would be close to the Palacio Nacional. As a four-story building on the Zócalo, the market would tower over the Palacio Nacional and thus diminish the perceived power of the state. Worse, it would spell disaster for the allure of the Zócalo, especially if Chavez would not adhere to the neocolonial style befitting the surrounding architecture. City officials also believed that the proposal would endanger the business of the big department stores such as Palacio del Hierro and Sanborns. In the end, Sáenz convinced the president to vote down the project.[47]

But this was not the only plan for new markets in the centro. Inhabitants of the zone could finally look forward to a new market when construction of the Mercado Abelardo Rogríguez began on February 6, 1933. The DDF acquired a lot on Venezuela, Carmen, and Rodríguez Puebla Streets the size of a quadruple block surrounding the old Colegio de San Gregorio, part of the Jesuit San Pedro y San Pablo complex dating back to 1573. The plans for the market included two freestanding pavilions with refrigeration for the sale of fish and poultry alongside a general building at the center containing a civic center, a civil registry, a day-care center, and a theater. During the colonial period, the Colegio de San Gregorio had instructed indigenous people in catechism and literacy through plays and musical performances. Conserving the sixteenth-century cloisters thus honored the area's history as a place of educational entertainment. Antonio Muñoz García, the architect in charge of designing and building the market, explained that in saving the convent as part of national patrimony, his proposal for the complex was conceived in harmony with the architectural environment of the colonial barrio.[48]

Located in the poor, east sector of the historic district, the market would tend to the needs of rural migrants not only in terms of food distribution but also architecturally. The building was to be executed in the neocolonial style, which most architects found the most appropriate for a new nationalistic architecture that was also befitting of the colonial centro. The two-story market reflected the aims of architects like Carlos Obregón Santacilia, who called for a "horizontal architecture" that reflected authentic "Mexican culture," that is, responded to the needs of rural migrants who were "accustomed to open spaces and to constructions that grow horizontally, where the sun and green spaces predominate; nature and human being are the most important."[49] In other words, the market—in order to be authentically Mexican—should invoke feelings and visions of camposcape.

Before tackling the Mercado project, Muñoz García, then head of the Office of Buildings and Monuments of the Division of Public Works, had observed how inadequate markets "caused disequilibrium in the organism of the city." Instead of a public service, these markets had been merely a source of pesos for city administrators who granted licenses arbitrarily to any vendor and thus were responsible for an eruption of street vending. Due to heavy taxation and poor planning, stalls with luxury goods such as cloth occupied the space inside markets, while basic foodstuffs were pushed onto the streets. Impromptu markets had sprung up in streets and parks, which, along with the frequently enumerated health risks and traffic jams, constituted an eyesore for the city's tourists. In order "to prevent the future growth of the city," the DDF had to control market activities, advised Muñoz García. Moreover, he urged that the beauty of the historic district be saved by rescuing what he called its "colonial jewels" from the degradation of being put to commercial use.[50]

Muñoz García, one of the foremost proponents of aesthetic principles in setting the guidelines for urban renewal, hoped to empty architecture of political messages. He favored simple designs that reduced time and construction costs and produced beautiful and healthy surroundings.[51] In keeping with this philosophy, he outfitted the Mercado with a modernist and Art Deco interior. The solution to the organization of the building was differentiating between its interior and exterior, with the result that the windows and arches of the building's facade did not correspond to the interior space. Instead, the design sought to recover and unify the building's many different architectural styles with a colonial surface, that is, a "colonial skin." The Mercado would furnish the densely populated barrio with a state-of-the-art, modern market that would beautify the barrio by eliminating the "ugly barracks of the ambulantes" and conserve colonial monuments as part of national patrimony.[52]

The hybrid architectural styles and spaces in the Mercado symbolized that revolutionary reform served to harmonize functionalism, order, history, and beauty. As we saw in the previous chapter, Muñoz García rejected the idea that all modern architecture should conform to a functionalist style. Instead, he agreed with cultural engineers such as José Vasconcelos, who were instrumental in introducing neocolonial architecture in constructing new buildings by advocating for a colonial style as a mixture between Spanish and indigenous that would produce a homogeneous national identity. Muñoz García's multifaceted design inspired alternate readings, depending on one's ideological and physical position vis-à-vis the market. The DDF's promotional photographs of the Mercado emphasized the traits that reformers wished to inculcate: the stark neocolonial facade harked back to a colonial desire for order; its Deco theater communicated the mestizo modernity of Deco bodies, entertainment, and beauty; and its sober and functional interior design served industry, progress, and health.[53]

In many ways, DDF officials envisioned the Mercado as a large educational facility, one that would inculcate proper hygiene, organization, productivity, and historical memory. Sáenz believed that the market would thus help society's poorest and most vulnerable, the female vendors and their children. Planners hoped to house women inside the market and place their children in a new day-care center and school, where they would be instructed in proper hygiene and basic literacy. For children who were still too young for such activities, the market would provide beds and a place of recreation. In addition to serving poor women, reformers hoped to inculcate modern behaviors and eliminate the inefficiency of the old markets, which, they believed, left customers confused in terms of spatial organization of foodstuffs and other products. By subjecting vendors to the interior space of the building itself, Sáenz hoped to instill a better work ethic and a modern, productive life philosophy: to live better, present themselves more effectively, and take better care of their merchandise. This was a large task, he noted, but one that the DDF pursued so that women who suffered much in obtaining their daily bread could improve morally, economically, and socially.[54] Sáenz maintained that modern and rational use of space would "awaken the vendor's stimulus" to better display her wares and sell superior merchandise, which would in turn improve not only commercial activity but also social interactions among vendors in the area. Strict regulations would spell out the obligations of both consumers and vendors in the market.[55]

Sáenz was not alone in his belief that the marketplace itself, in both a literal and a figurative sense, functioned as a space of moral instruction. Planning and architectural literature published under the auspices of the DDF narrated that markets had a long history as sites of socialization within colonial and national projects. The architect Francisco Bulman wrote in 1930 that Spaniards deemed the creation of markets a necessity in inculcating new customs and facilitating "the fusion of the two races." According to Bulman, the Spanish used the Mexica tiangius as a blueprint to accomplish the acculturation of colonized groups. The markets' aesthetic qualities as places of peace and order, where fountains and gardens served to uplift the spirits of vendors and visitors, had facilitated the process of colonialization.[56]

Consequently, the presence of camposcape in the market echoed not only longings for the simpler life of the campo but also nostalgia for colonial relations that were perceived to have established peace, harmony, and order. Like architectural projects elsewhere, the new revolutionary architecture was marked by a tension between camposcape and industrialization. For instance, in designing buildings in Chicago, the celebrated U.S. architect Frank Lloyd Wright "was ultimately ambivalent" about whether to endorse the industrial city or, instead, to embrace the "nostalgic image of the American suburb as a new Arcadia," creating a "domestic architecture of rural innocence." Once they were off the streets and housed in a modern structure, market women could perform camposcape by engaging in productive work. Thus, even though it was not built along the vertical, elongated style of Art Deco, the Mercado was conceived as female space, a container of "surplus women." Even if, apart from its theater, the Teatro del Pueblo, the Mercado did not bare the fine lines of the nude Deco body, it contained female bodies in an idealized setting reminiscent of the campo and the past. In its bid for camposcape, the Mercado endorsed spectacle in which urban campesinas performed an idealized but consumable version of the campo.[57] Time spent in the market was not merely an exercise in grocery shopping; it was to be a transformative experience, one in which performance of authenticity went hand-in-glove with revolutionary socialization.[58]

In addition to creating an instant nostalgia and ideas of Mexican authenticity afforded by camposcape, reformers hoped that the new markets would function as sites of knowledge in bridging the rural and the urban, creating new desires, and serving as an "educative spectacle" of cosmopolitan values. The incorporation of the Centro Cívico Álvaro Obregón into the Mercado provided reformers with a direct means to instruct both vendors and the inhabitants of neighboring barrios in revolutionary values. The center, previously housed in the Palacio Nacional, was formed from six civic centers located in the city's "centers of vice," that is, in barrios such as Tepito. These centers educated thousands of workers of both sexes, who engaged in "aesthetic and cultural preparation to elevate workers' moral and intellectual level." In 1934, the dedication and enthusiasm of the roughly thirty thousand alumni had reportedly reached such high levels that they formed groups to assist teachers in public schools. The leaders of civic centers, besides taking charge of the mission to uplift the character of the worker and to instill patriotism and revolutionary memory through art education, books, exhibits (including student paintings), lectures, and festivals, also concerned themselves with anti-alcohol campaigns and the protection of children. Women were encouraged to enroll in home economics courses especially designed to serve the needs of specific barrios to optimize practical application of the learned material.[59]

Of these cultural and civic centers, the Álvaro Obregón center engaged most actively in political education through the Teatro del Pueblo. In 1933, before moving to the Mercado, the civic center offered free lectures every night of the week, and in 1931 the PNR used the center to hold the first of three feminist congresses in the capital.[60] The inclusion of Teatro del Pueblo within the structure of the Mercado resulted from the Álvaro Obregón center's previous successes in drawing extremely large crowds to its cramped facilities. Sáenz proudly reported to President Rodríguez that the theater within the Mercado, which had a seating capacity of fifteen hundred and was outfitted with equipment required by modern stage design, was built as a premier theater geared to contemporary needs. In the social realm, the civic center concentrated its efforts on its special mission of orienting workers and peasant groups toward the state by staging festivals on Sundays in the theater, and periodically, with the Teatro del Pueblo acting ensemble, it facilitated excursions to the different delegations of the Federal District to give lectures that centered on social themes.[61]

THE THEATER IN THE MARKET

The Teatro del Pueblo was inaugurated in December 1934, a time when most theaters were being converted into cinemas. Despite this trend, the new theater would use the more traditional entertainment form as a tool in intellectual formation and provide the popular classes of the centro's heavily populated neighborhoods with the "aesthetic education" that they so needed, according to the *Revista de Revistas* article that covered its inauguration. Initially, however, members of the popular classes stayed away from the People's Theater. Of the roughly ten thousand visitors who milled around the stands during the *feria nacional* (national festival) of the Mercado's grand opening, only fifty found their way to the second-floor theater to watch *Los amigos del Señor Gobernador*, a social satire starring Gloria Iturbide. In stark contrast, carpa owners made ample profits from enthusiastic spectators who overran the festively lit tent theaters right outside the market.[62]

The new revolutionary state approached theater in much the same way that colonial administrators had: as a tool of education, acculturation, and pacification. Throughout the 1920s, the cultural programs that spearheaded the institutional phase of the revolution aimed at molding hearts and minds to forge a truly revolutionary citizenry. The creation of theaters such as the Teatro Lindbergh in the Condesa and the Teatro del Pueblo in the Mercado (as well as other playhouses in the city, such as Hidalgo and Bellas Artes) was a conscious effort on the part of the new administrators to educate capitalinos in revolutionary objectives. In order to reach out to an impoverished and suffering working class, the PNR also used radio and film as means to tie entertainment closer to state educational objectives, yet theater remained supreme. Compared to watching movies that cost between from 60 centavos to 1.50 pesos, about the average daily wages of a laborer, theater was cheap. In 1931, President Ortiz Rubio and his wife staged numerous benefit shows in the capital's finest theaters, such as El Iris, where circus, puppet theaters, and other spectacles sought to raise the spirits of working-class children. Early childhood education specialist (and later diplomat and minister) Amalia G. C. de Castillo started a series of theatrical activities for the DDF's Oficina de Educación y Recreaciones Populares (Office of Education and Popular Recreation) in 1929. Her "popular recreations," including drama contests for workers, were staged in schools, parks, prisons, and workers' centers. As part of this effort, poet and playwright Bernardo Ortiz

Mentellano created and directed a puppet theater, El Periquello, to travel the city's parks and schools throughout the year. This division within the DDF was also responsible for the construction of several temporary structures, such as the Carpa Morelos at the edge of the notorious La Bolsa neighborhood. Designed by Obregón Santacilia and furnished with backdrops by Diego Rivera, Carpa Morelos was the first of these traveling theaters owned and operated by the DDF. Inaugurated by Gloria Iturbide, it offered plays for and by workers on Saturday nights. In 1931 the PNR organized "cultural Sundays" in Teatro Hidalgo where the Department of Education established the Teatro Orientación. Even educational acting companies that performed infrequently shared in the mainstay of revolutionary repertoire, such as *Emiliano Zapata* (1932), which also dominated performances in the Teatro Lindbergh and Teatro del Pueblo.[63]

The inception of the theater in the Mercado thus marked the convalescence of a set of strategies to harness the lure of spectacles at the service of the new state. The DDF's Acción Social (Commission of Social Activities) used the Teatro del Pueblo to educate members of labor and campesino organizations. In addition to the "Sunday festivals" and educational tours of the Federal District, the Teatro del Pueblo offered artistic training and dance performances that gave residents of the city the chance to participate. These programs figured prominently in the annual performance of *La creación del quinto sol y el sacrificio gladiatorio* (The creation of the fifth sun and the gladiatorial sacrifice), an "indigenous" play staged by more than three thousand actors on the ruins of the pre-Columbian site of Teotihuacán.[64] By staging these enormous historical plays at the archaeological site, the Teatro del Pueblo attempted to urge "city Indians" and other working-class folk to enact a campo of the past—camposcape—and inculcate revolutionary historical memory. Rafael M. Saavedra had founded the Teatro Regional Mexicano (Mexican Regional Theater) under sponsorship of the Department of Education in 1921 after establishing the open-air theater at Teotihuacán. Supposedly constructed by local indigenous groups, theaters such as Teatro Regional Mexicano in San Juán Teotihuacán formed part of an effort by rural schoolteachers to instruct indigenous campesinos in "moral hygiene" and warn them against the dangers of alcohol. Plays in the open-air theaters were performed in both Spanish and indigenous languages and drew upon the colonial traditions of missionary theater. Contemporary dramaturge Rodolfo Usigli criticized these theaters as separatist and argued that, because their nationalist message kept indigenous people unaware of larger theatrical trends, they would not help to integrate indigenous people into the modern nation. He also questioned whether this type of theater would emancipate "the Indian" and whether it could incorporate the new ethnic ideal as part of the quest for the new Mexican citizen.[65]

Staging theater in marketplaces was not new. In Europe this tradition dated back to ancient times, and until well into the eighteenth century, theater and market were closely related. Large markets such as Bartholomew Fair in England came under middle-class scrutiny because of the nefarious influence of "obscene, lascivious and scandalous" market plays on the larger theater world.[66] In Latin America the historical development of theatrical entertainment similarly was tied to public festivals in "temporarily appropriated or liminalized" public spaces, where outdoor theater originated in elaborate public celebrations and pageants. Even privately owned theaters that staged variety shows were at times converted into public, accessible space due to low admission fees. Yet, these "democratic forms" of popular theater, no matter where in the world, ran up against the policing and disciplining measures of the state.[67]

The DDF used the Teatro del Pueblo to neutralize class tensions by raising a political consciousness that sought to attract working-class capitalinos to their version of revolutionary reform. While market women in the Mercado's main hall participated in performing camposcape, the Teatro del Pueblo aimed to instill a specific, official historical memory that rendered the revolution as a unified, nationalist effort with shared objectives that transcended concerns of class. Civic activities in the 1930s centered on patriotic commemorations and historic celebrations. PNR members organized ceremonies that paid tribute to great men who struggled for emancipation, interspersed with lectures and talks on the liberation brought by the evolution.[68]

The presence of the Centro Cívico Álvaro Obregón thus reflected a trend in which "los nombres de hombres" and "male monuments" memorialized the revolution. By naming the civic center after the "Caudillo of the Revolution" and changing the market's name from Mercado Carmen to Mercado Abelardo Rodríguez, city planners honored the building as masculine and national space. Besides its name, the legacy of the Álvaro Obregón civic center's ties to the Palacio Nacional inscribed the Teatro del Pueblo as a political space dedicated to the revolutionary generals and their links to national power. The stress on the cult of heroes in the civic center's curriculum sought to intensify patriotic feelings and underscore the importance of great men to the market as revolutionary space. By publicizing biographies of great men and organizing outings to monuments honoring fallen heroes, the civic center hoped to "awaken love for the city" and educate inner-city residents about their place in the nation's history.[69] Moreover, the many political functions and benefits staged around the memory of the nation's leaders underscored the importance of state-organized theater as a place of masculine power.

State theaters such as the Teatro del Pueblo, Hidalgo, and Lindbergh glorified the exploits of great men and tied these to both the revolution and the state. The first official function in remembrance of Emiliano Zapata was a vigil in 1930 at the Álvaro Obregón civic center before its integration in the Mercado. On July 17, 1933, Teatro Hidalgo was the site of the celebration commemorating the fifth anniversary of Obregón's death. The ceremony included a speech by historian Luis Araiza and utilized the theater as a place of high drama to conjure the spirit of the departed caudillo and transform the stage of entertainment into the platform of high politics. In his closing, Araiza emphasized the need to bring the leader back to life: "Álvaro Obregón! We want to revive you in this moment; here are the people that are your soul. Here is your spirit that is the revolution." The Teatro del Pueblo also staged commemorations, party functions, and political speeches. On January 21, 1936, Hernán Laborde, speaking on the occasion of the twelfth anniversary of Lenin's death, invoked another dead male war hero to explain revolutionary objectives.[70] In addition to being able to accommodate a large number of people, theaters were ideal locations for political functions in terms of ritual. Already imbued with the history of spectacle, which evoked expectations of emotional responses, theaters such as Teatro del Pueblo were the perfect setting for political drama.

The revolutionary leadership was not alone in appropriating spaces of leisure for political purposes. Mexico had a long history of leaders using playhouses for political functions, as evidenced by the numerous constitutions that had been signed in the stately Teatro de la República, in Querétaro, and the use of other theaters for political rallies. In an effort to separate entertainment from politics, legislation dating to 1891 prohibited theaters from staging benefit functions for authorities and functionaries. The custom, however, was revived shortly afterward, and this would continue, as revolutionary use of theaters was no different. Calles spoke in Teatro Iris during a rally in 1923, proving that even privately owned theaters proved useful to politicians. Theaters were important political spaces, and the Teatro del Pueblo's emphasis on politically charged, didactic plays thus fit into a larger tradition.

The Teatro del Pueblo represented a space dedicated to official, male history and precluded performances of revistas, tandas, bataclán, or other female frivolities, which, and not ironically, took place in carpas directly outside the market. When speakers in the Teatro del Pueblo addressed female workers, even the powerful Frente Único Pro-Derecho de la Mujer (United Front for Women's Rights), they stressed that "the great role" of Mexican intellectual women was to incorporate youth and students into the socialist movement.[71] The Mercado's ideologically charged camposcape of female space allowed authorities to contain politically volatile market women and female vendors—and, perhaps inadvertently, appropriated female space and female spectacle—to further the gendered messages of revolutionary reform.

The murals in the Mercado represented another attempt at revolutionary education and, with their depiction of rural people and places, resonated with the structure's overall gesture toward camposcape. By 1934 the buildings and walls of the centro had enjoyed a relatively long history of revolutionary murals. Mexican muralism as a public art debuted during the late 1910s and early 1920s in the church of the colonial Jesuit complex San Pedro y San Pablo (later the Hemeroteca Nacional de México, or National Library), across the street from the Mercado, where Roberto Montenegro painted murals in a European modernist style. During the early 1920s, José Vasconcelos declared that art should be aesthetically and physically accessible to workers and peasants. Following this, in word rather than deed, the new government commissioned murals as decoration for places that technically constituted public spaces, such as the Department of Education offices, the National Preparatory School, and the Palacio Nacional, buildings that members of the lower classes rarely frequented. No market had ever been selected as a mural site, making the Mercado's murals, which were painted in 1935 and 1936, unique.

In 1934 the muralist movement was more than fifteen years old, and its practitioners were divided over what murals should depict and how they should be painted. José Clemente Orozco and David Alfaro Siquiros in particular opposed Diego Rivera's glorification of nationalism, which closely conformed to the government's nationalist agenda. Rivera increasingly resorted to a romanticized indigenismo—especially during the 1930s, when he managed to get all the major government contracts—that, according to critics, buried the contradictions within the revolutionary project.[72] For the Mercado, however, the DDF hired a large group of young artists, some of them Rivera's students, to paint murals designed to teach the popular classes the value of proper nutrition. The contract was negotiated under President Rodríguez, but painting did not start until Lázaro Cárdenas took office in January 1935, and was completed the next year.

For the Mercado's murals, ten painters—six Mexican nationals, four foreigners, and two women—covered approximately 4,500 square meters (nearly 48,500 square feet) of wall and ceiling space, mainly at the entrances, vestibules, patios, and hallways of the principal market building. Even though the artists were the direct or indirect heirs of Rivera, most opted for new ways of painting and attempted to further politicize the medium. The murals differed little from Rivera's style, but they were far more radical and critical in addressing the exploi-

FIG. 22. Ángel Bracho, *Los mercados*, mural painting in the Mercado
Abelardo Rodríguez. Photo by the author.

tation of workers and campesinos. Unlike Rivera's grand murals in prominent political places that depicted the course of Mexican history as nationalist origination mythos, these paintings were meant to educate the proletariat without converting the images into folklore or objects for tourist consumption. Within the ongoing narrative of food production, struggles of workers appeared in the Mercado murals that especially criticized the contemporary crisis of cereal shortages and the detrimental influence of capitalism.

Due to their radical content, the murals faced considerable opposition during their creation. Overt socialist messages against fascism and Nazism abounded, especially in the work of Japanese American Isamu Noguchi, whose masterpiece, *Historia de México*, was a three-dimensional piece fashioned out of cement and plaster replete with clenched fists, swastikas, and skeletons that depicted the evils of fascism.[73] In 1936 new DDF regent Cosme Hinojosa suspended the project, but a consortium of eighty-five painters opposed the decision. In addition, leaders of the teachers unions urged President Cárdenas to show solidarity with the Mercado artists because of their eminent educational work for the masses. Members of the influential Liga de Escritores y Artistas Revolucionarios (League of Revolutionary Writers and Artists) also protested.[74]

The overarching theme of the murals was not the socialism of the urban proletariat, however, but the campo. Works with titles such as *Los mercados* by Ángel Bracho (see fig. 22), *Influencia de las vitaminas* by Antonio Pujol, *Escenas populares* by Ramón Alva Guadarrama, *Las labores del campo* by Grace Greenwood Ames, *Los alimentos y los problemas del obrero* by Pedro Rendón, and *La industrialización del campo* and *Los mercados* by Raúl Gamboa glorified not only the struggles of campesinos but also the purity and beauty of country life. The vibrant colors that showcased the campesinos' healthy bodies and the lush depiction of vegetation, fruits, and vegetables marked the murals of markets and the campo and contrasted sharply against the drab colors and macabre rendering of the horrors and poverty that are featured in the murals of urban life. Even Noguchi's innovative cement relief, so different in style and color, highlights the contrast between fascism and an agricultural scene. Hence, the Mercado murals not only aimed to "bring art to the people" but also delivered special messages about the importance of the market in sustaining urban life with a focus on market workers and consumers as productive citizens bringing the campo to the city.

Even if it captured and reflected a living present rather than the idealized past of Rivera's indigenismo, the imagery imbued with renewed revolutionary fervor served the vendors in the Mercado as much as it validated the state that had commissioned the art.[75] The murals, in complementing the jumble of colors of fruit and produce with the smells and sounds of the countryside that permeated the market, reminded its visitors and workers that mexicanidad was alive and well in the centro histórico. Moreover, as most market workers and customers were women, the Mercado connected notions of female space with the beauty of the campo but situated their well-being within the state that had furnished them this place.

The Mercado proved to be a signature project, perhaps the era's most important attempt at urban renovation in the capital. Its architecture, art, and educational and cultural spaces achieved an expression of power that served to legitimize the revolutionary government and, by deploying powerful symbols in its murals and design, evolved into a symbol of governmental power itself. Architecture, art, and the creation of public space altered the city as a tool in achieving the consolidation of the revolution. Not only did the PNR use political means to secure revolutionary continuity, but building projects also gave form to the institutions required in the institutionalization of revolutionary ideas.[76] The Mercado functioned equally as an investment opportunity and as a revolutionary veneer for conservative politics. Although the federal government, the DDF, and PNR leadership all promoted the Mercado as a noble attempt to deliver the gains of the revolution to the city's poor, the market paid homage to a "wily capitalist." As governor of Baja California, Abelardo Rodríguez had made a fortune as a bootlegger and casino investor.[77]

The construction of the Mercado indeed involved more than molding revolutionary citizens. A less transparent but no less important objective of the project was to increase the value of real estate in the vicinity, raise tax revenues for the DDF's Oficina de Mercados (Office of Markets), and widen and lengthen streets to allow for greater and more efficient circulation of cars and buses. A 1933 DDF report mentioned that construction for the Mercado would extend and streamline Venezuela Street, thereby establishing an important link for motorized traffic between the eastern and western segments of the city. Urban-reform policies of clearing streets, whether of vendors, markets, or buildings, were not a new strategy in dealing with congestion, but by the early 1930s, when car sales started to increase significantly and public transportation became a necessity to residents and city planners alike, it gained urgency.[78] The planners also hoped to increase city revenues. After property and business taxes, market dues were the third-largest source of revenue for the city. However, the DDF budget saw a shortfall of 119,957 pesos due to lost market tax revenue for the 1932 fiscal year, and the treasury again missed out on 84,528 pesos in 1933 for the same reason. City administrators were optimistic that projected tax revenue for the Mercado Abelardo Rodríguez and the new market of the colonia Del Valle would more than make up for 1933's deficit.[79]

The Mercado proved even more lucrative for the jefe of the DDF. FYUSA, the company he owned with Calles, secured the rights to build the Mercado as part of large government contracts such as the Centro Escolar Revolucionario, the Supreme Court building, and the Mercado Melchor Ocampo. FYUSA executed most of the signature projects of the era, and Sáenz thus stood to profit from this ambitious urban overhaul. By 1935 the DDF had spent 1,554,170 pesos on the Mercado alone.[80] Apart from revolutionary concerns with social reform, the Mercado thus was also the result of profit incentives of new political elites who used public works for personal gain, and in that sense was not much different from the private business interests that undergirded the development of colonia Condesa.

Nonetheless, the Mercado addressed community needs and, unlike the majority of functionalist architecture of its day, was conceptualized as part of the surrounding barrio. The needs of motorized traffic received special attention within the designs, but Muñoz García and the members of the DDF planning commission also considered the plight of pedestrians. As Jane Jacobs would posit decades later, the reformers viewed the accessibility of the market within the neighborhood from the perspective of a pedestrian on daily rounds, something of particular importance to women.[81] Unable to spend billions of pesos on new low-income housing to benefit all needy people, the DDF opted to alleviate some of the centro's most pressing problems by building a public market that had the potential of functioning as an alternative homescape for market women and their children.

CONCLUSION

A Casasola photo of the Mercado on its inauguration day depicts a dynamic scene (see fig. 20). The image shows the market's entrance, slightly off-center, with a sizable group of people ready to cross the threshold; the adjacent streets have filled with cars and simply dressed but modern-looking people. The photo does not show the entire market, but rather the general atmosphere of the moment. Unlike the governmental blueprints and photos of the market, the barrio has come alive, and the market has become part of the city.[82] In keeping with the photo's message, Sáenz and his DDF associates felt that the Mercado was indeed a great success and that it set a marvelous example to inspire future market reforms. Inspired by the Mercado, the DDF built five additional markets throughout the city, mostly in working-class neighborhoods, and some of the Mercado's services and special features were duplicated in other markets, including La Lagunilla, Tepito, and La Merced, even twenty years later. The fiesta that accompanied the inauguration of the Mercado was deemed such a sensation that the DDF granted vendors permission to organize similar, annual festivals to coincide with national celebrations.[83]

The initial euphoria, particularly on the part of DDF officials, hardly forms a sufficient indicator of how successful the urban reformers were in what they had set out to accomplish. The community reaped a number of direct rewards from the Mercado, as did the DDF. The increased quantity of affordable, quality foodstuffs helped to meet the needs of low-income consumers and aided city officials in forging a "social peace" through governmental intervention into food distribution.[84] The introduction of water, electricity, and pavement resulting from the extension of Venezuela Street constituted another welcome benefit for residents. The facility's sheer size and diverse functions had a significant impact on the surrounding area. The Mercado drastically altered the urban landscape of the surrounding barrios, and—as a vibrant public space—it forged and strengthened community ties, functioning as a point of gravitation for social, economic, and educational activities. During the remainder of the 1930s, the Mercado thrived and maintained its prominence as a signature project.[85] In April 1938, when Lázaro Cárdenas nationalized the petroleum industry, the Mercado served as the focal point for the famous "Colecta," the public collection of moneys to offset the indemnification of debt owed to oil companies. The Committee for National Economic Redemption would start its daily evening torchlit march from the Teatro del Pueblo to tour the centro and collect funds. If historical memory serves correctly, the market represented an *ágora popular*, an open, public marketplace that furnished the city not only with food but also with "social and spiritual services."[86] The neighborhood surrounding the Mercado has affectionately come to be known as "Abelardo." Hence, although the creation of markets was reminiscent of ill-fated Porfirian strategies, the Mercado integrated the barrios of the centro by furnishing the popular classes with a large place of social and economic interaction that strengthened communities.[87]

Despite these successes, the Mercado—as well as subsequent market reform—fell short of expectations and even had some harmful consequences. The goal of ridding the centro of street vendors, which planners shared with their Porfirian predecessors, failed to be realized. The Mercado proved unable to halt the rise of the informal economy in the area, let alone eradicate it. As late as the 1960s (and in certain areas up until the massive "cleanup" efforts financed by Carlos Slim started in 2000), women sold tacos, beans, tortillas, and enchiladas out of their houses or on the street. Furthermore, new markets like the Mercado did not eliminate food shortages. A perhaps unforeseen but nonetheless grave outcome was the proliferation of vecindades in the centro. Slums, necessary to house the many manual laborers involved in market work, persisted because of markets, and not despite them. In some cases, the creation of market buildings contributed to destitution of ambulantes. Most vendors were accommodated in the new markets, but those who had used their stalls as living quarters were left homeless. After World War II, increased governmental regulations resulted in limiting vendors' earnings. Crime also remained a dire problem. Although retired policemen patrolled the public markets, the area continued to be a part of the underworld and illegal activities.[88] Well into the new century, "Mafia-like organizations" attempt to control the Mercado and the surrounding barrio.[89]

The reformers' philosophy of creating a modern, productive citizenry contradicted their decision to give women only limited spaces to become full-fledged citizens. While the capital's cityscape was a negotiated and, ultimately, inclusive product, the creation of the Mercado occurred without community input, and instead constituted a top-down effort in forging revolutionary change. The market afforded the inhabitants of the centro, including women, significant benefits— better food, a healthier place to work, some education, child care, and perhaps a strengthened sense of community—but these advances came at a price. Some vendors and other barrio members lost their living space or were forced to join the swelling numbers in the slums, and increased taxation and regulation of market activity decreased vendors' earnings and autonomy. Revolutionary rhetoric contrasted sharply with the reality of governmental corruption and the persistence of urban poverty, yet Sáenz and the DDF planning commission took on public-works projects that the public sector ignored.[90] The market, a complex project from its inception, had mixed results.

As a multi-use public space, the Mercado Abelardo Rodríguez promoted the peaceful coexistence of different elements within revolutionary reform efforts in Mexico City. Its architecture, a jumble of conflicting styles, functioned as a metaphor of the multiplicity of revolutionary spaces and corresponding projects. The Teatro del Pueblo, housed in the remnants of a colonial ecclesiastic complex, not only conformed to legislation to safeguard national patrimony but also served as a place to educate workers and other lower-class barrio residents. In this capacity, it maintained important historical links with the San Pedro y San Pablo Jesuit institution and its mission to convert the indigenous population, signaling—however subtly—a continuation of the colonial project to civilize marginal groups. The functionalist day-care center and nursery school, with its emphasis on practical and scientific education for the neighborhood's youngest members, symbolized an investment in the future and the continuation of the revolution. The modernist interior of the market and pavilions aimed at instilling productivity, efficiency, and cleanliness, while the murals—regardless of their more radical messages—both legitimized modern values as revolutionary and modernized camposcape in redeeming the market as a modern reincarnation of the tianguis with its time-less, indígena, and near primordial quality of Mexican essence. Finally, the neocolonial facade suggested that a harmony of these divergent spaces and objectives was possible by respecting tradition, order, na-tion, and—above all—the revolutionary leadership.

The symbolic harmony of the Mercado was enhanced by important discourses of gender and space. While named after a male revolutionary general, the market first and foremost memorialized female space. As a public market with private features, the Mercado had been envisioned by urban reformers as a particularly beneficial place for female vendors. City officials wished to keep families strong by providing care for the small children of the female merchants, so that mothers did not have to divide their attention between their business and their children, a matter—the officials noted—that resulted in "a detriment to one or the other."[91] By housing female vendors indoors, male revolutionar-ies believed that they had eliminated some of the danger zones for female vendors and their children and had saved them from making a spectacle of themselves.

The market, however, performed its own spectacle. Neither a site of transgression and dirt nor a museum of commodities on display, the market was a site of performative interchanges.[92] As an outpost of the campo in the city, the Mercado was living camposcape. In its architectural hybridity, its colorful murals romanticizing the countryside, and its feast of sounds, smells, and sights provided by market women and female vendors, the facility echoed visual discourses that represented the campo and the city as gendered realms of stark contrast. The continued emphasis on the city and the campo as distinct spheres that characterized discourses of the entertainment world sharpened perceived tensions between the rural and the urbane, tradition and modernity, indigenismo and mestizaje. Like the camposcape of Parque México, the camposcape of the Mercado sought to neutralize these tensions.

Patrice Olsen argues that city-building in Mexico City remained a negotiated process that favored inclusion, especially on the street level, where contrasts, such as those provided by markets, functioned as "picturesque landscapes."[93] Despite the contradictions between perceptions of rural migrants in the city and romanticized ideas of the countryside, the camposcape of markets proved irresistible to urban audiences and foreign tourists alike. As we will see in the next chapter, during the remainder of the 1930s the entertainment industry increasingly solidified the idea that the nation's essence resided in the countryside. With the rise of the masculine state came a change of what camposcape would look like, however. Not the tehuana of the south, but the *charro* of the north—the main protagonist of Mexico's Golden Age of cinema—would take the lead in the remasculinization of the campo, and with it, revolutionary and national identity.

Palacio de Bellas Artes

On May 3, 1934, the Mexico City daily *El Universal* dedicated its weekly magazine to the imminent inauguration of the Palacio de Bellas Artes (Palace of Fine Arts). Bellas Artes would not open its doors until after the summer, but excitement in the city was building as the structure neared the end of its thirty-year journey toward completion. On the cover of the magazine, the enormous edifice appeared small, held by a coy, white Mexican beauty in traditional clothing. Bellas Artes indeed stirred national sentiments. In response to a media contest to determine what spectacle should inaugurate the new national theater, Antonio Gomezanda—director of the Instituto Musical—offered the fatherland what he labeled a "purely nationalist work." Gomezanda, trained at the finest schools in Europe, proudly announced in his letter to Narciso Bassols, director of the Department of Education, that his opera *La primera opera ranchera mexicana* (The first Mexican ranch opera) was inspired by contemporary Mexican literary, musical, social, and scenic depictions of the ranchos of the interior. Here, Gomezanda explained, he had encountered the nation's "purest traditions, the least foreign influence, and the most splendid campo."[1] Even if both *El Universal*'s cover (fig. 23) and Gomezanda's opera tied Bellas Artes to the campo, their camposcapes proved significantly different. Unlike the cosmopolitan folkloric female figure, Gomezanda depicted Bellas Artes' future as a masculine camposcape where rancheros and charros wrested the authentic countryside from tehuanas and other female indígenas. Both visions, however, proved prophetic.

At the time the Bellas Artes was completed, the performed campo, no matter how insipid, was still largely a female realm. However, as

FIG. 23. Cover, *Universal Ilustrado*, May 3, 1934.

the camposcape of tehuanas gradually gave way to the land of the charros, it began to undergo a masculine reinterpretation. Throughout the 1930s, city audiences learned to embrace an idealized countryside where dashing cowboys dominated the landscape as well as the silver screen, a trend that would accelerate through the Mexican-made feature film *Allá en el rancho grande* (1936). The masculinization of camposcape through the *ranchera* genre also served as a vehicle to instill perceptions of the revolution as a memorial to its fallen heroes. Bellas Artes, in search of viable forms of national entertainment that would not offend bourgeois sensibilities, turned more and more to this genre in fulfilling its promise to the revolution by elevating nationalist sentiments that increasingly aimed at uplifting lower-class morality.

Completed and inaugurated just months prior to the Mercado Abelardo Rodríguez, the Palacio de Bellas Artes in many ways presents us with a mirror to the Mercado. The road to the completion of Bellas Artes, the first official national theater to open its doors since the 1880s, was an arduous one. Designed and partially built during the late Porfiriato, it suffered from major structural weaknesses that had to be remedied before reconstruction could commence, and this required enormous financial commitments on the part of the DDF. Despite financial pressures in the midst of an economic recession and the engineering challenges that the structure posed, city leaders never wavered in fulfilling those commitments. The reason for this had to do with the type of spectacle that Bellas Artes offered. In contrast to the highly popular carpas and the burlesque theater, which faced increasing governmental censorship over the course of the 1930s, the productions of Bellas Artes celebrated a mexicanidad that políticos could live with. Because Bellas Artes often staged plays about or set in markets, productions hinged on the understanding of the campo as site of national identity. Like its Porfirian shell that hid a blatant Art Deco interior, Bellas Artes championed Deco bodies in its representation of indigenismo, using form instead of color in embodying the nation.

Nationalist market scenes staged in Bellas Artes, however, did not resemble the revolutionary theater performed in the Mercado. With the rise of sound cinema, the persistent popularity of carpas, and governmental hesitation to dedicate the new national theater to the lower classes, the brand of drama exemplified by Bellas Artes became an elite affair that inscribed the western part of the centro histórico with neo-Porfirian qualities. Under the strain of the popularity of cinema, theater increasingly became problematic as a tool in educating the lower classes, especially as it also catered to elite desires for upscale drama and opera. Within the larger framework of entertainment in the 1930s, Bellas Artes set the stage for the entry of a new masculinity predicated on the glorification of the revolutionary war hero that reached its apex in Mexico's cinematic Golden Age.

(RE)BUILDING A NATIONAL THEATER

The construction of the Palacio de Bellas Artes involved an arduous and drawn-out process, though this was largely unforeseen at the time. The new theater was conceived primarily as a showcase of Porfirian greatness, and its inauguration was planned to coincide with the centennial celebration of independence in 1910.[2] Working with the Italian architect Adomo Boari, the Porfirian government planned on erecting a structure that, with a seating capacity of nearly two thousand, would be the largest of its kind in the world and hence surpass the Opéra Nacional de Paris, which served as its main inspiration. Before starting on his designs, Boari toured famous theaters in Europe to study the latest stage designs, and he consulted with drama experts in order to perfect a stage suited for opera, ballet, comedies, and large history plays.[3] While Boari designed the new theater, federal and city officials surveyed the city for a suitable place for the venue. The planners eventually settled on a site adjacent to Alameda Central that would bring together the axes that formed the Porfirian city: the Paseo de Reforma, Plateros Street, and Juárez Street, which connected the affluent neighborhoods of Roma and Juárez to the Zócalo.[4]

This location was not only a felicitous choice in terms of anchoring the sociopolitical geography of the Porfiriato; it also enhanced the Art Nouveau appeal of the theater as a site of female history. Like the Mercado many years later, the new national theater would occupy the remains of a colonial church complex. Although the Mercado was housed at the site of the former San Pedro y Pablo colonial complex, the future Palacio de Bellas Artes was situated on the ruins of the Convento de Santa Isabel, built in 1680. In addition to female religiosity, the site was inscribed in popular memory as a place of "public women." After the Liberal Reform Laws were passed, city officials closed Santa Isabel in 1860 and converted its cloisters into public dormitories for single mothers, while the remainder of the building housed a silk factory that employed young female workers.[5]

The site was set aside for a national theater in the late nineteenth century, but in 1901 it was leveled when Porfirio Díaz decided to erect a more ostentatious structure in celebration of the 1910 centennial of independence. The idea that the new national theater would occupy female space in the city was strengthened in the popular imagination when construction workers came upon the physical remains of the convent's founder, Catalina Peralta. Reminiscent of a scene out of a Gabriel García Márquez novel, the bricklayers gazed in awe on a body mere moments away from final disintegration, dressed in clothes made of the finest embroidery and covered in religious paraphernalia. Peralta's body was not the only one that surfaced, though, and it soon became clear that many nuns had been buried under the convent.[6] The future Bellas Artes, an homage to entertainment, thus sat on female burial ground.

In addition to its unusual site, the theater was designed to communicate a sense of feminine space. Due to Boari's strict adherence to Art Nouveau, the theater exuded what contemporaries considered feminine charm. In borrowing the European style, Porfirians embraced a "feminine" aesthetic that represented opulence and civility, which was thought to elevate the city and the regime to the status of Paris. The Porfirian penchant for ornate fin de siècle furnishings of houses and public buildings was not lost on the Italian architect, who— being also awarded the commission to design the Palacio de Correos across from the new theater—looked to eclectic and elaborate styles made up primarily of European elements. The Palacio de Correos (completed in 1907), for instance, was made up of a complex mix of Spanish Renaissance Revival, Plateresque, Venetian Gothic Revival, Moorish, and Art Nouveau styles. For the design of the theater, Boari did not stray far from his European sensibilities, opting for an exotic, orientalist structure—which some likened to a Byzantine basilica— dominated by ornamentation steeped in organic design articulated through feminized landscapes.[7] The choice of white Italian marble, the building's rounded forms, and the theater's elaborate decorations softened its starker neoclassical design. Massive marble bas-relief on the main facade showed nude women as allegories of harmony, inspiration, and music, as did the oversized marble statues that flank the main entrance and occupy the building's numerous niches (fig. 24).[8] For contemporary Porfirians, the design communicated the ascendency of Art Nouveau and "the reign of ornamentation."[9]

Feminine cityscapes permeated the larger structure around the theater and radiated from its stage to the spaces far beyond its large marble walls. Boari's plans centered on creating a large, open interior where exotic plants exemplifying the architectural organic designs would convert the theater into a lush, indoor garden. Here, Boari hoped, visitors could engage in contemplation, conversation, and romance. The virtual garden would be bathed in natural light streaming from the glass domes in the ceiling, which would also permit the audience to show off their fashion sensibilities. The garden would extend to the esplanades and terraces surrounding the building, where plants and flowers would adorn porticos and *miradores* (lookout points). Boari envisioned that the gardens would also serve as an excellent backdrop for masked balls during Carnival.[10] While the gardens did not yet aspire to the camposcape that the revolution would link to indigenismo as an expression of Mexican identity, they greatly informed the national theater as a place of pastoral pleasures.

The charms of verdant tranquillity permeated plans for the entire structure of Bellas Artes, but its greatest asset in articulating Mexican camposcape stood within the theater's inner sanctum. The crystal curtain, the theater's most unique Art Nouveau feature, led European ideas of landscape to Mexican memories, and European decorum to Mexican performance. The permanent stained-glass curtain, created by the famous Tiffany Studio of New York, contains over a million pieces of glass and weighs more than twenty-one tons. Moved by two electric engines, the curtain cost nearly 100,000 pesos.[11] Installed in 1910, the glass mosaic showed the famous Popocatépetl and Iztaccíhuatl towering over the Valley of Mexico. The volcanoes, named after the Aztec warrior and his sleeping princess of a pre-Cortesian legend reminiscent

FIG. 24. Palacio de Bellas Artes, detail, constructed in 1908. Photo by the author.

of Romeo and Juliet, inscribed the stage with an indigenous landscape tied to the glories of Aztec Tenochtitlan. Gerardo Murillo, who had renamed himself Dr. Atl during the armed phase of the revolution and would become instrumental in launching the mural movement, designed the curtain.[12] The volcanoes, especially the Popo, featured prominently Dr. Atl's murals in an attempt to anchor indigenismo in landscape painting and elevate Mexico's pre-Columbian past.

Despite the building's bid for splendor, pomp, and circumstance, the project faced considerable criticism from its inception. After Díaz laid the cornerstone in 1905, newspapers responded with slogans such as "destruction for construction" that they deemed emblematic of Porfirian beautification measures in the city. The slogan was often invoked by critics of the regime, who understood that the old national theater was being demolished largely because of plans to widen Cinco de Mayo Avenue, thereby sacrificing national patrimony for the sake of capitalist development.[13] To make matter worse, construction ran into major financial and structural problems early on. The federal government allowed for 4 million pesos covering four years of construction, but actual costs quickly exceeded the budget. The white marble alone cost more than 200,000 pesos. The decision to use the heavy stone also made additional support necessary, and a concrete base and metal skeleton designed by the New York architect W. H. Wirkimire was put in place by the Miliken Brothers company from Chicago. Despite the sturdy base, the structure starting sinking even before its completion. At a pressure of 1.5 kilograms per square centimeter (roughly 21 pounds per square inch), the base needed repeated cement injections. Six years later, and at the outset of the revolution, the unfinished building had already sunk between nearly two meters. Due to revolutionary turmoil, budget constraints, and structural problems, work was suspended in 1913.[14]

With the sinking, obsolete Porfirian theater, both the revolution and the city had inherited a seemingly worthless treasure. By 1932, when construction resumed, the "marble monster" had cost Mexican taxpayers more than 20 million pesos. The fact that it sat incomplete, useless, and sinking into the city's unstable soil presented the revolutionary leadership with what the city's foremost journalists called "a sad spectacle."[15] Engineer and minister of finance Alberto Pani, by his own admission, was responsible for breathing new life into the project. Upon encountering the problematic edifice, he decided to embark on the momentous task of claiming the enormous structure for the revolution.[16] The executive branch decided that not only the revolution but also the capital city should claim this Porfirian inheritance. On October 8, 1931, President Pascual Ortiz Rubio delivered the unfinished theater into the hands of DDF administrators. Taking control of the national theater and what would transpire in it, the DDF promised to complete the project within two years.[17] This meant that, once again, the city shouldered the financial burdens and administrative responsibility for a cultural space that operated in service of the state.

Reconstruction efforts proved difficult. Pani had little love for the actual building, which he considered an exercise in bad taste and as "weak as the political and social regime in which it had its origin." As an all-too-visible holdover of the *ancien régime*, the theater presented Pani with a formidable challenge. In 1932 the country faced a severe economic crisis that forced Pani, then serving his second term as minister of finance, to work within the confines of what he considered a severely limited budget. Looking back in 1941, he proudly announced that under his direction the completion of Bellas Artes had cost a mere 7 million pesos, about a third of what had been spent on the structure during its Porfirian building phase.[18] Despite the financial burdens, resuming the project also generated economic opportunity. The modifications of the building provided the lower classes with about five thousand construction jobs, and construction contracts also led to an influx of commercial activity in the area.[19]

Of the thirty years it took to finish Bellas Artes, scholars consider the third phase, from 1932 until 1934, the most important in the gestation of the building. Pani changed the name of the structure from Teatro Nacional to Palacio de Bellas Artes to indicate the demise of the Porfirian concept of a national theater in favor of an inclusive, multipurpose institution of fine arts that would showcase the accomplishments of the revolution through concerts, lectures, expositions, and spectacles.[20] His plans envisioned that the structure would accommodate a museum of plastic arts, a conference hall, an exposition hall, a museum of books, a museum of popular art, and a restaurant. By gathering a variety of art forms that had been isolated from each other in one place and connecting a range of existing schools and academies through a governmental department housed in the structure, revolutionary art could truly fulfill its potential as a force of nationalism. In occupying Porfirian space, Bellas Artes showed that the revolution made Porfirian structures productive by filling them with revolutionary objectives.[21]

Like Muñoz García in his design for the Mercado, Pani envisioned Bellas Artes as a monument to the revolution as well as a means of educating the lower classes. First, Pani hoped to democratize the structure by simplifying its ornamentation in an effort to "suppress societal differences." Second, he planned to redesign the theater in favor of a multi-use space that allowed for instructing the working-class capitalinos in artistic formation through multiple venues. This entailed converting the vast, open interior into a constellation of halls dedicated to a plurality of art forms. Architects Frederico Mariscal, who had also designed and built the Teatro Iris, and Mario Pani, nephew to Alberto, were in charge of completing the structure's interior. Mariscal and Mario Pani had to drastically modify the interior in order to transform the building into its envisioned multipurpose design, which was considered a radical idea and emblematic of the revolution itself.[22]

DECO INDIGENISMO

In 1908, in direct response to the elaborate style of Art Nouveau, the Viennese architect Adolf Loos had condemned all ornamentation as a crime. Together with Josef Hoffmann, he developed what he called a new, rational architecture based on bare, geometric designs expressed by simple lines that would evolve—among other modernist architectural genres—into Art Deco. As demonstrated in chapter 5, Art Deco defied both traditional architecture and rigid functionalism, and it appeared to appease some of the Mexican architects who were divided over what style would best exemplify a revolutionary national character. In the architectural debates in Mexico during the late 1920s and early 1930s, Art Deco was thought to usher in a transitional period and provided opposing camps with a conciliatory position. Even with its connections to global capitalism and U.S. and European culture, Deco was able to express nationalist objectives and could be adapted to local realities.

Art Deco fit many different situations and lent itself well to commercial incentives, luxury interiors, and public buildings alike. According to the architectural historians Manfredo Tafuri and Francisco dal Co, Art Deco's "extenuating play of ascending lines, the recuperation of a large variety of ornamental solutions, and the use of refined materials all resulted in an adequate solution of incorporating the new taste and new quality of the chaotic flux of the masses and metropolitan consumerism."[23] The style expressed a quest for modernity without offending more provincial bourgeois sensibilities of moderation and need for easy assimilation. From President Calles's administration onward, a number of architects developed what Patrice Olsen has deemed "a fusion of Art Deco and pre-Hispanic elements." Examples were to be found in a new fire station that sported two black stone masks that represented the gods of fire and water, inspired by Olmec statues. Examples in ornamentation of doorways, windows, and staircases surfaced in the colonia Condesa. Of all of these efforts, Bellas Artes proved the most beautiful and successful.[24] Instead of a straightforward "fusion," however, the interior of Bellas Artes was a testament to Art Deco's versatility and its infatuation with primitivism, which allowed for the mapping of indigenismo onto its linear designs.

Due to the enormous open space within the walls of an exterior styled after outmoded architectural traditions, Pani and Mariscal had ample to room to engage in "the play of ascending lines." Mario Pani, who looked to Carlos Obregón Santacilia's work in the Deco colonia Condesa and the equally Deco Banco de México a mere two blocks from Bellas Artes, had studied at the prestigious École nationale supérieure des Beaux-Arts (School of Fine Arts) in Paris and was a firm proponent of introducing Art Deco into Mexico City. Yet, he would take his love for the style to an entirely new level in redesigning the interior of Bellas Artes. The choice of new ornamentation and materials such as bronze, copper, and onyx from Hidalgo and pink marble from Querétaro indicated that Pani embraced a highly evolved, bourgeois, consumerist style of Deco to lend

FIG. 25. Deco indigenismo, interior of the Palacio de Bellas Artes, designed by
Mario Pani, 1933. Photo by the author.

the nation's foremost center of art a palatable indígena identity. Serpen-
tine manifestations of Quetzalcoatl graced window arches, and depictions of the Nahua rain god Tlaloc and Mayan Chaac masks in warm
bronze and copper appeared on stark vertical lines on the theater's
main entrance, door handles, and light fixtures (see fig. 25). Echoing the
Deco bodies of the bataclán, especially the stylized mestizo Deco bodies
drawn by Cabral and the Deco indígenas in Casasola photographs, Bellas Artes' female space had been recuperated and modernized—made
linear and legible as healthy and beautiful—through Art Deco and
made nationalist and historic through indigenismo.

With its brilliant, luxurious indigenista Art Deco interior, Bellas

Artes had become a modern palace dedicated to the revolution. Historian Thomas Benjamin argues that Bellas Artes constituted a "glorious art nouveau monument" that was "Boari's (and Mexico's) true monument to Porfirio Díaz."[25] While Boari (and Porfirian Mexicans) certainly had intended for it to be that, its Art Deco interior repudiated those claims. On the outside, Bellas Artes still looked like a giant "creampuff" that spoke to the frills of Porfirian decadence, but the "true heart" of its interior, with its Deco indigenismo, belonged to the revolution. Upon its completion, the outwardly neoclassical structure had been invested with revolutionary camposcape and Deco modernism, thus bridging two contrary and oppositional political regimes.[26]

No contemporaries commented on the underlying reasons to resort to Art Deco in the design of the Mercado's Teatro del Pueblo and the Bellas Artes complex, yet the decision reflected the strong ties between Art Deco and the world of entertainment, not only in Mexico but also in a global context. Lucy Fischer notes the long relationship between entertainment and architecture in various permutations, from the more straightforward relationship of set designs to depictions of cities. In her analysis of Busby Berkeley films, especially his elaborate modernist metropolitan stage sets, scenes superimposing female faces over skyscrapers, and female dancers' bodies morphing into a city skyline, Fischer finds these were linked with the linear style of Art Deco. In short, the fantastical elements of the Deco style reminded spectators of the Deco building as a theatrical set, and both invoked the sleek figure of a woman as an architectural ornament.[27]

Some modernist architects working in Latin American cities also conceived of urban reform and the construction of buildings as designing stage or film sets. For example, Donat Agache's plan for the overhaul of Rio de Janeiro's city center included a layout of wide streets and large lots with high-rises that would "produce a decorative set," featuring two monumental columns and a stairway "as if in theatrical scenery." Agache also valued skyscrapers "as a form able to produce a decorative effect." Le Corbusier was taken with the grandeur of the continent and the seemingly limitless possibilities for a modernist future after witnessing Josephine Baker's "variety show act" in São Paulo. "The ebony goddess" apparently moved him to tears and led him to create a design for Rio that would "reflect and collect its American identity," as a theatrical scene of a "fully green" urban organism where human bodies in motion would form "the strongest instrument of memory."[28]

The interior of Bellas Artes, with its dramatic staging of indigenismo and its gleaming metal doors, railings, and light fixtures, was itself a cinematic experience. The floor plan, which still allowed unencumbered views of the Marotti glass-and-iron roof as well as the balconies of the three ascending floors, connected by sweeping onyx marble staircases, resembled a fantasy land film decor, or certainly would not have been out of place in a grand Hollywood movie. Stylized Deco calla lilies—the national flower—informed the large glass-and-bronze illumination columns reminiscent of the film sets in *Metropolis* that stretched from the floor to the building's high ceiling.

As the refashioning of Bellas Artes was under way, not all capitalinos could muster enthusiasm for the new "Palace of Beautiful Arts," yet the majority of criticism came from conservatives. Editorials in *La Prensa* took issue with Mariscal's and the Panis' concept of space. Discussing the building as they would a body, commentators stated that what the DDF considered reforms were nothing less than "shameful amputations" and "mutilations." They pointed to the new staircase as a ridiculous contraption completely contrary to the style of the building, and criticized the installation of separate halls as "dark, badly ventilated rooms of deplorable aesthetic condition." It was clear to *La Prensa*'s editorial staff that revolutionary reform had compromised Bellas Artes' health. Boari's vistas of uncluttered pastoral space had been usurped by Alberto Pani's fragmented and obscure rooms left to darkness after the domes were plastered over with reinforced concrete, thus obstructing the natural light that had been part of the original design. The new interior shape of the building, found one journalist, was a radical attack on national architecture.[29] Contrary to its new name, which communicated both art and beauty, Bellas Artes' altered body was found to be neither pretty nor healthy.

In spite of the radical alteration of the interior, however, Alberto Pani's strategy for Bellas Artes retained Boari's ideal of the theater as camposcape. While not explicitly commenting on his reasons for doing so, Pani clearly understood his efforts to re-create Bellas Artes as part of inserting a site of idealized countryside in the rapidly growing metropolis. Forging ties between the art complex and spaces of market activities, Pani placed a flower-and-fruit market right outside of Belles Artes' main entrance, which connected the building to Alameda Park. Also, Pani planned to outfit La Merced with a fine arts annex that would extend Bellas Artes' reach to the tenement communities of the poor east side of the centro. The Mercado de Artes Populares (Market of Popular Arts), part of Bellas Artes' Museo de Arte Popular (Museum of Popular Art), not only extended the Palacio de Bellas Artes to the lower-class barrio and the large market, but did so as a way to "fix national patrimony" to the marketplace. Like that of the Mercado, the presence of Bellas Artes in La Merced would cultivate the practice of private enterprise among the many worker associations tied to the market.[30] Perhaps these efforts were not as strange as they seemed. The entanglements between market and theater were historically rooted in the ancient and medieval city, where markets were the sites for theatrical performances ranging from comedy to mystery play. According to Lewis Mumford, "the marketplace recaptured the function of the earliest forum or agora."[31]

THE MARKET OF THE THEATER: "MÉXICO DE SERAPE"

The Palacio de Bellas Artes finally opened its doors on September 29, 1934. The elaborate inauguration program started in the morning when Abelardo Rodríguez officially opened the theater while the Orquesta Bellas Artes played the national anthem, after which the president toured the many galleries, museums, and exhibits throughout the building. The festivities suffered a major setback, however, when the guest of honor had to duck the many bottles and stones thrown at him by angry protesters directly outside the main entrance. After pelting the president, the enraged crowd broke windows in an attempt to enter the building. In response, police and firefighters resorted to heavy-handed efforts to calm and disperse the mob. After the disturbance had been quelled, the inaugural program, which had cost in excess of half a million pesos, resumed in the evening with such illustrious guests as Hollywood movie stars Dolores del Río, Ramón Novarro, and Douglas Fairbanks.[32]

Despite Antonio Gomezanda's enthusiastic offer, no national ranchera operas graced the stage of the Palacio de Bellas Artes on its opening night. Instead, Bellas Artes started its tenure as the national theater with the comedy *La verdad sospechosa* (*Suspicious Truth*, directed by Alfredo Gómez de la Vega), the Ballet of Monte Carlo, and the Andalusian flamenco star "La Argentinita."[33] The real star of the show, however, was the camposcape at the center of the revamped building. The state-of-the-art (and General Electric–created) light shows dazzled audiences as they brought to life the grand spectacle of the Popo and Itza on the famed crystal curtain. Due to ingeniously placed mirrors, the pre-Columbian volcanoes were bathed alternately in the pink hues of sunrise or the orange tones of sunset. A voice-over narrating the history of pre-Columbian peoples, especially the journey of the Aztecs to the Valley of Mexico and the foundation of Tenochtitlan, accompanied the light shows.[34]

Despite the dramatic overtures to nationalism, Bellas Artes did little to implement Pani's vision of attracting lower-class citizens and developing a truly national theatrical tradition. Bellas Artes' theatrical ensemble, Teatro de Orientación (Theater of Guidance), offered plays by Cervantes, Shakespeare, Chekhov, and O'Neill for the more discriminating tastes. Formed under the auspices of literary luminaries Xavier Villaurrutia and Salvador Novo, the intellectually sophisticated theater group hoped to elevate theater as art to counteract the negative effects of commercial productions that, in the opinion of stage and film director Julio Bracho, trailed fifty years behind current developments elsewhere.[35] Bracho—who advised the board of Bellas Artes in selecting suitable plays—was even more critical of some young Mexican playwrights, whose still immature work, he believed, suffered from severe weaknesses. For instance, in assessing Victoriano Martínez Lara's play *Sangre de patria* (Blood of the fatherland), which depicted the struggles of a poor campesino family during the revolution, Bracho condemned the play for its weak characters, illogical plot, and bad grammar.[36] In keeping with discriminate tastes, the new national theater would—apart from the occasional foreign literary play—be home to Italian operas, *Salomé*, Russian ballet, and numerous returns of "La Argentinita."[37] In response, the press increasingly criticized Bellas Artes for offering nothing more than operas and ballets. Comedy, the "flower of artistic spectacle" and the spirit of national sentiments, according to one theater critic, was left without the proper home it so needed.[38]

If Bellas Artes' repertoire of opera and ballet catered exclusively to the middle and upper classes, it was because comedies popular with working-class audiences did not receive the approval of revolutionary leaders. In reviewing Bellas Artes' performance as Premier Theater of the Nation for the year 1937, an anonymous columnist in *El Universal* commented that even though the revistas of the comedian Roberto Soto in Bellas Artes could not satisfy the scrutiny of the government's educational objectives in cultivating good taste, they remained popular with audiences. Soto's humor, commented the columnist, made up for the less than inspiring mainstay of regional dances and other "sins of pretense" in Bellas Artes.[39]

Despite Bellas Artes' penchant for folkloric regional dances that could be construed as popular entertainment, critics believed that these offerings did not express an authentic Mexican national identity. In an effort to present a Mexico constructed for tourists, they argued, the Department of Fine Arts bent and twisted authentic national artistic expressions to serve the interests of the revolutionary elite. This "México de Serape," deemed journalists, did not originate in the tastes of the popular classes but in the middle-class "perversions of popular artistic sentiment." Thus, one writer concluded, the revolutionary agenda of the state failed not by protecting bourgeois art per se but by protecting bourgeois interpretations of popular art that resulted in "mediocre affectation."[40] In short, the camposcape of Bellas Artes, which fit the objectives of the Department of Education and government officials keen on attracting tourist dollars, alienated the city's theater critics, social commentators, and working-class audiences.

If Bellas Artes served bourgeois and tourist consumption of what most of Mexico City press deemed facile folklore, teachers from the Department of Education used other performative spaces in the building to acclimatize the popular classes to refined art. Yet even if Pani's plans for exhibition space focused on the edification of popular art and crafts as the national art form, Bellas Artes' permanent art collection consisted largely of murals fashioned by the movement's principal artists. As explored briefly in the previous chapter, muralism among all arts was thought to best express revolutionary sentiments and was most recognized as uniquely Mexican.[41] Yet muralism in Mexico was nearly an exclusively male domain. Despite the brief incursion of the Greenwood sisters working in the Mercado and the largely unrecognized work of María Izquierdo, muralism stayed within the confines of male painters. The movement, while multifaceted in style, content, and practitioners, became consolidated in the work of the Tres Grandes—Diego Rivera, José Clemente Orozco, and David Alfaro Siquieros—which exacerbated the masculine outlook of mural painting in Mexico and mirrored the gender dynamics that underpinned the institutionalization of the revolution.

Like the Mercado, Bellas Artes was outfitted with murals upon its completion. Unlike the murals in the Mercado, which focused on ongoing struggles of the urban working class and campesinos, were seen by working-class market-goers, and were painted by a group of young and eclectic artists, the wall painting in Bellas Artes were a largely elite affair. The Department of Fine Arts started to acquire murals for its permanent collection in 1934, at a time reflecting a more conservative stage in the development of the work by the Tres Grandes after their bid for didactic impact and political radicalism had reached its apex. Even if the murals were categorized as revolutionary art for public consumption by the popular classes, they expressed the rise of a nationalist bourgeoisie rather than constituting "art for the masses." With the institutionalization of the revolution, muralism—at least as expressed by the Tres Grandes—became part of the state apparatus. Against the backdrop of the problem of nationhood and modernity, the Tres Grandes turned to definitions of Mexican identity and history, appropriating and consolidating the past into epic narratives that told Mexicans who they were.[42]

In addressing Mexico's history, revolutionary muralism not only participated in new constructions of indigenous identities but also portrayed visions of modern Mexico by addressing political and social issues in the present and of possible futures. As the movement progressed, representations of campesino lives, especially in Rivera's work, made way for a glorification of indigenous traditions and idealization of revolutionary inclusion of indigenous groups. This shift was expressed not only in terms of style, such as Rivera's adoption of pre-Columbian arrangements of space, but also in choice of subject matter. Here, the focus was principally on the indigenous past and contemporary indígena practices, such as fiestas and markets.[43] In Bellas Artes, this indigenista camposcape was positioned alongside a growing infatuation with modernism and modernization.

Exhibited on the second floor above the main halls, murals with historic themes concentrate on pre-Columbian indigenous cultures, conquest, and mestizaje. For instance, indigenist tropes abound in Siqueiros's diptych *Tormento de Cuauhtémoc y Apoteosis de Cuauhtémoc* (*The Torment of Cuauhtémoc* and *The Apotheosis of Cuauhtémoc*), an homage to the resistance of the last Aztec ruler and testament to Spanish cruelty and tyranny. Read together, the images reveal that the tortured indigenous hero will rise again to lead his people, a reference to indigenista politics of the revolutionary era that sought to liberate the Indian. The allegorical female figure in Siqueiros's *Nueva democracia* (*The New Democracy*), by contrast, focuses on the mestizo nature of the Mexican nation that looks to European traditions, such as the French Revolution, for inspiration in establishing a free, and new, democratic system.

The earliest murals commissioned for Bellas Artes dealt not only with indigenist and historic topics but also with the promises and perils of modernity. On the third floor, José Clemente Orozco's *Catharsis* (1934), fashioned for Bellas Artes' permanent mural collection, uses emblematic dangers of technology and mass culture to criticize the social degradation forged by modern society; it points to the cathartic fires and destruction that are necessary to purify society. On the second floor, Rivera's *El hombre en el cruce de caminos* (Man at the crossroads, 1934) depicts a human-controlled machine that appears to destroy the Earth's natural resources in order to enrich the industries of the wealthy North, symbolized by gambling, debauched white capitalists who oppose rallying, socialist workers. The mural, re-created for Bellas Artes after the 1933 original in New York City's Rockefeller Center was destroyed on orders of Nelson Rockefeller due to Rivera's refusal to remove the figure of Lenin, is a polemical sketch of the grand schema of early-twentieth-century history, illustrating the global forces in which Mexico finds, and must place, itself.

The reincarnation of the mural in Belles Artes entails a series of interesting juxtapositions where gender serves to structure class differences. In *El hombre en el cruce de caminos*, Rivera literally places a man at the center of the world, at the controls of a machine that orders the universe. Radiating outward from the man/machine in the center, a series of scenes depicts life in the industrialized North on the left against the socialist utopia on the right, in which women and men alternate in embodying capitalist or socialist values. Directly to the right of the man/machine is a panel in which Lenin unites colored male workers juxtaposed with gambling older white women. The top panels show socialist women of all racial backgrounds rising up against an army men wearing gas masks. Harking back to Rivera's earlier work, such as *La noche de los ricos* (Night of the rich), bad women incite capitalist vice, while good communist women are healthy, strong, and devoted mothers and workers. Interestingly, Rivera replaced the teachers in the Rockefeller Center design with a scene from a nightclub to show the debauchery of the rich.[44] Orozco's *Catharsis* highlights a white and nude prostitute amid death and destruction, indicating that overt female sexuality is at the core of corruption that needs to be destroyed and cleansed. As a middle-aged and heavily bejeweled woman, with her face contorted in sarcastic laughter and legs spread wide, this central figure represents a public woman who inspires terror reminiscent of *Detectives'* fear-inducing imagery of prostitutes and other loose women thought to occupy Mexico City's underworld.

Like theater productions staged in Bellas Artes, its murals were intended as public art for the enjoyment and education of the popular classes. However, similar to the regional dances and ranchera operas, most murals—especially when housed in the same space—reduced popular imagery into folklore or objects for tourist consumption. Despite their creators' best intensions, and even when overtly political, the murals often succumbed to a staid polemics that solidified notable male historical figures as the nation's great heroes and used anonymous female bodies as allegorical figures who—depending on their sexual mores—either liberated or disgraced the nation. Rivera's visions of an idealized pre-Columbian past wove history, fantasy, and memory into a golden tapestry of nostalgia and myth that increasingly formed the visualization of national identity. Rather than capturing and reflecting a living present, as his students had done or had attempted at the Mercado, they staged an idealized past as desired by the federal and city governments. In this, muralism formed an integral part of the contemporary modernist fascination in Europe and the United States with the exotic and primitive. Moreover, the institutionalization of the Tres Grandes—and their male-centered visual histories and views of modernity—also meant that the revolutionary legacy was one in which women occupied restricted physical and ideological spaces.

REVOLUTIONARY MASCULINITY:
ALLÁ EN EL RANCHO GRANDE

In many ways, the tensions between modernity and its celebration of camposcape that dominated the Bellas Artes' murals were indicative of the changing representations of camposcape. The gendered dimensions of camposcape in particular were changing in other visual narratives and cultural shifts at large. During the 1920s, cinema started its rapid ascent as the city's preferred form of entertainment, but it was not until the early 1930s, with the start of sound cinema, that film overtook theater in Mexico. Many playhouses, such as Salon Rojo, had shown movies as part of their theatrical offerings from the 1910s onward, yet by the mid-1930s many of these venues showed films exclusively. After the completion of Bellas Artes, El Iris lost its place of prominence and succumbed to financial pressures. El Iris entered into a contract with the U.S. media company RCA to show four movies a week. La Iris, too, moved from the stage to the screen. Like many other stage actresses of her time, Esperanza Iris embarked on a movie career by the early 1930s, playing maternal roles in fairly successful features such as *Mater noster* (Our mother, 1936) and *Noches de gloria* (Glorious nights, 1938), often to critical acclaim.[45]

If by the 1930s theaters symbolized outdated traditions, movies signaled the start of the modern era. In 1931 the Federal District counted fourteen theaters and seventy cinemas.[46] By 1938, even famed theaters such as Iris, Colón, Principal, Regis, María Guerrero, and Politeama had succumbed to the lure and popularity of the movies.[47] By 1942, journalists commented that theaters were virtually empty. With Deco bodies ensconced in film, young capitalinos flocked to the silver screen to behold close-ups of their idols kissing each other without restraint or modesty. Raised on cinema, the young person did not understand or love theater, complained theater critics, and thus ignored it all together.[48]

Despite the lure of Hollywood, early Mexican films looked more like stage productions than many film aficionados realized. Still in its infancy when Bellas Artes opened, Mexican film would come into its own by the late 1930s, not only as a successful industry but even more as a cultural product that would attract a large audience, especially after the release of Fernando de Fuentes's blockbuster *Allá en el rancho grande* (Out on the big ranch, 1936). A romantic musical written by none other than revista author Antonio Guzmán Aguilera (also known as Guz Águila), this comedy of errors tells the story of two good friends, the owner and the ranchhand of the Rancho Grande, who fall in love with the same girl. Set on a hacienda in an unidentified, amorphous campo in northern Mexico, de Fuentes's rural world is filled with a new array of regional types to whom, according to one critic, "the revolution did not appear as important as parties, rodeos, and songs." The film picked up on, and became emblematic of, one of the principal themes within "México de Serape" that informed the remaining revistas popular with working-class audiences and tourists.

Leaving the china poblanas and tehuanas to the *jarabe tapatío* (traditional dance from Jalisco) and zandugas of the future Bellas Artes' Ballet Folklórico, the changing camposcape influenced by "México de Serape" became more and more imbued with the charros on the frontier ranchos of the vast northern landscapes.

In addition to changing the imagined rural landscape from an indigenous realm to the land of charros, *Rancho grande* also set a new tone for the gendered dynamics of camposcape. In its depiction of the world of the charro, Guz Águila and de Fuentes codified a set of gender stereotypes as crucial elements of the comedia ranchera. Introducing the soon-to-be-famous character of the singing cowboy (a role that defined the careers of later screen idols Jorge Negrete and Pedro Infante), the film depicts a mythical campo dominated by social bandits, dashing cowboys, mestizo campesinos, and beautiful but naive young women. In this romanticized world, masculine honor and homosocial friendships trump politics, social issues, and class status. The singing charro embodied all the qualities of desirable, virile Mexican masculinity. As an honest, hardworking hacienda owner, the charro—unlike the double-crossing lower-class urban pelado immortalized by comedians such as Cantinflas—not only revalorized the campo as a simpler, purer place but also tied it to masculine honor. Women, especially the film's main female protagonist, functioned as objects of tension that tax male friendships. In terms of female character development, *Rancho grande* is a Cinderella story of a meek, barely noticed young campesina who turns into a swan to command male attention. In many ways, *Rancho grande* harked back to the paternalistic past of the Porfiriato, when benevolent but strict fathers were in control and everyone knew his or her proper place. This entailed that women, who generally had not fared well as independent, successful protagonists in Mexican film, receded even further into the background.

Once they were ensconced in the highly popular comedia ranchera, these gendered types gained even more staying power. As critics attest, with its "lavish, dreamlike" cinematography and its timeless feel, *Rancho grande* "built a brand new mythical Mexican identity almost singlehandedly."[49] Placing the Hollywood cowboy in an easily recognizable setting for Mexican audiences, the rancho, it married song to film so successfully that it launched an entire new musical genre, the *canción ranchera*, anticipated by Antonio Gomezanda when he offered up his ranchero opera to inaugurate Bellas Artes. The film also put Cinematográfica Latino Americana, S.A. (CLASA) on the map as Latin America's main studio and paved the way to the advent of Mexican cinema, which reached its apex in the 1940s—the much-touted Golden Age of Mexican cinema.

In many ways, the charro spoke to the desire for new masculinities in the wake of the revolution, when new norms of male behavior emerged that had their roots in the revolutionary struggle against an aging patriarch.[50] As we saw in previous chapters regarding the heroic masculinity celebrated in monuments, the female masculinity that followed on the heels of stars such as Dietrich and Garbo, along with notable upsets in gender roles in general, the revolution itself appeared to have had a large role in masculinizing society. Demonstrating the links between the revolution and the fashioning of new masculine identities, Gabriela Cano argues that critical situations such as revolutionary combat, where "manners and reserves were abandoned," forged both strong homosocial bonds and a more combative masculinity, which allowed fellow revolutionaries to gain status within the brotherhood of the armed forces.[51]

Ranchera films followed on the heels of cinematic, theatrical, and other visual representations enshrining popular heroes such as Villa, Zapata, Obregón, and Carranza as the revolutionary family, even if they had little in common other than the fact that they had been soldiers. Moreover, the popularity of the charro was emblematic of the ascent to national power of middle-class administrators who—like future president Miguel Aléman—had not fought in the armed struggle and stood in need of an image that would lend them revolutionary appeal. The allure of the male camposcape allowed these "junior men" to identify with the charro as a signifier of revolutionary, heroic masculinity that communicated strength and virility. In national political circles, the term *charrismo* quickly came to indicate the top-down structure of labor unions tied to the state, where unscrupulous labor leaders entered into bossist manipulation of the rank and file under the guise of patriotic loyalty and national development.[52] According to scholars such as Salvador Oropesa, the "charro nationalism" that came of age during the Cárdenas years was "a paradoxical mixture of the new consumerism coming from the United States and folklorism of the charros." Moreover, even though this charro nationalism was tied to a popular culture defined in rural terms, its expressions— "radio, cinema, boxing, wrestling, bullfighting, cabaret, café de chinos, carpa . . . and the red light district"—were clearly urban.[53] Yet the very contradictions and "paradoxes," especially in validating the class dimensions of national politics, worked in tandem and were mutually constitutive in the modification of camposcape, which—despite historic continuities—was retooled as a heroic, historic, and, above all, masculine space.

The placid landscapes of "México de Serape" celebrated in the ranchera genre that propelled Mexican cinema to its Golden Age increasingly became a construct of insipid nationalist theater that reflected little more than a conservative political desire to maintain Mexico's image as a virtual, unspoiled campo. Instead of the edenic garden of the female indígena, however, camposcape had become the land of the white or mestizo male ranchero. Meanwhile, the presence of the campo in the city was policed ever more stringently. While Bellas Artes relied more and more on the fame of its Ballet Folklórico, and movies showed Pedro Negrete in charro films, city markets faced tightening restrictions. Aarón Sáenz's well-publicized fight against poverty, disease, and unsightly women on the street had done much to inspire hope for a healthier—and certainly prettier—Mexico City, even if problems remained. In the light of an indigenous feminine camposcape giving way to a male mestizo and campesino one, it is all the more interesting that Cárdenas's tenure as president is known as a period that forged ties between Mexico City and the campo that were both enduring and yet never again replicated. Cárdenas, according to John Ross, realized that the urban proletariat of *chilangos* and the campesinos were merely two sides of the same coin and that chilangos "deep down" were really campesinos.[54] The campesino-like qualities of the chilangos, however, especially when robbed by the city of their camposcape honor and innocence, were perceived as ever more problematic.

"EVERYTHING IN ITS RIGHT PLACE"

Because the elites viewed the lower-class countryside as backward, Alberto Pani's vision for Bellas Artes' role in acculturating the lower-class chilangos proved increasingly problematic. Following an incident involving vandalism and theft, Cárdenas ordered on February 8, 1938, that no more union meetings or other political gatherings would be permitted to take place in Bellas Artes. During a union gathering, workers had reportedly extinguished their cigarettes on the plush carpets and then made off with some crystal and bronze decorations that they had dislodged from the upscale boxes. In response, Cárdenas decreed that political meetings be moved to the Teatro Hidalgo, which, according to journalists reporting on the new ordinance, had a longer tradition of hosting union functions and was old and devoid of luxury furnishing. The incident raised pertinent questions. Should only the bourgeois have access to the national theater? Had the revolutionary leadership not stated that Bellas Artes was a space for the use of the popular classes?[55] Debates raged in the press about the validity of the executive decision and the nature of Bellas Artes as a public institution, reflecting the larger contest over urban space in the center of the capital, the legacy of camposcape, and the discourse of health, beauty, and female bodies that connected these themes.

By the end of the 1930s, Bellas Artes no longer appeared a proper place for the popular classes.[56] One side of the debate held that Bellas Artes was not the place to host workers' festivals and other celebrations that had nothing to do with art. Opening up "the First Theater of the Nation" to these type of activities, argued proponents of this position, was as preposterous as "proposing to have trapeze and flying swings around the Column of Independence, an exhibit of livestock in Chapultepec Park, and a fair in the National Palace." As one journalist commented, it was important to have "everything in its right place." Others concluded that the incident at the union gathering showed that Bellas Artes had not followed its designated course and that authorities prioritized property over people.[57] Bellas Artes, commented *Gráfico* columnist "Jubilo," suffered from two types of harmful elements: those who ruined carpets, and those who had elevated objects to the level of obsession and adhered to the belief that everything, and everybody, should be in its "right" place.[58]

Pani's objective of dedicating Bellas Artes to the popular classes had met with opposition early on. Even before the new theater had opened its doors, pundits had questioned whether Bellas Artes would fulfill its role in furnishing the popular classes with upstanding entertainment. Noting that the new national theater only had two thousand seats, they jokingly proposed to repeat shows often, admit spectators on a first-come, first-served basis, and refrain from charging admission.[59]

Theater aficionados blamed not only the workers but also DDF administrators for the general state of malaise in Bellas Artes. Playwrights and cronistas, among them illustrious names such as Armando de María y Campos and Xavier Villaurrutia, wrote President Cárdenas of their dismay at the lack of efficiency at Bellas Artes in a letter published in the city's foremost newspapers. They cited lack of proper management for the disarray of the Department of Fine Arts, which had been unable to implement its program for 1937. Due to the absence of centralized authority, they argued, offerings at Bellas Artes were arbitrary and smacked of favoritism, and the shows it did offer were at the whim of private enterprise and lacked the quality befitting a national theater. Bellas Artes neither fulfilled its obligation in terms of education nor served as a model for the nation's youth. They advised the president to form an honorary committee drawn from prominent artists, who, together with the director, would select the shows in accordance with the tourist season. In addition, supplementary government funds would help to limit the detrimental role of private business.[60]

Following the incidents of vandalism, public scandals, and protests, the Department of Fine Arts did undergo a drastic reorganization. Cárdenas revoked its independence and returned it to the leadership of the Department of Education.[61] Among the new staff were Rudolfo Usigli as head of theater, Nellie Campobello as director of the dance school, and Bellas Artes' new jefe, Celestino Gorostiza, who was put in charge of an investigation into the "nation's folkloric traditions," especially with respect to pre-Cortesian, indigenous music.[62] Gorostiza also consulted with private enterprise to combat the general state of decadence of theaters and restore theater to its former glory. In comparison with the progress that had been made in the other arts since the revolution, theater was deemed a failure. In order to remedy the situation, Gorostiza hoped to make Bellas Artes a central force in the production of theater by Mexican artists.[63]

This overhaul of Bellas Artes, unfortunately, ran into trouble early on. In the summer of 1938 the Department of Education provoked an uproar by refusing to host the farewell concert of the popular culture icon Augustín Lara. Lara, a bolero singer who had risen to fame by working in cabarets and composing songs that the Education Department deemed morally suspect, protested the decision, but the director of the department remained firm in his opinion that "negative elements" such as Lara would undermine his efforts at elevating the tastes of Mexico's citizenry.[64] Editorials opposed the renewed focus on politicization of theater, especially theater in service of the state. In order to clear the "miasma of pestilence" that was political theater, whether communist, socialist, even just "revolutionary," theater should just be art for art's sake.[65]

Bellas Artes remained a problematic space in many other respects as well. In 1938 reports indicated that the structure itself was weak and that in case of an earthquake it would not only suffer irreparable damage but also collapse or sink further into the ground. Little recourse existed to prevent the decline of the building into the unstable soil of Mexico City's ancient lake bed. Engineers advised that a solid cement base would be the only remedy to save the building.[66] These structural weaknesses caused public concern again in 1941, when, due to the seemingly unstoppable downward tilt of the building, a block of marble fell into the orchestra in the middle of a performance. Worse, authorities appeared largely indifferent to the issue of public safety. The Department of Education had not spent any of its 6-million-peso budget set aside for repairs to remedy the problem. Bellas Artes needed to close its doors, proposed the daily *Excélsior*, or face the possibility of operating as an "underground theater."[67] A series of cement injections could not defy gravity or fortify the unstable soil; Bellas Artes was sinking.[68]

Bellas Artes' reputation was clearly sinking as well. The tales of fraud and disorder involving the highest administrators of the Department of Fine Arts reached a fever pitch in 1941 when reports of a wave of thefts by Bellas Artes personnel served to illustrate the incompetence of its director, Fermín Cuéllar. Besides theft of costumes, including women's lingerie, beauty products, and even the chairs of the presidential box, Bellas Artes seemed to be a site of decadence and decay, where employees engaged in after-hours parties to drink, engage in orgies, and wreak other havoc.[69] Even respected dancer Nellie Campobello was implicated in fraud, discovered entertainment inspectors. Although she earned a full salary from the Department of Education, she informally charged her students additional tuition.[70]

A group of actors also came forward to accuse the Department of Fine Arts of fraud and deception. The Cuadro Dramático Popular (People's Theater Group), geared toward educating the city's workers, maintained that from their inception in 1936 they had performed on numerous occasions for the Department of Education yet had not been paid nearly the wages stipulated by their contracts. The small and sporadic cash payments they did receive had forced them to lead a hand-to-mouth existence.[71] Even more scandalous, they stated, Bellas Artes shelled out exorbitant sums to foreign groups to perform in the national theater. While humble Mexican actors of the Cuadro Dramático Popular were starving, the Russian ballet company Daniel grossed 150,000 pesos for its performances in the theater, even when paying a mere 3,600 pesos to cover rent, electricity, and service personnel.[72]

In the end, the state's efforts at theatrical renewal seemed to bear little fruit. A Partido de la Revolución Mexicana (PRM) committee largely composed of the directors of various governmental departments, such as the Department of Education, the Department of Fine Arts, and the Departamento Autónomo de Prensa y Publicidad (Department of Press and Publicity), sought once again to breathe new life into national theater by developing a genuine popular theater at the service of the "most humble masses of the nation."[73] The committee hoped to form a new theater group, construct a new theater to house the group, and start a drama school to instruct new actors. The school would also serve to rejuvenate Bellas Artes as a national theater by using material from Mexico's popular imagination, "so rich, delectable and picturesque."[74] The educational venue, however, was not completed until 1946, when Department of Education director Jaime Torres Bodet inaugurated the School for Theater Arts. Like others who had tried to uplift the morals of lower-class audiences through the arts, Torres Bodet hailed theater as a "living school for adults," especially for members of the popular classes.[75]

As with the Deco structures in colonia Condesa, the architectural debates on building Deco bodies, and the female camposcape of the Mercado, the physical condition of Bellas Artes was articulated not only through issues of class—such as the vandalism of the country-bumpkin chilangos without manners—but also through gender. Female performance came to the rescue in addressing the class tensions that undergirded the discourse of Bellas Artes and its problematic positioning as a space that was either too elevated for the unrefined manners of the working-class chilangos or, instead, should serve as a force of civilizing them. The building shone in its role as a focal point for nationalism and popular support for the Cárdenas administration when, in 1938, Amalia Solórzano, wife of the president, moved the Colecta from the Teatro del Pueblo to Bellas Artes.[76] The Colecta, which represented an enormous public outpouring of financial and especially emotional support for Cárdenas's nationalization of the oil industry, in many ways once again turned Bellas Artes into female space. On April 12, thousands of women of all social classes gathered in front of Bellas Artes to donate everything from chickens and piggybanks to wedding rings and other jewelry. The performative quality of this enormous crowd of impassioned women, a near "stadiogenic event" without a stadium, enshrined Bellas Artes even more in the popular imagination as a place of female spectacle.[77] If Bellas Artes was "in ruins" and "diseased," it was because her sumptuous, female body had not been properly taken care off.

This notion reflected the changing nature of censorship. Although censorship had focused on political issues in the 1920s, especially when it involved political satire and jokes directed at local politicos, by the late 1930s city officials were ready to shut down theaters on grounds of transgressing boundaries of sexual morality. Moreover, they drew on a well-rehearsed revolutionary discourse of health and safety precautions to condemn adult entertainment as pornography. Because bataclanesque revistas had ingrained the idea that political satire went hand-in-glove with female nudity, city inspectors faced less opposition censoring shows on the basis of immoral content than for their political messages.

In the late 1930s, bataclanesque entertainment was not limited to cabarets. In February 1938 Bellas Artes was the site of a vaudeville show, which theater critics considered a funny but undignified spectacle in the nation's "first theater."[78] Sexualized female spectacle such as vaudeville and bataclanesque theater—infused with popular understandings that connected it with political satire—was out of place, theater critics deemed, in Bellas Artes. Revolutionary ideas of women's place and role in society linked women to the preservation of order and tradition, qualities thought to have great importance in stemming the onslaught of modernity. With Mexico City on the verge of becoming a full-fledged modern metropolis in the late 1930s, female commentators such as Teresa de Cepeda regarded the big city as a magnifying glass of human behavior. Whereas the small pueblo inspired purity and even equality, vice and degradation flourished in the modern city with its contrasts and anonymity. Because de Cepeda believed that women were the great moral agents of humankind, she argued that women—especially poor women—should inspire order. Mexican women—perhaps primitive, argued de Cepeda, but humble—would save Mexico from the corruption that had befallen other modern nations.[79]

As social roles for women were proscribed again more traditionally from the late 1930s onward, Bellas Artes became less and less a place of women's history or activism. Instead, female spectacle became contained in the theater's Ballet Folklórico. In regional dances such as the jarabe tapatia from Jalisco, the zanduga from Oaxaca, and the huanpango from Veracruz, women represented various regions of the nation woven into a comprehensive, folkloric camposcape. By 1952, dancer and choreographer Amalia Hernández had founded the Ballet Moderno de México, which eventually became the highly successful Ballet Folklórico of today. Hernández, the daughter of a revolutionary general, was trained in classical and modern ballet by illustrious teachers such as Sybine from Anna Pavlova's dance company and the Ballet d'Opéra de Paris's Madame Dambré, yet she found her calling when studying with Bellas Artes dance sensation La Argentinita starting in 1934. Her biography states: "She was moved, instead, by the songs and dances she experienced in her father's land during her journeys outside of the city.... Her contemporary Mexicanism, vibrating with a mestizo resonance, was already defined and on the surface of colorful Mexico. And soon, she started to understand that in the corners, mountains and valleys of her country, in those little towns that come alive in large festivities, represented a treasure not yet explored."[80] By 1959, Hernández's Ballet Folklórico became part of the Instituto Nacional de Bellas Artes, which President Miguel Alemán had established in 1947. Although Hernández was to be the most important proponent of modernizing ethnic and regional dances into a rich tapestry of national dance tradition, Bellas Artes clearly had a longer history of "staging the folkloric."[81]

Keeping in mind the discourses that connected Bellas Artes with female space, ranging from its ancient history as a convent to *Vea*'s photographs of scantily clad Deco-bodied women in front of the illustrious building, and from reports of feminist congresses housed in Bellas Artes to the nationalist outpouring of women sacrificing for the patria, we can discern a trajectory whereby female bodies represented not only urban space and urban reform but also a historical arc that bridged understandings of women's bodies and cosmopolitan modernity as well as female space in service of the nation. Combined representations of women and space not only fixed multiple meanings of changing gender roles onto the path of desired Western modernity but also showed where these had their limits. Bellas Artes, which had been symbolic of female space upon its inception, reworked Deco bodies into new conceptualizations of camposcape in which men could be charismatic, powerful charros and women's bodies represented the standardized physical features of folkloric Mexico through dance performances by the increasingly popular Ballet Folklórico.

CONCLUSION

In the wake of World War I, European architects—rethinking the role of theaters within the overall concept of the "world city"—started to build new theaters as monuments of peace. Inspired by Richard Wagner's *Gesamtkunstwerk*, theaters—such as the Grosses Schauspielhaus in Berlin, which seated five thousand spectators—were thought to play an important function in sustaining a healthy urbanism.[82] Alberto Pani similarly believed that the resurrection of a national theater, especially when complemented by an array of visual arts, a *palace* of fine arts, would exercise a redeeming influence on the Mexican population. This civilizing influence was not derived simply from the plays to be performed and art to be shown, but was communicated through the physical structure of the building itself. Completed and inaugurated just months before the Mercado Abelardo Rodríguez was finished, the Palacio de Bellas Artes in many ways functioned as a mirror to the Mercado. While Bellas Artes' modern and luxurious indigenista Deco interior communicated modern cosmopolitanism, its camposcape—like that in the Mercado—showed strong nationalist overtures. By the mid-1930s, visual indigenismo had coalesced into a highly nationalist camposcape that could be performed across race and class, and it was largely women who engaged in its performance.

Like the *Universal* cover that depicted a lovely, cosmopolitan, and white indígena (re)presenting the new Palacio de Bellas Artes, the building radiated a new nationalist, folkloric femininity. Although the glamorous cover girl had her hair braided in traditional indígena style and was dressed in a *huipil* (traditional blouse worn by indigenous women in central and southern Mexico), her white skin, nonsensical bow, painted red lips, and polished nails indicated that she was no longer a tehuana, the exotic other from Mexico's southern realms. Instead, the cover demonstrates that vague indicators of an indigenous identity now amounted to regional folklorism that was sufficient to infuse the new national theater with authentic mexicanidad. Bellas Artes, built on the site of a colonial convent and female bodies, and with an Art Nouveau exterior reminiscent of Porfirian divas, implied ongoing links between the modern city and female bodies. Yet, Deco shapes and designs and ideological connections to the modern world of entertainment, along with bataclanas and explicit models of female sexuality such as *Vea*'s nude Irma, showed that Bellas Artes belonged to a new, revolutionary age of chicas modernas.

However, this feminized, even if whitened, indigenismo increasingly gave way to a camposcape made up of male protagonists. Gomezanda's vision of Bellas Artes' future as the site of a masculine camposcape in which ranchos and charros dominated the stage and screen proved prophetic. With the success of *Allá en el rancho grande*, nationalist representations increasingly depicted a campo ruled by mythical, macho charros, a place where revolutionary heroes were born and the (new, improved) country was forged. The ranchera genre, which came to dominate Mexico's cinematic Golden Age, taught urban audiences to embrace an idealized countryside where dashing charros dominated the landscape as well as the silver screen. Situated within Mexican performance, Bellas Artes set the stage for a new masculinity predicated on glorification of the revolutionary war hero.

Despite the dramatic overtures to nationalism, Bellas Artes did little to implement Pani's vision to attract the lower classes or develop a truly national theatrical tradition. Like the decorations of its interior, Bellas Artes' display of Deco indigenismo communicated a mediated modernity that looked more to consumer tastes than to the realities of race and class. Similarly, the murals of the Tres Grandes that filled the halls of Bellas Artes' permanent exhibits had moved toward a glorification of modernization and a celebration of an indigenous past rather than its present, rendering these as gender-polarized visual narratives. In its infatuation with a camposcape that catered to elite desires for upscale drama and opera and to tourists in search of "México de Serape," Bellas Artes undermined much of its credibility with theater critics and lower-class audiences alike. Yet, like the Deco structures in colonia Condesa, the architectural debates on building

Deco bodies, and the female camposcape of the Mercado, the physical condition of Bellas Artes was articulated through not only issues of class—such as the vandalism of the country-bumpkin chilangos without manners—but also through gender.

By the end of the 1930s, the upset in gender roles had been, or was being, repaired. The discourse of women as moral gatekeepers of the nation-state was as old as the nation itself, but such sentiments did not become commonplace in Mexico's daily newspapers until the mid- to late 1930s, a trend that intersected with a rise in censorship. New DDF theater regulations also contained measures aimed at policing undesirable sexual behavior as part of a larger understanding of deviancy and transgression. Due to the visibility of Bellas Artes as the nation's official theater, the issue of proper management epitomized the desire on the part of governmental officials to keep everything, and everyone, in its right place. The productions of Bellas Artes staged a mexicanidad that the political leadership could live with. With the rise of sound cinema, the persistent popularity of carpas, and governmental hesitation to dedicate the national theater to the lower classes, the brand of drama exemplified by Bellas Artes became an elite affair, one that relegated the feminized world of tipos mexicanos to folklore, consigned indigenous struggles to the past, and allowed for the entry of a new masculinity symbolized by the charro.

Conclusion

DECO BODIES, *CAMPOSCAPE*,
AND RECURRENCE

In August 2003, Mexicana Airways' magazine, *Vuelo*, published a story on the plans for renovating Mexico City's centro histórico. Describing the 500-million-peso project that would refurbish a vast majority of the centro's streets and buildings, the author noted the importance of beautiful women. The renewal of the area, according to the commission, would be greatly enhanced by the visibility of "curvaceous brunettes and blondes" to attract a bohemian population that would infuse the area with a touch of chic and a sense of metropolitan modernity. Attractive women would turn the dilapidated and, according to the author, dangerous area of the centro into the rival of the thriving colonia Condesa, known for its haute cuisine, hip bars, and largely white and affluent clientele and inhabitants.[1]

The short article, amply illustrated with a large photo spread speaking to the centro's stately and sophisticated urbanity, clearly sought to promote these recently embarked upon urban-renewal efforts. Financed in large part by billionaire Carlos Slim (one of the world's richest men), the project launched a large-scale attempt to both revitalize and rescue the historic district through the Fundación del Centro Histórico de la Ciudad de México (Mexico City Historic Center Foundation). Having bought several dozen colonial buildings in the historic district, Slim's foundation—in partnership with the DDF, which was then headed by Partido de la Revolución Democrática's Andrés Manuel López Obrador—completed a full renovation of about thirty-four blocks around the Zócalo (mostly the north end of the centro).[2] Although the project included large public works, such as the overhaul of the area's drainage system and water supply, much effort went into beautification efforts. The foundation restored facades on more than five hundred historic buildings, refurbished walkways for pedestrians, created new lofts to attract young, elite professionals, and subsidized the construction of upscale restaurants, boutique hotels, and designer stores.[3] With these revitalization efforts, however, also came an increase of cleanup and control: security cameras in public areas, a new mayor's residence on the Zócalo, and—most visibly—the removal from the centro's streets of undesirable elements such as the homeless, the poor, and street vendors. The last group in particular, a very vocal and visible obstacle to the project, was removed in an effort to curb both the "chaos" in the centro and its flourishing underground economy, what Carlos Monsiváis referred to as "making popular market places of the streets."[4]

This pattern of public works, beautification modeled on female bodies, removal of street vendors, and the two-pronged approach of renewal and preservation presents us with the echoes of a bygone era, especially in the face of Mexico's much touted re-democratization of the early twenty-first century. Indeed, *Vuelo*'s and the commission's initially inexplicable connection between female bodies and buildings starts to make sense when we compare it to Mexico City of the 1920s and 1930s, when modern Deco-bodied women informed and were incorporated into plans for urban reform. New conceptions of femininity that came out of revolutionary struggle as well as transnational ideas of the New Woman influenced the physical shape that the city would take. Not only women's new roles in the public sphere (or at least a perception thereof) but also their new looks in terms of fashion, makeup, and body shape reverberated in cityscapes. While women's increased mobility worried revolutionary leaders and led to efforts to contain undesirable behavior, the new bodily contours of the flapper girls who made their entry into Mexico at this time formed an aesthetic blueprint for new forms of architecture and urban space.

From about 1900 until 1940 (the late Porfiriato through the years of the institutional revolution), the capital city experienced drastic changes, a shifting social and cultural geography that was the result of both structural and ideological forces. Due to massive rural-to-urban immigration, the start of large public-works projects, the creation of new colonias such as Condesa, the overhaul of infrastructure, the construction of markets, and the completion of monuments and commercial buildings, the transformation of Mexico City in the 1920s and 1930s was especially dramatic. The small town of half a million before the revolution, in a peripheral region of third-world status, grew into the "post-apocalyptic" urban Leviathan of the Americas. This rapid growth, so often believed to have been the unintended result of industrialization starting in the 1940s, clearly had a larger historic, gendered blueprint dating back to the beautification efforts of the 1920s and 1930s.[5]

As the most recent overhaul of the centro shows, urban reform in Mexico City still invokes notions of female beauty and still appears to require the presence of female bodies to render these reforms successful. *Deco Body, Deco City* demonstrates that ideas about female beauty are more important than most historians recognize. First, Deco bodies fulfilled an important role in fashioning new, modern, capitalist subjects. In 1925, when the theater production *Voilá Paris: La ba-ta-clán* heralded the arrival of the Deco body in Mexico City, it was quickly taken up as representative of a distinct urban modernity. Long, sleek, and toned, Deco bodies connected Mexico to global currents and new aesthetics of modern industry and the machine age. As a prime mnemonic device in the visualization of the modern girl, the Deco body formed the "bedrock" of her visibility, identity, and ability to travel the globe.[6] The Deco body became a signifier of a larger gendered discourse that functioned as a blueprint to model oneself on in the quest for bodily perfection. In their celebration of athleticism, discipline, and productivity, Deco bodies enticed Mexican women to exercise, consume new products, and become attractive New Women; they aestheticized the modernity of early-twentieth-century global capital.

More than a vehicle to reform women, the ideas about female beauty inherent in Deco bodies not only informed larger discourses of modernity itself but also aimed at accommodating modernity and nationalism. Deco bodies symbolized what new revolutionary elites and leaders deemed desirable traits of modernity by which they sought to remake the country: productivity, discipline, health, sophistication, cleanliness, education, simplification, and consumption. Strong, athletic, and beautiful, Deco bodies represented attractive vectors on which to plot Mexico's path toward modernity. Even if it was a transnational cultural phenomenon that originated in Europe and the United States, the Deco body could readily be adapted to local realities. The beauty of Deco bodies depended on form, not color. Inhabited by mestizas, trumping form over color, they helped the revolutionary government equate modernity with the "new" revolutionary mestizo nation.

Moreover, the Deco aesthetic in this new female beauty ideal informed larger—what at first glance seem gender-neutral and structural—developments, such as urban reform, the production of habitable space, and desirable environments. This city of the future had gendered overtones that figured prominently within debates over larger social reform. The conceptualization of the city as female space where Deco bodies represented a daring, new, and bare modernist architecture resulted in the planning and construction of new buildings in the centro and the refurbishing of existing structures and neighborhoods such as upscale colonia Condesa. Building a utopian, revolutionary city was an aesthetic project that looked to female bodies for its inspiration, but it was also a moralistic project that attempted to contain women's mobility.

Why did ideas about female beauty guide these processes? Most notably, Deco bodies were successful in producing a variety of desires, ranging from sexual to capitalist, self-actualist to nationalist. In the 1920s and 1930s, the enormous increase in visual culture influenced by the advent of cinema, mass marketing, and technological advances in print and photography was indicative of the advent of a scopophilic age. The fact that theater and cinema generated Deco bodies contributed to their enormous popularity as emblems of urban modernity. Through the long-running theater and fashion phenomenon of bataclanismo, Deco bodies changed the way the city was imagined. As a new form of revista theater, which had been popularized by divas such as Esperanza Iris and María Conesa, bataclanismo informed the inhabitants of Mexico City of current events and mirrored, as well as defined, metropolitan life. As both a space of sociability and a challenge to normative discourses, revistas facilitated the transition from divas to Deco bodies. Through visual media, Mexican women, like their counterparts elsewhere, learned to dress, use makeup, slim down, and even consider plastic surgery as they beheld the Deco bodies of female entertainment stars. In the barrage of visual materials that propagated a new beauty ideal for women, Deco bodies and the city were intertwined and illustrated that metropolitan modernity depended on the physical and behavioral aspects of a new femininity; the visibility of women's movement in urban, public spaces was a requisite for modernity.

As emblems of cosmopolitanism and the city at large, Deco bodies were the latest product of a genealogy of artistic and ideological discourses that historically had equated women's bodies with desirable space. Dating as far back as conquest/exploration narratives of the colonial era, which depicted terra incognita as conversant with indigenous female bodies through allegorical figures representing the new nation-states of the nineteenth century, territory was rendered as a female construct, devised by men and for men to command. Camposcape, a quintessential Mexican adaptation of this larger discourse, identified indigenous women—as tipos—with the countryside, which coalesced into a representation of the Mexican nation-state, and into what best exemplified mexicanidad.

In adapting and nationalizing modernist discourses, revolutionary elites reformulated older, Porfirian forms of camposcape that equated exotic, rural landscapes with indígenas and the past. Invoking the uncomplicated pastoral pleasures of the idealized garden, camposcape represented, in Michel Foucault's terminology, a quintessential heterotopia. Reminiscent of eighteenth- and nineteenth-century orientalist pleasure gardens, camposcape placed racial others in an exotic countryside and in a highly gendered configuration. Revolutionary camposcape popularized regional tipos such as the tehuana and reinvented rural culture for mass consumption in urban areas to still—or awaken—the longing for a purer, simpler, life. Moreover, through art and ideas about physical culture, camposcape provided an ideological realm where female nudity was acceptable and healthy. The presence of camposcape in discourses of nudism represented an enacted indigenismo, a vivified pastoral of timeless women where nudity was innocent and pure and where, consequently, matters of race were elided by aesthetics of gender.

Although urban Deco bodies were in tension with this camposcape due to the juxtaposition of the campo against the city, they ultimately came to perform it in urban settings. The romanticized version of the campo staged by the Deco body contrasted sharply with generally poor, destitute, and desperate rural female migrants who arrived in the capital city in great numbers during the 1910s and 1920s. The large and long process of rural-to-urban migration that accelerated during the revolution brought rural culture to the heart of the city as a shared and lived reality. Migrants brought saints to protect their vecindades, curanderos to heal their bodies and minds, tianguís to procure daily necessities, and a set of behaviors and morals that the revolutionary state viewed as unhealthy and unproductive. Despite their rural origins, the real-life, poor indigenous women on the city streets did not embody a state-constructed ideal of camposcape but rather the painful spectacle of Mexico's most visible colonial legacy.

The performance of camposcape by Deco bodies as romanticized tehuanas erased, or at least obfuscated, the uncomfortable presence of real-life indígenas, whom most middle-class urbanites knew mostly in city settings as servant girls, market vendors, beggars, or third-class prostitutes, and neutralized racial and class tensions within the revolutionary project. By modernizing camposcape, they eased the middle-class discomfort at the presence of poor indigenous women in the city. In the service of the nation-state, and through the tipos of revolutionary art, commercial imagery, and film and theatrical productions that glorified indígenas, Deco-bodied urban women performed camposcape as a spectacle of modernity. In addition, the Mexicanization of Deco bodies in bataclanismo paved the way for a new, mestizo modernity by defining, as well as erasing, differences of modernism's "exotic others."

Deco bodies expressed a mestizo modernity that celebrated cosmopolitanism while staying in the bounds of revolutionary nationalism, thereby offering a way to neutralize the tension between indigenismo and mestizaje.

In the face of the stark realities of urban life, the search for perfect camposcape vis-à-vis the desired cosmopolitanism represented by Deco bodies mirrored race and class tensions within the revolutionary city. As symbols of urban modernity, Deco bodies spoke a "cartographic language" and functioned as mimetic symbols on the map of the city. Yet the meanings ascribed to these symbols were indeterminate and harbored the contradictions, ambivalences, and tensions inherent in modernity itself. Due to polite society's preoccupation with female nudity and sexuality in the wake of bataclanismo, Deco bodies also communicated the shadow side of modernity. When incarnated by the flapper, a being thought to be given to the unbridled excesses of sex, sin, drinking, and drugs, nude Deco bodies were—especially in the wrong place—accused of attracting crime, violence, and the darkness of the underworld. The depiction of female bodies as sexualized urban landscapes in "men's magazines" such as *Vea* fueled concerns over "public women." By portraying the city as an environment dominated by Deco bodies, magazines like *Vea* mapped geographies of desire onto the modern metropolis as spaces that both informed and hampered urban (re)form. In short, if female, indigenous nudity in artistic representations of camposcape was deemed beautiful and pure, representations of nude, Deco-bodied modern girls in the city constituted "promis-ciudad," the pornography of the underworld.

The confusion over the meaning of the multivalence, indeterminacy, and paradoxes within Deco body representations in urban space reflected a set of divergent, and often conflicting, agendas inherent in urban-reform efforts. The flurry of urban projects between 1929 and 1934 showed that, on the one hand, the conceptualization of the city as female space likened Deco bodies to modern buildings and eroticized the new architectural forms associated with global modernity; on the other hand, sexualized Deco bodies led revolutionary officials to believe that in the burgeoning and rapidly changing city, every thing and every body should be kept in its right place. The increased number of poor, destitute female migrants in the capital city complicated the new state's plans in reforming women, whom they sought to return to the private sphere. The stress on domesticity as nationalist discourse was integral in envisioning a hierarchy of spaces that privileged nation building as public male domain while sanctioning the space of the bourgeois home as a primary building block in national development. The reimplementation of the zonas libres and designated areas of market activity aimed at containing the mobility of poor women reflected these concerns.

In addition to the decision to uphold the zonas libres, reformers in Mexico City created a historic district to safeguard national patrimony. The new centro histórico would serve as a mnemonic device where monuments, place-names, and colonial patrimony dedicated to iconic male heroes would keep national history alive. Urban planning not only illustrated the tension between the need to preserve history (create public memory) and the urge to modernize cityscape but also demonstrated how these processes inscribed gender in and onto the city, using concerns about changing gender roles to direct and legitimize state and private investments. The centro histórico allowed the state to control what transpired in the capital's center and clear its streets of undesirable activities associated with female spectacle: carpas, prostitution, and street vending.

Markets and theaters, imbued with attractive spectacle, received special attention within overall urban-reform plans. The main market complex built during the 1930s, the Mercado Abelardo Rodríguez, was to represent a microcosm of revolutionary reform, especially according to state directives to protect public health, women, and the procreative, nuclear family. Urban planners envisioned the Mercado as a particularly beneficial place for female vendors: a public market with private features. Although revolutionary leaders were concerned about public-health issues, they also feared that "public women" would undermine their efforts to strengthen nuclear families in which women would fulfill their patriotic duty to the state as mothers and wives. City officials wished to maintain family unity by providing day care for the small children of the female merchants. In policing markets, authorities sought to enforce class and gender hierarchies, sexual repression, and the separation of commerce from entertainment.

As an outpost of the campo in the city, the Mercado represented living camposcape. Beyond their practical functions in facilitating urban growth, markets such as the Mercado Abelardo Rodríguez (which contained an actual Art Deco theater) were envisioned as theaters by developers because of their performative quality as camposcape. These qualities—carnivalesque excitement, colorful displays, and invitations for social gathering—tied the city to the countryside as an undefined, living past. Indeed, the camposcape of markets proved irresistible to urban audiences. By the mid-1930s the national theater in the newly completed Palacio de Bellas Artes started staging folkloric productions that celebrated the campo as site of national essence. In contrast to the highly popular and politicized entertainment of the carpas and burlesque theaters, which faced increasing governmental censorship as the decade advanced, the productions of Bellas Artes celebrated a mexicanidad acceptable to government officials. Despite its campo-focused repertoire, Bellas Artes championed Deco-tecture as its main architectural style and Deco bodies in its representation of camposcape in embodying the nation.

The centrality of female beauty, not only in the construction of desirable modern femininities but also in the larger movements within modernity, such as nationalism, global capitalism, and urbanization, has a number of consequences. The processes by which particular ideas of feminine beauty shape, manipulate, and serve nationalist and capitalist development shed light not only on the gendered nature of modernization but also on how modernity itself depended on the visibility of femininity. During a crucial time in Mexico's sociopolitical development—the change from a nineteenth-century dictatorship to an institutionalized revolution—preoccupation with changing gender roles became more pervasive because of modernity projects inherent in state formation, not in spite of them. Because the revolution upset gender norms, revolutionary leaders made a conscious effort to return to "traditional" gender norms by way of a "modernization of patriarchy," which structured much revolutionary reform and ensured that women's rights would take a backseat to the fortification of the middle-class family as the platform for national development.

Urban reform, informed by concerns over women in public, female physiques, and beautification, did not prove successful, even by the standard of meetings its own aims. The Mercado did not rid the centro of street vendors. Market reforms generally did little to halt the rise of the informal economy in the eastern part of the centro histórico or diminish the promiscuity associated with market activity.[7] Up until 2010, when vendors were removed as part of Slim's cleanup plan for the centro, vendor activity crowded the centro's streets and blocked traffic. Crime rates in the neighborhood surrounding the Mercado were high and hindered commercial activity in the market. Yet the promise of markets as instruments in urban renewal as well as in preserving a living past also continue. Today the Mercado is listed as a tourist attraction in *Lonely Planet* and other U.S. and European tour guides, and it is one of the first results to come up on a Google search on Mexican markets.[8] Slim's latest urban-reform project, the Plaza Mariana, reminds one of the Mercado in many ways. Situated next to the Basilica de Guadalupe, arguably the city's and nation's most sacred space with clear female foundations, the complex is to house an evangelical educational center, a museum, and a market.

The Plaza Mariana project demonstrates that post-revolutionary notions that wedded place to gender, and representations of femininity to both markets and modernization, proved more lasting and successful. Even if an unintended outcome, urban-reform efforts of the 1920s and 1930s and new expressions of gender identities were mutually constitutive. At a time that saw the creation of new forms of femininity, urban planning either affirmed or attempted to contain new gender roles and cemented these conventions into urban landscapes in ways that still have currency today. The ideological constructs that pit campo against city continue to resonate in debates over migration today where rural subjectivities overlay those of race and class, and the continued quest to modernize rural people survives well into our postmodern age.[9] In the aftermath of the revolution, Mexico—as a country, a new state, a people, and a city—had to come to terms with the disruption of existing class and race divisions. This, however, was a gendered process. The city of the future had gendered overtones that figured prominently within debates over larger social reform that addressed both the promises of the revolution and preoccupations with modernization.

Ultimately, the larger significance of Deco bodies, camposcape, and gender performance is what they tell us about sweeping historical processes as urbanization, state building, and modernization, especially in the face of today's problems and pressures. The quest for modernity was, and still is, informed by gender politics, not merely one that affects gender norms.[10] The fact that femininity is still identified with formulations of beauty that not only form the bedrock of women's identities but also continue to position them as vehicles of capitalist development presents clear challenges to viable women's liberation projects. The story of Mexico City's Deco bodies, camposcapes, and gender performance, along with the reverberations of these tropes in contemporary mass-renovation projects in the same city, forces us to take seriously the category of gender—as idealized, practiced, governed, and performed—as a central strand in modernization processes of urbanization, industrialization, and national development.

NOTES

ABBREVIATIONS

AGN-APR-AR   Archivo General de la Nación, Mexico City, Administración Pública de la República, Lázaro Cárdenas

AGN-APR-LC   Archivo General de la Nación, Mexico City, Administración Pública de la República, Abelardo Rodríguez

AHDF-DP   Archivo Histórico del Distrito Federal, Mexico City, Diversiones Públicas

AHDF-EI   Archivo Histórico del Distrito Federal, Mexico City, Esperanza Iris

AHSSA-SP-SJ   Archivo Histórico de Secretaría de Salubridad Pública y Asistencia, Mexico City, Salubridad Pública, Servicio Jurídico

FPECFT-APEC   Fideicomiso Plutarco Elías Calles y Fernando Torreblanco, Mexico City, Archivo Plutarco Elías Calles

FPECFT-FAO   Fideicomiso Plutarco Elías Calles y Fernando Torreblanco, Mexico City, Fondo Alvaro Obregón

FPECFT-FSG   Fideicomiso Plutarco Elías Calles y Fernando Torreblanco, Mexico City, Fondo Soledad González

NARA   National Archives and Records Administration, Washington DC

INTRODUCTION

1. Gortari Rabiela and Franyuti, "Imágenes de la ciudad," 1–2; see also Garza, *Imagined Underworld*, 14.
2. Garza, *Imagined Underworld*, 13.
3. Johns, *City of Mexico*, 12.
4. Piccato, "Paso de Venus," 206.
5. Garza, *Imagined Underworld*, 32.

6. Piccato, "Paso de Venus," 206.

7. Johns, *City of Mexico*, 11.

8. Usigli, *Mexico in the Theater*, 94. Usigli notes that the Coliseum became independent from the Royal Hospital for Illegitimates in 1822 and was controlled by city thereafter.

9. Johns, *City of Mexico*, 18, 23.

10. Gortari Rabiela and Franyuti, "Imágenes de la ciudad," 4.

11. Garza, *Imagined Underworld*, 15.

12. Piccato, "Paso de Venus," 203–4, 206, 209.

13. Gortari Rabiela and Franyuti, "Imágenes de la ciudad," 2.

14. Garza, *Imagined Underworld*, 15, 16.

15. Tenorio-Trillo, "1910 Mexico City Space," 170.

16. Bliss, *Compromised Positions*.

17. Kandell, *La capital*, 448; "And That It Is Custom Makes It Law," 129. Porter states that between 1880 and 1921 the majority of migrants to Mexico City were women.

18. Bliss, *Compromised Positions*, 33, 36. At the start of the revolution, more than 15 percent of women in the capital were registered as prostitutes.

19. Rosenthal, "Spectacle, Fear and Protest," 43; Lear, "Mexico City" (*Journal of Urban History*), 475–76.

20. Lear, *Workers, Neighbors, and Citizens*, 305–12.

21. Olsen, *Artifacts of Revolution*, 17.

22. Cruz Rodríguez, *Crecimiento urbano y procesos sociales*, 122–23, 129.

23. Olsen, *Artifacts of Revolution*, 8.

24. Gortari Rabiela and Franyuti, "Imágenes de la ciudad," 15; Ayuntamiento de Ciudad de México, *Memoria de H. Ayuntamiento* (1926), 65, 66.

25. "Ley de organización del distrito y territories federales" (Tlalpam, DF, 1925) Capítulo VIII: 41–2, in FPECFT-APEC, file 1, Inventario 1467, Legajo 1.

26. "La supresión de municipio libre en la Ciudad de México," Ayuntamiento de Ciudad de México, *Memoria de H. Ayuntamiento* (1926), 15.

27. Olsen, *Artifacts of Revolution*, 31.

28. "Francisco Serrano to Calles," June 30, 1927, in FPECFT-APEC, file 1, Gaveta 23, Inventario 1467, Legajo 1.

29. Davis, *Urban Leviathan*, 25; Lear, "Mexico City" (*Journal of Urban History*), 463; Cruz Rodríguez, *Crecimiento urbano y procesos sociales*, 131–32, 133.

30. Olsen, *Artifacts of Revolution*, 62, 102.

31. Acevedo de Iturriaga, "Dos muralismos," 44; Olsen, "Artifacts of Revolution," 137; Olsen, "Sáenz Garza," 1326–27.

32. In 1925, Mexico City's population surpassed one million. Oropesa, *The Contemporáneos Group*, 122.

33. Brenner and Leighton, *The Wind That Swept Mexico*, 80; Beals, *Mexican Maze*, 151.

34. Davis, "The Modern City," 55.

35. J. C. Scott, *Seeing Like a State*, 82; Mignolo, *The Idea of Latin America*, xix, xiii, xi.

36. Olsen, "Artifacts of Revolution," 20; Rosenthal, "Spectacle, Fear and Protest," 47, 49; Meskimmon, *Engendering the City*, 1.

37. See Viqueira Albán, *Propriety and Permissiveness*; Beezley, *Judas at the Jockey Club*; Matthews, *The Civilizing Machine*; Tenorio-Trillo, *Mexico at the World's Fairs*.

38. Monsiváis, "Mexico City," 11, emphasis added.

39. Joseph and Nugent, *Everyday Forms of State Formation*. Also see scholarship by Joy Elizabeth Hayes, Joanne Hershfield, Alan Knight, Julia Tuñón, Mary Kay Vaughan, and Anne Rubenstein,

40. Rubenstein, "Mass Media and Popular Culture," 639, 641.

41. See Salas, *Soldaderas in the Mexican Military*.

42. Vaughan, "Modernizing Patriarchy"; Deutsch, "Gender and Sociopolitical Change."

43. See Rubenstein, *Bad Language*.

44. See Soto, *The Mexican Woman*; Macías, *Against All Odds*; Salas, *Soldaderas in the Mexican Military*; Blum, *Domestic Economies*.

45. Vaughan, "Modernizing Patriarchy"; Deutsch, "Gender and Sociopolitical Change," 259–307.

46. Conor, *Spectacular Modern Woman*, 61.

47. Chase quoted in Olsen, *Artifacts of Revolution*, 110.

48. Debord, *Society of the Spectacle*, 12–13.

49. Butler, *Gender Trouble*; Butler, *Bodies That Matter*.

50. Mexican women learned about successful businesswomen such as Helena Rubinstein, who by the late 1930s headed a cosmetics empire. "Nuevo mundo: La Señora Gana Mas," *El Nacional*, December 21, 1941, 8. Joanne Hershfield remarks that most of the merchandise on display in large department stores in Mexico City was of U.S. or European origin. See Hershfield, *Imagining the Chica Moderna*.

51. *Indigenismo* refers to a movement in arts and sciences tied to the state valorizing indigenous heritage and culture. *Mestizaje* refers to race mixing, in particular between white or European and indigenous, yet is also sometimes used in a cultural context.

52. Grosz, *Space, Time, and Perversion*, 108.

53. While camposcape is not directly related to Arjun Appadurai's use of the suffix "scape," it does share his notion of "scapes" as "building blocks" of imagined worlds. See Appadurai, *Modernity at Large*, chapter 2.

54. Bonfil Batalla, *Mexico Profundo*; see also Debroise, *Mexican Suite*. These garden-like spaces also recall Michel Foucault's notion of heterotopia. See Foucault, "Of Other Spaces."

55. Delpar, *Enormous Vogue*; Rochfort, *Mexican Muralists*; on mestizo modernity, see Hedrick, *Mestizo Modernism*.

56. Pilcher, *Cantinflas*.

I. PERFORMANCE

1. "El Sr. Carranza asistio a la inauguracion del Teatro 'Esperanza Iris,'" *Excélsior*, May 26, 1918, 1.

2. Gortari Rabiela and Franyuti, "Imágenes de la ciudad," 1–2; Garza, *Imagined Underworld*, 14.

3. Garza, *Imagined Underworld*, 13.

4. Johns, *City of Mexico*, 15.

5. Johns, *City of Mexico*, 12.

6. Garza, *Imagined Underworld*, 32, 8, 3.

7. Piccato, "Paso de Venus," 211.

8. Buffington and Piccato, "Tales of Two Women," 402–3.

9. Piccato, "Paso de Venus," 234.

10. McCleary, "Culture and Commerce," 269.

11. Nesvig, "The Lure of the Perverse," 9–10, 12, 14.

12. G. Wood and, "Symbols of the Sacred," 82, 88.

13. See Piccato, "El Chalequero"; and Garza, "Dominance and Submission."

14. Piccato, "Paso de Venus," 228; Garza, "Dominance and Submission," 82–83.

15. Piccato, "Paso de Venus," 238.

16. Viqueira Albán, *Propriety and Permissiveness*, 58.

17. Usigli, *Mexico in the Theater*, 75.

18. Viqueira Albán, *Propriety and Permissiveness*, 45, 48, 61.

19. McCleary, "Culture and Commerce," 325–26.

20. McCleary, "Culture and Commerce," 350.

21. M. Can-Can [Gutiérrez Nájera], "Crónica humorística: Memorias de un vago," *El Cronista de México*, November 20, 1880.

22. Usigli, *Mexico in the Theater*, 75,84–85, 90–91, 105, 110.

23. Usigli, *Mexico in the Theater*, 138–39, 141.

24. See Glenn, *Female Spectacle*; Ullman, *Sex Seen*.

25. Glenn, *Female Spectacle*.

26. E. Alonso, *María Conesa*, 8, 39, 50, 51.

27. E. Alonso, *María Conesa*, 66, 8, 10.

28. AHDF-EI, box 16, file 4; "Con Juanito Palmer," *Mefistófeles*, February 26, 1918, 7, 13.

29. Rico, *El Teatro Esperanza Iris*, 64, 66. In this, Iris was not alone; actress and impresario Virginia Fábregas owned her own theater just down the street from El Iris, and Mimí Derba started Mexico's first movie production company, Azteca Films.

30. Monsiváis quoted in E. Alonso, *María Conesa*, 9. Mimí Derba produced a film about the gang, using their name as its title.

31. Gutiérrez Nájera, "Humoradas dominiciales," *Partido Liberal*, December 20, 1885, 2–3.

32. El Duque Job [Gutiérrez Nájera], "Memorias de un vago," *La Libertad* año, September 30, 1883, 1–2.

33. Gortari Rabiela and Franyuti, "Imágenes de la ciudad," 1–2.

34. Dueñas Herrera, *Las divas*, 17; Alonso, *María Conesa*, 57.

35. Counted among these theaters were the Principal, Arbeu, and Fábregas, as well as the famous Coliseo and the Gran Teatro Nacional in 1842 by President Santa Anna; the area would soon have two more palaces of entertainment: El Palacio de Bellas Artes and El Iris. Usigli, *Mexico in the Theater*, 97.

36. Viqueira Albán, *Propriety and Permissiveness*, 44.

37. McCleary, "Culture and Commerce," 236–38.

38. McCleary, "Culture and Commerce," 260, 261–62.

39. Johns, *City of Mexico*, 34, 51; Marroquín y Rivera quoted in Johns, *City of Mexico*, 32.

40. Johns, *City of Mexico*, 75.

41. M. Gutiérrez Nájera, "Desde la torre a la plaza," *El Nacional*, April 5, 1881, 2.

42. El Duque Job [Gutiérrez Nájera], "Humoradas dominiciales," *El Partido Liberal*, October 30, 1887, 1–2.

43. El Duque Job [Gutiérrez Nájera], "Crónica color de Venus," *La Libertad*, December 10, 1882, 2.

44. El Duque Job, "Crónica color de Venus."
45. I found evidence of this in the many advertisements for the Iris and other theaters that offered cheap seats.
46. Puck [Gutiérrez Nájera], "Lo del día, Cuadros plásticos," *El Universal,* August 19, 1891, 1.
47. Johns, *City of Mexico*, 29.
48. M. Can-Can, "Crónica humorística," 667–68.
49. Frú-Frú [Gutiérrez Nájera], "Bis! Bis!" *El Nacional,* May 21, 1882, 1–2.
50. M. Can-Can, "Crónica humorística," 699–700.
51. M. Can-Can, "Crónica humorística," 677, 668.
52. M. Can-Can, "Crónica humorística," 699–700.
53. Piccato, "Paso de Venus," 225.
54. José Vasconcelos mentioned in Carballo, *El cuento mexicano.*
55. Usigli, *Mexico in the Theater*, 90, 102. Usigli states that *The Revue of 1869*, performed on January 30, 1870, was the first Mexican revista.
56. Oropesa, *The Contemporáneos Group*, 121, 122. Oropesa says that the revista genre represented "a necessary transition between a rural and urban country" and "anticipated the values of mass culture."
57. *Revista* more commonly translates as "magazine."
58. Usigli, *Mexico in the Theater*, 118.
59. Debroise, *Mexican Suite*, 118–19.
60. McCleary, "Culture and Commerce," 355, 182, 183.
61. Usigli, *Mexico in the Theater*, 117; Johns, *City of Mexico*, 58, 96.
62. Usigli, *Mexico in the Theater*, 140–41.
63. Monsiváis, Foreword, 12.
64. McCleary, "Culture and Commerce," 3.
65. Usigli, *Mexico in the Theater*, 122.
66. Salvador Novo, *Excélsior*, February 15, 1929, 7.
67. E. Alonso, *María Conesa*, 73, 93, 92, 94, 99.
68. Ayuntamiento de Ciudad de México, *Informe de H. Ayuntamiento* (1923), 281.
69. Ayuntamiento de Ciudad de México, *Memoria de H. Ayuntamiento* ((1925).
70. Ayuntamiento de Ciudad de México, *Memoria de H. Ayuntamiento* (1925), 14.
71. AHDF-DP, "Teatros," vol. 812, file 1661/25.
72. The play dealt with the marriage of two pelados who rob a bank in the city and return to the campo, where they ridicule an array of high-placed officials (representatives, the *regidor* [municipal council member], a

general, etc.). Except for the governor of the Federal District, these officials were not identified by name.

73. AHDF-DP, "Teatros," vol. 812, file 1757.

74. AHDF-DP, "Teatros," vol. 812, file 1661/41.

75. AHDF-DP, "Teatros," vol. 812, file 1661/27, 32.

76. Salvador Novo, *Excélsior*, February 15, 1929, 7.

77. AHDF-DP, "Teatros," vol. 812, file 1667.

78. Pilcher, *Cantinflas*, 30.

79. AHDF-DP, "Teatros," vol. 812, files 1708 and 1721; see also Pilcher, *Cantinflas*,
24.

80. AHDF-DP, "Teatros," vol. 812, file 1667.

81. AHDF-DP, "Teatros," vol. 812, files 1735 and 1720.

82. Socorro Merlín quoted in Pilcher, *Cantinflas*, 25.

83. AHDF-DP, "Teatros," vol. 812, files 1706 and 1692.

84. AHDF-DP, "Teatros," vol. 812, file 1661/24.

85. Zedillo Castillo, *El teatro*, 95.

86. Juan Palmer to Mario Sánchez, June 29, 1917, in AHDF-EI, box 16, file 4;
AHDF-EI, box 3, file 7; Rico, *El Teatro Esperanza Iris*, 47, 52, 53.

87. "De Telon adentro," *Gráfico*, February 18, 1917, 13. See also AHDF-EI, box 16,
file 7, and box 25, file 2; Rico, *El Teatro Esperanza Iris*, 49.

88. Rico, *El Teatro Esperanza Iris*, 54, 85, 73.

89. AHDF-DP, "Teatros," vol. 812, file 1661.

90. Berlanstein, *Daughters of Eve*, 131.

91. "Kaleidoscopio de la semana," *Revistas: El Semanario Nacional*, September
2, 1933; "Intrascendencias semanales," *Diversiones*, September 30, 1933, 3. *La
Prensa*, August 30, 1939.

92. "Intrascendencias semanales," *Diversiones*, September 30, 1933, 3, describes
how Iris, after the loss of one of her sons, has given a benefit concert
for the victims of the Tampico hurricane: "Esperanza Iris, alma de raza,
Mexicana de corazon: Bendita seas!" By 1929, the series of farewells and
comebacks of Esperanza Iris were legendary. Salvador Novo joked that
Iris "redoncontravuelve a redoncontradespedirse de 'su' público" (re-
contra-comeback to re-contra-leave) yet again with the operetta *The Merry
Widow*. *Excélsior*, March 23, 1929, 5.

93. See *Filmografica*, January 5, 1935, 35.

94. Butler, *Gender Trouble*; Butler, *Bodies That Matter*.

95. E. Alonso, *María Consea*, 73. See also López Sánchez and Rivas Guerrero,
Esperanza Iris.

2. BATACLANISMO

1. Butler, *Gender Trouble*; Butler, *Bodies That Matter*.
2. I borrow the term from Hedrick, *Mestizo Modernism*.
3. Rico, *El Teatro Esperanza Iris*, 66.
4. *Gazeta de Noticias* (Rio de Janeiro), August 6, 1922, 6. See also Travassos and Corrêa do Lago, "Darius Milhaud." Rasimi explained that a scene which showed "masked characters, puppeteers with big heads, [and] a black barman" was "supposed to be in New York" (but was not meant to offend that "friend-country" either). Rasimi argued that Darius Milhaud, "one of the most vibrant friends of Brazil, known for such delicate melodies as *Saudade do Brasil*," would not have intended anything disrespectful.
5. *Gazeta de Noticias*, August 6, 1922, 5; *Revista da Semana*, August 5, 1922. The *Gazeta de Noticias*, August 5, 1922, ran ads on page 8 for both *Paris chic* and *Phi-Phi*, which was playing at the same time in Teatro Republica. Iris thus must have seen, or at least been aware of, the bataclán and its success in Rio. Departing Rio fortified with Carlito's Jazz Band, a group of Brazilian musicians fronted by percussionist Carlos Blassifera, the bataclán troupe left to perform in São Paulo. The ensemble returned to Rio in 1926 with another grand spectacle, *C'est Paris*, and toured São Paulo, Salvador, and Recife. Travassos and Corrêa do Lago, "Darius Milhaud."
6. While earlier theater productions, especially revistas, had merely alluded to female nudity with actresses dressed in body stockings, the bataclanas performed "sans maillots," i.e., without the flesh-colored body stockings usually worn.
7. *Gazeta de Noticias*, August 6, 1922, 6, described the splendor of the costumes, which appear to have represented "a fantastic luxury for us, little accustomed to big installation/sets," because in all of the acts "one discovers a savoir-faire of rare intelligence on the part of the female director of the bataclán." *Revista da Semana*, August 12, 1922, "Semana Teatral," opened with a review of the revista *Paris chic*: "It was a very happy occasion, with delicious increments." It was described as genero music-hall "songs, picturesque duets jocular scenes, stylish dances, and fantastic costumes." "a true parade of gran gala, an example of divine chic and feminine caprice."
8. Quoted in Zedillo Castillo, *El teatro*, 93.
9. Zedillo Castillo, *El teatro*, 93.

10. Attended primarily by middle-class audiences in more upscale theaters, revistas were also favored in working-class theaters and carpas. *Voilá Mexique: El Rataplan* translates as "Here is Mexico: The rat manifesto." The word *plan* was frequently used in Mexico to outline political programs, especially during the revolution, e.g., Emiliano Zapata's *Plan de Ayala*. Dueñas Herrera, *Las divas*, 25. Rico suggests that bataclanismo fit the period's changing social climate of "indiscreet looks, parody, temptation between the stage and the public, the *vacilón* [party-goer] as lifestyle, strong and seductive perfume, flight of husbands, red plumage and the cabaret as place of refuge." Rico, *El Teatro Esperanza Iris*, 101–2.

11. *El Rataplan* included songs such as "El Tuli," which used "the jazz craze" with its "wagging" to liken politicians to rats and monkeys. See Miranda, *Del rancho al bátaclan*, 39. For instance, theater production such as *De México a Cuba* (1928) invoked the bataclán. Also, the popular men's magazine *Mujeres y Deportes* reported that María Rivera, a onetime star of adult entertainment clubs in Plaza Garibaldi, "undressed her life" in her 1938 autobiography, *Frine criolla*, as she had her body on the stage. "Una tiple cuenta su vida!" *Mujeres y Deportes*, February 12, 1938, 22.

12. Usigli, *Mexico in the Theater*, 123.

13. Dueñas Herrera, *Las divas*, 25–26; Zedillo Castillo, *El teatro*, 95. Rico finds that the incongruities between the stock revista types and the imported chorus girls reflected the general contradictions in Mexican society. Rico, *El Teatro Esperanza Iris*, 106. With the more risqué performances around the city, El Iris continued with profitable light spectacle, staging variety shows and piquant comedies such as U.S. follies performances, *Kiss-me* and *Yes-Yes*. In the latter half of the 1930s bataclanismo gave way to pornographic burlesque, which flourished in lowbrow theaters such as Apolo and Tivoli.

14. Zedillo Castillo, *El teatro*, 95.

15. Zeitz, *Flapper*, 153–54.

16. Chanel's *garçonne* style would have remained largely unknown, catering only to the rich and eccentric, had it not been for the entrance of hundreds of thousands of European and American women into the workforce during and after World War I.

17. Conor, *Spectacular Modern Woman*, 19, 25; Cheng, *Second Skin*, 3.

18. For a biographical article and analysis of Cabral and his work, see Barrow, Barrow, and Katz, "Ernesto Cabral." For references to Cabral's later works, see Zolov, "Jorge Carreño's Graphic Satire."

19. For a detailed discussion of the many guises of the modern woman in Mexico, see Hershfield, *Imagining the Chica Moderna*.

20. Barrow, Barrow, and Katz, "Ernesto Cabral," 17. Having come of age during the late Porfiriato, Cabral irreverently used his training at the famed Academy of San Carlos to draw political cartoons for weeklies, and he quickly earned fame with his caustic caricatures. President Francisco Madero so feared the artist's work that he sent him off with a generous scholarship to study in Paris. Like Diego Rivera (and sometimes with Rivera), Cabral spent some of the most turbulent years of the revolution in Paris, living the bohemian life of the Latin Quarter. As the cultural attaché to the Mexican consulate, Cabral later traveled to Spain and Buenos Aires, where he remained until 1918.

21. Barrow, Barrow, and Katz, "Ernesto Cabral," 18.

22. Conor, *Spectacular Modern Woman*, 110.

23. Barrow, Barrow, and Katz, "Ernesto Cabral," 20.

24. Barrow, Barrow, and Katz note that during the lengthy time Cabral worked for *Excélsior* he masterfully wove all he had absorbed into a signature style. "Ernesto Cabral," 24.

25. A. M. Alonso, "Conforming Disconformity," 465.

26. Hershfield, *Imagining the Chica Moderna*, 12. See also Gallo, *Mexican Modernity*, chapter 1.

27. Peiss, *Hope in a Jar*, 152–54; Conor, *Spectacular Modern Woman*, 23; Hershfield, *Imagining the Chica Moderna*, 67.

28. Enstad, *Ladies of Labor*; Conor, *Spectacular Modern Woman*, 112, 128; Fitzgerald quoted in Zeitz, *Flapper*, 158.

29. Hershfield, *Imagining the Chica Moderna*, 59.

30. Enstad, *Ladies of Labor*, 52, 161, 181; Peiss, *Cheap Amusements*; Conor, *Spectacular Modern Woman*, 112; Hershfield, *Imagining the Chica Moderna*, 41. Hershfield agrees that even if lower-class women could not afford most foreign fashion and luxuries advertised in magazines or displayed at Palacio de Hierro, they understood "the freedom to window-shop."

31. Vaughan, "Introduction: Pancho Villa," 23; Gallo, *Mexican Modernity*, 201–26.

32. "Circular 550," November 14, 1927, in AHSSA-SP-SJ, box 8, file 1.

33. Salvador Novo, "Los feos concursos de belleza," *México al Día*, December 1, 1935, 36–37.

34. Hershfield, *Imagining the Chica Moderna*, 33, 59; see also Conor, *Spectacular Modern Woman*, 119, 120.

35. Novo, "Los feos concursos de belleza," 36–37; Hershfield, *Imagining the Chica Moderna*, 51–52.

36. *Selecta* (Rio de Janeiro), August 16, 1922.

37. Conor, *Spectacular Modern Woman*, 8, 106–7.

38. See, for example, "Las calles del ayuntamiento," *El Universal Ilustrado*, December 22, 1932, 43; and "Intrascendencias semanales," *Diversiones*, September 26, 1931. Hershfield, *Imagining the Chica Moderna*, 51–52, agrees that it was not merely the clothes,but also the body type of the models that taught Mexican women how to be modern.

39. Conor, *Spectacular Modern Woman*, 19, 25.

40. *Universal Ilustrado*, May 3, 1934, 69. This might have resulted in part from the fact that active ingredients in most whitening creams, such as potassium cyanide, lead, uranium, arsenic, mercury, and other substances deemed "poisonous and noxious," were outlawed by article 2 of the 1931 Sanitary Code. January 20, 1931, in AHSSA-SP-SJ, box 11, file 7.

41. Novo, "Los feos concursos de belleza," 36–37.

42. Beauvoir quoted in Conor, *Spectacular Modern Woman*, 32, emphasis added.

43. Seltzer, *Bodies and Machines*, 114–15; Fischer, *Designing Women*, 32; Cheng, *Second Skin*, 8.

44. Cheng, *Second Skin*, 122; Kracauer quoted in Conor, *Spectacular Modern Woman*, 124, 152. Conor writes: "This correspondence between body parts and working tools reflected the fragmentation of the industrialized body through the atomized tasks of the Fordist conveyer belt" (124).

45. Lungstrum, "Metropolis and the Technosexual Woman," 135; Mulvey, "Pandora," 60.

46. Seltzer, *Bodies and Machines*, 13; Conor, *Spectacular Modern Woman*, 157.

47. "La mujer mexicana ha entrado de lleno por la senda del deporte," *El Universal*, December 7, 1931, 9; "Mas deportes, menos vicios," *Mujeres y Deportes*, August 18, 1934, 3–4.

48. Conor, *Spectacular Modern Woman*, 115.

49. Carmina, "Cómo reducir las caderas y el abdomen," *Mujeres y Deportes*, November 3, 1934, 5; "Las reglas de salud a que se sujeta para no perder la linea," *Mujeres y Deportes*, December 8, 1934, 21.

50. Gleber,"Female Flanerie"; Conor, *Spectacular Modern Woman*, 114. Conor quotes Elizabeth Wilson (*The Sphinx in the City*): "only by becoming part of the spectacle can you truly exist in the city" (114).

51. Cheng, *Second Skin*, 25, 141; Conor, *Spectacular Modern Woman*, 153; Bordo, *Unbearable Weight*, 160.

52. Bordo, *Unbearable Weight*, 163–64.

53. Bordo, *Unbearable Weight*, 186, 206; Cheng, *Second Skin*, 141, 122; Bordo also has shown how social anxiety over feminine bodies occurs at times when women gain certain measures of independence and assert them- selves socially and politically.

54. Conor, *Spectacular Modern Woman*, 138, 164, 153.

55. "Belleza feminina: El cutis es el mayor atractivo. Hay que quidarlo como un tesoro," *El Hogar*, May 29, 1929.

56. Conor, *Spectacular Modern Woman*, 132.

57. Conor, *Spectacular Modern Woman*, 42, 112.

58. "Reglamento para el registro y certíficación de medicinas de patente, especialidades, y productos de tocador, higienicos de belleza, y demas similares," in AHSSA-SP-SJ, box 11, file 7; "Circular 550," November 14, 1927, in AHSSA-SP-SJ, box 8, file 1.

59. "En los templos de la belleza," *Mujeres y Deportes*, January 1, 1938, 66–73; "Norma Shearer: A los 30 años comienza la vida de la mujer," *Mujeres y Deportes*, July 7, 1934, 20; "Belleza feminina."

60. Novo, "Los feos concursos de belleza," 36–37; Carmina, "Para ellas," *Mu- jeres y Deportes*, August 11, 1934.

61. The slogan "Salud es Belleza = Belleza es Salud" accompanies advertise- ments for beauty products in contemporary Mexican media.

62. Conor, *Spectacular Modern Woman*, 33, finds that "men act and women appear," which "keeps intact the alignment of sexual difference with the subject/object binary."

63. "Asi las miran in Yanquilandia: Este usted de acuerdo?" *Mujeres y Deportes*, January 8, 1934, 94. See also Widdifield, *Embodiment of the National*; and Poole, "An Image of 'Our Indian.'"

64. Salvador Novo, *Revista de Revistas*, September 8, 1929, 5.

65. Rubenstein, "The War on 'Las Pelonas.'" *Pelonas* literally means "bald women," but this term was used to refer to any woman who cut her hair short.

66. Braids were considered a crucial element in the construction of tradi- tional Mexican femininity.

67. Conor, *Spectacular Modern Woman*, 46, argues that "the 1920s were a cusp decade in which women's public presence increased dramatically." Salva- dor Novo, *Revista de Revistas*, September 8, 1929, 5; Pilcher, *Cantinflas*, 22; for prostitution zones in Mexico City, see Bliss, *Compromised Positions*.

68. Pilcher, *Cantinflas*, 20; Salvador Novo, "Que hacer los Domingos," *Nuestra Ciudad*, August 1930, 6–7; *Diversiones*, August 13, 1932, 15. In 1932, the attraction of outdoor street theater spoke to the imagination of capitalinas as the "Jaime Nunó alley" became the epicenter of spectacles en vogue.

69. Weinbaum et al., *Modern Girl around the World*, 6; Hershfield, *Imagining the Chica Moderna*, 5; see also Conor, *Spectacular Modern Woman*, 19.

70. Mahieux, *Urban Chroniclers*, 141.

71. Mahieux, *Urban Chroniclers*, 1.

72. Cube Bonifant, "A flor de pupila," *El Universal Ilustrado*, September 29, 1921, 21.

73. Mahieux, *Urban Chroniclers*, 127, 139–40, 143; Bonifant, *Marquesa*, 35.

74. Cube Bonifant, "Feminismo a toda vela," *El Universal Ilustrado*, October 20, 1921, 34; Cube Bonifant, "Sólo para mujeres," *El Universal Ilustrado*, December 8, 1921.

75. Mahieux, *Urban Chroniclers*, 25, 140,141–42, 148; Cube Bonifant, "Vanidad de vanidades!" *El Universal Ilustrado*, July 14, 1921, 12. Before trying her hand at journalism she had "dabbled in theater" and appeared in a few plays. In 1923 she starred (in the role of a journalist) in the film *La gran noticia*, directed by her *Ilustrado* publisher Noriega Hope. Although the film lent her great visibility, she expressed a "distaste for filmmaking" and never acted in a film again.

76. Bonifant, *Marquesa*, 33, 34, 36.

77. Cube Bonifant, "Tempestad en una melena," *El Mundo*, April 21, 1923, 6.

78. Cube Bonifant, "Cuestiones filosas y peliagudas," *El Mundo*, April 23, 1923, 6.

79. Bonifant, *Marquesa*, 38.

80. Mahieux, *Urban Chroniclers*, 9, 22.

81. Bonifant, "Feminismo a toda vela," 34; Mahieux, *Urban Chroniclers*, 128, 146, 148; Bonifant, *Marquesa*, 65–68, 75.

82. By the 1930s, Bonifant had left behind her bad-girl persona as well as her "women only" columns and converted herself into a highly respected film critic.

83. Mahieux, *Urban Chroniclers*, 128.

84. Piccato, *City of Suspects*, 113. While divorce became legal in 1915, this did not have much significance, especially in the Federal District, where marriage rates were lower than in the rest of the country, because many lower-class men and women did not marry.

85. Carmina, "Para ellas, sección a cargo de Carmina, la amiga sincera de la mujer," *Mujeres y Deportes*, July 7, 1934, 10–11.

86. *El Universal* (1930) quoted in Piccato, *City of Suspects*, 113; "Hay demasiadas tentaciones," *Mujeres y Deportes*, August 18, 1934; "La poligamio progresiva de los artistas de Hollywood," *Revista de Revistas*, July 8, 1934, 35; Halberstam, *Female Masculinity*.

87. *Mujeres y Deportes*, August 25, 1934; "Marlene sin pantalones," *Mujeres y Deportes*, July 7, 1934, 22. *Universal Ilustrado*, April 6, 1933, 26, shows a picture of Dietrich with the caption: "The disquieting Marlene, who now does not take off her pants, even when going to sleep."

88. "Las cartas entre novios," *La Familia*, January 15, 1935, 22; "Consejas a las casadas," *La Familia*, December 7, 1935, 59. Oddly, although its target audience was female, this women's magazine also published an advice column, "Consejas a las casadas," in which an anonymous male author taught men how to write decent love letters to their betrothed. While his advice overall was to keep the letters short, sincere, and happy in the hope of "provoking expectations," the piece seemed to express doubts about the affections of the modern woman: "I know that many female readers don't share this opinion, but masculine hearts feel much more deeply the troubles of being loved than those of the other sex." *La Familia*, December 7, 1935, 59.

89. Carmina, "Para ellas," *Mujeres y Deportes*, August 18, 1934, 10; "La muchacha moderna," *El Hogar*, May 29, 1929, 20.

90. Carmina, "Para ellas," 9, 13; "Norma Shearer: A los 30 años comienza la vida de la mujer," *Mujeres y Deportes*, July 7, 1934, 5.

91. Stallybrass and White, *Politics and Poetics*, 25.

92. Hershfield, *Imagining the Chica Moderna*, 14.

93. Conor, *Spectacular Modern Woman*, 30.

94. On the performance of indigenismo in portraiture, see Poole, "An Image of 'Our Indian.'"

95. Cheng, *Second Skin*, 11, 47.

96. See Delpar, *Enormous Vogue*.

3. CAMPOSCAPE

1. The contestants of beauty pageants organized in an attempt to stimulate indigenismo were known as *indias bonitas*. For a discussion of these beauty contests, see López, "India Bonita Contest," which traces the first india bonita contest to 1921 and argues that these pageants sought to inculcate

a national identity based on the idea that all Mexicans shared, and should honor, their indigenous past.

2. Johns, *City of Mexico*, 38. James Garza notes that Santa Anita was also a bustling working-class hangout, with plenty of restaurants and pulquerías. It was not until 1896 that it attracted more upper-class visitors (gente de razón) after police started to enforce order in the town. Also, Canal de la Viga's "unofficial purpose was as a working-class park." Garza, *Imagined Underworld*, 21.

3. Manuel Rámirez Cárdenas, "Santa Anita; colores y flores," *El Globo*, April 4, 1925, 1.

4. Pilcher, *Cantinflas*.

5. For examples of sexualized and feminized landscape in early modern European depictions of the Americas, see the image *America*, ca. 1575, by Jan van der Straet, cited in McClintock, *Imperial Leather*, 25. For discourses on rituals of possession in European colonization of the Americas, see Seed, *Ceremonies of Possession*.

6. See Widdifield, *Embodiment of the National*.

7. G. Wood and Greenhalgh, "Symbols of the Sacred."

8. Solomon-Godeau, "Going Native," 314, 316, 319.

9. Debroise, *Mexican Suite*, 116, 117.

10. Linati, *Trajes civiles, militares y religiosos*.

11. For examples, see Brasseur, "The Didjazá," 83.

12. Terry, *Terry's Guide to Mexico*, 858–59. The quotes are from the original 1909 description of the Isthmus of Tehuantepec.

13. Brasseur, "The Didjazá," 83.

14. G. Wood and Greenhalgh, "Symbols of the Sacred," 86.

15. Chassen-Lopez, "Juana Cata."

16. Ramos, *El perfil del hombre*.

17. Debroise, *Mexican Suite*, 115; Bartra, "Stuffing the Indian Photographically."

18. Creswell, *Place*, 11, 10.

19. In her analysis of Josephine Baker's nudity onstage, Cheng alludes to a modernist nostalgia in the primitivist "dream of second skin—of remaking one's self in the skin of the other." Within the visual tropes of modernism, she explains, "Baker's famous nakedness begins to look less and less apparent," because race functions as covering: "the flirtation with the idea of race-as-surface that can be added on or taken off." Cheng, *Second Skin*, 58, 59.

20. See, among many works on Mexican's cultural revolution, scholarship by Joy Elizabeth Hayes, Joanne Hershfield, Alan Knight, Julia Tuñón, and Mary Kay Vaughan,

21. Sierra, "The Creation of a Symbol," 84–85.

22. The lure of the tehuana as camposcape partly originated from the mistaken notion that Zapotec culture of the isthmus constituted a matriarchy, an idea perpetuated far into the twentieth century.

23. Beals, *Mexican Maze*, 15; Toor, *Toor's Guide to Mexico*, 206.

24. Toor, *Toor's Guide to Mexico*, 207.

25. Covarrubias, "Mirando hacia el sur."

26. Díaz del Castillo, *Conquest of New Spain*, 215, 235.

27. Kotkin, *The City*, 114–16. Cortes deemed markets to constitute crucial nodes of social and economic activity; in rebuilding the city he changed the marketplaces into plazas.

28. *Tipos mexicanos* were derived from *costumbrismo*, a Latin American form of genre painting. The genre was characterized by a full-frontal view of the subject placed at the center of the composition, a "snapshot" styled with the subject's predictable, theatrical poses.

29. Debroise, *Mexican Suite*, 117, 118.

30. Stallybrass and White, *Politics and Poetics*, 119.

31. Porter, "And That It Is Custom Makes It Law," 115.

32. Garza, *Imagined Underworld*, 12–13.

33. Quoted in López Rosado, *Los servicios públicos*, 213.

34. López Rosado, *Los servicios públicos*, 213.

35. Terry, *Terry's Mexico*, 297, 293.

36. Markets in early modern Europe proved dangerous places. See Stallybrass and White, *Politics and Poetics*, 138.

37. Beals, *Mexican Maze*, 151; Toor, *Toor's Guide to Mexico*, 78–79.

38. Irigaray quoted in Noble, "Zapatistas en Sanborns," 369.

39. Cuevas-Wolf, "Guillermo Kahlo and Casasola," 202; Noble, "Zapatistas en Sanborns," 366.

40. Marino, "Representaciones del zapatismo," 257.

41. Caplow, "Twentieth Century Photography," 28.

42. Cuevas-Wolf, "Guillermo Kahlo and Casasola," 203.

43. Ross, *El Monstruo*, 110–13, 128.

44. Meskimmon, *Engendering the City*, 13.

45. "Dispareles cuando menos lo piensan," *Mujeres y Deportes*, January 22, 1938, 57. With new technology and reduced costs of cameras that were

small and thus highly portable, this was a snap, said reporters. As a disembodied eye, the photographer represented a technology of power not unlike Michel Foucault's reading of the Panopticon, especially since sight observation underpinned much of scientific method. Meskimmon, *Engendering the City*, 12–13, 18.

46. "Dispareles cuando menos lo piensan," 57.

47. Lacey, "The 1921 Centennial Celebration," 208.

48. Andrew Donovan II, U.S. Vice Consul, "Regulations Regarding Photographing Artistic Property in Mexico," October 10, 1934, Consular Reports to the Department of State, 812.4035/15, NARA; Consulate N. Laredo, Mex., "Regulations Governing Tourist Traffic by Automobile into Mexico," April 17, 1934, Consular Reports to the Department of State, 812.4035/16, NARA.

49. See Poole, "An Image of 'Our Indian'"; López, "India Bonita Contest." Cube Bonifant's reports from the campo also illustrate that indias bonitas pageants were an urban phenomenon that was brought to the campo by reporters and photographers from Mexico City. Bonifant, "Una fuga a la provincia," *El Universal Ilustrado*, March 17, 1921, 56.

50. "De donde es la mujer mas bonita de la republica," *Mujeres y Deportes*, August 25, 1934, 7.

51. Tuñón, "Femininity, *Indigenismo*, and Nation," 95.

52. Rivera's mural series at the Autonomous University at Chapingo, considered by most art critics as exemplary of the height of Mexican muralism, celebrates the female form as an allegory of the Earth, the nation, and timeless space.

53. Rochfort, *Mexican Muralists*, 75.

54. Oropesa, *The Contemporáneos Group*, 98. Elena Poniatowska, quoted in Oropesa, describes the scene eloquently: "Lupe with a bulging abdomen, breasts swollen from a recent pregnancy" (98).

55. Rivera quoted in Oropesa, *The Contemporáneos Group*, 98.

56. Seltzer, *Bodies and Machines*, 28.

57. Bonifant, "Una fuga a la provincia," 42.

58. Cube Bonifant, "Una pequeña Marquesa de Sade para un Oscar Wilde pequeño," *El Universal Ilustrado*, April 21, 1921, 9. Cube literally doesn't "feel well" after looking at the rural girls in "transparent" clothes.

59. Hooper Irask, "El culto del nudismo en Alemania" *Heraldo de Cuba*, July 3, 1932, 4.

60. Irask, "El culto del nudismo," 4.

61. Irask, "El culto del nudismo," 4.

62. "Piensase establecer en Mexico la primera colonia nudista autorizada," *La Prensa*, December 7, 1938, 11.

63. "Piensase establecer en Mexico la primera colonia nudista autorizada," 11.

64. Conor, *Spectacular Modern Woman*, 170.

65. L. F. Bustamante, "Ya hay nudistas en México," *Gráfico*, November 9, 1937, 12.

66. Carlos del Rio, "Algo mas sobre el campo de nudismo que hay en Mexico," *Gráfico*, November 30, 1937, 12.

67. Irask, "El culto del nudismo," 4.

68. Salvador Novo, "Por la desnudez hacia la perfección: El movimiento nudista en Alemania y Francia," *Resumen*, July 1, 1931, 17–19, 43.

69. Perhaps in an unconscious effort to discourage nudism in Mexico, the press announced the arrival of the first nudist camp on Mexican soil at various intervals throughout the 1930s. The first report located the first colony in Baja California in 1932, made up of eighty Mexican couples along with the "Yankees" who had financed the initiative. While the state of Baja California allowed the foundation of the colony, it prohibited its members from making their practices public. The reporter predicted that this colony would grow rapidly despite the prohibition, as the colonists advertised quite heavily in the United States on behalf of the nudist lifestyle. "La primera colonia de 'nudistas,'" *La Prensa*, January 11, 1932, 11. *Gráfico* heralded the second arrival of nudism on Mexican shores. Teacher Esperanza F. de Lara, "the prophet of Mexican naturalism," openly advertised and discussed the practice during public talks in Mexico City. Bustamante, "Ya hay nudistas en México," 12. One Nels Holmes founded the third "first" colony in Cuernavaca. "Piensase establecer en Mexico la primera colonia nudista autorizada," 11.

70. L. F. Bustamante, "Los nudistas de Mexico proyectan su unificación para afianzar su causa," *Gráfico*, November 15, 1938, 12. Carlos Marín Foucher identified indígenas as morally and physically perfect. Foucher quoted in Knight, "Racism, Revolution, and Indigenismo," 92. He added that they were "almost perfect, biologically speaking."

71. Bustamante, "Los nudistas de Mexico," 12.

72. Early in his tenure as president, Cárdenas embarked on a morality campaign, which included closing casinos and brothels throughout the republic. See Cabeza de Baca and Cabeza de Baca, "The 'Shame Suicides' and Tijuana."

73. By 1935, U.S. nudist aficionados had gone from a silent minority to an outspoken movement of three million Americans—of which half were practicing nudists—who openly campaigned against governmental restrictions and had "militant plans" to convert the masses.

74. Don Catrino, "Este mundo de mis pecados," *Gráfico*, June 13, 1939, 12.

75. "La primera colonia de 'nudistas,'" *La Prensa*, January 11, 1932, 11; Bustamante, "Ya hay nudistas en México," 12.

76. Bustamante, "Los nudistas de Mexico," 12.

77. Del Rio, "Algo mas sobre el campo de nudismo," 12.

78. Salvador Dorantes, "El nudismo, remora de la industria," *El Nacional*, December 16, 1935, 8.

79. "El nudismo es solo pretexto burdo," *Gráfico*, August 19, 1939, 12.

80. "La ciencia estudia a los nudistas," *Mujeres y Deportes*, January 29, 1938, 55.

81. "La ciencia estudia a los nudistas," 55.

82. Dorantes, "El nudismo," 8.

83. "El crimen del nudismo," *Mujeres y Deportes*, October 20, 1934.

84. This loosely translates as "the most beautiful farm flower." Ejidos, however, were rural communal landholdings associated with pre-Columbian notions of landownership that featured heavily in revolutionary reform.

85. Distrito Federal, *Memoria presentada* (September 1935–August 1936), 247.

86. Toor, *Toor's New Guide to Mexico*.

87. Augustín Yáñez, "Espejismo de Juchitán," reprinted in *Artes de México* 49 (2000): 90–92; Sergei Eisenstein, "La vida," reprinted in *Artes de México* 49 (2000): 83.

88. Pratt, *Imperial Eyes*, 4. Pratt defines contact zones as "social spaces where disparate cultures meet, clash, and grapple with each other, often in highly asymmetrical relations of domination and subordination" (4).

89. Rubenstein, *Bad Language*, 28, 44, 46–47, 54, 85.

4. PROMIS-CIUDAD

1. *Vea*, the imperative of the verb *ver*, "to see," does not quite translate to "see" here. Rather, it indicates an active way of seeing in a manner of "taking in a scene," so I have translated it as "look."

2. "La cita," *Vea: Semanario Moderno*, December 7, 1934, 24.

3. "Palabras de presentación," *Vea: Semanario Moderno*, November 2, 1934, 2.

4. See Vargas, *La casa de cita*.

5. French, "A History of Playboy Magazine."

6. Cheng, *Second Skin*, 46.

7. Ullman, *Sex Seen*, 104–5.

8. Grosz, *Space, Time, and Perversion*, 108.

9. See, for instance, *Frente-a-Frente*, *Futuro*, and other leftist magazines.

10. Shell, *Church and State Education*, 88.

11. Rubenstein, *Bad Language*, 16, 78–80, 83. Rubenstein argues that engaging with printed material was itself "evidence of the reader's participation in modernity" (78). This also meant that readers believed there was nothing wrong with reading racy comics or magazines.

12. On Catholic women and their relationship with the church, also see works by Nicole Sanders, Mary Kay Vaughan, and Stephanie Mitchell and Patience Shell.

13. Shell, *Church and State Education*, 119, 124.

14. AGN-APR-LC, vol. 704, fol. 31.

15. The entanglement of discourses on female sexuality and nationalism of the 1930s seems to have been a forerunner of more intense censorship efforts of the 1940s. Claire Fox argues that by the 1940s there were established links that tied subversive female sexuality, in the form of the "exotica" female cabaret or nightclub dancer, to anti-foreign political sentiments. Fox, "Pornography and 'the Popular,'" 144–45.

16. AGN-APR-LC, vol. 704, fol. 31. Article 33 of the 1917 Mexican Constitution states in part that "non-nationals may not interfere in the political matters of the country in any way."

17. AGN-APR-LC, vol. 704, fol. 31. See also Fujigaki Cruz and de León Banuet, *Asamblea de ciudades*, 150.

18. Andes, "A Catholic Alternative to Revolution," 553.

19. Zeitz, *Flapper*, 280; Ullman, *Sex Seen*, 19; Halberstam, "MacDaddy, Superfly, Rapper," 113. See also Maines, *The Technology of Orgasm*.

20. Conor, *Spectacular Modern Woman*, 83; Kendrick, *The Secret Museum*, 195–96, emphasis added.

21. Foucault, *The History of Sexuality Volume I*; Foucault, *Discipline and Punish*.

22. Cheng, *Second Skin*, 120; Kendrick, *The Secret Museum*, 188.

23. Conservative women's unified stance in condemning magazines like *Vea* has been explained as potentially due to the failure to secure political rights. Carlos Monsiváis believes that "once political defeat became inevitable, women on the right concentrated their efforts on practicing religious teachings and promoting censorship" (14). See Olcott, Vaughan, and Cano, *Sex in Revolution*, 14, 26, 30. In *Bad Language*, Rubenstein argues that, beginning in the 1930s, popular culture represented a safety valve for

the PRM/PRI regime. By allowing disenfranchised Catholic conservatives to take an active role in social criticism concerning morality issues, and agreeing to to their pleas to censor pornography, the regime siphoned off their discontent.

24. *Vea* maintained this price until it was banned, in 1937. Circulation rates are unknown. See Wilkie, *The Mexican Revolution*, for equivalency rates of Mexican peso in 1934. A contemporary story on minimum wages stated that on average, cashiers started at fifteen pesos per month, and drivers averaged twenty pesos per month. Luis F. Bustamante quoted in Hershfield, *Imagining the Chica Moderna*, 125. In *Naked Ladies*, 14, Rubenstein notes that in the early to mid-1930s most comic books cost about ten centavos, which amounted to about a quarter of an average worker's hourly salary.

25. Hunt, "Obscenity and the Origins of Modernity," 357.

26. Hunt, "Obscenity and the Origins of Modernity," 356, 357.

27. Freud, *Five Lectures*, 43. Freud coined the term *psychoanalysis* in 1906, but it was not until after the publication of his *Introductory Lectures on Psycho-Analysis* (1917) and *The Ego and the Id* (1923) that he secured a wide audience and became a household name in the United States and Europe.

28. Ullman, *Sex Seen*, 38, 44.

29. Weekly magazines such as *Mujeres y Deportes* and *Detectives* regularly featured articles translated into Spanish written by U.S. authors that analyzed the behavior of women, often Hollywood stars, in the context of theories by Freud and Adler. In *The History of Sexuality*, Foucault defies the prevailing perception of sex as silenced or repressed by implicating Freudian theory and practice in the rise of normalized sexuality (that of the heterosexual married couple).

30. Kendrick, *The Secret Museum*, 207; see also Freud, *Five Lectures*, 47, 49. Freud proposed a specific sequence of phases to reach sexual maturity. According to Freud, masturbation, while healthy in children, constituted perverse behavior in adults and was thus considered a disorder.

31. Knopp, "Sexuality and Urban Space," 151. Quoting Henning Bech, Knopp states that this type of sexuality is "only possible in the city" because it requires "the dense and permanent cluster of heterogeneous human beings in circulation."

32. Salvador Novo, editorial, *Excélsior*, February 15, 1929, afternoon edition, 7.

33. Kendrick, *The Secret Museum*, 208. Kendrick draws on Stephen Marcus's formulation of *pornotopia* as a utopian fantasy where "space and time only measure the repetition of sexual encounters, and bodies are re-

duced to sexual parts and the endless possibilities of their variation and combination."

34. "Historia de teatro en México," *Artes y Historia México*, f://www.arts-history .mx.

35. Avila and Serrano, "Las racionistas," 52.

36. "Hay Teatro Mexicano?" *Universal Ilustrado*, May 23, 1933, 19: "daughters of slime, tropical obscenities, afro-cuban stupidities."

37. Knopp, "Sexuality and Urban Space," 152–53.

38. "Calendario de 'Diversiones,'" *Diversiones*, July 9, 1932, 14.

39. Mario Fuentes to Lázaro Cárdenas, April 7, 1939, in AGN-APR-LC, vol. 415.13, fol. 33.

40. "Historia de teatro en México"; see also Merlín, "La censura en las carpas de México," for an examination of the DDF commissions.

41. Salvador Novo, an openly gay writer (member of the vanguard, modernist writers collective the Contemporáneos), theater critic, and social commentator, seemed to have been able to acquire the respectability and credibility to weigh in on such sensitive issues as pornography.

42. Salvador Novo, *Excélsior*, February 15, 1929, afternoon edition, 7.

43. "Historia de teatro en México."

44. Lawrence quoted in Kendrick, *The Secret Museum*, 204. On the cultural meanings of dirt, see Mary Douglas's *Purity and Danger* as well as Stallybrass and White's *Politics and Poetics*.

45. Cheng, *Second Skin*, 114, 115; Mulvey, "Pandora," 69; Conor, *Spectacular Modern Woman*, 75.

46. Lefebvre, *The Production of Space*, 32–33.

47. "Numerosas viciosos en el fumadero de opio," *El Universal*, June 10, 1931, 9.

48. Armando Salinas, "Lacras metropolitanas en el mundo del hampa," *Mujeres y Deportes*, February 26, 1938, 24–25.

49. "Mientras México duerme," *Mujeres y Deportes*, January 22, 1938, 34–36.

50. "Personas sospechosas," March 11, 1932, in AHSSA-SP-SJ, box 30, file 24.

51. "Mientras México duerme," 34–36; Salinas, "Lacras metropolitanas," 24–25.

52. Seltzer, *Bodies and Machines*, 96.

53. "En casa de Venus," *Detectives*, June 4, 1934, 15.

54. "En casa de Venus," 18.

55. "En casa de Venus," 18.

56. Bliss and Blum, "Adolescence," 167.

57. Oropesa, *The Contemporáneos Group*, 109.

58. Cheng, *Second Skin*, 37, 39, 65; Conor, *Spectacular Modern Woman*, 26–27, 29, 32. "It is the young girl's ability to double, to 'exist outside' herself, that enables her to see herself as an object and thus to find erotic transcendence" (32).

59. Seltzer, *Bodies and Machines*, 93; Conor, *Spectacular Modern Woman*, 29, 65, 70.

60. See O'Malley, *The Myth of the Revolution*, for early scholarship on revolutionary constructions of masculinity.

61. Salinas, "Lacras metropolitanas," 24–25; see also Piccato, "El Chalequero."

62. On London, see McClintock, *Imperial Leather*; and Walkowitz, *City of Dreadful Delight*. On New York, see Stansell, *City of Women*.

63. Rio de Janeiro's bohemian quarter, Lapa, enjoyed great popularity with middle- and upper-class men. Rago, *Do cabaré ao lar*; Caulfield, *In Defense of Honor*.

64. Wilson, *The Sphinx in the City*, 3; Freud, *Five Lectures*, 16; Knopp, "Sexuality and Urban Space," 152. Knopp states that Henning Bech also credits modern medicine and psychoanalysis with sexualizing the urban experience.

65. See chapter 2, figures 6–7.

66. Conor, *Spectacular Modern Woman*, 11, 16–17, 55, 63–69.

67. Seltzer, *Bodies and Machines*, 18; Bliss and Blum, "Adolescence," 164, 165.

68. Bliss, *Compromised Positions*, 65–66.

69. AHSSA-SP-SJ, box 17, file 19.

70. AHSSA-SP-SJ, box 17, file 19.

71. Junta de Obreros, Industriales, Propretarios y Vecinos de las calles de Cuauhtemotzín y adyacentes and Comision Mixta-Pro-Turismo to Department of the Interior, November 14, 1929, in AHSSA-SP-SJ, box 17, file 19. The group again protested against the zone on February 20, 1930, and wrote President Pascual Ortíz Rubio on May 15, 1930.

72. "Codigo Sanatario 1927–1928," in AHSSA-SP-SJ, box 10, file 5.

73. Dr. Sanroman to Departamento de Salubridad Pública, n.d., in AHSSA-SP-SJ, box 7, file 3.

74. Bliss and Blum, "Adolescence," 174–75.

75. Department of Public Health, Judicial Division, to Department of the Federal District, October 10, 1929, in AHSSA-SP-SJ, box 17, file 19.

76. Report of Judicial Division to Department of Public Health, 1926–1929, in AHSSA-SP-SJ, box 7, file 3.

77. Dr. Sanroman to Department of Public Health.

78. "Reglamento hotels," September 25, 1934, in AHSSA-SP-SJ, box 40, file 24.

79. In *Soldaderas in the Mexican Military*, Salas notes that female communists and union members insisted that Mexican women could only improve their condition by working through established party channels, and condemned feminism as "a bourgeois tactic," while some feminists labored intensely to create a united feminist front.

80. Macías, *Against All Odds*, 114–15, 118, 129, 137.

81. Olcott, *Revolutionary Women*, 3.

82. Rosario Sansores, "Congresas feministas," *La Familia*, January 15, 1935, 14.

83. "Proteccion a las mujeres," *El Hogar*, August 5, 1929, n.p.

84. "Proteccion a las mujeres."

85. "Proteccion a las mujeres."

86. Bliss and Blum, "Adolescence," 166, 167–68.

87. Piccato, *City of Suspects*, 125, 126. Conviction rates for (prosecuted) rape were very low, and this apparently changed little between 1900 and 1940.

88. Piccato, *City of Suspects*, 129.

89. Piccato, *City of Suspects*, 105. Piccato finds that violence against women was not only part of a patriarchal social and cultural structure but that it resulted from the enormous changes Mexico City underwent from 1900 to 1940.

90. Piccato, *City of Suspects*, 128, 127.

91. Piccato, *City of Suspects*, 130.

92. J. W. Scott, *The Politics of the Veil*, 156.

93. Cheng, *Second Skin*, 35.

94. McClintock, *Imperial Leather*, 72.

5. PLANNING THE DECO CITY

1. Gortari Rabiela and Franyuti, "Imágenes de la ciudad," 5, 7, 13.

2. Reese, "Urban Development of Mexico City," 159.

3. Gortari Rabiela and Franyuti, "Imágenes de la ciudad," 7, 11; Reese, "Urban Development of Mexico City," 158.

4. Olsen, *Artifacts of Revolution*, 4; Reese, "Urban Development of Mexico City," 158. Reese dates Roma and Condesa to 1902 as middle-class colonias.

5. Reese, "Urban Development of Mexico City," 160.

6. Olsen, *Artifacts of Revolution*, 54, 19. Olsen states that de la Lama seemed fairly unscrupulous; he "offered to compensate" an ayuntamiento member, who ended up refusing the deal, "in a very generous manner" (19).

7. Arturo De Saracho to Calles, August 31, 1926, in FPECFT-APEC, file 8: Legajo 1/3, Inventario 1474. The former Calles mansion now houses the

historical archives of the Fideicomiso Plutarco Elias Calles y Fernando Torreblanca.

8. Parque México was first known as Parque General San Martín.

9. Olsen, *Artifacts of Revolution*, 54.

10. Departamento del Distrito Federal (Mexico), *Boletín de Obras Públicas*, July 1930, 18–19; see also Ayuntamiento de Ciudad de México, *Informe de H. Ayuntamiento* (1926), 192, 68.

11. Salvador Novo, "Que hacer los Domingos," *Nuestra Ciudad*, August 1930, 6–7.

12. Reese, "Urban Development of Mexico City," 165. The first "comprehensive urban plan" in 1930 sought to increase health conditions and unused space acreage was to be transformed into parks, gardens, and municipal markets.

13. Reese, "Urban Development of Mexico City," 161; Seltzer, *Bodies and Machines*, 18, 19.

14. Departamento del Distrito Federal (Mexico), *Boletín de Obras Públicas*, July 1930, 20–21. On governmental use of radio, see Sluis, "Revolution and the Rhetoric of Representation."

15. Shell, *Church and State Education*, 164.

16. After visiting the park and theater, I found the estimate of eight thousand spectators to be high.

17. The Casa de Orientación, a correctional facility, provided delinquent young women with training as seamstresses to set them on a course toward an honest life. Distrito Federal, *Informe* (1934).

18. Johns, *City of Mexico*, 86; Gortari Rabiela and Franyuti, "Imágenes de la ciudad," 21.

19. Excerpts from *El banquete de palacio* quoted in Carballo and Martínez, *Págines sobre la Ciudad de México*, 223.

20. Incidentally, Esperanza Iris maintained a residence in Condesa on Oaxaca Street.

21. Cube Bonifant, "En la colonia Roma," *El Universal*, September 14, 1928, first section, 3.

22. Debord, *Society of the Spectacle*, 125, 112; Colquhoun, *Modern Architecture*, 149, 152; Mumford, *The City in History*, 325.

23. Reese, "Urban Development of Mexico City," 160; Salvador Novo, *Nuestra ciudad mía*, quoted in Carballo and Martínez, *Págines sobre la Ciudad de México*, 280; Friedeberg, *De vacaciones por la vida*, 35–36.

24. Olsen, *Artifacts of Revolution*, 54.

25. G. Wood and Greenhalgh, "Symbols of the Sacred."

26. Sola-Morales, "Barcelona," 336; Vanke, "Arabesques," 123.

27. *Jugendstil* was the German term for, and contemporary with, Art Nouveau.

28. Johns, *City of Mexico*, 18, 23.

29. Friedeberg, *De vacaciones por la vida*, 31–34.

30. Colquhoun, *Modern Architecture*, 51.

31. Colquhoun, *Modern Architecture*, 33, 87.

32. Colquhoun, *Modern Architecture*, 99.

33. Olsen, *Artifacts of Revolution*, 23.

34. Le Corbusier quoted in J. C. Scott, *Seeing Like a State*, 106, 107, 115.

35. Almandoz, *Planning Latin America's Capital Cities*, 34, 35, 36, 105.

36. Olsen, *Artifacts of Revolution*, xvi, 2.

37. Anda Alanís, "Preservation of Historic Architecture," 61.

38. Olsen, *Artifacts of Revolution*, 5.

39. Olsen, *Artifacts of Revolution*, 5, 6, 7.

40. Olsen, *Artifacts of Revolution*, 9, 10, 11.

41. Olsen, *Artifacts of Revolution*, 20–21, 22.

42. Instituto Nacional de Bellas Artes, *Pláticas sobre arquitectura*.

43. Instituto Nacional de Bellas Artes, *Pláticas sobre arquitectura*, 50, 53. Architects like Mariscal were mostly political conservatives who feared communism and believed that functionalism came close to emulating communist architecture.

44. Instituto Nacional de Bellas Artes, *Pláticas sobre arquitectura*, 11, 15, 20, 21, 24–27, 60 and 98.

45. Colquhoun, *Modern Architecture*, 141, 13, 16, 18.

46. Greenhalgh, *Art Nouveau*, 431–32, 436; Fischer, *Designing Women*, 11–12.

47. *Pláticas sobre arquitectura*, x; Olsen, *Artifacts*, xvi, 2.

48. Secretaría de Educación Pública (Mexico), *Boletín de Instrucción Pública*, July–September 1913, 306–7.

49. Secretaría de Educación Pública (Mexico), *Boletín de Instrucción Pública*, May 10, 1903, 95, 97, 92–93, 342, 345.

50. Secretaría de Educación Pública, *Boletín de Instrucción Pública*, July–September 1913, 234–36. The first prize was a certificate and one hundred pesos in cash.

51. Secretaría de Instrucción Pública y Bellas Artes, *Boletín de Educación*, November 1915, 6, 13, 161–62.

52. Olsen, *Artifacts of Revolution*, 22, 25.

53. Mumford, *The City in History*, 11–12, 12, 16, 97, 43, 100–101, 105.

54. Grosz, *Space, Time, and Perversion*, 116.

55. In his report to Emperor Augustus, *De architectura* (known today as *Ten Books on Architecture*), Vitruvius outlined the modalities of desirable buildings as based on ideal human proportions that the perfectly shaped human body should adhere to, which are most clearly evident in his discussion of columns. Looking to Greek examples, he created a gendered division of that beauty. The standard "Doric column came to exhibit the proportion, soundness and attractiveness of the male body." The temple in honor of Diana, however, called for the column lengths and appearance adapted to female "slenderness," a more "lofty appearance," and incorporated "for the capital, as for hair, . . . draped volutes on either side to resemble curled locks" . . . "and . . . flutes down the whole trunk of the column to mimic, in matronly manner, the folds of the stola." In this way, found Vitruvius, the Greeks devised two types of columns, one masculine, the other Ionian and "of womanly slenderness, ornamentation, and proportion." Even more ornate and feminine was the Corinthian column, which—Vitruvius tells us—"imitates the slenderness of *a young girl*, because young girls, on account of their age, can be seen to have even more slender limbs and obtain even more charming effects when they adorn themselves." Vitruvius, *Ten Books on Architecture*, 47, 55, emphasis added.

56. Vitruvius, *Ten Books on Architecture*, 56.

57. Vitruvius, *Ten Books on Architecture*, 56. Vitruvius explains that the "architectural ornament" follows the logic and design of the columns; i.e., the columns thus appear a central part/focal point of ancient architecture.

58. Quoted in Zedillo Castillo, *El teatro*, 93.

59. See Mumford, *The City in History*, 27; and Lefebvre, *The Production of Space*.

60. Grosz, *Space, Time, and Perversion*, 104, 109, 108; Grosz, "Bodies-Cities," 242.

61. Colquhoun, *Modern Architecture*, 21, 101; Gallo, *Mexican Modernity*, 188.

62. Cheng, *Second Skin*, 25.

63. Cheng, *Second Skin*, 36, 78.

64. Olsen, *Artifacts of Revolution*, 24.

65. Cheng, *Second Skin*, 35.

66. Olsen, *Artifacts of Revolution*, 16, 85.

67. *Pláticas sobre arquitectura*, vii.

68. *Pláticas sobre arquitectura*, 60.

69. *Pláticas sobre arquitectura*, 59–60.

70. Fischer, *Designing Women*, 27; *Pláticas sobre arquitectura*, 60.

71. Mark Winokur quoted in Fischer, *Designing Women*, 25.

72. *Pláticas sobre arquitectura*, 82, 83.

73. Olsen, "Issues of National Identity."

74. Olsen, *Artifacts of Revolution*, 35, 67.

75. Olsen, *Artifacts of Revolution*, 63, 64, 65.

76. Olsen, "Revolution in the Streets," 130; Olsen, *Artifacts of Revolution*, 67.

77. Gallo, *Mexican Modernity*, 170, 171, 172.

78. *Pláticas sobre arquitectura*, 2; Gallo, *Mexican Modernity*, 184.

79. Cheng, *Second Skin*, 102.

80. Gallo, *Mexican Modernity*, 189; Olsen, *Artifacts of Revolution*, 28.

81. Gómez Mayorga quoted in Olsen, "Issues of National Identity"; Olsen, *Artifacts of Revolution*, 33; Olsen, "Revolution in the Streets," 120.

82. *Pláticas sobre arquitectura*, 22, 29–30, 33.

83. Olsen, *Artifacts of Revolution*, 66, 67.

84. Olsen, *Artifacts of Revolution*, 16.

85. Olsen, "Saving the Past," 11.

86. Olsen, *Artifacts of Revolution*, 30. Anáhuac Construction (the recipient of the contract for building the national highway), founded by General Almazán and directed by Calles, was another.

87. Oles, "Noguchi in Mexico," 16, 17, 18; Olsen, *Artifacts of Revolution*, 33, 62.

88. This analysis is based on the Foreign Club ad that appeared in *Mujeres y Deportes*, November, 17, 1934. Advertisements like this appeared frequently in both newspapers and magazines. I am indebted to Eric Schantz for the reference to Rita Cansina Hayward's performance in the club before her arrival in Hollywood.

89. Olsen, "Artifacts of Revolution," 44, 45, 152–53.

90. Acevedo de Iturriaga, "Dos muralismos," 44; Olsen, "Artifacts of Revolution," 137; Olsen, "Sáenz Garza," 1326–27.

91. Olsen, "Artifacts of Revolution," 18, 19; Mumford, *The City in History*, 302.

92. Almandoz, *Planning Latin America's Capital Cities*, 32.

93. Olsen, *Artifacts of Revolution*, 3, 61, 101.

94. Olsen, *Artifacts of Revolution*, 61, 9.

95. Distrito Federal, *Memoria del ddf* (1932–33), 170–71.

96. Monnet, "La parole et le geste," 96; Olsen, *Artifacts of Revolution*, 103, 116, 154. Davis, *Urban Leviathan*, 77; Olsen, "Artifacts of Revolution," 124.

97. Olsen, *Artifacts of Revolution*, 103; Olsen, "Artifacts of Revolution," 116, 154; Monnet, "La parole et le geste," 99.

98. J. C. Scott, *Seeing Like a State*, 88–89, 94, 113.

99. J. C. Scott, *Seeing Like a State*, 95, 104, 109, 112,

100. J. C. Scott, *Seeing Like a State*, 119.

101. Unlike the adjacent Zona Rosa, Condesa's streets bore the names of Mexican states, and its restaurants specialized in regional Mexican cuisine that demonstrated a new pride in lo mexicano.

6. MERCADO ABELARDO RODRÍGUEZ

1. Distrito Federal, *Informe* (1934), 142.

2. Toor, *Toor's Guide to Mexico*, 78–79; "Deutsch Praises Mexico," *New York Times*, August 4, 1934.

3. Born, *The New Architecture in Mexico*, 52–53.

4. Market women were among the most vocal proponents of women's activism in the 1930s, and they reacted strongly against the domesticating efforts inherent in market reform.

5. Porter, "And That It Is Custom Makes It Law," 124, 125; Lear, "Mexico City: Popular Classes," 78.

6. Porter, "And That It Is Custom Makes It Law," 112, 115, 125, 116–17, 127–28.

7. Ochoa, *Feeding Mexico*, 25.

8. López Rosado, *Los servicios públicos*, 213.

9. Lear, "Mexico City" (*Journal of Urban History*), 469; Lear, *Workers, Neighbors, and Citizens*, 78.

10. López Rosado, *Los servicios públicos*, 212–13; Eckstein, *The Poverty of Revolution*, 45.

11. Rangel M., *La Merced*, 69, 71, 73–74, 79–80.

12. Rangel M., *La Merced*, 77, 79.

13. "Mercados," Ayuntamiento de Ciudad de México, *Memoria de H. Ayuntamiento* (1925), 205; "Mercados," Ayuntamiento de Ciudad de México, *Memoria de H. Ayuntamiento* (1926), 70–71.

14. Inspector del Servicio Sanitario de Mercados, "Dictámes inspecciones mercados," August 4 and 17, 1922, in AHSSA-SP-SJ, box 8, file 8.

15. Friedeberg, *De vacaciones por la vida*, 34.

16. Report by Inspector Castillo Nájera, July 27, 1922, in AHSSA-SP-SJ, box 8, file 8; AGN-APR-LC, file c549.3/16.

17. Olsen, *Artifacts of Revolution*, 102.

18. Director of Department of Public Health to Mayor's Office, August 21, 1922, in AHSSA-SP-SJ, box 8, file 8.

19. Olsen, *Artifacts of Revolution*, 109.

20. "Mercados," Ayuntamiento de Ciudad de México, *Memoria de H. Ayuntamiento* (1926), 70–71; AHSSA-SP-SJ, box 2, file 10.

21. "Informe al Jefe de Seccion Juridico," December 18, 1928, in AHSSA-SP-SJ, box 14, file 20.

22. Dr. Daniel Ríos Zertuche, "Higiene en la Ciudad de México," December 30, 1933, in AHSSA-SP-SJ, box 37, file 3.

23. Alberto Olague Soria to Abelardo Rodríguez, n.d., in AGN-APR-AR, file 616/15.

24. López Rosado, *Los servicios públicos*, 264–65; Beals, *Mexican Maze*, 159–60; Thomas D. Bowman, U.S. Consul General, "Sanitary Measures in Mexico," August 24, 1935, Consular Reports to the Department of State, 812.124/10, NARA.

25. Distrito Federal, *Informe* (1933), 119; Distrito Federal, *Informe* (1934), 89–90; Olsen, "Artifacts of Revolution," 164, 165.

26. Rojas Loa O., "La transformación de la zona central," 230.

27. Lear, "Mexico City: Popular Classes," 56, 91–92.

28. Beals, *Mexican Maze*, 152, 24; Eckstein, *The Poverty of Revolution*, 48.

29. Tenorio Trillo, "1910 Mexico City," 177.

30. The report did not specify what tenements it referred to, but the commission included photographs of the vecindad Las Inditas on Rodríguez Puebla Street, directly across from the future market. Distrito Federal, *Informe* (1934), 90.

31. Oropesa, *The Contemporáneos Group*, 104.

32. Vázquez Ramírez, *Organización y resistencia popular*, 98.

33. AGN-APR-AR, file 139.74/2.

34. AGN-APR-AR, file 562.1/155 and file 616.7/6.

35. Vázquez Ramírez, *Organización y resistencia popular*, 97.

36. Vázquez Ramírez, *Organización y resistencia popular*, 39, 99, 103, 109, 111.

37. Rangel M., *La Merced*, 86.

38. Vázquez Ramírez, *Organización y resistencia popular*, 97, 98, 112, 114, 117, 118.

39. Vázquez Ramírez, *Organización y resistencia popular*, 81.

40. Casasola, *Historia gráfica*, vol. 4, no. 2714.

41. AGN-APR-AR, file 610/3.

42. AGN-APR-AR, files 616/4, 616/15.

43. "Mexico City Markets Always Full of Life," *New York Times*, February 16, 1930.

44. Distrito Federal, *Informe* (1934), 89–90.

45. Mumford, *The City in History*, 97, 43, emphasis added.

46. "Great Building Era for Mexico City," *New York Times*, July 15, 1934.

47. AGN-APR-AR, file 160/8.

48. Distrito Federal, *Informe* (1933), 136.

49. Olsen, *Artifacts of Revolution*, 66, 67.

50. Antonio Muñoz García, "Los mercados de la capital," *Boletín de Obras Públicas*, December 1930, 270–85.

51. Instituto Nacional de Bellas Artes, *Pláticas sobre arquitectura*, 54, 57.

52. Olsen, "Artifacts of Revolution," 165, 166; Acevedo de Iturriaga, "Dos muralismos," 42, 46.

53. "Architecture: The Twentieth Century," *Encyclopedia of Mexico*, 90, 92; Casey, *The Fate of Place*.

54. Acevedo de Iturriaga, "Dos muralismos," 44; Distrito Federal, *Informe* (1934), 89–90.

55. Distrito Federal, *Informe* (1934), 89–90, 142.

56. Francisco Bulman, "La situación de la ciudad en lo relativo a mercados," *Boletín de Obras Públicas*, August/September 1930, 81–83.

57. Debord, *Society of the Spectacle*, 112.

58. Colquhoun, *Modern Architecture*, 53.

59. For instance, in cultural center number 3 in colonia Morelos, where most of the students were domestic servants and workers, classes focused on cooking and sewing. Distrito Federal, *Informe* (1933), 160, 162; Distrito Federal, *Memoria del ddf* (1935), 169; Distrito Federal, *Informe* (1934), 142.

60. Distrito Federal, *Memoria del ddf* (1935), 169; Casasola, *Historia gráfica*, vol. 4, no. 2714.

61. Distrito Federal, *Memoria del ddf* (1936), 242–43, 244.

62. Roberto "el Diablo," "La semana teatral: Un nuevo teatro," *Revista de Revistas*, December 9, 1934, 33.

63. Vázquez Ramírez, *Organización y resistencia popular*, 45; Usigli, *Mexico in the Theater*, 131–32, 133.

64. Due to its resounding success, the actors repeated the performance in the bullring El Toreo in Mexico City. Distrito Federal, *Memoria presentada*, 144.

65. Usigli, *Mexico in the Theater*, 123–25.

66. Stallybrass and White, *Politics and Poetics*, 33–34, 62.

67. Weis, *Latin American Popular Theatre*, 94–95.

68. Distrito Federal, *Memoria del ddf* (1936), 242–43, 244.

69. Distrito Federal, *Informe* (1934), 147.

70. O'Malley, *The Myth of the Revolution*, 58; "Homenaje, 1933" in FPECFT-FAO, II 060400 6 5155 1; "Laborde, Hernán (líder comunista)," in FPECFT-FSG, file 414, Inventario 356, Legajo 1.

71. Usigli, *Mexico in the Theater*, 104.

72. Acevedo de Iturriaga, "Dos muralismos," 47; Ruíz, *La Plaza de Loreto*, 47; Kandell, *La capital*.

73. Noguchi, an artist and landscape architect, produced his first work of public art for the MAR; he had been involved in designing work for the Public Works of Art Project in the United States. See Oles, "Noguchi in Mexico."

74. AGN-APR-LC, file 609/262.

75. Acevedo de Iturriaga, "Dos muralismos," 48.

76. Olsen, "Artifacts of Revolution," 23; Acevedo de Iturriaga, "Dos muralismos," 45.

77. Oles, "Noguchi in Mexico,"16, 17, 18. Oles calls the the Mercado "Mexico City's most important urban renovation project of the 1930s" (16).

78. Acevedo de Iturriaga, "Dos muralismos," 40; Distrito Federal, *Informe* (1933), 120; Distrito Federal, *Informe* (1934), 89–90; Cruz Rodríguez, *Crecimiento urbano y procesos sociales*, 123; Lacey, "The 1921 Centennial Celebration," 204.

79. "Seccion Analítica de Ingresos y Egresos, No. 1," Distrito Federal, *Informe* (1933), tables 27 and 33; Distrito Federal, *Informe* (1934), 46.

80. Distrito Federal, *Memoria del ddf* (1935), 79–80.

81. J. C. Scott, *Seeing Like a State*, 134, 140; Meskimmon, *Engendering the City*, 27. Jacobs, a staunch critic of architectural functionalism, believed that diversity, complexity, and cross-use of public space would make streets, neighborhoods, and public space in general more exiting and desirable.

82. Casasola, *Historia grafíca*, vol. 3.

83. Distrito Federal, *Informe* (1934), 142–43, 153; Distrito Federal, *Memoria del ddf* (1935), 44–45; Toor, *Toor's Guide to Mexico*, 78–79.

84. Ochoa, *Feeding Mexico*, 7, 29.

85. Casey, *The Fate of Place*, 315; Olsen, "Saving the Past," 7.

86. Ross, *El Monstruo*, 184 ; "Recuperan murales," *La Mañana*, http://www.elmanana.com.mx/notas.asp?id=72823.

87. Olsen, "Artifacts of Revolution," 149.

88. Eckstein, *The Poverty of Revolution*, 44, 50; Rojas Loa O., "La transformación de la zona central," 235; Ochoa, *Feeding Mexico*, 59.

89. James Oles, interview by the author, June 28, 2001.

90. Olsen, "Saving the Past," 9; Olsen, "Artifacts of Revolution," 167.

91. Distrito Federal, *Informe* (1934), 142.

92. Stallybrass and White, *Politics and Poetics*, 37, 38–39, 41, 42.

93. Olsen, "Saving the Past," 9.

7. PALACIO DE BELLAS ARTES

1. AHSEP Departamento Bellas Artes Serie Teatro 95/30, January 12, 1933.

2. Alberto J. Pani, "El Palacio de Bellas Artes," *El Universal*, February 12, 1941, 9.

3. Ulloa del Río, *Palacio de Bellas Artes*, 19–20.

4. Ulloa del Río, *Palacio de Bellas Artes*, 26.

5. Ulloa del Río, *Palacio de Bellas Artes*, 25, 28–29.

6. Ulloa del Río, *Palacio de Bellas Artes*, 34, 35.

7. Ulloa del Río, *Palacio de Bellas Artes*, 22.

8. Teresa Gurza, "Como nació y creció Bellas Artes," *El Día*, August 30, 1980.

9. Johns, *City of Mexico*, 18, 23.

10. Ulloa del Río, *Palacio de Bellas Artes*, 23–24.

11. AHSEP-BA 4910/10/2 May 25, 1934.

12. Gurza, "Como nació y cerció Bellas Artes."

13. Usigli, *Mexico in the Theater*, 117.

14. Gurza, "Como nació y cerció Bellas Artes."

15. "El Teatro Nacional," *El Nacional*, November 27, 1932, 8.

16. Pani, "El Palacio de Bellas Artes," 9.

17. "El Teatro Nacional paso el Depto. Del Distrito," *El Universal*, October 9, 1931, 9.

18. Pani, "El Palacio de Bellas Artes," 9.

19. "Cuatro millones de pesos para dos grandes obras capitalinas," *Excélsior*, August 19, 1932, 10.

20. Manfredo Tafuri and Francisco dal Co quoted in Víctor Jímenez, "El Palacio de Bellas Artes en 1930: Viejas piedras, nuevas ideas," *Mexico en el Tiempo*, March/April 1998, 18–25.

21. Gurza, "Como nació y cerció Bellas Artes."

22. Tafuri and dal Co quoted in Jímenez, "El Palacio de Bellas Artes," 23.

23. Jímenez, "El Palacio de Bellas Artes," 23.

24. Olsen, *Artifacts of Revolution*, 54.

25. Benjamin, *La Revolución*, 123.

26. "El Teatro Nacional," *El Nacional*, November 27, 1932, 8.

27. Fischer, "City of Women," 113–15, 117–19.

28. Almandoz, *Planning Latin America's Capital Cities*, 102, 103, 36, 104.

29. "Atentado incredible: Estan destruyendo el Teatro Nacional," *La Prensa*, September 23, 1932, 11.

30. "Atentado incredible," 10.

31. Mumford, *The City in History*, 307.

32. Ulloa del Río, *Palacio de Bellas Artes*, 83–84.

33. "Un cuarto siglo de teatro en México," *El Universal*, October 1, 1941, 9.

34. Ulloa del Río, *Palacio de Bellas Artes*, 85.

35. AHSEP-BA-ST 492/50, "Teatro de Orientación, Temporada 1934."

36. AHSEP-BA-ST 401/35, 1936.

37. "Un cuarto siglo de teatro en México," 9.

38. "El resurgimiento del teatro," *El Universal*, October 30, 1941, 9.

39. "Por el ojo del llave: Las bellas artes y el estado," *El Universal*, January 1, 1938, 9.

40. "Por el ojo del llave," 9.

41. Rochfort, *Mexican Muralists*.

42. Rochfort, *Mexican Muralists*, 84.

43. Rochfort, *Mexican Muralists*, 59.

44. Rochfort, *Mexican Muralists*, 132.

45. *Mundo Cinematográfico* 7 (March–April 1936): 67–68.

46. "Solo hay en el Republica un teatro o cine por cada dieciseis mil habitants," *Excélsior*, March 1, 1931, 10.

47. "Tenaz oposición para que no sean convertidos yam as teatros en salones de cine," *Excélsior*, June 24, 1938, 10.

48. Luvio Mebdieta y Nuñez, "La agonia del teatro," *El Universal*, December 5, 1942, 9.

49. J. Luis Rivera, review of *Allá en el rancho grande*, http://w-cinema.blogspot .com/2008/11/all-en-el-rancho-grande-1936.html.

50. See O'Malley, *The Myth of the Revolution*, for early scholarship on revolutionary constructions of masculinity.

51. Cano, "Unconcealable Realities of Desire," 38, 40.

52. For an in-depth treatment of charrismo, see Niblo, *Mexico in the 1940s*.

53. Oropesa, *The Contemporáneos Group*, 120.

54. Ross, *El Monstruo*, 175–77.

55. Jubilo, "Acotaciones del momento: No mas mitines ni asambleas en el Teatro de Bellas Artes," *Gráfico*, February 9, 1938, 12.

56. Editorial, *Excélsior*, February 7, 1938, 10.

57. Editorial, "La rehabilitación de la Palacio de Bellas Artes," *El Universal*, February 10, 1938, 9.

58. Jubilo, "Acotaciones del momento," 12.

59. "Avisos a tiempo," *El Universal*, August 8, 1934, 9.

60. "El teatro de Bellas Artes no responde a su objeto," *El Universal*, January 9, 1938, 9.

61. "Pasa a ser dependencia de educación," *El Nacional*, February 24, 1938, 8.

62. "Se reorganiza ya el Departamento de Bellas Artes," *Excélsior*, March 3, 1938, 10.

63. "Loable esfuerzo en pro de la actividad teatral," *El Nacional*, October 20, 1938, 8.

64. "Se oponen a que Augustín Lara trabaje en el Bellas Artes," *El Nacional*, July 29, 1938, 8.

65. Editorial, *Excélsior*, October 22, 1938, 10.

66. "El Teatro de Bellas Artes, en peligro de hundirse," *El Nacional*, October 24, 1938, 8.

67. "Inminente es la clausura del Palacio de B. Artes," *Ultimas Noticias de Excélsior*, July 16, 1941, 14.

68. "Por todas partes hay grietas que le dan un feo aspecto de ruina," *La Prensa*, July 18, 1941, 12.

69. "Ya regrasoron los sillones," *El Universal*, February 4, 1941, 9.

70. "El Palacio de Bellas Artes bajo el voraz sindicalismo!" *La Prensa*, February 10, 1941, 11.

71. "El asunto de Bellas Artes," *El Universal*, February 10, 1941, 9.

72. "El Bellas Artes, magoneado por una empresa extranjera," *La Prensa*, February 21, 1941, 11.

73. "Consejo para el teatro popular," *Excélsior*, August 13, 1938, 10.

74. "Como functionara el consejo nacional del Teatro Popular," *El Nacional*, August 31, 1938, 8.

75. Francisco Pasolargo,"El teatro, elemento indispensable para la educación popular," *El Nacional*, July 16, 1946, 8.

76. Ross, *El Monstruo*, 184.

77. Gallo, *Mexican Modernity*, 210. "Stadiogenic events" is Gallo's wording for theatrical gatherings in stadiums where large groups of people would be incited to nationalism.

78. "Teatros," *Diversiones*, February 12, 1938, 5.

79. Teresa de Cepeda, "La mujer y la moral," *Excélsior*, August 9, 1942, 10.

80. "Ballet Folklórico de México/Amelia Hernández," http://www.ballet folkloricodemexico.com.mx.

81. Zolov, "Discovering a Land," 241.

82. Colquhoun, *Modern Architecture*, 93.

CONCLUSION

1. "Renace el centro histórico: 500 milliones de pesos invertidos en 34 man-zanas," *Vuelo*, August 2003, 38–46.

2. Geri Smith, "Mexico City Gets a Face-lift," *Business Week*, May 2004, http://www.bloomberg.com/bw/stories/2004-05-23/mexico-city-gets-a-face-lift.

3. Ron Butler, "Center of Belated Attention," *Economist*, September 2002, 37.

4. Monsiváis, "Mexico City," 10. During Mayor López Obrador's administra-tion, when big developers like Slim "shared decision making power with public officials," "street vendor dissatisfaction soon became a political problem for the mayor because this highly organized and large constitu-ency was known to be a strong base for the PRD [Partido de la Revolu-ción Democrática]." Davis, "The Modern City," 74.

5. For growth of Mexico City since 1940 due to structural forces, see Ward, *Mexico City*.

6. In places as far apart and culturally diverse as Australia, Japan, the Neth-erlands, and Mexico, the use of catchphrases such as "maintaining the line" conveyed similar beauty and especially dietary strategies to achieve or enhance the ideal female shape. Conor, *Spectacular Modern Woman*, 156. Also see Silverberg, "After the Grand Tour." Having grown up in the Netherlands during the 1970s, I know that "to be on the line" ("aan de lijn") was standardly used to mean dieting, slang that went back to my grandmother's youth during the 1920s.

7. As late as the early 1980s, about four thousand women worked the streets around La Merced market as prostitutes. Rangel M., *La Merced*, 90.

8. "Mercado Abelardo Rodríguez," *Lonely Planet*, http://www.lonelyplanet .com/mexico/mexico-city/sights/art/mercado-abelardo-rodriguez#ixzz 2FGKou52s.

9. The Dutch historian and social critic Geert Mak posits that the modern-ist split of these separate and diametrically positioned spaces eclipses Jürgen Habermas's emphasis on the importance of public and privates spheres. The current immigration flows into northern Europe do not rupture the mystique of Western modernity due to their composition of Muslim, Mediterranean, and brown peoples. The important element in

their identity as "non-modern" people, argues Mak, is their rural origin. Mak, "Een kleine geschiedenis van een novembermaand: Het moment waarop in Nederland de kelders open gingen," NCR *Handelsblad*, November 27, 2004.

10. In *The Politics of the Veil*, Joan Scott also notes the importance of gender, specifically, femininity, to the formulation of modernity. Women's sexual liberation became a distinct marker of Western modernization in the twentieth century, with liberal capitalist societies measuring gender equality by the barometer of female sexual liberty and, moreover, sexual availability.

BIBLIOGRAPHY

ARCHIVAL SOURCES

Archivo General de la Nación, Mexico City
Administración Pública de la República
LÁZARO CÁRDENAS
ABELARDO RODRÍGUEZ
Archivo Histórico de la Secretaría de Educación Pública, Mexico City
Departamento de Bellas Artes
Archivo Histórico del Distrito Federal, Mexico City
Diversiones Públicas
Esperanza Iris
Archivo Histórico de Secretaría de Salubridad Pública y Asistencia, Mexico
City
Salubridad Pública
SERVICIO JURÍDICO
Fideicomiso Plutarco Elías Calles y Fernando Torreblanco, Mexico City
Archivo Plutarco Elías Calles
Fondo Alvaro Obregón
Fondo Soledad González
National Archives and Records Administration, Washington DC. Records of
the Department of State Relating to the Internal Affairs of Mexico, 1910–
1929. File 812.

PUBLISHED SOURCES

Acevedo de Iturriaga, Esther. "Dos muralismos en el mercado." *Plural* 11 (Octo-
ber 1981): 40–50.
Almandoz, Arturo, ed. *Planning Latin America's Capital Cities, 1850–1950.* New
York: Routledge, 2002.

Alonso, Ana María. "Conforming Disconformity: 'Mestizaje,' Hybridity, and the Aesthetics of Mexican Nationalism." *Cultural Anthropology* 19, no. 4 (2004): 459–90.

Alonso, Enrique. *María Conesa*. Mexico City: Océano, 1987.

Anda Alanís, Enrique X. de. "The Preservation of Historic Architecture and the Beliefs of the Modern Movement in Mexico: 1914–1963." *Future Anterior* 6, no. 2 (2009): 58–73.

Andes, Stephen J. C. "A Catholic Alternative to Revolution: The Survival of Social Catholicism in Post-Revolutionary Mexico." *The Americas* 68, no. 4 (2012): 529–62.

Appadurai, Arjun. *Modernity at Large: Cultural Dimensions of Globalization.* Minneapolis: University of Minnesota Press, 1996.

Avila, Arturo, and Luis Martinez Serrano. "Las racionistas," from *De México a Cuba* (1928). In *Del rancho al bátaclan: Cancionero de teatro de revista, 1900–1940*, ed. Jorge Miranda. Mexico City: SEP/Museo Nacional de Culturas Populares, 1984.

Ayuntamiento de Ciudad de México (Mexico). *Informe de H. Ayuntamiento.* Mexico City: n.p., 1923.

———. *Informe de H. Ayuntamiento.* Mexico City: n.p., 1926.

———. *Memoria de H. Ayuntamiento.* Mexico City: n.p., 1925.

———. *Memoria de H. Ayuntamiento.* Mexico City: n.p., 1926.

Balderston, Daniel, and Donna J. Guy. *Sex and Sexuality in Latin America.* New York: New York University Press, 1997.

Barrow, Joanne, Randy Barrow, and Fred Katz. "Ernesto Cabral." *Comic Art* 4 (Fall 2003): 14–31.

Bartra, Roger. *Blood, Ink, Culture: Miseries and Splendors of the Post-Mexican Condition.* Durham NC: Duke University Press, 2002.

———. "Stuffing the Indian Photographically." *History of Photography* 20, no. 3 (Autumn 1996): 236–39.

Beals, Carleton. *Mexican Maze.* Philadelphia: Lippincott, 1931.

Beezley, William H. *Judas at the Jockey Club and Other Episodes of Porfirian Mexico.* Lincoln: University of Nebraska Press, 1987.

Beezley, William H., and Linda Ann Curcio, eds. *Latin American Popular Culture: An Introduction.* Wilmington DE: SR Books, 2000.

Beezley, William H., and David E. Lorey, eds. *Viva Mexico! Viva La Independencia! Celebrations of September 16.* Wilmington DE: SR Books, 2001.

Benjamin, Thomas. "From the Ruins of the Ancien Regime: Mexico's Monument to the Revolution." In *Latin American Popular Culture: An Introduc-*

tion, ed. William H. Beezley and Linda A. Curcio-Nagy, 169–82. Wilmington DE: SR Books, 2000.

———. *La Revolución: Mexico's Great Revolution as Memory, Myth, and History*. Austin: University of Texas Press, 2000.

Berlanstein, Lenard R. *Daughters of Eve: A Cultural History of French Theater Women from the Old Regime to the Fin De Siècle*. Cambridge: Harvard University Press, 2001.

Bliss, Katherine E. *Compromised Positions: Prostitution, Public Health, and Gender Politics in Revolutionary Mexico City*. University Park: Pennsylvania State University Press, 2001.

Bliss, Katherine E., and Anne S. Blum. "Adolescence, Sex, and the Gendered Experience of Public Space in Mexico City." In *Gender, Sexuality and Power in Latin America Since Independence*, ed. William French and Katherine Bliss, 163–86. Lanham MD: Rowman and Littlefield, 2006.

Bloomer, Kent C., and Charles W. Moore. *Body, Memory, and Architecture*. New Haven: Yale University Press, 1977.

Blum, Ann S. *Domestic Economies: Family, Work, and Welfare in Mexico City, 1884–1943*. Lincoln: University of Nebraska Press, 2010.

Bonfil Batalla, Guillermo. *Mexico Profundo: Reclaiming a Civilization*. Austin: University of Texas Press, 1996.

Bonifant, Cube. *Una pequeña Marquesa de Sade: Crónicas selectas (1921–1948)*. Ed. Viviane Mahieux. Mexico City: Direccíon de la Literature UNAM/CONACULTA Consejo Nacional para la Cultura y las Artes, 2009.

Bordo, Susan. *Unbearable Weight: Feminism, Western Culture, and the Body*. Berkeley: University of California Press, 1993.

Born, Esther. *The New Architecture in Mexico*. New York: William Morrow, 1937.

Bourdieu, Pierre. *Photography: A Middle-Brow Art*. Stanford CA: Stanford University Press, 1990.

Boylan, Kristina. "Gendering the Faith and Altering the Nation: The Unión Femenina Católica Mexicana and Women's Revolutionary and Religious Experiences (1917–1940)." In *Sex in Revolution: Gender, Politics, and Power in Modern Mexico*, ed. Gabriela Cano, Jocelyn Olcott, and Mary Kay Vaughan, 199–224. Durham NC: Duke University Press, 2006.

Brasseur, Charles. "The Didjazá." *Artes de México* 49 (2000): 83.

Brenner, Anita. *Your Mexican Holiday: A Modern Guide*. New York: Putnam, 1932.

Brenner, Anita, and George Ross Leighton. *The Wind That Swept Mexico: The History of the Mexican Revolution, 1910–1942*. New York: Harper and Brothers, 1943.

Brettle, Jane, and Sally Rice. *Public Bodies/Private States: New Views on Photography, Representation, and Gender Photography, Critical Views*. Manchester: Manchester University Press, 1994.

Broude, Norma, and Mary D. Garrard, eds. *The Expanding Discourse: Feminism and Art History*. New York: Icon Editions, 1992.

Buffington, Robert, and Pablo Piccato. "Tales of Two Women: The Narrative Construal of Porfirian Reality." *The Americas* 55, no. 3 (January 1999): 391–424.

Bunker, Steven B. *Creating Mexican Consumer Culture in the Age of Porfirio Díaz*. Albuquerque: University of New Mexico Press, 2012.

Butler, Judith. *Bodies That Matter: On the Discursive Limits of "Sex."* New York: Routledge, 1993.

———. *Gender Trouble: Feminism and the Subversion of Identity*. New York: Routledge, 1990.

Cabeza de Baca, Vincent, and Juan Cabeza de Baca. "The 'Shame Suicides' and Tijuana." *Journal of the Southwest* 43 (2001): 603–35.

Calhoun, Craig J. *Habermas and the Public Sphere*. Cambridge: MIT Press, 1992.

Cano, Gabriela. "Unconcealable Realities of Desire: Amelio Robles's (Transgender) Masculinity in the Mexican Revolution." In *Sex in Revolution: Gender, Politics, and Power in Modern Mexico*, ed. Jocelyn Olcott, Mary Kay Vaughan, and Gabriela Cano, 35–56. Durham NC: Duke University Press, 2006.

Cano, Gabriela, and Georgette Emilia José Valenzuela. *Cuatro estudios de género en el México urbano del siglo XIX*. Mexico City: Universidad Nacional Autónoma de México Miguel Ángel Porrúa, 2001.

Caplow, Deborah. "Twentieth Century Photography: Tradition and Change." Master's thesis, University of Washington, 1992.

Carballo, Emmanuel. *El cuento mexicano del siglo XX: Antología*. Mexico City: Empresas Editoriales, 1964.

Carballo, Emmanuel, and José Luis Martínez. *Págines sobre la Ciudad de México, 1469–1987*. Mexico City: Consejo de la Crónica de la Ciudad de México, 1988.

Cárdenas, Leopoldo Ramírez. *Mexico: Viñetas de ayer*. Mexico City: Editorial Imprenta Casas, S.A., n.d.

Careaga Soriano, Teresa María. *Mi México de los veinte*. Toluca: Universidad Autónoma del Estado de México, 1994.

Casasola, Gustavo. *Historia gráfica de La Revolución Mexicana, 1900–1960*. 4 vols. Mexico City: Editorial F. Trillas, 1962.

Casey, Edward S. *The Fate of Place: A Philosophical History*. Berkeley: University of California Press, 1997.

Caulfield, Sueann. "The Birth of Mangue: Race, Nation, and the Politics of Prostitution in Rio de Janeiro, 1850–1942." In *Sex and Sexuality in Latin America*, ed. Daniel Balderston and Donna J. Guy, 86–100. New York: New York University Press, 1997.

———. *In Defense of Honor: Sexual Morality, Modernity, and Nation in Early-Twentieth-Century Brazil*. Durham NC: Duke University Press, 2000.

Chakel, Amy. "The Cronica, the City, and the Invention of the Underworld: Rio de Janeiro, 1889–1922." *Estudios Interdisciplinarios de America Latina* 12, no. 1 (2001).

Chassen-Lopez, Francie. "Juana Cata." Lecture, Oaxaca Summer Institute, June 2009.

Cheng, Anne Anlin. *Second Skin: Josephine Baker and the Modern Surface*. New York: Oxford University Press, 2011.

Colquhoun, Alan. *Modern Architecture/Oxford History of Art*. New York: Oxford University Press, 2002.

Conor, Liz. *The Spectacular Modern Woman: Feminine Visibility in the 1920s*. Bloomington: Indiana University Press, 2004.

Covarrubias, Miguel. "Mirando hacia el sur." *Artes de México* 49 (2000): 26–37.

Creswell, Tim. *Place: A Short Introduction*. Malden MA: Blackwell, 2004.

Cruz Rodríguez, María Soledad. *Crecimiento urbano y procesos sociales en El Distrito Federal (1920–28)*. Mexico City: Universidad Autónoma Metropolitana, Unidad Azcapotzalco, Departamento de Sociología, 1994

Cuevas-Wolf, Cristina. "Guillermo Kahlo and Casasola: Architectural Form and Urban Unrest." *History of Photography* 20, no. 3 (Autumn 1996): 196–207.

Davis, Diane E. "From Avenida Reforma to the Torre Bicentenario: The Clash of "History" and "Progress" in the Making of Modern Mexico City." In *Mexico City through History and Culture*, ed. Linda A. Newson and John P. King, 55–84. Oxford: Oxford University Press, 2009.

———. "The Social Construction of Mexico City: Political Conflict and Urban Development, 1950–1966." *Journal of Urban History* 24, no. 3 (March 1998): 364–415.

———. *Urban Leviathan: Mexico City in the Twentieth Century*. Philadelphia: Temple University Press, 1994.

Dawson, Alexander S. *Indian and Nation in Revolutionary Mexico*. Tucson: University of Arizona Press, 2004.

Debord, Guy. *The Society of the Spectacle*. New York: Zone Books, 1995.

Debroise, Olivier. *Mexican Suite: A History of Photography in Mexico*. Austin: University of Texas Press, 2001.

Debroise, Olivier, Lola Alvarez Bravo, James Oles, and University of Arizona. Center for Creative Photography. *Lola Alvarez Bravo: In Her Own Light*. Tucson: Center for Creative Photography, the University of Arizona, 1994.

Delpar, Helen. *The Enormous Vogue of Things Mexican: Cultural Relations between the United States and Mexico, 1920–1935*. Tuscaloosa: University of Alabama Press, 1992.

Deutsch, Sandra M. "Gender and Sociopolitical Change in Twentieth-Century Latin America." *Hispanic American Historical Review* 71 (May 1991): 259–307.

Díaz del Castillo, Bernal. *The Conquest of New Spain*. New York: Penguin Books, 1963.

Distrito Federal (Mexico). *Informe presidencial y memoria del Departamento del Distrito Federal*. Mexico City: n.p., 1933.

———. *Informe presidencial y memoria del Departamento del Distrito Federal*. Mexico City: n.p., 1934.

———. *Memoria del Departamento del Distrito Federal*. Mexico City: n.p., 1932–33.

———. *Memoria del Departamento del Distrito Federal*. Mexico City: n.p., 1935.

———. *Memoria del Departamento del Distrito Federal*. Mexico City: n.p., 1936.

———. *Memoria presentada al H. Congreso de la Union por el period Sept. de 1935 a Augosto de 1936*. Mexico City: n.p., 1936.

Dore, Elizabeth, and Maxine Molyneux. *Hidden Histories of Gender and the State in Latin America*. Durham NC: Duke University Press, 2000.

Douglas, Mary. *Purity and Danger: An Analysis of Concepts of Pollution and Taboo*. London: Routledge, 2003.

Dueñas Herrera, Pablo. *Las divas en el teatro de revista mexicano*. Mexico City: Asociación Mexicana de Estudios Fonográficos, Dirección General de Culturas Populares, 1994.

Eckstein, Susan. *The Poverty of Revolution: The State and the Urban Poor in Mexico*. Princeton NJ: Princeton University Press, 1977.

Encyclopedia of Mexico: History, Society, Culture. Vol. 2. Chicago: Fitzroy Dearborn, 1997.

Enstad, Nan. *Ladies of Labor, Girls of Adventure: Working Women, Popular Culture, and Labor Politics at the Turn of the Twentieth Century*. New York: Columbia University Press, 1999.

Fischer, Lucy. "City of Women: Busby Berkeley, Architecture, and Urban Space." *Cinema Journal* 49, no. 4 (Summer 2010): 111–30.

———. *Designing Women: Cinema, Art Deco, and the Female Form*. New York: Columbia University Press, 2003.

Flores Rivera, Salvador. *Relatos de mi barrio: Autobiografía*. 2nd ed. Mexico City: EDAMEX, 1988.

Foucault, Michel. *Discipline and Punish: The Birth of the Prison*. New York: Vintage, 1979.

———. *The History of Sexuality Volume I: An Introduction*. New York: Vintage, 1990.

———. "Of Other Spaces." http://foucault.info/documents/heteroTopia /foucault.heteroTopia.en.html.

Fowler-Salamini, Heather, and Mary K. Vaughan. *Women of the Mexican Countryside, 1850–1990: Creating Spaces, Shaping Transition*. Tuscon: University of Arizona Press, 1994.

Fox, Claire F. "Pornography and 'the Popular' in Post-Revolutionary Mexico: The Club Tívoli from Spota to Isaac." In *Visible Nations: Latin American Cinema and Video*, ed. Chon. A. Noriega, 143–73. Minneapolis: University of Minnesota Press, 2000.

Franco, Jean. *Plotting Women: Gender and Representation in Mexico*. New York: Columbia University Press, 1989.

French, Howard. "A History of Playboy Magazine: The Girls Next Door; Life in the Centerfold." New Yorker, March 22, 2006.

Freud, Sigmund. *Five Lectures on Psycho-Analysis*. Ed. and trans. James Strachey. 1909. New York: Norton, 1961.

Friedeberg, Pedro. *De vacaciones por la vida: Memorias no autorizadas del pintor Pedro Friedeberg*. Mexico City: Trilce Ediciones CONACULTA, 2010/2011.

Fujigaki Cruz, Elsa, and Ricardo de León Banuet. *Asamblea de ciudades: Años 20s/50s, ciudad de México*. Mexico City: Museo del Palacio de Bellas Artes/ Consejo Nacional para la Cultura y las Artes, 1992.

Gallo, Rubén. *Mexican Modernity: The Avant-Garde and the Technological Revolution*. Cambridge: MIT Press, 2005.

García Canclini, Néstor, Alejandro Castellanos, and Ana Rosas Mantecón. *La Ciudad De Los Viajeros: Travesías E imaginarios urbanos, México, 1940–2000*. Mexico City: Universidad Autónoma Metropolitana Editorial Grijalbo, 1996.

Garza, James A. "Dominance and Submission in Don Porfirio's Belle Epoque: The Case of Luis and Piedad." In *Masculinity and Sexuality in*

Modern Mexico, ed. Anne Rubenstein and Victor Macías, 79–100. Albuquerque: University of New Mexico Press, 2012.

———. *The Imagined Underworld: Sex, Crime, and Vice in Porfirian Mexico City*. Lincoln: University of Nebraska Press, 2007.

Gleber, Anke. "Female Flanerie and the Symphony of the City." In *Women in the Metropolis: Gender and Modernity in Weimar Culture*, ed. Katharina Von Ankum, 67–88. Berkeley: University of California Press, 1997.

Glenn, Susan A. *Female Spectacle: The Theatrical Roots of Modern Feminism*. Cambridge: Harvard University Press, 2000.

Gonzalez Obregón, Luis. *Las calles de México*. Mexico City: Impresa M. León Sánchez, 1924.

Gortari Rabiela, Hira, and Regina Hernández Franyuti. "Imágenes de la ciudad: Colonias Roma y Condesa." *Boletín Fideicomiso Archivos Plutarco Elías Calles y Fernando Torreblanca* 16 (May 1994).

Greenhalgh, Paul, ed. *Art Nouveau, 1890–1914*. London: V&A, 2000.

Grosz, Elizabeth A. "Bodies-Cities." In *Sexuality and Space*, ed. Beatriz Colomina, 241–54. New York: Princeton Architectural Press, 1992.

———. *Space, Time, and Perversion: Essays on the Politics of Bodies*. London: Routledge, 1995.

Guy, Donna J. *Sex & Danger in Buenos Aires: Prostitution, Family, and Nation in Argentina*. Lincoln: University of Nebraska Press, 1991.

Halberstam, Judith. *Female Masculinity*. Durham NC: Duke University Press, 1998.

———. "MacDaddy, Superfly, Rapper: Gender, Race, and Masculinity in the Drag King Scene." *Social Text* 52/53 (Fall/Winter 1997): 104–31.

Hayes, Joy Elizabeth. *Radio Nation: Communication, Popular Culture, and Nationalism in Mexico, 1920–1950*. Tucson: University of Arizona Press, 2000.

Hedrick, Tace. *Mestizo Modernism: Race, Nation and Identity in Latin American Culture, 1900–1940*. Newark NJ: Rutgers University Press, 2004.

Hefley, James C. *Aarón Sáenz; Mexico's Revolutionary Capitalist*. Waco TX: Word Books, 1970.

Hershfield, Joanne. *Imagining the Chica Moderna: Women, Nation, and Visual Culture in Mexico, 1917–1936*. Durham NC: Duke University Press, 2008.

Hunt, Lynn. "Obscenity and the Origins of Modernity, 1500–1800." In *Feminism and Pornography*, ed. Drucilla Cornell, 355–80. Oxford: Oxford University Press, 2000.

Illades, Carlos and Ariel Rodríguez Kuri. *Ciudad de México: Instituciones, actores sociales, y conflicto político, 1774–1931*. Zamora, Michoacán: El Colegio

de Michoacán; Azcapotzalco: Universidad Autonoma Metropolitana–
Azcapotzalco; Iztapalapa: Universidad Autonoma Metropolitana–
Iztapalapa, 1996.

Instituto Nacional de Bellas Artes (Mexico). *Pláticas sobre arquitectura (1933)*.
2nd ed. Centro Histórico, Mexico City: Consejo Nacional para la Cultura
y las Artes: Instituto Nacional de Bellas Artes, Dirección de Arquitectura
y Conservación del Patrimonio Artístico Inmueble, 2001.

Jímenez, Armando. *Sitios de rompe y rasga en la Cuidad de México*. Mexico
City: Editorial Oceano de México, S.A., 1998.

Jímenez, Víctor. "El Palacio de Bellas Artes en 1930: Viejas piedras, nuevas
ideas." *Mexico en el Tiempo*, March/April 1998.

Johns, Michael. *The City of Mexico in the Age of Díaz*. Austin: University of
Texas Press, 1997.

Joseph, G. M., and Daniel Nugent. *Everyday Forms of State Formation: Revolution and the Negotiation of Rule in Modern Mexico*. Durham NC: Duke
University Press, 1994.

Joseph, G. M., Anne Rubenstein, and Eric Zolov. *Fragments of a Golden Age:
The Politics of Culture in Mexico since 1940*. Durham NC: Duke University
Press, 2001.

Kandell, Jonathan. *La Capital: The Biography of Mexico City*. New York: Ran-
dom House, 1988.

Kendrick, Walter. *The Secret Museum: Pornography in Modern Culture*. New
York: Viking Penguin, 1987.

King, John. *Magical Reels: A History of Cinema in Latin America*. New ed.
London: Verso, 2000.

Knight, Alan. *The Mexican Revolution*. 2 vols. Cambridge, UK: Cambridge
University Press, 1986.

———. "The Mexican Revolution: Bourgeois? Nationalist? Or Just a 'Great
Rebellion'?" *Bulletin of Latin American Research* 4 (1985): 1–37.

———. "Racism, Revolution, and Indigenismo: Mexico, 1910–1940." In *The
Idea of Race in Latin America, 1870–1940*, ed. Richard Graham, 71–113. Austin: University of Texas Press, 1990.

Knopp, Lawrence. "Sexuality and Urban Space: A Framework for Analysis." In
Mapping Desire: Geographies of Sexualities, ed. David Bell and Gill Valen-
tine, 136–49. London: Routledge, 1995.

Kotkin, Joel. *The City: A Global History*. New York: Modern Library, 2006.

Kristeva, Julia. *Powers of Horror: An Essay on Abjection*. New York: Columbia
University Press, 1982.

Kuzio, Barbara Allen. "President Abelardo Rodríguez (1932–1934): From Maximato to Cardinismo." MA thesis, Portland State University, 1997.

Lacy, Elaine C. "The 1921 Centennial Celebration of Mexico's Independence: State Building and Popular Negotiation." In *Viva México! Viva La Independencia!: Celebrations of September 16*, ed. William H. Beezley and David E. Lorey, 199–232. Wilmington DE: SR Books, 2001.

Landes, Joan B., ed. *Feminism, the Public and the Private*. Oxford: Oxford University Press, 1998.

Lauderdale Graham, Sandra. *House and Street: The Domestic World of Servants and Masters in Nineteenth-Century Rio De Janeiro*. Cambridge, UK: Cambridge University Press, 1988.

Lear, John. "Mexico City." *Journal of Urban History* 22, no. 4 (May 1996): 454–93.

———. "Mexico City: Popular Classes and Revolutionary Politics." In *Cities of Hope: People, Protests, and Progress in Urbanizing Latin America, 1870–1930*, ed. Ronn Pineo and James A. Baer, 53–87. Boulder: Westview Press, 1998.

———. *Workers, Neighbors, and Citizens: The Revolution in Mexico City*. Lincoln: University of Nebraska Press, 2001.

Lefebvre, Henri. *The Production of Space*. Oxford, UK: Blackwell, 1991.

Linati, Claudio. *Trajes civiles, militares y religiosos de Mexico (1828)*. Mexico City: Imprenta Universitaria, 1956.

López, Rick A. "The India Bonita Contest of 1921 and the Ethnicization of Mexican National Culture." *Hispanic American Historical Review* 82, no. 2 (2002): 291–328.

López Rosado, Diego G. *Los servicios públicos de la Ciudad de México*. Mexico City: Editorial Porrúa, 1976.

López Sánchez, Sergio, and Julieta Rivas Guerrero. *Esperanza Iris: La Tiple De Hierro (Escritos 1)*. Mexico City: Instituto Nacional de Bellas Artes, 2002.

Low, Setha M. *On the Plaza: The Politics of Public Space and Culture*. Austin: University of Texas Press, 2000.

Lungstrum, Janet. "Metropolis and the Technosexual Woman in Weimar Modernity." In *Women in the Metropolis: Gender and Modernity in Weimar Culture*, ed. Katharina Von Ankum, 128–44. Berkeley: University of California Press, 1997.

Macías, Anna. *Against All Odds: The Feminist Movement in Mexico to 1940*. Westport CT: Greenwood Press, 1982.

Mahieux, Viviane. *Urban Chroniclers in Modern Latin America: The Shared Intimacy of Everyday Life*. Austin: University of Texas Press, 2011.

Maines, Rachel P. *The Technology of Orgasm: "Hysteria," the Vibrator, and Women's Sexual Satisfaction*. Baltimore: Johns Hopkins University Press, 2001.

Marino, Daniela. "Representaciones del zapatismo en la Ciudad de México: Los discursos fotográficos y del rumor." *Historia Mexicana* (Colegio de México) 190, no. 2 (October–December 1998).

Massé, Patricia. "Photographs of Mexican Prostitutes." *History of Photography* 20 (1996): 231–34.

Matthews, Michael. *The Civilizing Machine: A Cultural History of Mexican Railroads, 1876–1910*. Lincoln: University of Nebraska Press, 2014.

McCleary, Kristen L. "Culture and Commerce: An Urban History of Theater in Buenos Aires, 1880–1920." PhD diss., University of California, Los Angeles, 2002.

McClintock, Anne. *Imperial Leather: Race, Gender, and Sexuality in the Colonial Conquest*. New York: Routledge, 1995.

McKee Irwin, Robert. "The Centenary of the Famous 41." In *The Famous 41: Sexuality and Social Control in Mexico, 1901*, ed. Robert McKee Irwin, Edward J. McCaughan, and Michelle Rocío Nasser, 169–92. New York: Palgrave MacMillan, 2003.

Merlín, Socorro. *Vida y milagros de las carpas: La carpa en México, 1930–1950*. Mexico City: Instituto Nacional de Bellas Artes; Centro Nacional de Invest. y Document. Teatral R. Usigli, 1995.

Meskimmon, Marsha. *Engendering the City: Women Artists and Urban Space*. London: Scarlet, 1997.

Meyer, Jean A. *The Cristero Rebellion: The Mexican People between Church and State, 1926–1929*. Cambridge: Cambridge University Press, 1976.

Meyer, Michael C., and William H. Beezley. *The Oxford History of Mexico*. Oxford, UK: Oxford University Press, 2000.

Mignolo, Walter D. *The Idea of Latin America*. Malden MA: Blackwell, 2005.

Miranda, Jorge, ed. *Del rancho al bátaclan: Cancionero de teatro de revista, 1900–1940*. Mexico City: SEP/Museo Nacional de Culturas Populares, 1984.

Mitchell, Stephanie, and Patience Shell, eds. *The Women's Revolution in Mexico, 1910–1953*. Lanham MD: Rowman and Littlefield, 2009.

Monnet, Jerôme. *La ville et son double: Images et usages du centre: La parabole de México*. Paris: Editions Nathan, 1993.

Monsiváis, Carlos. Foreword. In *María Conesa*, by Enrique Alonso. Mexico City: Océano, 1987.

———. "Mexico City: Space to Mourn, Time to Spend." In *Mexico City through History and Culture*, ed. Linda A. Newson and John P. King, 9–17. Oxford: Oxford University Press, 2009.

Monsiváis, Carlos, and John Kraniauskas. *Mexican Postcards*. London: Verso, 1997.

Mora, Carl J. *Mexican Cinema: Reflections of a Society*. Rev. ed. Berkeley: University of California Press, 1989.

Moreno Toscano, Alejandra, ed. *Investigaciones sobre la historia de la ciudad de México*. Mexico City: Instituto Nacional de la Antropología e Historia, 1974.

Mulvey, Laura. "Pandora: Topographies of the Mask and Curiosity." In *Sexuality and Space*, ed. Beatriz Colomina, 53–72. New York: Princeton Architectural Press, 1992.

Mumford, Lewis. *The City in History: Its Origins, Its Transformations, and Its Prospects*. San Diego: Harcourt, 1961.

Nesvig, Martin. "The Lure of the Perverse: Moral Negotiation of Pederasty in Porfirian Mexico." *Mexican Studies/Estudios Mexicanos* 16, no. 1 (Winter 2000): 1–39.

Niblo, Stephen R. *Mexico in the 1940s: Modernity, Politics, and Corruption*. Lanham MD: Rowman and Littlefield, 2000.

Noble, Andrea. "Zapatistas en Sanborns (1914): Women at the Bar." *History of Photography* 22, no. 4 (Winter 1998): 366–70.

Ochoa, Enrique. *Feeding Mexico: The Political Uses of Food since 1910*. Wilmington DE: SR Books, 2000.

Olcott, Jocelyn. *Revolutionary Women in Postrevolutionary Mexico*. Durham NC: Duke University Press, 2005.

Olcott, Jocelyn, Mary Kay Vaughan, and Gabriela Cano, eds. *Sex in Revolution: Gender, Politics, and Power in Modern Mexico*. Durham NC: Duke University Press, 2006.

Oles, James. "Noguchi in Mexico: International Themes for a Working-Class Market." *American Art* 15, no. 2 (Summer 2001): 10–33.

Olsen, Patrice Elizabeth. "Artifacts of Revolution: Architecture, Society, and Politics in Mexico City, 1920–1940." PhD diss., Pennsylvania State University, 1998.

———. *Artifacts of Revolution: Architecture, Society, and Politics in Mexico City, 1920–1940*. Lanham MD: Rowman and Littlefield, 2008.

———. "Issues of National Identity: Obregon, Calles and Nationalist Architecture 1920–1930." Paper presented at the Conference of Latin American Studies Association, 1997.

————. "Revolution in the Streets: Changing Nomenclature, Changing Form in Mexico City's Centro Histórico and the Revision of Public Memory." Paper prepared for the Latin American Studies Association meeting, Chicago, 1998.

————. "Sáenz Garza, Aarón." *Encyclopedia of Mexico*, 1326–27.

————. "Saving the Past, Denying the Present? Cárdenas, Development, and Preservation in Mexico City, 1934–1940." Paper presented at the Rocky Mountain Council for Latin American Studies, January 12–15, 2000.

O'Malley, Ilene V. *The Myth of the Revolution: Hero Cults and the Institutionalization of the Mexican State, 1920–1940*. Westport CT: Greenwood Press, 1986.

Oropesa, Salvador A. *The Contemporáneos Group: Rewriting Mexico in the Thirties and Forties*. Austin: University of Texas Press, 2003.

Overmeyer-Velásquez, Mark. "Espacios públicas y mujeres publicas: La regulación de prostitución en la cuidad de Oaxaca, 1885–1911." *Acervos* 20 (Winter 2000): 20–26.

Peiss, Kathy Lee. *Cheap Amusements: Working Women and Leisure in Turn-of-the-Century New York*. Philadelphia: Temple University Press, 1986.

————. "Girls Lean Back Everywhere." In *The Modern Girl Around the World: Consumption, Modernity, and Globalization*, ed. Alys Eve Weinbaum, Lynn M. Thomas, Priti Ramamurthy, Uta G. Poiger, Madeleine Yue Dong, and Tani E. Barlow (The Modern Girl Around the World Research Group), 347–53. Durham NC: Duke University Press, 2008.

————. *Hope in a Jar: The Making of America's Beauty Culture*. New York: Metropolitan Books, 1998.

Piccato, Pablo. "'El Chalequero' or the Mexican Jack the Ripper: The Meanings of Sexual Violence in Turn-of-the-Century Mexico City." *Hispanic American Historical Review* 81, nos. 3–4 (August 2001): 623–51.

————. *City of Suspects: Crime in Mexico City, 1900–1931*. Durham NC: Duke University Press, 2001.

————. "'El Paso de Venus por el disco del Sol': Criminality and Alcoholism in the Late Porfirato." *Mexican Studies/Estudios Mexicanos* 11, no. 2 (Summer 1995)

Pilcher, Jeffrey M. *Cantinflas and the Chaos of Mexican Modernity*. Wilmington DE: SR Books, 2001.

Poole, Debra. "Cultural Diversity and Racial Unity in Oaxaca: Rethinking Hybridity and the State in Post-Revolutionary Mexico." Paper presented at the Oaxaca Summer Institute for Mexican History, Oaxaca, June 2001.

————. "An Image of 'Our Indian': Type Photographs and Racial Sentiments in Oaxaca, 1920–1940." *Hispanic American Historical Review* 84, no. 1 (2004): 37–82.

Porter, Susie S. "'And That It Is Custom Makes It Law': Class Conflict and Gender Ideology in the Public Sphere, Mexico City, 1880–1910." *Social Science History* 24, no. 1 (2000): 111–48.

Pratt, Mary Louise. *Imperial Eyes: Travel Writing and Transculturation*. London: Routledge, 1992.

Rago, Margareth. *Do cabaré ao lar: A utopia da cidade disciplinar: Brasil, 1890–1930*. Rio de Janeiro: Paz e Terra, 1985.

Ramírez Plancarte, Francisco. *La Ciudad de México durante La Revolución Constitucionalista*. 2nd ed. Mexico City: Ediciones Botas, 1941.

Ramos, Samuel. *El perfil del hombre y la cultura en México*. 3rd ed. Mexico City: Espasa Calpe Mexicana, 1965.

Rangel M., José de Jesús. *La Merced: Siglos de comercio*. Mexico City: Cámera Nacional de Comercio de la Ciudad de México, 1983.

Reese, Carol McMichael. "The Urban Development of Mexico City." In *Planning Latin America's Capital Cities, 1850–1950*, ed. Arturo Almandoz. New York: Routledge, 2002.

Rico, Araceli. *El Teatro Esperanza Iris: La pasión por las tablas*. Mexico City: Plaza y Valdés, 1999.

Rochfort, Desmond. *Mexican Muralists: Orozco, Rivera, Siqueiros*. San Francisco: Chronicle Books, 1998.

Rojas Loa O., José Antonio. "La transformación de la zona central, Ciudad de México: 1930–1970." In *Ciudad de México: Ensayo de construcción de una historia*, ed. Alejandra Moreno Toscano. Mexico City: Instituto Nacional de Antropología e Historia, 1978.

Rosenthal, Anton. "Spectacle, Fear, and Protest." *Social Science History* 24, no. 1 (2000): 33–73.

Ross, John. *El Monstruo: Dread and Redemption in Mexico City*. New York: Nation Books, 2009.

Rubenstein, Anne. *Bad Language, Naked Ladies, and Other Threats to the Nation: A Political History of Comic Books in Mexico*. Durham NC: Duke University Press, 1998.

————. "Mass Media and Popular Culture in the Postrevolutionary Era." In *Oxford History of Mexico*, ed. William H. Beezley and Michael Meyer, 637–70. Oxford: Oxford University Press, 2000.

———. "The War on 'Las Pelonas': Modern Women and Their Enemies, Mexico City, 1924." In *Sex in Revolution: Gender, Politics, and Power in Modern Mexico*, ed. Jocelyn Ollcott, Mary Kay Vaughan, and Gabriella Cano, 57–80. Durham NC: Duke University Press, 2006.

Rubin, Gayle. "Thinking Sex: Notes for a Radical Theory of the Politics of Sexuality." In *Pleasure and Danger: Exploring Female Sexuality*, ed. Carole S. Vance, 267–319. New York: HarperCollins, 1993.

Ruíz, Sonia L. de. *La Plaza de Loreto*. Mexico City: Instituto Nacional de Antropología e Historia, Departamento de Monumentos Coloniales, 1971.

Ryan, Mary P., and American Council of Learned Societies. *Women in Public Between Banners and Ballots, 1825–1880*. Baltimore: Johns Hopkins University Press, 1992.

Sanders, Nicole. *Gender and Welfare in Mexico: The Consolidation of a Postrevolutionary State (1937–1958)*. University Park: Penn State University Press, 2011.

Salas, Elizabeth. *Soldaderas in the Mexican Military: Myth and History*. Austin: University of Texas Press, 1990.

Scott, James C. *Seeing Like a State: How Certain Schemes to Improve the Human Condition Have Failed*. New Haven: Yale University Press, 1999.

Scott, Joan Wallach. *The Politics of the Veil*. Princeton: Princeton University Press, 2007.

Seed, Patricia. *Ceremonies of Possession in Europe's Conquest of the New World, 1492–1640*. Cambridge: Cambridge University Press, 1995.

Shell, Patience A. *Church and State Education in Revolutionary Mexico City*. Tucson: University of Arizona Press.

Seltzer, Mark. *Bodies and Machines*. New York: Routledge, 1992.

Sierra, Aída. "The Creation of a Symbol." *Artes de México* 49 (2000): 84–85.

Silverberg, Miriam. "After the Grand Tour: The Modern Girl, the New Woman, and the Colonial Maiden." In *The Modern Girl around the World: Consumption, Modernity, and Globalization*, ed. Alys Eve Weinbaum, Lynn M. Thomas, Priti Ramamurthy, Uta G. Poiger, Madeleine Yue Dong, and Tani E. Barlow (The Modern Girl Around the World Research Group), 354–61. Durham NC: Duke University Press, 2008.

Sluis, Ageeth. "Revolution and the Rhetoric of Representation: Gender Construction in Mexican Radio and Cinema, 1920–1940." MA thesis, University of Wyoming, 1997.

Sola-Morales, Ignasí. "Barcelona: Spirituality and Modernity." In *Art Nouveau, 1890–1914*, ed. Paul Greenhalgh, 334–45. London: V&A, 2000.

Solomon-Godeau, Gail. "Going Native: Paul Gauguin and the Invention of Primitivist Modernism." In *The Expanding Discourse: Feminism and Art History*, ed. Norma Broude and Mary D. Garrard, 314–31. New York: Icon Editions, 1992.

Soto, Shirlene Ann. *The Mexican Woman: A Study of Her Participation in the Revolution, 1910–1940*. Palo Alto CA: R&E Research Associates, 1979.

Stallybrass, Peter, and Allon White. *The Politics and Poetics of Transgression*. London: Methuen, 1986.

Stansell, Christine. *City of Women: Sex and Class in New York, 1789–1860*. Champaign: University of Illinois Press, 1987.

Tenorio-Trillo, Mauricio. *Mexico at the World's Fairs: Crafting a Modern Nation*. Berkeley: University of California Press, 1996.

———. "1910 Mexico City: Space and Nation in the City of the *Centenario*." In *Viva Mexico! Viva La Independencia! Celebrations of September 16*, ed. William H. Beezley and David E. Lorey, 167–98. Wilmington DE: SR Books, 2001.

Terrés, María Elodia. *La Ciudad de México: Sus orígenes y desarrollo*. Mexico City: Editorial Porrúa, 1977.

Terry, T. Philip. *Terry's Guide to Mexico: The New Standard Guidebook to the Mexican Republic, with Chapters on the Railways, the Airways, and the Ocean Routes to Mexico*. Rev. ed. Boston: Houghton Mifflin, 1931.

———. *Terry's Mexico: Handbook for Travelers*. Mexico City: Sonora News Company, 1909.

Toor, Frances. *Frances Toor's Guide to Mexico*. New York: R. M. McBride, 1936.

———. *Frances Toor's New Guide to Mexico*. Mexico City: Francis Toor Studios, 1946.

Travassos, Elizabeth, and Manoel Aranha Corrêa do Lago. "Darius Milhaud e os compositores de tangos, maxixes, sambas e cateretês." *Revista Brasileira* 11, no. 43 (April–June 2005). http://daniellathompson.com/Texts/Le_Boeuf/boeuf.pt.15–16.htm.

Tuñón, Julia. "Femininity, *Indigenismo*, and Nation: Film Representation by Emilio 'El Indio' Fernández." In *Sex in Revolution: Gender, Politics, and Power in Modern Mexico*, ed. Jocelyn Olcott, Mary Kay Vaughan, and Gabriela Cano, 81–98. Durham NC: Duke University Press, 2007.

———. *Mujeres de luz y sombra en el cine mexicano: La construcción de una imagen (1939–1952)*. Mexico City: Colegio de México: Instituto Mexicano de Cinematografía, 1998.

————. *Los rostros de un mito: Personajes femeninos en lLas Películas de Emilio Indio Fernández*. Mexico City: Conaculta: Instituto Mexicano de Cinematografía, 2000.

Ullman, Sharon R. *Sex Seen: The Emergence of Modern Sexuality in America*. Berkeley: University of California Press, 1997.

Ulloa del Río, Ignacio. *Palacio de Bellas Artes: Rescate de un sueño*. Mexico City: Universidad Iberoamericana, 2000.

Usigli, Rodolfo. *Mexico in the Theater*. University MS: Romance Monographs, 1975.

Vanderwood, Paul J. *Juan Soldado: Rapist, Murderer, Martyr, Saint*. Durham NC: Duke University Press, 2004.

Vanke, Francesca. "Arabesques: North Africa, Arabia, and Europe." In *Art Nouveau, 1890–1914*, ed. Paul Greenhalgh, 114–25. London: V&A, 2000.

Vargas, Ava, ed. *La Casa de Cita: Mexican Photographs from the Belle Epoque*. London: Quartet, 1986.

Vaughan, Mary Kay. *Cultural Politics in Revolution: Teachers, Peasants, and Schools in Mexico, 1930–1940*. Tucson: University of Arizona Press, 1997.

————. "Introduction: Pancho Villa, the Daughters of Mary, and the Modern Woman: Gender in the Long Mexican Revolution." In *Sex in Revolution: Gender, Politics, and Power in Modern Mexico*, ed. Jocelyn Ollcott, Mary Kay Vaughan, and Gabriella Cano, 21–34. Durham NC: Duke University Press, 2006.

————. "Modernizing Patriarchy: State Policies, Rural Households, and Women in Mexico, 1930–1940." In *Hidden Histories of Gender and the State in Latin America*, ed. Elizabeth Dore and Maxine Molyneux, 194–214. Durham NC: Duke University Press, 2000.

Vázquez Ramírez, Esther Martina. *Organización y resistencia popular en la Ciudad de México durante la crisis de 1929–1932*. Mexico City: Instituto Nacional de Estudios Históricos de la Revolución Mexicana, 1998.

Villagrán García, José. "Ideas regentes en la arquitectura actual." *Arquitectura/México* 48 (December 1954): 195.

Vincent, K. Steven, and Alison Klairmont-Lingo. *The Human Tradition in Modern France*. Wilmington DE: SR Books, 2000.

Viqueira Albán, Juan Pedro. *Propriety and Permissiveness in Bourbon Mexico*. Trans. Sonya Lipsett-Rivera, and Sergio Rivera Ayala. Wilmington DE: SR Books, 1999.

Vitruvius. *Ten Books on Architecture*. Ed. Ingrid D. Rowland and Thomas Noble Howe. Cambridge, UK: Cambridge University Press, 2001.

Walkowitz, Judith R. *City of Dreadful Delight: Narratives of Sexual Danger in Late-Victorian London*. London: Virago Press, 1992.

Ward, Peter. *Mexico City: The Production and Reproduction of an Urban Environment*. London: Belhaven Press, 1990.

Weinbaum, Alys Eve, Lynn M. Thomas, Priti Ramamurthy, Uta G. Poiger, Madeleine Yue Dong, and Tani E. Barlow, eds. (The Modern Girl around the World Research Group). *The Modern Girl around the World: Consumption, Modernity and Globalization*. Durham NC: Duke University Press, 2008.

Weis, Judith E., ed. *Latin American Popular Theatre: The First Five Centuries*. Albuquerque: University of New Mexico Press, 1993.

Widdifield, Stacie G. *The Embodiment of the National in Late Nineteenth-Century Mexican Painting*. Tucson: University of Arizona Press, 1996.

Wilkie, James W. *The Mexican Revolution: Federal Expenditure and Social Change since 1910*. Berkeley: University of California Press, 1970.

Wilson, Elizabeth. "Bodies in Public and Private." In *Public–Privates: New Views on Photography, Representation, and Gender*, edited by Jane Brettle and Sally Rice. Manchester: Manchester University Press, 1994.

———. *The Sphinx in the City*. Berkeley: University of California Press, 1991.

Winokur, Mark. *American Laughter: Immigrants, Ethnicity and the 1930s Hollywood Film Comedy*. New York: St. Martin's Press, 1996.

Wood, Andrew Grant. *Revolution in the Street: Women, Workers, and Urban Protest in Veracruz, 1870–1927*. Wilmington DE: SR Books, 2001.

Wood, Gishlaine, and Paul Greenhalgh. "Symbols of the Sacred and Profane." In *Art Nouveau, 1890–1914*, ed. Paul Greenhalgh, 73–91. London: V&A, 2000.

Zedillo Castillo, Antonio. *El teatro de la Ciudad de Mexico Esperanza Iris: Lustros, lustres, experiencias y esperanzas*. Mexico City: Socioculture D.D.F., 1989.

Zeitz, Joshua. *Flapper: A Madcap Story of Sex, Style, Celebrity and the Women Who Made America Modern*. New York: Three Rivers Press, 2006.

Zolov, Eric. "Discovering a Land 'Mysterious and Obvious': Renarrativizing of Postrevolutionary Mexico." In *Fragments of a Golden Age: The Politics of Culture in Mexico since 1940*, ed. Gilbert Joseph, Anne Rubenstein, and Eric Zolov, 234–72. Durham NC: Duke University Press, 2001.

———. "Jorge Carreño's Graphic Satire and the Politics of 'Presidentialism' in Mexico during the 1960s." *Estudios Interdisciplinarios de América Latina y el Caribe* 17, no. 1 (2006): 13–38.

INDEX

Page numbers in italics refer to illustrations.

Art Deco style: camposcape and, 117; Deco body and, 70, 72, 77; entertainment industry, associated with, 269–70; Mercado Abelardo Rodríguez and, 227, 238–39; in Mexico City architecture, 17, 179, 184, 186, 188, 190, 196–97, 204–7, 208–10, 218–19; origins of, 266; Palacio de Bellas Artes, Deco indigenismo interior of, 259, 266–71, 268, 289–90; visible female sexuality and, 156

Art Nouveau style, 57, 69–70, 98, 104, 108, 190–92, 197, 202, 216, 260, 261–62

athletics, participation in, 80, 96, 129

Atl, Dr. (Gerardo Murillo), 264

Azcapotzalco, 53

Azteca Films, 309n29

Baker, Josephine, 98, 142, 269–70, 319n19

Balbuena, 10, 213, 214

Ballet Folklórico, 124, 143, 279, 281, 287–88

Ballet Moderno de México, 288

Banco de México, 207, 267

La Banda de Automovil Gris (The Gray Car Gang), 36, 309n30

Baratillo, 114–15

Barreda, Gabino, 28, 29

barrios populares, 1, 6, 8

Bartra, Roger, 108

Basilica de Guadalupe, 302

Bassols, Narciso, 257

bataclanismo, 20, 61–66, 296; architecture and the Deco body, 202; Cabral and, 69–72, 71; Cabral's

Conflicto en el tráfico and, 165; camposcape and, 101, 132–33; Deco body and, 61, 62, 66, 68, 86, 96–97, 138, 182; defined, 61–62, 96; introduced to Latin America, 62–66; La Iris and, 59, 62, 63; new concepts of femininity and physical beauty derived from, 61–62, 64–66, 86, 96–97; nudity and, 63, 66, 101, 312n6; revista genre reformed by, 64–66; visible female sexuality in *Vea* and, 138, 142, 153–54, 157; *Voilá Paris*, 17, 61, 62, 63–66, 96

Bauhaus, 192, 195

Beals, Carlton, 10, 11, 12, 111, 116

beauty pageants and india bonita contests, 85, 101, 124, 132–33, 318n1, 321n49

Beauvoir, Simone de, 77

Bech, Henning, 325n31, 327n64

Beezley, William, 5

Belem prison, 28, 214, 230, 235

Benjamin, Thomas, 269

Beristáin, Leopoldo, 58

Berkeley, Busby, 64

Bernhardt, Sarah, 32, 33

Blassifera, Carlos, 312n5

Bliss, Katherine, 165

Blum, Ann, 165

Boari, Adamo, 191, 251, 260, 269, 270

Boccioni, Umberto, 202

La Bolsa (barrio), 6, 8, 28–29, 114, 243

Bonfil Batalla, Guillermo, 18

Bonifant, Cube: Cabral and, 89–92, 172–73; camposcape and, 127, 321n49, 321n58; on Colonia Condesa, 188; Deco body and,

317n75, 317n82; on feminists and feminism, 89, 91, 92; life and career of, 3, 87–92

Bordo, Susan, 81, 316n53

Bosque de Chapultepec, 156, 185, 186, 282

Bourbon Reforms, 30

Bow, Clara, 67

boxing matches, 55

Boylan, Kristina, 145

Boytler, Arcady, 160

Bracho, Ángel, *Los mercados*, *248*, *249*

Bracho, Julio, 272–73

Brasseur, Charles, 106

Brenner, Anita, 11, 12

Brooks, Louise, 67, 162

Buenos Aires, Argentina, 39, 46–47, 193

Buffington, Robert, 27

bullfighting, 30, 40, 88, 91, 187, 281

Bulman, Francisco, 239

burlesque, 153–54, 158, 160, 163, 259, 301, 312n13

Burnham, Daniel, 192

Butler, Judith, 15–16, 60, 80

Cabral, Ernesto García (El Chango; the monkey), 268; career of, 68–69, 314n24; collapsing discourses of female modernity, 174; *Conflicto en el tráfico* (Traffic incident), 164–67, *165*, 171; Cube Bonifant and, 89–92, 172–73; Deco body and, 68–72, *70*, *71*, *73*; signature style of, 314n24

Café Colón, 86

Café Globo, 188

calla lilies, 270

Calles, Plutarco Elías, 8, 184–85, 188, 206, 212, 216, 246, 251, 267, 332n86

Calles Torreblanca, Hortensia, 185

Campillo, José, 65

Campobello, Nellie, 283, 285

camposcape, 18–19, 20, 101–35; bataclanismo and, 101, 132–33; Deco bodies and, 101, 102, 103, 123, 124–25, 132–33, 134, 298–99; defined, 18, 102; gendered nature of, 102, 103–9, *107*, 111–16, *117*, 118–20, *119*, 123–24, 133–35, 256, 297–98; health and hygiene associated with, 103, 111, 129–30; in high art, 102–3, 110, 111–14; history and origins, 103–9; imagining camposcape in the city, 102–3, 109–18, *117*, 135; marketplace and, 102–3, 111–20, *117*, *119*, 122–23, 134–35, 223, 231–32, 240, 255–56; Mexican Revolution and, 109–10, 116–18, 120–21; Mexico City's chilangos and, 281–82; migration to Mexico City and, 229–30; modernity and, 18–19, 108–9, 119; murals of Mercado Abelardo Rodríguez celebrating, *248*, 249–50; nudity and, 20, 101, 102, 103, 109, 124–32, *126*, 133–34, 158; Palacio de Bellas Artes and, 257–59, 271, 272, 273, 275; Parque México, Colonia Condesa, 179, *180*, *181*, 185–87, 189, 190, 201, 210, 215, 219–20; in photojournalism, 102–3, 118–24, *119*; remasculinization of, 256, 257–59, 277–88, 290, 291; Santa Anita festivals and, 101–2, 132–33; tehuanas, 46, 105–8, *107*, 110–11, 114, 133, 134–35, 320n22;

Hidalgo (now Doctores), 8, 267
Hinojosa, Cosme, 249
Hipódromo, 179, 184, 185, 187, 189, 190, 209
historical preservation, 179–81, 207, 216–17
Hoffmann, Josef, 266
El Hogar, 82, 95, 173
Holmes, Nels, 322n69
homosexuality, 44, 326n41
Hotel Regis, 207
Humboldt, Alexander von, 26, 104
hybridity: of architecture, 197, 208–9, 219, 238, 255; of modern women, 87; in theater, 48, 51, 55, 57, 65

india bonita contests and beauty pageants, 85, 101, 124, 132–33, 318n1, 321n49
indigenismo: architecture and urban reform, 220; camposcape and, 18, 102, 103, 110, 113, 132; Deco body and, 85, 97–98; Deco indigenismo, 266–71, 268; defined, 308n51; Mercado Abelardo Rodríguez and, 247, 250; mestizaje and, 17, 220, 256, 299; Palacio de Bellas Artes and, 259, 262, 264, 266–71, 268; theater and, 46, 308n41
Las Inditas (vecindad), 334n30
Infante, Pedro, 279
informal economy, 1, 21, 225, 253, 294, 302
infrastructure, urban reform characterized as, 227
Instituto Nacional de Bellas Artes, 288

Iris, Esperanza: Art Nouveau and, 191; background and career, 35–36; bataclanismo and, 59, 62, 63, 138, 312n5; charitable works, 58–60, 311n92; Conesa compared, 58; debut performance of, 25–26; as diva, 3, 20, 33, 38, 59–60, 67, 297; in Mexican Revolution, 49; in movies, 59, 278; Palavicini and, 199; personal life, 58–59, 311n92; photo, 34; retirements of, 58, 59, 311n92; in revistas, 47, 51; Teatro Iris, 20, 23–25, 24, 36, 52, 55–59, 62, 191, 196, 242, 246, 266, 277–78, 309n35
Iturbide, Gloria, 242, 243
Izquierdo, María, 274
Iztaccíhuatl, 262–64, 272

jacalones (makeshift theaters), 39, 41, 53
Jack the Ripper, 163
Jacobs, Jane, 252, 336n81
Jaime Nunó alley, 317n68
Jiménez y Ortega, Augustín, 142
Jockey Club, 5, 44, 184, 187
Johns, Michael, 5
journalism: Cube Bonifant, career of, 3, 87–92; Deco body in, 68–73, 70, 71, 73; on divorce, marriage, and female agency, 93, 95–96; female masculinity in, 94; photojournalism, 102–3, 118–24, 119, 320n45; public behavior and female beauty, influence on concepts of, 37, 40; street spectacle criticized by, 40, 41. *See also* visible female sexuality in *Vea*; *specific periodicals*

muralism in Mexico, 246–52, *248*, 249–50, 274–77
Murillo, Gerardo (Dr. Atl), 264
Museo de Arte Popular, 271

El Nacional (newspaper), 146
La Nacional (high rise), 156, 179, 205, 207, 209, 235
National Authors Association, 133
National Preparatory School, 247
Nazism, 249
Negrete, Jorge, 279
neocolonial architectural style, 194–96, 237, 238
Netzahualcoyotl Street, 168
Neue Sachlichkeit (New Objectivity), 204
New Woman, 2, 28, 32, 66, 67, 68, 69, 294, 295
New York Times, 234, 235
Noguchi, Isamu, *Historia de México*, 249–50, 336n73
Noriega Hope, Carlos, 88, 317n75
Novarro, Ramón, 272
Novo, Salvador, 75, 76–77, 84, 85, 86, 88, 129–30, 153, 155, 189, 272, 311n92, 326n41
nudism, 128–32, 133–34, 158, 201, 322n69, 323n72
nudity: acceptability of representations of, 125, 128–29, 142, 148; architectural minimalism, bareness, and the Deco body, 179, *181*, 182, 202–10, 219; bataclanismo and, 63, 66, 101, 312n6; camposcape and, 20, 101, 102, 103, 109, 124–32, *126*, 133–34, 158; gender and, 131–32, 133–34; health and

hygiene associated with, 128, 129, 131–32, 133; male perception of female body and, 43. *See also* visible female sexuality in *Vea*

Oaxaca, 46, 105, 111, 124, 188, 287
Obregón, Álvaro: Centro Cívico Álvaro Obregón, Mercado Abelardo Rodríguez, 240–41, 245; funerary monument for, 214, 215; in Monumento a la Revolución, 216; ranchera films and, 280; Teatro Hidalgo and, 245; at theater, 49; urbanization and urban reform programs under, 8, 9, 211, 215
Obregón Santacilia, Carlos, 206, 209, 237, 243, 267
Oficina de Espectáculos (Office of Entertainment), 155
O'Gorman, Juan, 195, 196, 209
Olague Soria, Alberto, 228–29
Olsen, Patrice, 8, 190, 197, 207, 209, 214, 256, 267, 328n6
orientalism, 18–19, 33, 102, 106–8, 114, 170, 190, 219, 261, 297
Oropesa, Salvador A., 126, 281, 310n56
Orozco, José Clemente, 69
Orrin Brothers and Circus Orrin, 39, 182–83
Ortíz Mentellano, Bernardo, 242–43
Ortíz Monasterio, Manuel, 208
Ortiz Rubio, Pascual, 214, 242, 265

Palacio de Bellas Artes, 257–91, 301; Art Nouveau exterior, 191, 260, 261–62; camposcape and, 257–59, 271, 272, 273, 275; class discourse and, 272–73, 282–84, 286; criticism of, 270, 273; Deco body and, 288–89; Deco indigenismo interior, 259, 266–71, 268, 289–90; design and construction, 259, 260–66, 284–85; exterior female figures, 262, 263; as female space, 260–62, 263, 268, 286–88; Mercado Abelardo Rodríguez compared, 259–60, 266, 274, 277, 289; murals at, 274–77; *New York Times* on, 235; opening of, 257, 258, 271–72; remasculinization of camposcape and, 256, 257–59, 277–88, 290, 291; reorganization and overhaul, 282–86; revolutionary aims of, 242; rise of cinema and, 277–82; theater in Mexico City and, 5, 10, 21, 47, 55, 56, 309n25; theatrical offerings at, 272–73; visible female sexuality and, 137, 143, 156

Palacio de Correos, 261

El Palacio del Hierro (department store), 5, 207, 236, 314n30

Palacio Nacional, 26, 156, 207, 215, 236, 240, 245, 247

Palafox, Silvano, 205–6, 209, 215, 219

Palavicini, Felix, 199

Palmer, Juan, 36

Panama Street, 168

Pani, Alberto, 265–66, 270–71, 272, 274, 282, 283, 289, 290

Pani, Mario, 266, 267

Paquin, 146

Paramo, José, 130

Parían (market), 188

La Parisina. *See* Conesa, María

Parque España, Colonia Condesa, 185

Parque México, Colonia Condesa, 179, *180*, *181*, 185–87, 189, 190, 201, 210, 215, 219–20, 256

Partido de la Revolución Democrática, 293

Partido de la Revolución Mexicana (PRM), 285

Partido Nacional Revolucionario (National Revolutionary Party or PNR), 80, 171, 212, 234, 241–44, 250

Paseo de Reforma, 260

paving of streets, 227

Pavlova, Anna, 57, 288

pelonas (short-haired women), 86, 90, 95, 316n65

Peralta, Angela, 31

Peralta, Catalina, 261

performativity. *See* entertainment industry; spectacle and performativity; theater

El Periquello (puppet theater), 243

petroleum industry, nationalization of, 253, 286

photojournalism, 102–3, 118–24, *119*, 320n45

Piccato, Pablo, 27, 174, 328n89

Pimentel y Fagoaga, Fernando, 183

Plateros Street (now Avenida Madero), 4–5, 44, 260

Playboy, 141, 142

plays and show titles: *Los amigos del Señor Gobernador*, 232; *Au revoir*, 63; "Baile de los Cuarenta y Uno," 44; *Le boeuf sur le toit*, 63; *Cachez-Ça*, 64; *C'est Paris*, 312n5; *Chin-Chun-Chan*, 47; *El Congreso*

1931) and, 150–52, *151*, 156, 164; architecture and, 202, 205; camposcape nudity contrasted with, 158, 178; "La cita" (The date; short story), 137, 141; "decent women" and prostitutes, difficulty distinguishing, 177–78; Deco body and, 138, 141–42, 147, 152, 153, 155, 156, 157, 175, 176, 178, 182; feminism and female mobility and safety, 156, 171–76; health and hygiene issues, 155; heteronormativity underwritten by, 141, 152–53, 175–76; meaning of *Vea*, 323n1; modernity, efforts to map, 164–75, *166*, 177–78; pornography, concept of, 141, 149–50, 155; price and circulation of *Vea*, 149, 325n24; psychoanalytic theory and, 152–53, 164; resistance to and censorship of, 145–50, 324n15, 324n23; standards of female beauty in, 140–45, *144*, 156–57; underworld in other periodicals and, 155–56, 158–64; urban space and, 137–39, *139*, *140*, 143, 153–58, 176–77

Vitruvius, 200–202, 331n55

Viuda de Florez, Elise Gomez, 172

El Volador (market), 115, 225, 236

Vuelo, 293, 294

Wagner, Richard, 289

Waite, Charles, *Selling Gorditas at Guadalupe* (ca. 1900), 118–20, *119*

western district, 4–6, 27, 38–39, 40

White, Allon, 96–97, 113

whiteness, 72, 84, 85, 96, 97, 98, 119–20, 124, 134, 141, 149, 150, 177, 179, 276, 281, 289–90, 293

Wilde, Oscar, *Salomé*, 33, 273

Wilhelmy, Amelia, 53

Wilson, Elizabeth, 164, 315n50

Winokur, Mark, 205

Wirkimire, W. H., 264

women. *See* gender

Woolf, Virginia, 148

Wright, Frank Lloyd, 192, 240

Yáñez, Augustín, 134

Zapata, Emiliano, 121, 187, 216, 243, 245, 280, 313n10

zarzuelas, 30–31, 41–42, 45

Ziegfeld Follies, 17, 61, 78

Zócalo, 4–5, 6, 26, 27, 38, 39, 40, 153, 156, 167, 188, 215, 216, 217, 221, 225, 236, 260, 293, 294

Zola, Emil, *Nana*, 29

CPSIA information can be obtained
at www.ICGtesting.com
Printed in the USA
FFOW04n1054160116
20534FF